MAPPING
THE ETHICAL
TURN

MAPPING THE ETHICAL TURN

A Reader in Ethics, Culture, and Literary Theory

Edited by

TODD F. DAVIS AND KENNETH WOMACK

UNIVERSITY PRESS OF VIRGINIA
Charlottesville and London

The University Press of Virginia
© 2001 by the Rector and Visitors of the University of Virginia
All rights reserved
Printed in the United States of America on acid-free paper
First published 2001

9 8 7 6 5 4 3 2 1

Library of Congress Cataloging-in-Publication Data

Mapping the ethical turn : a reader in ethics, culture, and literary
theory / edited by Todd F. Davis and Kenneth Womack.
    p. cm.
Includes bibliographical references and index.
    ISBN 0-8139-2055-8 (alk. paper)—ISBN 0-8139-2056-6 (pbk. : alk. paper)
    1. Criticism—Moral and ethical aspects. 2. Literature, Modern—20th
century—History and criticism. I. Davis, Todd F., 1965– II. Womack,
Kenneth.
    PN98.M67 M37 2001
    801'.95—dc21

                                                            2001002051

For Neneng, Shelly,
Noah, and Nathan

CONTENTS

PREFACE

Reading Literature and the Ethics of Criticism

TODD F. DAVIS AND KENNETH WOMACK

> This is not a time for professors of literature to ignore the judgments of human passions.
>
> —Ihab Hassan

THE TITLE of this volume—*Mapping the Ethical Turn*—is not meant to suggest that only in recent years have we seen a shift toward the marriage of ethical thought and literary study. Rather, as with the meaning of the verb *to map,* this volume, in certain ways, seeks to tell a story that highlights a terrain that has always been there. Ethical critics, like cartographers, do not necessarily discover or make a territory but, instead, describe and give shape to what has always existed.

While more obvious forms of an ethical or moral criticism are easily accounted for by the scholarship of such figures as F. R. Leavis and Northrop Frye, many critics during the poststructuralist era have doggedly and determinedly sought to place distance between themselves and any mention of an ethical or moral perspective in their work. Of course, such a response seems only natural when understood in the context of the demise of modern humanism, its failure in the face of two world wars, the proliferation of nuclear weapons, the horror of genocide and holocaust, and the oppression of peoples whose narratives somehow fell outside the bounds of an Anglo- or Eurocentric point of view. Yet to pretend that the ethical or moral dimensions of the human condition were abandoned or obliterated in the shift to postmodernity certainly seems naïve. Part of being human involves the daily struggle with the meanings and consequences of our actions, a struggle most often understood in narrative structures as we tell others and ourselves about what has transpired or what we fear will transpire in the future. As creatures driven by story, we find ourselves immersed in narrative in almost every aspect of our lives. The act of telling stories—the gesture to represent what all too often is unrepresentable, ineffable—grounds and distinguishes human activity. Thus, it would be ludicrous to imagine that readers of literature over the past several decades somehow disengaged their ethical faculties as they encountered their culture's grand narratives. What *has* changed over the course of the twentieth century in our discussion of ethics and literature is the simplistic, uncomplicated prescription of external ethical forces regarding so many different literatures and cultures.

Today, the ethical consideration of a given work of literature ranges from the close reading of the text itself—particularly in terms of the dilemmas and conundrums presented in the lives of the characters that we encounter there—to the ethical questions that the story raises in the reader's own life beyond the margins of the text. Ethical criticism, at other times, focuses upon the life of the author and how his or her own ethical or moral commitments have shaped the construction, production, and performance of narrative. Some critics included in the present volume question whether ethical considerations have any place in literary study at all. Yet by raising such issues these same critics have already affirmed that ethical questions remain central to the act of literary criticism. Their questions and the doubt that drives them are themselves integral to the notion of an ethical criticism. In the end, if there is any single defining characteristic in the ethical turn that marks contemporary literary studies, it resides in the fact that few critics wish to return to a dogmatically prescriptive or doctrinaire form of reading. Our past failures make such hubris unattractive. Instead, ethical criticism appears to be moving, in all of its various forms, toward a descriptive mode, a dialogue between what has occurred in the past and what is alive and in process at the present.

Divided into four descriptive sections, *Mapping the Ethical Turn* traces the interpretive, pedagogic, and theoretical concerns inherent in the study of literature and ethics, as well as its natural interdisciplinary connections with other modes of criticism. Although many of the essays in the present volume meaningfully illustrate Tobin Siebers's contention that "the heart of ethics is the desire for community" (202), the contributions in *Mapping the Ethical Turn*'s first section, "Theory and the Ethics of Literary Study," demonstrate the ways in which our conceptions of ethics and the scholarly value of ethical criticism remain matters of significant debate. In "A Humanistic Ethics of Reading," Daniel R. Schwarz usefully differentiates between an *ethics of reading* and an *ethics while reading*. In addition to illustrating the hermeneutic activities involved in ethical reading and interpretation, Schwarz accounts for the recent revival of the Anglo-American humanistic tradition. Wayne C. Booth's "Why Ethical Criticism Can Never Be Simple" explores the "undeniable" power of narrative to change our lives—for good or ill. In addition to noting that ethical judgments are inevitably "controversial," Booth underscores the value of ethical criticism as a means for understanding narrative's capacity for registering an ethical and aesthetic impact upon the human condition. Charles Altieri's "Lyrical Ethics and Literary Experience" addresses the centrality of the lyrical as a means for measuring our emotional and ethical responses to literary experience. Altieri problematizes ethical criticism's role in the theoretical project, arguing that our surrender to its interpretive aims may succeed in establishing passive strictures of morality and the sublimation of our capacity for rendering sound aesthetic judgments. In "Exactly and Responsibly: A Defense of Ethical Criticism," Martha C. Nussbaum responds to Richard A. Posner's attacks upon the interpretative validity and intellectual integrity of ethical criticism. Drawing upon Henry James's idea that in the act of "putting" things "exactly and responsibly" the novelist is at all times an ethical and political being, Nussbaum argues that the appeal of aesthetic detachment, which Posner parades as a kind of saving grace, is itself not innocent of political motivations.

The essays in the second section, "Confronting the Difficult: The Ethics of Race and Power," challenge conventional notions of race and power in terms of the often tenuous relationships between narrators and their audiences, between literary texts and the larger cultures in which they are received. Kathleen Lundeen's "Who Has the Right to Feel? The Ethics of Literary Empathy" discusses the ironic juxtaposition of empathy: in life, it is praised as a virtue, while the world of literary criticism often sees it as a form of cultural arrogance. Using Felicia Hemans's "Indian Woman's Death-Song," Lundeen explores the problematic nature of literary empathy and its ethical possibilities. James Phelan's "Sethe's Choice: *Beloved* and the Ethics of Reading" draws upon a rhetorical framework in an analysis of Toni Morrison's novel in order to account for Sethe's decision to kill her children and spare them the traumas of slavery. Phelan argues that this central crisis in *Beloved* establishes an ethical relation between implied author and audience in Morrison's novel. In "Moral Repair and Its Limits," Margaret Urban Walker juxtaposes her reading of Morrison's *Jazz* with the real-life project of moral repair that has transfixed a global audience: the spectacle and narrative of South Africa's Truth and Reconciliation Commission. Walker illustrates the manner in which reality and fiction both reveal hard choices and imponderable elements in the unavoidable and necessary human task of moral repair.

The contributions in the third section, "Making Darkness Visible: The Ethical Implications of Narrative as Witness," investigate the generic boundaries of fiction, film, and poetry as ethical constructs that bear witness to the horrors of the Holocaust and post-apartheid South Africa while also celebrating the endurance of the human spirit. In "Ethics before Politics: J. M. Coetzee's *Disgrace*," James Meffan and Kim L. Worthington examine the notion that ethics, for many commentators on South-African literature, is fundamentally political in conception. Drawing upon the philosophical insights of Emmanuel Levinas, Worthington and Meffan discuss the ways in which Coetzee continually resists a collapse of the ethical into the political, referring again and again to the necessary distinction between what he calls the writer's "social obligation" and the "ethical imperatives" that exceed politics. Todd F. Davis and Kenneth Womack's "The List Is Life: *Schindler's List* as Ethical Construct" explores the cultural response to *Schindler's List* by examining the relationship between the construction of Steven Spielberg's film and Thomas Keneally's novelized biography and the actual historical events that inspired such artful renderings. Demonstrating that ethics inevitably plays a role in determining the ways in which such stories may or may not be told, Davis and Womack argue that the manner in which we receive Holocaust narratives is itself decided by the ethical import of history's weight. In "Poets of Testimony: C. K. Williams and Jacqueline Osherow as Proxy Witnesses of the Shoah," Susan Gubar suggests that verse writers who concentrate on historical testimonials or deploy archival material serve as witnesses of the witnesses. Through close readings of two complex and quite powerful works—Williams's "Spit" and Osherow's "Conversations with Survivors"—Gubar underscores the ways in which men and women of letters approach the role of witness in quite different cadences, with quite distinct concerns.

The essays in the fourth section, "Ways of Seeing: The Diversity of Applied Ethical Criticism," demonstrate the interpretative range and power of ethical criticism. Drawing upon a diversity of disciplines—from ecocriticism, feminist studies, and linguistics to theories of collaborative life writing and moral philosophy—the contributors in this section provide readers with illustrative models of ethical criticism in practice and highlight its viability as a venue for engendering multidisciplinary readings. In "Forget the Phallic Symbolism, Consider the Snake: Biocentrism and Language in Margaret Atwood's 'Snake Poems,'" Ian Marshall challenges us to set aside anthropocentrism in favor of a more ethical biocentrism. In a reading of Atwood's "Snake Poems," Marshall examines the manner in which Atwood entreats readers to "consider the snake" as well as to comprehend the ethical properties inherent in nature and environmental studies. G. Thomas Couser's "Making, Taking, and Faking Lives: Ethical Problems in Collaborative Life Writing" contends that the ethical difficulties of collaborative autobiography are rooted in its nearly oxymoronic status. The partners' contributions, Couser writes, are not only different but incommensurate entities—on the one hand, lived experience mediated by memory and, on the other, the labor of eliciting, recording, inscribing, and organizing this material. In "The Scandal of Human Countenance: Witold Gombrowicz and Bruno Schulz in Exile from the Country of Forms," Adam Zachary Newton examines the various "silhouettes" of the self in works by Gombrowicz and Schulz. Newton devotes particular attention to the "intersubjective spaces" inherent in the human countenance, or "the face that begets other faces as well as the face of human encounter that transposes into the face of reading." In "Henry James, Moral Philosophers, Moralism," Cora Diamond traces the variousness of moral disagreement and the ways in which philosophers tend to see ethics in terms of the primary importance of judgment. For James, Diamond argues, the characterization of the distances that may exist between human beings in their moral lives proceeds altogether differently. Finally, J. Hillis Miller's "How to Be 'in Tune with the Right' in *The Golden Bowl*" discusses the manner in which ethical decisions and commitments are often signaled by utterances that are explicitly performative: promises, declarations, orders, wills, and the like—even lies and false signatures. Virtue is rarely rewarded in James's novels, Miller writes, and readers are often left pondering whether the characters acted rightly or whether they themselves would (or should) have behaved in the same way.

We owe special debts of gratitude to the many friends and colleagues who helped make this volume possible. We are particularly grateful for the encouragement and advice of Ervin Beck, Wayne Booth, Lee Ann De Reus, Marshall Gregory, Jim Harner, Jim Mellard, Dinty Moore, Dan Schwarz, Michael Wolfe, and Julian Wolfreys. The efforts of Carole Bookhamer, James Decker, and Matt Masucci on behalf of this volume are especially appreciated. *Mapping the Ethical Turn* would not have been possible without the support of travel grants provided by the administrations of Goshen College and Penn State Altoona. We are grateful to Paul Keim, Goshen College's vice-president of academic affairs, for a Goshen College Faculty Research Grant. Special thanks are also due to Kjell Meling, Penn State Altoona's associate dean and director of academic affairs, and the Altoona College Advisory Board for their assistance in the form of a course-load reduction and a Research Development Grant. In addition to the superb work of our copyeditor, Jane Curran, we are especially grateful to Cathie Brettschneider, Ellen Satrom, David Sewell, and the editorial staff of the University Press of Virginia for their enthusiastic support of our project. Finally, we are indebted to our parents—Joyce and Harold Davis and Sue and Fred Womack—for their role in first challenging us to ponder the kinds of ethical questions that inform this volume.

Permission has been kindly granted to reprint the following chapters: Charles Altieri, "Lyrical Ethics and Literary Experience," *Style* 32.2 (1998): 272–97; Wayne C. Booth, "Why Ethical Criticism Can Never Be Simple," *Style* 32.2 (1998): 351–64; G. Thomas Couser, "Making, Taking, and Faking Lives: The Ethics of Collaborative Life Writing," *Style* 32.2 (1998): 334–50; Cora Diamond, "Henry James, Moral Philosophers, Moralism," *Henry James Review* 18.3 (1997): 243–57; Kathleen Lundeen, "Who Has the Right To Feel? The Ethics of Literary Empathy," *Style* 32.2 (1998): 261–71; Adam Zachary Newton, "'Nothing But Face'—'To Hell with Philosophy'? Witold Gombrowicz, Bruno Schulz, and the Scandal of Human Countenance," *Style* 32.2 (1998): 243–60; Martha C. Nussbaum, "Exactly and Responsibly: A Defense of Ethical Criticism," *Philosophy and Literature* 22.2 (1998): 343–65; and James Phelan, "Sethe's Choice: *Beloved* and the Ethics of Reading," *Style* 32.2 (1998): 318–33.

Works Cited

Hassan, Ihab. *Radical Innocence: Studies in the Contemporary American Novel.* Princeton: Princeton UP, 1961.
Siebers, Tobin. *The Ethics of Criticism.* Ithaca: Cornell UP, 1988.

I

THEORY AND THE ETHICS OF LITERARY STUDY

A HUMANISTIC ETHICS OF READING

DANIEL R. SCHWARZ

W E ARE IN the midst of a humanistic revival or at least a neohumanist burst of energy. New Historicism and cultural criticism have paved the way for this turn by focusing on representation and mimesis. Not surprisingly, when the representation of a priori worlds becomes important, issues of how humans live and what they live for become central because they are what concern us as readers and teachers—sometimes in spite of ourselves. The representation of the relationship between author and reader is the representation of an ethical relationship.

As the high tide of rhetorical deconstruction receded and as Deconstruction was integrated into more mimetic approaches, hermeneutical questions have again come to the fore. Many of us were skeptical of deconstruction's moral *nolo contendere:* For who really reads in terms of discovering where meaning goes astray? Is that kind of engagement something other than reading, or a subcategory of picaresque reading, where the reader stands outside the text's imagined world as a carping cynic? In our teaching and reading, most of us, even while welcoming the important contributions of recent theory, supplement theoretically driven criticism with hermeneutical questions that ask, "What does this work mean?" "What does it signify for us?" and "How do the imagined worlds reflect anterior ones?" And these are all questions with ethical components.

Although the emphasis varies from critic to critic, we can identify several concepts shared by these humanists:

1. The form of a literary text—its style, structure, and narrative technique —expresses its value system. Put another way, form discovers the meaning of content.

2. A literary text is a creative gesture of the author. Understanding the process of imitating the external world gives us insight into the artistry and meaning of the text.

3. A literary text imitates a world that precedes the text, and the critic should recapture that world primarily by formal analysis of the text, although knowledge of the historical context and author is often important.

4. A literary text has an original meaning, a center, that can be approached, albeit perhaps not reached, by perceptive reading. The goal is to discover what the author said to the intended audience, as well as what the author says to us now. Acts of interpretation at their best—subtle, lucid, inclusive, perceptive—can bring that goal into sight, even while allowing for unintended meanings in what is now called the subtext.

5. Human behavior is central to most literary texts and should be a major concern of analysis. Although modes of characterization differ, the psychology and morality of characters must be understood as if the characters were metaphors for real people, for understanding others helps us to understand ourselves.

6. The inclusiveness, the depth, and the range of the literary text's vision is a measure of that text's quality.

As the new millennium begins, we need to acknowledge the important role that the Anglo-American humanistic tradition—stretching from Matthew Arnold and Henry James to J. Hillis Miller and Raymond Williams—has played and still plays in how many of us write and teach, especially in departments of English and American Literature.

The differences that separated various strands of Anglo-American criticism—formalist and historical—prior to the theoretical revolution of the 1970s seem less significant than they once did. Now we are able to see that the New Critics, Aristotelians, the *Partisan Review* group, contextualists, and literary historians share a number of important assumptions: authors write to express their ideas and emotions; the way humans live and the values for which they live are of fundamental interest to authors and readers; literature expresses insights about human life and responses to human situations, and that is the main reason why we read, teach, and think about literature.

Notwithstanding the theoretical revolution, these assumptions still play a powerful role in the classroom and even in the subtext of much of today's professional discourse. To be sure, the Anglo-American humanistic tradition was influenced by such European figures as Erich Auerbach and René Wellek and, in later years, by Jacques Derrida, Michel Foucault, Jürgen Habermas, and Jacques Lacan. But the basic critical principles of the most significant American figures in feminism (Elaine Showalter, Sandra Gilbert, and Susan Gubar), Marxism (Raymond Williams, Terry Eagleton, and Fredric Jameson), and poststructuralism (J. Hillis Miller, Geoffrey Hartman, and Harold Bloom) develop from the humanistic concepts defined above.

Texts demand ethical responses from their readers in part because *saying* always has an ethical dimension *and* because *we* are our values, and we never take a moral holiday from our values. We can no more ignore the ethical implications of what we read than we can ignore the ethical implications of life. But how does one discuss how one reads ethically? In practice, critics seeking a grammar of ethics have often focused on prose fiction, but one can, as Aristotle teaches us, find the ethical encounters and intersubjective relationships that form an important basis for those encounters in drama —and even in lyrics such as Marvell's "To His Coy Mistress" or Donne's "The Good Morrow." Yet many questions remain. Do we need to differentiate between the ethical implications of our response to short poems and the evolving effects—the proposing, modification, transformation, undermining, and reformation of patterns of meaning within narrative structures of prose fiction that we often do not read at one sitting? Does gender criticism address different kinds of ethical questions, in part because the canon of women's literature may have generic differences in some of its more confessional subjects and elliptical forms? Perhaps women writers, characters, and readers respond to different—more intuitive, less linear—ethical models. Might narrative ethics in Woolf, where a grammar of feeling dominates, differ from a narrative ethics in Dickens, where a grammar of motive dominates? Does cultural relativity determine the diverse responses of different readers to certain texts?

II

What unites ethical critics—Martha Nussbaum, Stanley Cavell, Richard Rorty, Wayne Booth, and, more recently, Adam Zachary Newton—is the premise of a strong connection between art and life. Rather than being divorced from life, our reading experience—if we read actively and with intelligence—is central to life and contributes to the development of the mature personality. Literature provides surrogate experiences for the reader, experiences that, because they are embodied within artistically shaped ontologies, heighten our awareness of moral discriminations. Yet, I suggest, what distinguishes moral philosophy from literature is its specificity, its nominalism, and its dramatized particularity.

Cavell, an American pragmatist, wishes to limit our ethical responses to the intersubjective relations *within* texts, and the work of such figures as Mikhail Bakhtin and Emmanuel Levinas has taken ethics in that direction. To some extent, that is the thrust of Newton's provocative *Narrative Ethics* (1995). But is a study of the immediacy of intersubjectivity a study of the range of reading ethics? Does it always account for nuances of form and the process of reading? Ethical criticism implies a transactive theory of reading where texts shape reader, and reader shapes text. Thus, narrative ethics also depends on the intersubjectivity of that transaction. We need, also, to differentiate between the ethical responses created by a structure of effects in the process of reading and the ethics of a reader resistant to the implications of that process, and to understand how and why the second response may take place after the reading—perhaps even years later when our retrospective view may make us realize a text's sexist or racist or homophobic implications.

Literature raises ethical questions that enable us to consider not only how we would behave in certain circumstances but also whether—even as we empathetically read a text—we should maintain some stance of resistance by which to judge that text's ethical implications. Although some artistic experiences allow for more of a moral holiday than others, even abstract art finally needs to be recuperated in human terms and regarding thematic issues. Literature calls upon us to respond fully, viscerally, with every dimension of our psychological and moral being.

Let us turn to an example where our ethics *demands* a response. When T. S. Eliot's speaker in the first stanza of his dramatic monologue "Gerontion" (1920) derides in most derogatory terms "the Jew"—drawing upon a rhetoric of insult to milk the stereotype of the Jew—we respond in multiple ways:

> I was neither at the hot gates
> Nor fought in the warm rain
> Nor knee deep in the salt marsh, heaving a cutlass,
> Bitten by flies, fought.
> My house is a decayed house,
> And the jew squats on the window sill, the owner,
> Spawned in some estaminet of Antwerp,
> Blistered in Brussels, patched and peeled in London.
> The goat coughs at night in the field overhead;
> Rocks, moss, stonecrop, iron, merds.
> The woman keeps the kitchen, makes tea,
> Sneezes at evening, poking the peevish gutter.

Devoting three lines to derogate the landlord with onomatopoeic verbs and participles—"squats," "spawned," "blistered," "patched," and "peeled"—is a gross example of the rhetoric of insult, prejudice, and defamation. Jews are associated in the passage with not only disease and decay but with lust and defecation. We stop and consider what this tells us about the narrator, whether we can attribute the words to an imperceptive speaker, whether the author is ironic, whether the dominant narrative of modernism adequately takes account of Eliot's anti-Semitism, whether a formal analysis ignores a critique of the cultural context in which such language was permissible, and, finally, whether the focus on formalism caused critics in the several decades following publication to ignore the inflammatory nature of this image—particularly after the Holocaust.

Notwithstanding its reliance on Bakhtin, Levinas, and Cavell, Anglo-American ethical criticism works partially within an Anglo-American critical tradition defined earlier by Robert Langbaum and Wayne Booth. Langbaum describes the tension between sympathy and judgment in *The Poetry of Experience: The Dramatic Monologue in Modern Literary Experience* (1957). But in part, because his subject was prose fiction, Booth is the more familiar and important prototype.

Beginning with *The Rhetoric of Fiction* (1961), Booth has always stressed the study of what works are made to *do* rather than the study of what works are made to *be*. In *The Company We Keep: An Ethics of Fiction* (1988), he adds the codicil that we as readers change and that we should acknowledge —both while reading and in our retrospective response—who we are and why we read as we do. In *The Company We Keep*, Booth regretted the then-current unwillingness to talk about the ethical effects of our reading experiences. What he proposed is not a one-dimensional ethic that condemns books as "good" or "bad" but a critical pluralism in which we can speak about what happens to each of us while we read and about why we prefer one text to another. He argued for the importance of considering the values of a reading experience: "Ethical criticism attempts to describe the encounters of a story-teller's ethos with that of the reader or listener" (8). The donnée of Booth's book is an incident at the University of Chicago when the late Paul Moses—a young assistant professor and a black man—objected to being expected to teach *Huckleberry Finn* because it was to him racist. Booth argues that, contrary to formalist critical ethos, we should consider what books do to readers: "Paul Moses's reading of *Huckleberry Finn*, an overt ethical appraisal, is one legitimate form of literary criticism" (4).

Booth is an articulate spokesman for a humanistic poetics that emphasizes how human readers respond to human subjects presented by human authors within an imagined world that represents—even if only as an illuminating distortion—anterior reality. He speaks of the experience of actual readers responding to actual texts, and his commonsense approach speaks, I believe, to the empirical experience of real readers: "In short, the ideal of purging oneself of responses to persons, the ideal of refusing to play the human roles offered us by literature, is never realized by an actual reader who reads a compelling fiction for the sake of reading it (rather than for the sake of obtaining material for an essay, dissertation or book)" (255–56). He argues, I believe correctly, that we respond to literary characterizations not as tropes but as representations of something anterior to the text: "When we lose our capacity to succumb, when we reach a point at which no other characters can manage to enter our imaginative or emotional or intellectual territory and *take over,* at least for the time being, then we are dead on our feet" (257). In our response to imagined worlds, do we not privilege our recognition of kinship with realized characters and our interest in their problems?

Booth uses the metaphor of friendship—the metaphor of *people meeting* as they share stories—to describe the interrelationship between readers and books during the process of reading: "Perhaps most obviously, this metaphor spontaneously revives a kind of talk, once almost universal, about the types of friendship or companionship a book provides *as* it is read" (170). He is concerned not only with the effect of narratives on audiences but on the tellers themselves: "Any story told with genuine engagement will affect its teller fully as much as it affects listeners" (42). According to Booth, "our reading friends vary according to seven criteria: the sheer *quantity* of invitations they offer us; the degree of *responsibility* they grant to us; the *degree* of intimacy in the friendship; the *intensity* of engagement; the *coherence,* or consistency of the proffered world; the *distance* between their world and ours; and the kind, or *range of kinds,* of activities suggested, invited, or demanded" (179–80). "In our living friends," he asserts, "we find these same variables" (180). Even those skeptical about seeing books as self-created texts, or as historical or cultural productions, may be uncomfortable with the ways that Booth anthropomorphizes books as if they were people and thinks of them as if they were human company. His voice is that of a traditional humanist inquiring about why and how we read; he is committed to reading as an essential activity and passionate in his enthusiasm for books that he admires.

As an Aristotelian, Booth regards ethics, rhetoric, and politics as inextricably related. The followers of Derrida and de Man have sought to define rhetoric as the study of tropes and semiology, as the study of how language means, and to separate both from hermeneutics, that is, what language means. But for Booth, rhetoric—as the art of persuasion *and* as the study of how language evokes meaning—cannot be separated from hermeneutics or ethics: "If 'virtue' covers every kind of genuine strength or power, and if a person's ethos is the total range of his or her virtues, then ethical criticism will be any effort to show how the virtues of narratives relate to the virtues of selves and societies, or how the ethos of any story affects or is affected by the ethos—the collection of virtues—of any given reader" (11). Booth believes that criticism is necessarily ethical and that not only feminists, blacks concerned with racism, and Marxists, but "even those critics who work hard to purge themselves of all but the most abstract formal interests turn out to have an ethical program in mind—a belief that a given way of reading, or a given kind of genuine literature, is what will do us the most good" (5). Of course, we all approach texts with preconceived ideologies of reading and of what we should be teaching. Every question we ask in our classrooms is an ethical and political question, deriving from our hierarchy of what is essential and what needs to be known. Are not our syllabi and reading lists political and ethical statements?

I believe that the close reading of texts—both from an authorial and resistant perspective—enables us to perceive more clearly. I believe in a continuity between reading texts and reading lives. I believe that the activity of critical thinking—not merely literary criticism—can be taught by the analysis of language. I believe in the place of the aesthetic. I believe that we can enter into imagined worlds and learn from them. Following Aristotle, I believe that the aesthetic, ethical, and political are inextricably linked.

III

Why did ethics virtually disappear from the universe of literary studies in the 1970s and 1980s? Was it in part the disillusionment of the Vietnam War that seemed to give the lie to the view prevailing after the Second World War that we could cultivate our minds and control our lives after the defeat of the Nazis and the Japanese? As critics, we once addressed both the ethics of reading and the ethics while reading, and that in part is what Arnold meant by "high seriousness," F. R. Leavis by such phrases as "tangible realism" and "bracing moralism," and Lionel Trilling by "the hum and buzz of implication."

Literary meaning depends on a trialogue among (1) authorial intention and interest, (2) the formal text produced by the author for a specific historical audience, and (3) the responses of a particular reader in a specific time. Texts mediate and condense anterior worlds and authors' psyches. The condensation is presented by words, words that are a web of signs that signify something beyond themselves; within a text, words signify differently.

Some words and phrases almost summon a visible presence; others are elusive or may barely even matter in terms of their representation—as in Joyce's encyclopedic catalogues in the "Cyclops" episode of *Ulysses*.

The context of any discourse determines the meaning—or should we say the epistemological and semiological value of the word or sentence? And once we use the word *value* are we not saying that words have an ethical quotient? Human agency—on the part of author, reader, or characters within real or imagined worlds—derives in part from will, from the idiosyncrasies of the human psyche and, in part, on cultural forces beyond the control of the individual. That is another way of saying that language is constituted and constituting, although it gives subjective human agency to the act of constituting. While we need to be alert to the implications of racist, sexist, and anti-Semitic nuances, we also need to stress reading the words on the page in terms of the demands made by the text's context and form—in particular, by its structure of effects or what I have called the *doesness* of the text.

If awareness of oneself and one's relationship to family and community —including one's responsibilities, commitments, and values—is part of the ethical life, then reading contributes to greater self-understanding. Reading complements our experience by enabling us to live lives beyond those we live and to experience emotions that are not ours; it heightens our perspicacity by enabling us to watch *figures*—tropes, that is, personifications of our fellow humans—who are not ourselves, but like ourselves.

When we enter into an imagined world, we become involved with what Nadine Gordimer has called "the substance of living from which the artist draws his vision," and our criticism must speak to that "substance of living." In Third World and postcolonial literature—and in politically engaged texts such as Wiesel's *Night* or Levi's *The Periodic Table*—this involvement is particularly intense. Thus, the interest in postcolonial and Third World literature—perhaps accelerated by Soyinka's and Walcott's Nobel prizes— challenges the tenets of deconstruction. Literature written at the political edge reminds us what literature has always been about: urgency, commitment, tension, and feeling. Indeed, at times have we not transferred those emotions to parochial critical debate rather than to our responses to literature? While the critical analysis of the gaps, fissures, and enigmas and of the free play of signifiers in the poetry of Wally Serote ("Death Survey") and Don Mattera ("Singing Fools") can never be intellectually irrelevant, we must focus, too, on those poets' status as persecuted blacks in the former regime of South Africa and the pain and alienation that they felt in the face of persecution. Nadine Gordimer has written—and Joyce might have said the same thing about Ireland—"It is from the daily life of South Africa that there have come the conditions of profound alienation which prevail among South African artists." When discussing politically engaged literature—be it Soyinka, Gordimer, Wiesel, or Levi—we need to recuperate historical circumstances and understand the writer's ordering of that history in his or her imagined world. We need to know not merely what patterns of provisional representation are created by language but the historical, political, and social grounds of that representation. We need to be open to hearing the often unsophisticated and unironical voice of pain, angst, and fear. When we read literature, we journey into an imagined land while at the same time remaining home. Reading is a kind of imaginative traveling; unlike real traveling, we are able to transport ourselves immediately back "home." Travel is immersive; home is reflective. How we take our imaginative journeys depends on how we are trained to read, as well as what we as readers do with the available data—how we sort it out and make sense of it. Although the text has a kind of stability because it cannot *change,* our ways of speaking about texts are always somewhat metaphoric.

Just as an author "rents" multiple linguistic systems to create what Bakhtin calls heteroglossia, the reader "rents" diverse interpretive strategies —or perspectives—depending upon his or her prior experience. But we each belong to multiple interpretive communities; and as we read, we draw upon our participation and experience in several interpretive communities. Not only do those interpretive communities change as well as modify and subvert one another, but our relationship to them varies from text to text. How we read texts—and the world—depends on an ever-changing hierarchy of interpretive strategies. These hierarchies constitute our reading of texts—and the world—even as they are constituted by it. That is, as we read, our interpretive strategies are challenged and modified even as they modify what we read. When reading criticism we need to be aware of the theoretical and methodological assumptions that produce a reading and examine whether we belong to the community of readers who share those assumptions.

Our ethics of reading needs to account for the subjectivity inherent in our reading. Indeed, subjectivity may idiosyncratically deflect us from the decision about which interpretive communities we shall use. Need we be self-conscious about the distinctiveness of our position as to the text that we are describing or to which we are responding? If someone were to read my interpretive criticism or come to my classes, he or she would be aware of my propensity for seeing texts in historical, mimetic, and formal terms —especially my propensity as a pragmatic Aristotelian to hear the voices of narrators and to stress the relationship between *doesness* and *isness.* And what about my personal background and experience? My biases and short-comings? Do I not have a greater professional and personal stake in some texts than in others?

What I am suggesting is that the reader as *Übermensch,* or super-reader, is a disguise for the human reader with all of his or her tics and quirks. Thus, if we wish to enter into a dialogue with other approaches, we need to understand the deflection caused by our subjectivity and that of the interpretive critics we read. It may be worth the effort to induce from each interpretive text a persona of the critic to see if we can explain his or her subjectivity and thus understand the critic's underlying perspective, approach, values, methods, and theory. That is, we must read critical texts as if they, too, were spoken by a human voice to a human audience, and—as if we were hearing a first-person narration—we must attend to what is missing or distorted.

IV

In considering ethical reading, I want to conclude by suggesting that we differentiate between an *ethics of reading* and an *ethics while reading.* For me, an ethics *of* reading includes acknowledging who we are and what our biases and interests are. An ethics *of* reading proposes that we interpret a given literary work by reading that text from multiple perspectives, acknowledging the differences between authorial and resistant readings, and understanding why and how the original audience might have responded and for what reasons. An ethics *of* reading realizes that original and contemporary audiences are polyauditory and that each of us is an interpretive community of one. It understands that the essential critical mantras "Always the text" and "Always historicize" may be at cross purposes. When what we choose to include on our syllabi has an ethical dimension, we are adhering to an ethics of reading. Thus, I will choose to select other Conrad works for my undergraduate lecture course than the unfortunately titled *The Nigger of the "Narcissus."*

An ethics *while* reading is different from an ethics *of* reading in its attention to a value-oriented epistemology. An ethics *while* reading implies attention to moral issues generated by events described within an imagined world. It asks what ethical questions are involved in the act of transforming life into art and perceives such issues as Pound's or Eliot's anti-Semitism and the patronizing racism of some American nineteenth- and early twentieth-century writers.

Let me tentatively propose five stages of the hermeneutical activities involved in ethical reading and interpretation. Even while acknowledging that my model is suggestive rather than rigorous, I believe that we do perceive in stages that move from a naïve response or surface interpretation to critical or in-depth interpretation and, finally, to understanding our readings conceptually and ethically in terms of other knowledge. Awareness of such stages enables us to read ethically and demonstrates how we progress from an ethics *while* reading to an ethics *of* reading, although, of course, the two concepts fertilize one another. My stages are:

1. *Immersion in the process of reading and the discovery of imagined worlds.* Reading is a place where text and reader meet in a transaction. As we open a text, we and the author meet as if together we were going to draw a map of an uncharted space. We partially suspend our sense of our world as we enter into the imagined world; we respond in experimental terms to the episodes, the story, the physical setting, the individualized characters as humans, and the telling voice. Although it has become fashionable to speak dismissively of such reading as "naïve," or the result of the "mimetic illusion," how many of us, in fact, do read in that way with pleasure and delight— and with ethical judgments? Who among us would be teaching and studying literature had we not learned to read mimetically?

2. *Quest for understanding.* Our quest is closely related to the diachronic, linear, temporal activity of reading. The quest speaks to the gap between "what did you say?" and "what did you mean?" In writing, as opposed to speech, the speaker cannot correct, intrude, or qualify; he or she cannot use gestures or adjust the delivery of his or her discourse. Because in writing we lack the speaker's help, we must make our own adjustments in our reading. As Paul Ricouer notes, "What the text says now matters more than what the author meant to say, and every exegesis unfolds its procedures within the circumference of a meaning that has broken its moorings to the psychology of its author" (191). In modern and postmodern texts, our search for necessary information will be much more of a factor than in traditional texts. In this stage, as we are actively unraveling the complexities of plot, we also seek to discover the principles or worldview by which the author expects us to understand the various behaviors of his or her characters in terms of their motives and values. Moreover, we make ethical judgments of inter-subjective relations *and* authorial choices.

3. *Self-conscious reflection.* Reflection speaks to the gap between "what did *you* mean?" and "what does *that* mean?" Upon reflection, we may adjust our perspective or see new ones. What the interpretive reader does—particularly with spare, allusive (as well as elusive and illusive) modern literature—is to fill the gaps left by the text to create an explanatory text or Midrash on the text itself. As Wolfgang Iser observes, "What is said only appears to take on significance as a reference to what is not said; it is the implications and not the statements that give shape and weight to the meaning" (qtd. in Suleiman and Crosman 111). While the reader half perceives, half creates his or her original "immersed" reading of the text, the reader retrospectively—from the vantage point of knowing the whole—imposes shape and form on his or her story of reading. The reader discovers its significance in relation to his or her other experiences, including other reading experiences, and in terms of the interpretive communities to which he or she belongs. The reader reasons posteriorly from effects to causes. The reader is aware of referentiality to the anterior world—how that world informs the author's mimesis—and to the world in which he or she lives. The reader begins—more in modern texts, but even in traditional texts—to separate his or her own version of what is really meant from what is said, and to place ethical issues in the context of larger value issues.

Here, Tzvetan Todorov's distinction between signification and symbolization is useful in defining how the reader moves from the imagined ontology to reflection: "Signified facts are *understood:* all we need is knowledge of the language in which the text is written. Symbolization facts are *interpreted:* and interpretations vary from one subject to another" (qtd. in Suleiman and Crosman 73). One notable problem is that, in practice, what is understood or judged by one reader as signified facts may require interpretation or a different ethical judgment by another.

4. *Critical analysis.* As Ricouer writes, "To understand a text is to follow its movement from sense to reference, from what it says to what it talks about" (214). In the process, we always move from signifier to signified; for no sooner do we understand what the original signifiers signify within the imagined world than these signifieds in turn become signifiers for larger issues and symbolic constructions in the world beyond the text. Each of us responds in terms of the *values* enacted by the text and, as with my example from Eliot's "Gerontion"—or, Pound's anti-Semitism—*resists* where texts disturb our sense of fairness.

Although the reader responds to texts in such multiple ways and for such diverse reasons that we cannot speak of a correct reading, we can speak of a dialogue among plausible readings. Drawing upon our interpretive strategies, we reflect on generic, intertextual, linguistic, and biographical relationships that disrupt linear reading; we move back and forth from the whole to the part. As Ricouer writes: "The reconstruction of the text as a whole is implied in the recognition of the parts. And reciprocally, it is in constructing the details that we construe the whole" (204). My responses to my reading are a function of what I know, what I have recently been reading, my last experience of reading a particular author, my knowledge of the period in which the author wrote as well as the influences upon his or her influence on others, *and* my current values. My responses also depend both on how willing I am to suspend my irony and detachment and enter into the imagined world of the text and on how much of the text my memory retains.

5. *Cognition in terms of what we know.* In a continuation of our fourth stage, we return to the original reading experience and text, subsequently modifying our conceptual hypotheses about genre, period, author, canon, themes, and, most of all, *values.* We integrate what we have read into our reading of other texts and into our way of looking at ourselves and the world. Here, we consciously use our values and our categorizing sensibility—our rage for order—to make sense of our reading experience and our way of being in our world. In the final stage, the interpretive reader may become a critic who writes his or her own text about the "transaction" between the self and the text—and this response has an ethical component.

Works Cited

Booth, Wayne C. *The Company We Keep: An Ethics of Fiction.* Berkeley: U of California P, 1988.
———. *The Rhetoric of Fiction.* 1961. Chicago: U of Chicago P, 1983.
Gordimer, Nadine. "The Arts in Adversity: Apprentices of Freedom." *New Society* 24.31 (1981): n.p.
Langbaum, Robert. *The Poetry of Experience: The Dramatic Monologue in Modern Literary Tradition.* New York: Norton, 1957.
Newton, Adam Zachary. *Narrative Ethics.* Cambridge: Harvard UP, 1995.
Ricouer, Paul. "The Model of the Text." *Social Research* 51.1 (1984): 185–218.
Suleiman, Susan, and Inge Crosman, eds. *The Reader in the Text: Essays on Audience and Interpretation.* Princeton: Princeton UP, 1980.

WHY ETHICAL CRITICISM
CAN NEVER BE SIMPLE

WAYNE C. BOOTH

> Auden's assertion that poetry doesn't make things happen is a tidy conceit
> for a melancholy afternoon's tea break, but as the prayers smoke from the
> mosque and the young thousands chant rap, my era will re-examine what is
> happening. Nor in that circum-audient air can one deny—terrifying, some
> of it—the power of prose.
>
> —Hortense Calisher

THIS ESSAY is one of many recent efforts, by myself and others, to challenge two critical schools popular through much of this century: those who think ethical judgments have nothing to do with genuine "literary" or "aesthetic" criticism, and those who think that ethical judgments about stories can never be anything more than subjective opinion. My thesis is thus double: ethical criticism is relevant to all literature, no matter how broadly or narrowly we define that controversial term; and such criticism, when done responsibly, can be a genuine form of rational inquiry. It is true that it will never produce results nearly as uncontroversial as deciding whether it rained in New York yesterday, or even whether President Clinton lied. What's more, many of its judgments, such as Plato's exaggerated attacks on Homer, will be rejected by most serious ethical critics. Yet when responsible readers of powerful stories engage in genuine inquiry about their ethical value, they can produce results that deserve the tricky label "knowledge."[1]

The very phrase "ethical inquiry" is for some thinkers an oxymoron. Ethical *indictment* of a story? Of course you can have that, as a personal expression. Ethical celebration? All right, if it will please a collection of fellow believers. But inquiry? The word implies the chance of arriving at established, decisive conclusions: *knowledge*. About ethics, many still claim, there can be no such conclusions—and thus no genuine inquiry about them. For some these days, the claim has been strengthened by a flood of aggressive and often carelessly performed denigrations of first-class works on grounds of sexism, racism, anti-Semitism, or "classism." Though seldom traveling under moral or ethical terminology, these intrusions of "ideological" interests have seemed to some a total corruption of the formal or structural standards that dominated criticism in midcentury.[2]

Meanwhile overconfident ethical or moral indictments and calls for censorship seem increasingly fashionable, many of them pursued so irrationally as to provide evidence that genuine inquiry flees whenever questions about ethics enter the room. The responses to those would-be censors are often equally subjective and opinionated, too often divorced from any serious digging into the potential dangers for readers who really listen to what the storyteller tells. (From here on I use the term "listen" to cover all serious engagement with stories, whether by readers or viewers or listeners.) Many of the defenders against censorship, resting strictly on First Amendment grounds, talk as if to engage in ethical or moral criticism is itself an act of censorship: once we step onto the slippery slope—"this story is ethically faulty"—the censors will bury our words and hurtle us onto the bottom.

More challenging efforts to rule out ethical criticism come from those who fear that it will destroy our most precious narrative possession: the "aesthetic" domain, the world of true art, a world that is not just different from the quotidian world of moral conflict but in effect far superior to it. As Wendy Steiner says in the conclusion to *The Scandal of Pleasure,* genuine art "occupies a different moral space" from the world of practical affairs. For her, since art is obviously "virtual," not concerned about "reality," it should not be subject to the kind of moral criticism we offer when everyday behavior in the so-called real world offends us (211).

What is striking, however, is that whether critics defend or attack ethical criticism, and whether or not "ideological" critics use ethical terms, nearly everyone concedes that no matter what we do or say about the ethical powers of art, those powers are real. Even the most ardent opponents of censorship or ethical criticism do not deny that many stories can actually harm at least some of those who "take them in." And even the most ardent attackers on immoral artworks imply by their every gesture that certain other works, in contrast, are not just morally defensible, not just beneficial, but essential to any full human life.

Claims about the transformative ethical power of all art are perhaps least questionable when we turn from "all art" to literary art, art that, because its very nature entails language loaded with ethical judgments, implants views about how to live or not to live. When the word "literature" is expanded to include all stories that we may listen to—not just novels, plays, and poems, but also operas, memoirs, gossip, soap operas, TV and movie dramas fictional and "real," stories heard in childhood—the power of narrative to change our lives, for good or ill, becomes undeniable.

That power is, however, tacitly denied by many a critic, simply by writing as if the ethical effects of stories are irrelevant to quality. In a recent and lengthy favorable account of the thirty novels by Stephen King, Mark Singer has not a word about what King's three hundred million copies sold have taught the world's mostly unsophisticated readers: about what actions are portrayed as really contemptible or admirable; about what views concerning aliens and phantoms are shown as naïve or sophisticated or mentally destructive; about what narrative devices are in effect ethical corruptions. The only ethical judgments Singer intrudes are against critics like me, what he calls "arbiters," who, "without bothering to read King, feel comfortable dismissing him as a hack."[3]

As my ambiguous use so far of the words "ethical" and "moral" suggests, one reason no progress is made in our battles is that too many reduce both terms to the narrowest possible moral codes. The essential issue for critics —perhaps in contrast with politicians—is not whether some part of a given story violates this or that moral code; rather, it is the overall effect on the *ethos,* the *character,* of the listener. And that effect is not to be measured by some simple study of overt behavior after listening: it must include the very quality of the life lived while listening.

Effects on actual behavior are extremely elusive and will, I suspect, never be conclusively demonstrated. It is true that whenever I ask adult readers if they can think of works that changed their lives in a significant way, whether recently or in childhood, almost all of them offer at least one powerful example. Sometimes they stress their regret ("How I wish I had not stumbled upon Jack Kerouac's *On the Road* when I was sixteen; I went 'on the road' for a full year, self-destructively").[4] More often they express deep gratitude ("Reading Tolstoy's *Resurrection* in my forties transformed my attitude toward religion; I had been an atheist for twenty years, and after reading that work—thank God!—I was not"). When the question is generalized—"Do you think that a large share of your ethical education, your construction as a person, was performed by stories, from infancy on?"—most answer decisively, "Yes." They agree that when we really engage with the characters we meet and the moral choices those characters face, ethical changes occur in us, for good or ill—especially when we are young.

To underline my point once again: no one who has thought about it for long can deny that we are at least partially constructed, in our most fundamental moral character, by the stories we have heard, or read, or viewed, or acted out in amateur theatricals: the stories we have really *listened* to. Their authors built their stories by creating *characters,* characters exhibiting an *ethos* that could be thought of as a collection of virtues and vices, presented as admirable or contemptible. Though many modern authors try to disguise this fact by dealing overtly with character qualities not ordinarily thought of in moral terms—such virtues as uncompromising pursuit of existential truth or honest probing of postmodernist mysteries—I can think of no published story that does not exhibit its author's implied judgments about how to live and what to believe about how to live.

The point is underlined when we think about how the world's most successful moral teachers have taken it for granted: they have chosen to tell stories. Rather than resorting to blunt, non-narrative preaching, they have implanted their messages into engaging narrative worlds. Although it is true that some moralizers have turned their tales into prosaic sermons, with simple summarizing moral tags, the most effective teachers—those who recognize moral complexities—have chosen narrative, with its inevitable ambiguities, as the chief vehicle.

Why did the authors of the Bible choose mainly to be storytellers rather than blunt exhorters with a moral tag at the end of each story? They did not rest with the laying down of bare codes, like a list of flat commandments. Though they sometimes tried the brief commandment line,[5] they more often told stories, like the one about a troubled, abandoned, child-hero who, as leader of his liberated people, almost botches the job of obtaining some divine rules printed on a tablet, and about a people who largely botch the job of receiving and abiding by them. The pious preachers did not just print out the sermons of a savior; they placed the sermons into a story, and they surrounded them with other stories, especially the one about how the hero himself grappled with questions about his status as savior, and about how he told scores of radically ambiguous parables that forced his listeners into moral thought. They did not openly preach that for God to be incarnated as a man entails irresolvable paradoxes; they *told a story* about how the God/man at the moment of supreme moral testing is ridden with doubt and cries out, as any of us would have done, "My God, my God, why has thou forsaken me?"

All those biblical authors must have known, perhaps without knowing what they knew, that serious stories educate morally—and they do so more powerfully than do story-free sermons. Just imagine how little effect on the world John Bunyan would have had if he had put into non-narrative prose the various messages embodied in *Pilgrim's Progress.*[6]

In short, the great tellers and most of us listeners have known in our bones that stories, whether fictional or historical, in prose or in verse, whether told by mothers to infants or by rabbis and priests to the elderly and dying, whether labeled as sacred or profane or as teaching good morality or bad—*stories* are our major moral teachers. Some stories teach only a particular moral perspective, one that can be captured with a moral tag, as in some of Aesop's fables and the simpler biblical tales. Many of them teach a morality that you and I would reject. But all of them teach, and thus in a sense they are open to moral inquiry, even when they do not seem to invite or tolerate it.

In the face of this general acknowledgment of stories' power, how could it happen that entire critical schools have rejected criticism that deals with such power? One obvious answer is that critics have wanted to escape the threatening flood of controversial judgments we land in as soon as ethical judgments are invited into aesthetic territory. Ethical judgments are by their nature controversial: the very point of uttering them is to awaken or challenge those who have missed the point. Consequently, whenever a feminist critic, say, judges a novel or poem to be sexist, she can be sure to be attacked by someone who sees her values as skewed. To praise or condemn for political correctness is widely scoffed at as absurd: political judgments are merely subjective. To judge all or part of a poem according to religious values is seen as even more absurd, since religious views are widely seen as even less subject to rational argument.

A second powerful reason for suppression is the fear already mentioned: that ethical criticism of any kind, even when critics agree with the proclaimed values, is an invasion of "aesthetic" territory. As Charles Altieri reports later in this collection, in "Lyrical Ethics and Literary Experience," to be seen as an ethical critic can trigger thoughtless responses from purists who fear that the "lyrical" or the "beautiful" will be sacrificed to preaching.

The third reason, my main interest in this essay, is too often overlooked in today's controversies. "Literature" itself is not just a controversial term: the works it covers are ethically and aesthetically so diverse, both in their intent and in their realization in multiple acts of listening, that any one critical method can at best "cover" no more than a fraction of actual works. The consequence is that a large share of attempted ethical criticism deserves to be attacked as unfair or irrelevant; methods and stances appropriate to one kind of story can be useless or destructive when applied to other kinds.

In what follows, I explore, for the five hundredth time in the history of criticism, some of the varieties of literary intention, as they inevitably reinforce the conflicts about ethical criticism. My basic argument is that only a fully developed critical pluralism—of principles, of methods, of purposes, and of definitions of subject matter—can ever reduce the quantity of pointless quarreling over ethical matters. Different genres, different intentions, invite or reject different ethical judgments.[7]

II

Even the word "intention" already lands us in deep controversy. The anti-intentionalists have dominated many fields in recent decades, as they have for the most part ignored the powerful arguments and distinctions made by William Empson, Ronald Crane, E. D. Hirsch, and others throughout the "New Critical" wars.[8] The most important of these distinctions, bungled by all of those who have declared the author and his or her intentions dead, is between the flesh-and-blood author whose intentions, whether or not recorded outside the work, are only loosely relevant to one's reading of the work, and the actualized text's intentions: what one can infer from the collection of choices that every work worth bothering about reveals. The author implied by those choices *made* them, consciously or unconsciously, and our judgments of the worth of any work depend on our decision, again conscious or unconscious, about whether the choices were good ones. Whether we use the word "intentions" or not, we are all dependent, in everything we say about a work, on an implied relation between our intentions and the intentions embedded in the author's choices.[9]

Now, as everyone who ever consults his or her own soul knows, our intentions in real life, as in any construction of a novel or poem, are manifold in kind and often confused or ambivalent in product. We are social selves, multiple selves, most of us moving always, or almost always, in many directions at once. Though sometimes we manage some degree of focus in daily choices, our genuine focusing usually comes when we move in the direction of artistic or technological production: the effort to pull the parts of life into some coherent interrelation. It is when we aim for a goal, especially when we try to *make* something coherent, that our multiplicity sometimes becomes reduced to a single, however complex, target. Like the badge-winning infantry rifleman I aimed to become in my World War II basic training, we concentrate so intently on the target that everything else is, for the time being, simply forgotten.

Artists—painters, musicians, novelists, poets—generally achieve something like that concentration, sloughing off many, though usually not all, of their rival selves. Many have testified to the way in which, as they pursue draft after draft, the manifold possibilities get reduced to a range of centered choices. Even those who have pretended to have no center, to celebrate their own uncontrollable richness, have in fact been forced, by the very nature of producing anything whatever, into a reduction of multiple or divided selves toward what critics used to call a "unity."

My favorite illustration of this point, one that I have printed several times before, was my encounter with Saul Bellow, back in 1962 or 1963. Memory reports it like this:

> WB: What are you up to, Saul?
> SB: Well, I'm spending about four hours a day revising a novel that's still much too long.
> WB: What'll it be called?
> SB: *Herzog.*
> WB: What are you actually doing, as you spend four hours a day revising?
> SB: Oh, just cutting out those parts of myself that I don't like.

It is important to remember that he was not only cutting out parts of his "self" that he did not like (actually his manifold manuscripts reveal several selves that he was wise to remove); he was cutting out parts of the book that did not harmonize with other parts of *that particular making.* He was changing the text's intentions, which slowly became a different thing from the flesh-and-blood author's original muddied intentions as he wrote many earlier drafts: a new, and presumably superior, self was being created.

It is the ignoring of that process by the "author-is-dead" crowd that has so often torn their criticism away from the ethical relation between the work, as published, and the reader. If there is no author, how can you talk about an ethical relation with anything? But if there is an author inflicting choices upon me, I have not only a right but a responsibility to think about whether those choices are ethically good or bad.

III

Once we revive the notion that texts do have intentions, we are still faced with a far more overwhelming multiplicity than most criticism acknowledges. Even the more sophisticated postmodernist works tend to lump all literature into a single pile, to be explored for this or that preconceived kind of data, as if all literary works were of the same kind. Such lumping is disastrous for every critical effort, but especially for ethical criticism. To judge a work as ethically praiseworthy or contemptible without determining its implied author's intent is like judging a dish of food not by tasting it but by how the waiter's description fits your preconceptions.

Of all the mistakes made by the enemies of ethical criticism, the most absurd is failing to recognize that a great proportion of what we call literary works are not only implicitly ethical, in the ways I have just described, but explicitly designed to elicit ethical responses. Unlike the authors of some lyrical poems and some playful or farcical stories, the authors of many works we consider worth our attention would feel offended if we ruled aside all consideration of ethical message (often in political form). Indeed, for some of our finest authors—Milton, Dante, Swift—*overt* message is the center, and for many others—Dickens, George Eliot, Tolstoy, Wallace Stevens, T. S. Eliot—to leave the work untouched by the message would be to miss the full experience.

Yet these works cannot be inviting the same ethical attention. The potential chaos requires us to turn to the distinctions that, as I said at the beginning, are disastrously ignored by those who would divorce the aesthetic from the ethical or moral.[10]

How many kinds of literary effect are there? It will be useful first to trace Sheldon Sacks's three, though to me they fall far short of exhausting the pile.

First, think of the absurdity of ruling out ethical criticism when we deal with works that are overtly polemical: stories that reveal themselves to every experienced reader as satires.[11] Such stories, if they earn any lasting interest, do exhibit a great many literary or aesthetic qualities: original style, gripping plots, amusing characters. But in reading them (or viewing dramatic productions), our attention is not primarily on the action they present as action but on the targets they are attacking. To read *1984* as a "novel," as if it were designed primarily to yield pleasure or excitement about its plot, is to be an ignorant reader. To engage in criticism of such a work without appraising the validity of Orwell's attack on various political and moral outrages would offend not only the implied author, "George Orwell." The flesh-and-blood author, Eric Blair, would call us just plain stupid. To discuss the movie *Dr. Strangelove* without addressing its satirical message might pass in some cinematographic quarters, but the makers of the film would feel simply bypassed.

The difference between such satires and other stories can be determined —when controversy arises—by whether or not all of the text's choices can be defended as in the service of the satirical point. In every satire, one finds elements that would not be justified if the point of it all were only to engage us in a powerful story. On the other hand, if the satirical force is in any detail sacrificed for the sake of heightening a beautiful, coherent plot, then the work is not fully a satire: it is either a bungled mixture or it has become

—something else. Whatever that something else is will be subject to ethical inquiry, but since it does not demand it openly, as the center of an appropriate response, the inquiry will itself be transformed into—something else, something radically different from what is invited by satire.

Turning from satire to a second kind, think how absurd it would be to rule out ethical considerations from any discussion of Dante's *Divine Comedy*, or Milton's *Paradise Lost,* or Toni Morrison's *Beloved* or *Paradise.* In all of those works, as in thousands of contemporary so-called novels, the central organizational point is not the effective action or plot, and also not a specific satirical target, but the probing or inculcation of an *idea* or collection of ideas the author is dramatizing. Although such works will never succeed without employing innumerable literary devices, including interesting story lines, the ultimate drive is toward patterning the world of ideas in a persuasive form. They are what Sheldon Sacks called apologues.

Just imagine how Toni Morrison must feel when critics misread and dismiss *Paradise* for having a muddied plot line, when what she wrote is an immensely complex, forbidding work that enforces, line by line, *thought* about race relations and about how forms of "white" violence have infiltrated the "black" world. To discuss her *Beloved* according to its novelistic structure, appraising it as either a gripping or moving or bungled story, without discussing one's agreement or disagreement with its ever-present penetrating thought, would be, I feel sure, offensive to the author—at least to the implied author.[12]

Moving beyond satire and apologue, we come to works that are designed to grip us as what Sacks called "actions": novels like those of Jane Austen or Cormac McCarthy or, moving down the line in quality, Agatha Christie or Louis L'Amour. Though they often contain satirical and apologic elements, those elements are subordinated to the center, which is the action—the engagement with characters who are themselves caught in an action that the proper reader comes to care about. Every detail, when examined closely, reveals itself as having been chosen to heighten the effect of the action, and thus of the reader's engagement with the story line. It is not surprising that many an author who has tried to write an effective action story has been furious when postmodernists and ethicists have imposed ethical criticism on this or that value implicit in the action or made explicit by heroes or narrators. Nor is it surprising that anti-ethical critics object strongly when we ethicists criticize first-class action-creators for anti-Semitism, racism, or sexism. For them, the beautifully formed action, conveyed in beautiful or witty or original style, is what counts. Consign the ethicists to hell, where they belong.

Unlike satires and apologues, action stories thus do not openly invite ethical criticism. They in effect imply a battle between the implied author and any ethical critic who comes plowing into the scene asking, "Is reading this story good or bad for you?" That battle must be conducted in ways entirely different from the encounters invited by satires and apologues.

So much for Sheldon Sacks's account of three major kinds of authorial invitation. Though Sacks himself never made this point, it is obvious to me that he was classifying fictions precisely as philosophers—from Plato through Kant to the present—have classified human goals in general: authors pursue either the good (through satire, attempting to make the world better), or the true (through apologue, teaching a truth), or the beautiful (through creating perfected actions or plots). Much controversy could be avoided if critics made clear just which of these three goals they pursue as they praise or condemn this or that story.

But these three piles are much too general to deal with the many different varieties of goods and truths and beauties that authors have pursued. For example, as Altieri argues (30), the trouble with too many defenses of ethical criticism, even those that honor one kind of beautiful structure, is that they have ignored the ethical import of one aspect, or kind, of the beautiful: what he calls the lyrical. Toward the end of his life, Sacks himself was exploring the need to add a fourth kind to his three, using Altieri's word for it. Reading and rereading Virginia Woolf's novels, he could not get them to fit under the labels of satire, apologue, or action. What they pursued was an evocation of the full aesthetic feeling of life when dramatized beautifully, but not as a coherent plot or action but rather almost like a series of beautiful illustrations. They did not really work as actions: readers were offered nothing remotely resembling a powerful plot. Even more obviously they did not work either as apologues, teachers of coherent thought, or as satires, attackers on sins or follies of the world. To judge this lyrical kind by the same standards one would apply to the other three would be, Sacks was beginning to suspect, a radical distortion.

But the expansion to this fourth kind still oversimplifies the landscape of story. It can never be reduced to a final list of kinds.[13] Though the kinds cannot be infinite, it seems clear that literary devices and qualities can be used in the effort by an author to achieve every conceivable (or defensible) effect: sheer farce, for the romping fun of it (a special form of "lyricism?"); sheer warning about impending disaster (a subversion of the pursuit of "goodness," but quite different from satires or apologues); stimulation of intense but disorganized thought and linguistic probing, as in *Finnegans Wake* (in the sense a pursuit of "truth," but a truth so diverse and un-pin-downable that no truth emerges; it would be absurd to condemn this novel because one or another line or character was considered morally offensive). With a little effort we can twist any literary experience into the service of improving thought, improving the world, or creating a new piece of beauty.

IV

The literary kind that I think is most important in all considerations of ethical criticism (and the one I care for most) has no label and is most resistant to simple ethical categories. When stories manage not only to engage us in serious thought about ethical matters, based on the reinforcement of certain ethical positions as admirable and others as questionable or indefensible, but also hook us into plots-of-conflict that are inseparable from that thinking, we meet what I consider the most admirable invitation to ethical criticism. The plot, in such stories, does not just present virtue and vice in conflict; the story itself *consists* of the conflict of defensible moral or ethical stances; the action takes place both within the characters in the story and inside the mind of the reader, as he or she grapples with conflicting choices that irresistibly demand the reader's judgment.

Take as a prime example the novels of Henry James, which are sometimes described as above morality or immune to ethical criticism. His tales are never moralistic, in the sense of being reducible to a simple code, obedience to which will produce ultimate blessing. On the other hand, they always reveal, to any careful reader, an extensive list of judgments about what constitutes defensible and indefensible human behavior. Nothing is more naïve than criticism of his works as if they were ethically neutral. Any reader of *Portrait of a Lady* who fails to judge Gilbert Osmond as a monstrously immoral villain would shock me and perhaps infuriate James. How can we think that any author who would revise, for a second edition, Osmond's view of Isabel from "as bright and soft as an April cloud" to "as smooth to his general need of her as handled ivory to the palm" was not wanting to guarantee a negative judgment of the manipulator.[14] At the same time, no reader can reduce the action to any easily resolved conflict between such a villain and our heroine. James thus doubles the plot: it is enacted both within the story as written and within the mind of the reader who engages fully with the dilemma faced by Isabel.

An even more striking example of this unnamed subclass of apologue, the thought-inducing action that resists reduction to summary or thesis, is

James's *The Wings of the Dove.* The plot cannot be summarized adequately, because it takes place in four different minds: within the mind of Kate Croy, as she experiences the conflicts in which James lands her throughout; within the mind of Merton Densher, as he experiences a different set of conflicts forcefully dramatized by the author; and within the minds of the reader and author as they experience the double conflicts of Kate and Merton and the intricacies of point of view that the complex story demands.

Some of the moral values of this novel are indeed as unequivocal as in any Sunday school tract or open apologue: for example, James implies but never states that it is always, in all circumstances, wrong to plot for the estate of a helpless dying woman by pretending to court her when you are really engaged to another woman. Merton knows it; James knows it; the readers James hopes for know it, though of course some will not catch it or will reject it when they do, perhaps deciding that it does not matter one way or another.[15] But what would James think of any critic who attempted to appraise the *literary* merit of *Wings* without mentioning the brilliance with which he places Kate's essential admirable qualities into moral decline. Criticism that ignores the ethical center of this aesthetic achievement is simply naïve. And ethical criticism that merely describes the conflicts, without permitting any statement of agreement or disagreement, is cowardly. Any reader who thinks Densher should have gone all the way with Kate's despicable plan should say so, up front, earning James's and my disapproval: the full aesthetic effect of the work *as intended* has been denied to any such reader, who may well reply: the novel is not as great as people say, because it touts that mistaken Puritan (or middle-class or Victorian) virtue.

It is from such disagreements that the most productive literary criticism can emerge. When undertaken seriously neither side is likely to feel fully victorious. Both sides will have learned something overlooked, either about the work itself or about the world of ethical values in which we all live. And both sides, whether in reading the work or in discussing it, are undergoing the ethical growth that serious encounters with such conflict can produce.

Nothing I have written here can be said to prove either of my two theses, if by prove we mean "move toward the impossibility of reasonable disagreement." Our cultural moment will ensure the production of many more claims, by the purists, that ethical and political views are irrelevant to literary judgment, and by the remaining defenders of the fact/value split that whenever values intrude, genuine knowledge and true rationality fly out the window. Intellectual fashions fade much more slowly than clothing styles. But while we wait patiently for the fading, we can continue to remind the purists and value-dodgers that whenever they engage with a story, privately or publicly, they encounter evidence that refutes their dogmas.

Notes

1. A few paragraphs that follow are slightly adapted from my recent article, "Of the Standard of Moral Taste: Literary Criticism as Moral Inquiry," collected in *In Face of the Facts: Moral Inquiry in American Scholarship,* edited by Richard Wightman Fox and Robert B. Westbrook. Permission for modified quotation has been granted by the Woodrow Wilson Center.

2. The most aggressive rejections of my most extensive work of ethical criticism, *The Company We Keep: An Ethics of Fiction,* came from purists and "aestheticists" who objected to such offenses as my criticizing Rabelais's sexism.

3. Have I really read King? Well, I've tried to.

4. When the recent Random House list of the one hundred greatest novels in English of the twentieth century was published, most of my friends joined my annoyance about seeing this poorly written, thoughtless book on that strange list. There you see again, as in my King comment: my own judgments will emerge throughout here, some of them perhaps chargeable as biases, and only some of them, unlike this one, defended with rational argument.

5. For examples that have caused endless trouble for commentators, Jews and Christians, and rich fodder for skeptics, see Judges 19–21 or Deuteronomy 21:18–21 and 22:20–22.

6. Some critics would say that Bunyan's story has only one message: embrace his one right version of Christianity. They should read this complex story again.

7. My engagement with critical pluralism here depends on years of living with "Chicago School" pluralists: Richard McKeon, Ronald Crane, and Elder Olsen were my mentors (see Crane's *Critics and Criticism, Ancient and Modern*); Sheldon Sacks was my colleague. His sadly neglected book, *Fiction and the Shape of Belief,* is most directly pertinent to my distinction of literary kinds.

8. Some who have not read Empson's *Seven Types of Ambiguity* carefully have reported it as anti-intentionalist. They should read it again.

9. Since I have publicly mocked some authors for referring to their own works too frequently, I hereupon resist offering any reference whatever to *The Rhetoric of Fiction,* a much-neglected work that explores the issues I am describing here.

10. See the essays engaging in ethical controversy by Richard Posner, Martha Nussbaum, and myself in the October 1998 issue of *Philosophy and Literature.*

11. Inexperienced readers do sometimes still read *Gulliver's Travels* as a travelogue or adventure story, breaking Swift's heart.

12. The only work I have met that deals adequately with the unique critical challenges presented by apologues that are called novels is David Richter's brilliant *Fable's End: Completeness and Closure in Rhetorical Fiction.*

13. See my "What Does It Take to Make a New Literary Species?" (11–12).

14. A great deal of James's later revisions for his New York edition were specifically addressed to heightening the reader's awareness of moral judgments. See especially what he does to the various choices of the manipulative narrator in *The Aspern Papers.*

15. For a full encounter with the ethical effects of reading *The Wings of the Dove,* see my "The Ethics of Forms: Taking Flight with *The Wings of the Dove*" in *Understanding Narrative,* edited by James Phelan and Peter J. Rabinowitz. For a further extensive discussion of this kind of "casuistical apologue"—to coin a label to which she might object and that will never catch on—see Nussbaum's discussion of James's *The Golden Bowl* in *Love's Knowledge* (125–47). For an excellent probing of moral issues in James's works, see Robert B. Pippin, *Henry James and Modern Moral Life.*

Works Cited

Booth, Wayne C. *The Company We Keep: An Ethics of Fiction.* Berkeley: U of California P, 1988.

———. "The Ethics of Forms: Taking Flight with *The Wings of the Dove.*" *Understanding Narrative.* Ed. James Phelan and Peter J. Rabinowitz. Columbus: Ohio State UP, 1994. 99–135.

———. "Of the Standard of Moral Taste: Literary Criticism as Moral Inquiry." *In Face of the Facts: Moral Inquiry in American Scholarship.* Ed. Richard Wightman Fox and Robert B. Westbrook. New York: Woodrow Wilson Center, 1998. 149–80.

———. *The Rhetoric of Fiction.* 2nd ed. Chicago: U of Chicago P, 1983.

———. "What Does It Take to Make a New Literary Species?" *Hypotheses: Neo-Aristotelian Analysis* 15 (1995): 11–12.

Calisher, Hortense. "Portrait of a Pseudonym." *American Scholar* 67 (1998): 53–61.

Crane, R. S., ed. *Critics and Criticism, Ancient and Modern.* Chicago: U of Chicago P, 1952.

Empson, William. *Seven Types of Ambiguity.* New York: New Directions, 1966.

Nussbaum, Martha C. *Love's Knowledge: Essays on Philosophy and Literature.* New York: Oxford UP, 1990.

Pippin, Robert B. *Henry James and Modern Moral Life.* New York: Cambridge UP, 2000.

Richter, David. *Fable's End: Completeness and Closure in Rhetorical Fiction.* Chicago: U of Chicago P, 1974.

Sacks, Sheldon. *Fiction and the Shape of Belief: A Study of Henry Fielding with Glances at Swift, Johnson, and Richardson.* Berkeley: U of California P, 1964.

Singer, Mark. "What Are You Afraid Of? Terror Is Stephen King's Medium, But It's Not the Only Reason He's So Popular—and So Frightening." *New Yorker* 7 September 1998: 56–67.

Steiner, Wendy. *The Scandal of Pleasure.* Chicago: U of Chicago P, 1995.

LYRICAL ETHICS AND LITERARY EXPERIENCE

Charles Altieri

W HAT SENSE can it make to attach the adjective "lyrical" to the term "ethics"? It is all too clear why those involved with the lyrical might want the attachment to ethics, for it seems as if literary criticism has to be able to idealize ethics now that it has manifestly failed to affect politics. Claims about ethics enable us to continue to feel good about ourselves by staking our work on values less easy to check up on: who can tell if the moral fiber of a literary audience undergoes some kind of modification? But why complicate that position by introducing the now largely neglected concern for anything distinctively lyrical within literary experience? In my case the answer is simply that I am angry and frustrated with the criticism and theory now arrogating to itself the aura that invoking "ethics" still seems to promise. Here, then, I attempt to provide reasons for these reactions and then use my criticisms in order to develop contrasts that I think offer readers an opportunity to speculate on how stressing qualities of ethos established by the lyrical can modify the relations we project between literary texts and moral philosophy.

Tony Cascardi once remarked to me that the only people to whom we should listen on the topic of ethics are those who are evidently embarrassed by their talk. Let me then begin by establishing the appropriate credentials. For literary critics, at least, this embarrassment can, or should, stem from taking ourselves as somehow spokespersons for self-congratulatory values in reading that are extremely difficult to state in any public language. And with this embarrassment there probably ought to be some self-disgust, since our claims to understand and use ethics seek a self-promoting and perhaps unwarranted dignity for what we do, while they also displace the domain of pleasures and thrills and fascinations and quirky sensualities that may in fact be what we produce for our clients. At the least, then, we need a theoretical stance that can acknowledge our self-interest without then succumbing to the temptation to defend ourselves by assuming the mantle of ironic distance.

This is where the lyrical becomes important. Emphasizing its centrality for literary experience allows us to stress modes of ethos capable of challenging the models of agency that dominate moral discourses. This challenge addresses the specific values philosophers bring to bear in that discourse as well as philosophy's tendency to make itself the arbiter of what differences make substantial differences in how criticism discusses values. More important, even to begin taking up the challenge criticism has to find new ways of showing how specific intricacies and pleasures that literary experience provides offer alternative means of making the corrections to practical experience now attributed to ethical reflection. I am tempted to claim that if we make the appropriate adjustments, critics will not have to be so desperately involved in what comes to seem a grand ethical dog show where we all get one turn around the arena before a table of discerning judges, judges who have probably forgotten what it feels like to be able to prance. But it is probably more accurate to claim only that this shift in critical perspective will at least lead us to do less harm than we do now because we need not promise moral worth but can stress simply those states that attentive pleasure makes available.

I

I have to start by attempting to clarify what I mean when I refer to ethical criticism in relation to literary studies. Ethical criticism occurs in at least three activities—in how individuals evaluate motives and actions in texts, in readers imagining or actually entering moral conversations about their assessments, and in the effort to link what readers and critics do to the discourses about morality carried out by professional philosophers. All three activities stage reading as a culturally vital practice because they require testing our moral vocabularies, making careful distinctions in our judgments, and even assessing public policies, at least in broad terms that reflect upon the ends that these processes serve and the imaginations about human value that go into shaping those ends. But all three activities also involve substantial risks of subordinating what might be distinctive within literary experience to those frameworks and mental economies that are attuned to modes of judgment shaped by other nontextual, and (usually) less directly imaginary, worldly demands.

Confronting these potential problems does not require melodramatic languages about shattering the self or pursuing polymorphously perverse sensibilities. It simply requires pushing back against the practices of ethical criticism to show what they negate and to provide a contrasting story of how literary experience celebrates and engages affective states much more in tension with our ideals of judgment than those cultivated by what we might call the new "emotion-friendly" versions of moral reason. In other words, it may be necessary now to push against claims about the ethical in the name of a richer model for approaching questions about ethos, so that one can envision ways that in the long run allow literary experience to affect what we take ethical judgment to involve.[1]

This is hardly a revolutionary proposal. No decent theorist on the relation between ethics and literary experience ignores the challenges I am trying to sharpen.[2] But, still, I want to claim that the challenge is rarely fully engaged. Clearly, ethical criticism often calls our attention to two aspects of literary experience that are central to many of the texts that matter to most of us, especially classic novels—a will to accurate and dense, relatively impartial, concrete description and a corresponding quest for a generalizing scope by which the text can establish an exemplary version of certain qualities of compassion and evaluative judgment. If criticism dwells only on these values, however, it offers little opportunity to extend beyond realistic narrative to engage what may be literature's major contribution to our appreciation of what is fundamentally at stake in ethical thinking. Literary modes like lyric often ask us to participate in states that are either too elemental or too transcendental or too absolute or too satisfyingly self-absorbed to engage ethical criticism. Yet these states can have enormous impact on how and why we are concerned with values of all kinds, including those that we pursue by ethical reasoning. Minimally, they bring to bear examples of positive intensities that any ethics might have to take into account. And at their richest these works explore the limitations of all judgmental stances by requiring complex blends of sympathy and distance and hence eliciting our fascination with extreme states of mind while complicating any possible grasp of how one might put such states into the categories of commensurability on which ethical judgment may ultimately depend.

Some of those energies are focused by acts of identification; others depend on where works situate us, that is, on the specific qualities of imaginative vitality offered by certain dispositions, including those states of transport once sustained by religious experience. In such cases participation entails maintaining substantial differences from the attitudes on which we rely in all of our practical judgments. We become attentive to the selves that are possible when we manage to deploy distinctive powers of mind and sensibility. And often the focus is much less on how we perceive or interpret the world beyond ourselves than on how we manage to achieve states of will or of satisfaction or of painful separation in relation to events and even to overall assessments about how life might be worth living. Through art (but not only through art) we learn to demand of ourselves something more grand and perhaps more threatening than that we be justified in our actions or that we be able to appreciate how others might be justified or not justified. And through art (but not only through art) we find the will engaged not simply in terms of languages of justification but also in terms of principles of satisfaction. These demands on the will cannot be met by determining that one has made the best decision among available options. Rather, for the moment one seems to see what it takes to make the world of a happy person different from that of an unhappy person, and then one understands how there is a dimension of ethics that cannot be put into words but must be approached by thinking about how we might understand Wittgenstein's dictum that ethics and aesthetics are one (*Tractatus Logico-Philosophicus* 6.421–6.43). And, conversely, the richer our alternative to standard ethical criticism, the better the case we can make that ethical analyses be limited to situations where we are concerned with the justification of specific actions or with the characterization of how we might go about making these assessments. More general questions about value then can be relegated to the general cultural theater where we have to acknowledge constant struggle not only over which specific aspects of ethos will prevail but also over which ways of determining among the values make the most practical sense.

I can summarize my project by claiming that I want to provide practical and nonmelodramatic ways of adapting to literary criticism Nietzsche's contrast between orientations shaped by a will to truth and orientations shaped by a will to power.[3] Therefore, I have to show how ethical criticism becomes subject to Nietzschean critique and to demonstrate how we can recuperate a good deal of what Nietzsche attributed to the will to power simply by concentrating on the conative aspects of those energies within our responses to art that cannot be located in the roles of spectator or judge. This, then, also requires altering the conceptual models we have for the emotions fundamental to the reading enterprise. Rather than dwelling within the parameters of approval and disapproval generated by empathy and sympathy, stressing conative states enables theory to explore how we participate in passions that range from fear and desperation and confusion about identification to the fullest models our culture has both for surrendering the self to what it attends to and for what Yeats called the "self-delighting, self-appeasing, self-affrighting" soul realizing "its own sweet will is heaven's will" ("Prayer for My Daughter"). As Yeats knew, it is precisely the relation between such states of soul and possible dispositions of will that makes the lyrical fundamental to the ethos within ethics: without it we may find ourselves comfortable judging others, but we will have impoverished terms for putting into our moral calculi what satisfactions are most important to pursue for and as ourselves.

II

Now it is time to be as specific as I can about the limitations within various versions of ethical literary criticism so that we appreciate at least the pressure to come up with alternative versions of how literary experience affects existential values. I suggest we begin by distinguishing four characteristic ways of performing ethical criticism. The first two are mirror images of one another. Each stresses the ethical importance of attending to dense concrete presentations of particular actions because such attention provides a powerful supplement to more abstract and categorical modes of ethical inquiry. At one pole we have an emphasis on how involvement in concrete situations enriches our capacities for making discriminations and keeps our judgments in close relation to the emotions of sympathy and empathy; at the other we have a deconstructive concern for an ethics of letting be that is acutely aware of the imperializing work usually done by professions of empathy and of sympathy since it is the responder who gets to specify what those emotions involve.

The first emphasis is particularly important for those who want literary experience to complement traditional ethical inquiry, since it promises to contour judgment to the dense texture of particular lives and hence can partially free us from the tendency within Anglo-American philosophy to rely on simple representative anecdotes as its means of testing moral values. And that shift, in turn, provides an alternative to the standard philosophical effort to base judgment on generalizations built by constructing and applying categorical frameworks to particular cases. Ethical literary criticism makes it clear that we simply cannot rely on such abstract principles for any aspects of experience without supplementing them with the more flexible, narrative-based modes of judgment that Aristotle characterized as *phronesis* (see Martha Nussbaum, *Love's Knowledge* 25–27 and 168–94). And where philosophy seeks impersonal and disinterested modes of judgment centered on the giving and testing of reasons, literary experience explores the degree to which our emotions can be heuristic features of the judgmental

process: we can be impartial without being unmoved (so long as our emotions are spectator emotions).[4]

Deconstructive and Levinasian ethical criticism is based on a very different notion of concreteness. More affected by Kantian aesthetics than by
ethical claims based on practical judgment, these theorists concentrate not
on dramatic situations but on the ethical force that one can attribute to the
purposiveness of the particular text as an authorial action. Here, the central
value lies in adapting oneself to strong particulars by letting them be, that is,
by coming to appreciate their power as the articulation of working desire,
which is manifest primarily as a direct function of the work's ability to ward
off the categories that moral judgment tries to impose. The ethical here is
sharply opposed to the moral, the domain of principle. Ethical values
emerge in reading because there we feel the violence of our will to make
texts mean something we can state abstractly while we also have to recognize the capacity of the desires working within textuality to resist that will.
Success in such reading then holds out the promise that we can adapt the
same attitudes toward society, keeping ourselves wary of the forms of violence that so easily mask as welfarist principles inattentive to the needs of
those for whom we see ourselves speaking.

Clearly, both perspectives have a good deal to offer literary criticism.
But they also leave us with substantial problems, making it impossible not
to have to reach out for additional theoretical terms. There arises immediately the question of how we reconcile the two quite different views of concreteness and the two quite different views of the values that ethical judgment seeks. Does dwelling on the denseness of particular actions afford a
richer model of ethical judgment, or does it encourage casuistries that evade
the clear and necessary application of principles? Once these two alternatives
emerge, we clearly cannot rely on the concrete experience of texts to help us
determine which one is to be preferred. For returning to the concrete case
for our answer will, in theory at least, produce endless regress unless one can
somehow relink such concreteness either directly to universals or to methods
of judgment that somehow have a more flexible version of generality built
into them. If we are to keep at the center of our inquiry the Aristotelian
concern for how we should live, we have to preserve as a background invoked
through the particulars some kind of larger framework of examples and
probably at least some principles that give resonance to the concepts of
good with which we want to work. Yet once we begin seeking explanatory
principles we put at risk the very concreteness that we want to celebrate.

There is then substantial pressure on traditional philosophy to articulate what roles it can play in establishing these principles and even in determining to what degree concrete cases can sanction our swerving from them.

Deconstructive theory seems capable of turning my objections to its interests, since it can insist that, unlike the discrimination view, it at least faces up to the gulf between particulars and supporting categorical principles. But its ways of engaging that gulf run a serious risk, for it seems as if the ideal of letting be takes on the function of a moral category and hence produces its own form of violence. More disturbing, deconstructive literary ethics has to face the problem of its so far not having done very much to specify what is so valuable about singularity per se in relation to literature or so necessarily destructive in the judicious use of categories. This version of ethical criticism may rely on the individualist values sustaining the modern philosophy that it is quick to reject. And if it is to attribute specific values to what singularities perform, deconstruction may have to find some rapprochement with the expressivist theory developed by Charles Taylor and others. This rapprochement would free deconstruction from relying on a binary opposition between singularity and the categorical and would enable it to stress what persons accomplish as they bend rather than break from the categories giving meaning to their actions.

III

Neither emphasis on concreteness can sustain a satisfying theoretical position. Deconstruction cannot even postulate much of an ethical theory for literary experience because it cannot supplement its commitment to singularity without falling into bad faith.[5] Discernment theories, on the other hand, invite conceptual elaboration, since they so clearly cry out for some account of the more general values that are at stake in our close concern with the elements that go into ethical judgments. But in my view these efforts only deepen the problem by showing how difficult it is to establish the necessary conceptual supplements. In order to show why we need alternative approaches to the value questions now consigned to ethical criticism, I now turn to the two basic forms I think such supplements can take.

The first conceptual structure for these supplements can be seen as a set of variants on perfectionist principles because its primary concern is with the versions of virtue and the qualities of life produced or reinforced by specific ways of reading. Stanley Cavell is the best-known thinker representing the relevant conceptual moves. But since I have written about him critically on other occasions and since to the best of my knowledge he does not identify himself as an ethical critic, I turn to the somewhat different but clearly related theorizing of Wayne Booth. There is no clearer rendering of how perfectionist ideals can be realized within literary examples, for Booth in *The Company We Keep* sees reading as fundamentally the exploration of desires we may come to desire[6]: "What sort of character, what sorts of habits, am I likely to take on or reinforce" as "I decipher this immensely compact bundle of actions, thought, and allusions?" . . . "What 'better desires' does it lead me to desire?" (274). Formulations like these enable Booth to provide a powerful answer to how texts mediate ethical values without his having either to subsume texts under general principles or to insist upon their close fit with moral philosophy. The values that matter emerge through comparisons we make among the qualities of experience in texts "that are both like and unlike" (70) each other. We appraise works by examining whether an experience can be seen as "*comparatively* desirable, admirable, lovable, or, on the other hand, comparatively repugnant, contemptible, or hateful" (71).

Such appraisal is not merely a matter of intuitions or the expression of sensibilities. Booth shows there are clear standards that enter our judgments, for ultimately ethical criticism asks how texts contribute to virtue. To address this concern, we have to begin with the issue of intentionality, for we cannot have virtue without agency. We have to postulate implied authors and then engage these authors in terms of the roles they might play in conversations about ethical values. Then the "key question in the ethics of narration . . . becomes: Is the pattern of life that this would-be friend offers one that friends might well pursue together?" (222). Now we have both an object of ethical reflection—the friendship relation—and an obvious locus for making assessments of texts. We are invited to ask whether the basic qualities of the text contribute to forging such imaginary friendships or if they present hindrances to friendship such as hidden designs or lack of respect for the audience or shoddy reflection on the activity presented. In either case Booth shows that by thinking about texts in terms of questions about the company we keep, we do not need abstract principles as grounds of their worth because we have clear personal measures based on how the modes of desire for desire they delineate stand up in relation to works to which they can be compared. We do not determine who our friends are because of the conditions they satisfy; rather, we determine who we are in terms of the quite concrete company we choose, and the company we reject. Responsibility remains a matter of individual self-definition, yet it brings with it appropriate contexts in which choices can be characterized and judged.

In my view, Booth's is a powerful theoretical position precisely because it appeals so directly to matters of ethos. Nonetheless, it is difficult to accept this figure of friendship as an adequate principle for either the qualities distinguishing individual valuations by readers or for the frameworks that give such choices public significance. First, this figure makes it difficult to have theory remain responsive to the full range of values explored by literary texts or to the often contradictory values that emerge within this range. Booth's concern for the company one keeps does support a limited pluralism (no single principle is likely to determine our range of friendships). But I suspect we would rather have some of the texts we value highly prove interesting enemies rather than all be admirable friends—not only because we want to be challenged but also because we want the fascination of engaging what refuses to contour itself to the models of dialogue that are allowed by a virtue-based model of friendship. More important, the idea of virtue as a primary criterion for the friends who contribute to happiness seems to me a somewhat pious and inaccurate one. Invoking "virtue" allows the appearance of combining plural possibilities with a generalizability based simply on examples and cultural traditions. Yet "virtue" proves an irreducibly equivocal concept because in one register it is simply a measure of power or conative strength, with no distinguishing "ethical" qualities, while in another it brings an aura of satisfying certain deep moral values in a society.

One can then use Booth for a Nietzschean reading of how literary experience becomes formative for certain groups highly conscious of how their sense of shared strengths makes them different from those bound to social mores. Or one can tilt one's sense of virtue as Booth himself does toward friendships that remain judgeable within moral frameworks, even if it foregrounds a set of examples rather than principles. But the more one tilts Booth's way, the more one undercuts the force of the level of intimacy that the figure of friends as a company seemed to afford. At most, virtue serves as a necessary but not sufficient condition of friendship because we choose our friends (if "choose" is the right word) for many positive qualities and in terms of many contingent aspects of our lives. Consequently, Booth's effort to keep the moral force of "virtue" can be said to confer on texts an awkward intimacy that is too public for most forms of affection and fascination while at the same time he fails to develop an adequate public model of what might count as virtue or satisfy specifically ethical conditions of judgment.

Given this ambiguity around "virtue" when it is definable only in terms of affective relations, it is not surprising that most philosophers seek different grounds for ethical criticism. Here, I concentrate on Martha Nussbaum's recent *Poetic Justice* because that book offers the most effective case I know for bringing narrative literature into close proximity with the concerns and the language of traditional moral philosophy. Getting clear on how this work matters and what we can learn from its limitations takes me somewhat more time than I have spent on Booth, but spending that time also demonstrates why it is ultimately necessary to return to the Nietzschean possibilities in Booth's argument if we are to preserve the sense of intimate stakes and concretizing passions for which Booth's theory provides a secure place.

Nussbaum's previous writings on literature and ethics had stressed the importance of concrete moral discrimination, but always with a keen sense of interpreting that concreteness as a contribution to concerns basic to "even . . . Kantians or Utilitarians" (*Love's Knowledge* 27).[7] Her more recent book is distinctive for its efforts to extend the "fit" between narrative fiction and moral philosophy beyond issues of judging individual actions to questions of public policy. There are, then, no better grounds on which to test the degree to which one can make literary concreteness a medium for more overtly generalized moral discourses. Nussbaum argues that reading narrative fiction actually provides "insights that should play a role (though not as uncriticized foundations) in the construction of an adequate moral and political theory," while at the same time the particular interpretive processes that the narratives invite help develop specific "moral capacities without which citizens will not succeed in making reality out of the normative conclusions of any moral or political theory, however excellent" (*Poetic Justice* 12). If it is to pursue these ends, ethical criticism has two basic tasks. It must establish a context for the literary text to operate in moral terms by bringing to bear the relevant issues formulated from within philosophy; then it must show how the text "exemplifies and cultivates abilities of imagination that are essential to the intelligent making" of the relevant "assessments, in public as well as private life" (52). For if literature really has philosophical force, then it ought to exercise that force in the same public domain that philosophical concepts try to influence. Where Booth talks of texts as friends, Nussbaum wants to create a context in which we can see deep links between the roles of reader and of judge.

Nussbaum's ability to realize the full implications of making moral claims for literary experience has a substantial downside. She in effect lays bare the underlying logic of this project and in the process raises very serious problems. Consider, for example, the fact that to make the arguments of *Poetic Justice* work she has to turn away from James and from Proust, the major figures of her earlier work on ethical criticism, to the Charles Dickens of *Hard Times*. While Dickens is clearly a major writer, there are few literary theorists who would want to use *Hard Times* as their exemplary text, for exactly the reasons that do tempt Nussbaum to make the effort. Where developing ethical claims from James and Proust require stressing the play of a very complex moral intelligence, developing claims for the Dickens of *Hard Times* entails stressing not so much the processes of judgment in particularly dense situations as the need to develop stances toward large social issues. Dickens is less interested in assessing how characters respond to intricate situations than he is in displaying how agents can respond adequately to the general social conditions making demands on them.

Such generalizing scope is not something to condemn, but neither is it something that most writers aspire to because of the limited means that fiction has at its disposal to create the appropriate effects. *Hard Times* gains its moral scope by its extraordinary ability to manipulate pathos and hence to position a responsive audience in a situation where it both registers suffering and understands plausible public causes of that suffering. Nussbaum, then, is quite right to argue that this novel shares with some contemporary philosophers the project of defending "an approach to quality of life measurement based on a notion of human functioning and human capability, rather than on either opulence or utility" (51). Dickens's pathos allows his fiction an immediate and compelling "measure of how people are doing" because he can bring emotional resonance to "questions of how well their form of life has enabled them to function in a variety of distinct areas, including but not limited to mobility, health, education, political participation, and social relations" (51). From this the leap to contemporary philosophy is not a large one:

> Since we read a novel like *Hard Times* with the thought that we ourselves might be in the character's position—since our emotion is based in part on this sort of empathic identification—we will naturally be most concerned with the lot of those whose position is worst, and we will begin to think of ways in which that position might have been other than it is, might be made better than it is. . . . If one could not imagine what it was like to be Stephen Blackpool, then it would be all too easy to neglect this situation as Bounderby does, portraying workers as grasping insensitive beings. Similarly, to take a case that will figure in my next section, if one cannot imagine what

women suffer from sexual harassment on the job, one won't have a vivid sense of that offense as a serious social infringement that the law should remedy. (91)

This stress on pathos allows the empathic imagination to leap directly to large value frameworks and produces an inherent socializing dimension for literary texts because it seeks imaginative agreement about ways of redressing the suffering. Yet I think it important to ask whether these advantages outweigh the disadvantages of letting our literary ethics be so dependent on that one emotional attitude. James, for example, is careful to make characters tempted by the appeal of pathos, such as Hyacinth Robinson, have to learn to make judgments critical of the temptations to self-righteousness that occur when one lets one's awareness of public issues outweigh the need for concrete self-understanding. And one could argue that this emphasis on pathos allows precious little room for a corresponding emphasis on the various modes of ethos that literary imaginations pursue. In fact, one could use this contrast between ethos and pathos as a basic way of challenging assumptions fundamental to Nussbaum's ethical criticism and perhaps to any criticism content to ally itself with moral philosophy. This contrast is especially important for clarifying the various roles that accounts of the emotions might play in our perspectives on literary values. For once pathos is the central link between the literary and the ethical, then Nussbaum's cognitive theory of emotions clearly provides the dynamic energies securing the interactions between the two domains. In my view, however, the costs exacted by this way of linking the domains makes it crucial that we turn from pathos to ethos and see what conceptions of emotion then best articulate the values provided by literary experience.

Nussbaum identifies three specific means by which the emotions elicited within literary narrative can support and extend the work of moral philosophy. The first is mentioned only in a passing remark, yet I think it has to play a major role in a full statement of her theory. I refer to the need to make moral sense of the simple but elemental fact that literature seeks to confer pleasure. What kind of pleasure instructs, especially when pathos is the vehicle of instruction? Nietzsche would suggest that we be suspicious of the kinds of pleasures we take in identifying with other people's suffering, since nothing secures bourgeois self-satisfaction so well as sympathy with those who lack the same possessions. Nussbaum is more generous and in some respects more subtle. She sees that pleasure affords a means of making identification attractive and hence of allowing us to orient cognitive interests toward suffering while resisting the need to locate the pleasure in our own melodramatic consciousness of ourselves as pity producers. For to the extent that we take pleasure in particular characters from underprivileged situations, we are likely to find their company attractive so that we are drawn further into their world and into sympathy with their interests (35). We do not have to let the pleasure be absorbed within our own senses of self-importance.

But any effort to link literary pleasure to moral philosophy brings back another version of the problem with concreteness that we have already considered. One has to be able to say which pleasures contribute to moral values and which do not: surely Plato's critique cannot be dismissed entirely. This is why Nussbaum links pleasure to her cognitive theory of emotions. If emotions can provide a kind of knowledge in their own right, then we can secure their role in moral thinking without prescribing in advance what emotions we will allow. And, indeed, there are many respects in which emotions produce knowledge and complement what on other grounds we establish as truths. Emotions establish salient conditions by stressing what might matter in particular perceptual fields, and they bring to bear belief contexts that we have to assess if we are to understand how and why particular options for actions might matter to us. The emotions organized by a sense of pathos provide excellent examples, for pathos attunes us to the facts contributing to someone's suffering and brings belief to bear that orients us toward specific actions if they prove true (just as pleasure facilitates identifications). As Nussbaum puts it, "The person deprived of the evaluations contained in pity seems to be deprived of ethical information without which such situations cannot be adequately, rationally appraised" (65). Yet because the emotions are bound to beliefs, they do not lock us into attitudes but can be modified by relevant information (such as information that the one bidding for our sympathy is faking it).

The greater the cognitive claims for emotions, however, the more pressing is that same old specter that its need to merge particularity and ideality makes ethical criticism vulnerable to critiques based on the dilemma of concreteness. Clearly, there are emotions that provide sustenance for reason. But how do we decide which emotions have the power to modify reason, especially when we are dealing with imaginary constructs? It seems as if these emotions have to be tested by reason in order to be worthy of having such an influence. But then what is to influence rationality must be influenced by rationality, and again we face a vicious circle. Nussbaum is not daunted. She turns to a version of Booth's position where specific human exemplars become the possible mediation defining how emotions can affect what we take reason to be. But rather than invoke the figure of the friend, she relies on Adam Smith's model of the "judicious spectator" because that enables her to tie emotions to dispositions of character. Focus, then, is not on how we come to desire to desire but on how we attach ourselves to the particular forms of idealizable desire that constitute ethical lives.

Smith develops his model in order to address the fact that many emotions obviously do not prove good guides for our actions, so to assure that the emotion is appropriate we have to determine that it is a "true view of what is going on" (74). Then we have to be sure that the viewer will not overdetermine that truth because of problematic private interests. Theory can make the appropriate distinctions if it can find a way of assuring that the emotion is that "of a spectator not a participant" (74). In a single stroke literary experience moves from being marginal to philosophy to having claims for centrality, since there is no better model for the psychic economies Smith calls for than the self-discipline fundamental to attentive reading. Reading reduces its object to banality if it simply imposes an individual's needs and desires. Conversely, the promise held out for readers requires that they assume spectatorial roles through which they manage both to feel the relevant emotions and to appreciate them for the energies and values that they organize. Reading shows how we can treat anger or grief or love as if we could identify with their intensities while at the same time maintaining the distance necessary to make judgments about and through our involvement in the particulars.

Suggestive as this account of reading is, Nussbaum is less interested in it than she is in the social implications she can draw from it. For once we accept its close relation to whatever remains disciplinary and social in the activity of reading, this figure of the "judicious spectator" allows us to project onto reading important social links to the entire dynamics of making social judgments. Hence, the dramatic climax of her book consists in an elaborate effort to show reading as a judicious spectator and provides a powerful model for making legal decisions. Judges have to know principles and procedures. But they also have to know the limitations of the abstractness built into principles and procedures, and they have to find ways to make those imaginative projections necessary for producing justice in particular situations (82). So if one can make literary experience an exemplar for the working of an impartial yet sympathetic judgment, one can then treat the "poetic imagination" as "a crucial agent of democratic equality" (119). This imagination not only tries to sympathize with all the relevant points of view; it also builds on its own impartiality to seek from that sympathy those actions that comprise the greater social good. And this imagination requires plural and qualitative terms based on those ideals of human flourishing that repeated acts of sympathy enable us to keep in the forefront of our vision.

IV

I dwell on Nussbaum at such length in part because I want to make readers feel a deep emotional problem that her theorizing about emotions in literature raises for me, and I think for the very practice of ethical criticism. On the one hand I am made uneasy by the self-confidence and imperialist philosophizing that reduces the great imaginative range of literary experience to the less intellectually demanding but quite important moral and political truths that a philosophy devoted to spreading the values of human flourishing can promulgate. On the other hand I am not happy with myself for being so easily seduced into the equally distressing arrogance of the literary critic appalled at our marvelous complexity being oversimplified merely because someone who has devoted her life to the project wants to use literature for making the world a better place in which to live for large segments of its population. I am forced to confront the fact that my view of literary experience can promise only moderate modifications in how some individuals view the world, so it cannot even approximate the kind of social impact that Nussbaum projects for these texts and that writers such as Dickens are, in fact, capable of producing. Yet I still want to argue that the very grandeur of her enterprise leads our attention away from those concrete processes by which literature does affect individual lives in ways that noble sentiments about public welfare simply cannot accomplish. Although my alternative perspective may not be able to demonstrate how literary experience makes better moral agents of us, it can show how that experience offers substantial values very difficult to get elsewhere.

In Nussbaum's story, on the other hand, literature can be replaced by any other means of training discernment and eliciting thoughtful pity. We do not even need literary examples to develop the theoretical importance of concentrating on plural qualitative measures of values. And although literature proves useful in resisting the utilitarian and rationalist models of assessment that Nussbaum attacks, its relevance in this regard stems less from the passions it mediates than from the inadequacies of those philosophical stances in the first place. Therefore, I think that by asking literary criticism to pursue clearly defined, public ethical ends we risk losing sight of what are usually the most compelling and most persuasive experiential qualities the relevant texts produce without gaining much more than ideological reinforcement for what has its driving energies and relevant conditions of judgment elsewhere.

My resistance to Nussbaum does not entail returning to some kind of aestheticism or adapting discourses about singularity and difference and empowerment. The literary values that I want to foreground hover in the shadows cast by work that overmoralizes them, so the best way to appreciate all that lyricism involves may be simply to reflect on why there might be good reasons to remain in constant struggle against ethical criticism. Such struggle promises not only to renew attention to particular qualities of literary experience but also to preserve a necessary tension between ethos and ethics perhaps necessary for an adequate grasp of how we make and maintain investments in the entire structure of concerns that ethical theory adjudicates. Therefore, I close by being as clear as I can on what I take to be three insuperable problems in contemporary ethical criticism, in the hope that we can deepen our appreciation of how literary experience is capable of challenging those philosophical stances that want to domesticate it so that it will submit to their conditions for praise.

We have already addressed the first problem, which lies in the logical structure of ethical criticism. This criticism insists on there being something distinctive in how concrete texts engage our moral attention, and yet it has to interpret the value of that engagement in terms of the very philosophical methods and generalizations from which the concrete reading deviates. As Derrida might put it, ethical theory wants the concrete both to establish values and to supplement value schemes, yet the very role of supplement undercuts the concreteness by making it dependent on abstractions and undercuts the abstractions by making them dependent for their realization on something that philosophy apparently cannot provide on its own. Because I have nothing more to say about the abstract form of this problem I next shift to a quite specific and, I think, telling manifestation of the issues that is brought into focus by Nussbaum and, indirectly, by Booth. When we realize how philosophy has to strain for the fit that melds it with literary experience, we also understand the pressure to let pathos take over from ethos, or to become the sole relevant ethos, and we understand why it is so tempting to vacillate between different meanings of "virtue." That realization in turn leads us to what I am claiming are the shadows or margins of ethical discourse, where we might value literary experiments in ethos precisely because they do not depend on the same kind of underlying distinctively moral sentiments as do examples drenched in pathos and, more important, because they allow us to appreciate imaginative states as directly affecting our experience of values without our having to postulate those underlying reasons. Examples of ethos make their appeal to us in terms of the dynamic capacities they afford our quite particular states of self-awareness as we explore the energies they make available, with no sanction beyond the intellectual, emotional, and intersubjective intensities a text affords.

There is no better contrast to the ethics of literary pathos than W. B. Yeats's "He and She," the sixth section of his poem "Supernatural Songs":

> As the moon sidles up
> Must she sidle up,
> As trips the scared moon
> Away must she trip:
> "His light had struck me blind
> Dared I stop."
>
> She sings as the moon sings:
> "I am I, am I;
> The greater grows my light
> The further that I fly."
> All creation shivers
> With that sweet cry. (286–87)

The first stanza tries to render something like the essence of pathos. For here, the character cannot speak for herself but must be represented by another, except for the one moment when she gets to utter her dilemma. And every move seems driven by forces to which the character is unwillingly bound. By the second stanza the very intensity of the pain seems to open a possible fascination with the opposite pole, with more assertive egocentric states that poetry might not only represent but also help focus. At first this stanza also depends on a narrator in order to situate the speaker. But after one line the content of the singing takes over from its visual representation, and the mode of consciousness within that singing then entirely dominates the scene. Just the absoluteness of the singing in turn suffices to produce an assertion of an "I" identical to itself: there seems simply no gap between the subject singing and the objective state that is the song made physical.

Technically speaking, such assertions cannot have any philosophical force, since only God can experience the complete coincidence of subjectivity and objectivity. But the poem is less interested in the truth of its assertion than in the energies and desires that it can make visible by the effort to purify song of everything but the "I" who as its singer, or better as its singing, manages to glimpse what it means to experience the coincidence of subject and object states. Although there is no empirical test of the truth of this assertion, there are considerable formal features of the poem that at least give a kind of substance to the desire itself. The utter simplicity of the situation, for example, shaped only by a contrast to the dependency of the first stanza, gives us a world in which there might be nothing but the singing, with all impurities driven away by the need to separate oneself from what the moon dominates. Here, lyric seems to approach its own inner possibilities—presenting not any one role, one version of ethos, but the essence of what any role becomes when it can be entirely the matter of song. And, as song, the poem's physical qualities deepen the all-absorbing nature of the "I am I." Long *I* sounds literally take the poem over, spreading the light produced by and as the "I" of the singing. That intensity in turn becomes so great that self-absorption cannot rest in narcissistic states. Just as the "she" of the first stanza is bound to the ways of the moon, the "I" of the second must return to its setting. Only now the self-absorption comes to constitute a fantasy lover bringing to creation its deepest sexual pleasure because finally creation has an opposite active enough to make its own presence felt and hence to make creation itself once again something to be loved and not merely feared or respected or moralized.

Had I the time, I would go on to poems that explore the same level of intensity attached to quite different emotional orientations. Yeats's "Lullaby," for example, completely absorbs the ego within that traditional folk form, using literary self-consciousness as its vehicle for giving itself a mode of absorption that extends far beyond what would suffice for moral judgment. But my one example is strong enough to allow my going directly to the generalization that what matters most in these literary states is not how they might be justified morally but how they justify themselves as invitations to imaginative participation within what the text elicits from its ways of bringing the world and the psyche into language. Excess lies down with extreme, precise care; no wonder creation shivers. And perhaps ethics can learn from this display. For it seems to me arguable that here we have a telling illustration of how the lyrical dimension of experience influences what Booth calls the desire for desires—not simply because specific states appeal to us but also because we encounter specific qualities of those desires that become exemplars for what a range of emotions might provide were we attuned to appreciate their intensities. Both ways of encountering emotional fields then have the power to affect how we adapt or modify ethical stances. Lyrical emotions can make certain states attractive because of the modes of self-identification that they allow—here, the best example may be the qualities of moral responsiveness that we find in the great epic poets. Or these emotions can affect ethics by giving us standards for what levels of emotional life we might find worth taking pride in as we explore possible dispositions, only some of which are thematizably moral. By this logic we might even claim that concerns about ethos prove central even to how we let ourselves be affected by pathos.

V

The second of the three basic problems I see facing ethical criticism provides a different path for linking literary affects to aspects of ethos not easily represented within ethical theory. The problem is simply the danger that criticism devoted to ethics will find itself not sufficiently honoring those affective qualities and values traditionally most important to writers and to the interpretive discourses fostered by their work. Considered logically, this problem repeats the same structure as that we saw in dealing with claims about concreteness. For on the one hand ethical criticism has to claim that it gives moral philosophy access to distinctive emotions mediating kinds of knowledge and of investment not available within the conceptual modes of judgment usually called upon by ethical theory. Yet while the emotions have to be different they also have to be contained, overtly or covertly, by the very rationality that they are seen as supplementing—hence, Nussbaum's reliance on the cognitive theory of emotions. But if we stop with the logical problems we might miss the force and possible social relevance of those literary emotions that do not so readily adapt to ethical theory. Therefore, I want to dwell on one particular instance of how the logical problem produces practical consequences.

I take as my example Nussbaum's use of Bigger Thomas in Richard Wright's *Native Son* because there we find the cognitive theory of emotions simply unable to deal with the intensities generated by the text, so that Nussbaum's effort to moralize emotions seems to repress some quite different and threatening aspect of emotional force. Nussbaum claims that readers of this text clearly find their emotional responses also serving as cognitive instruments—both in generating sympathy for Bigger and in pushing whites to examine their assumptions toward such young black males. And, Nussbaum shows, Wright is careful to complicate and qualify that sympathy so that it meets real-world conditions. Rather than make the easy appeal to figures of universal brotherhood, the novel demands we acknowledge the degree to which social factors have also made literal brotherhood very hard to envision, at least for bourgeois whites. The result of that demand is a deeper sympathy leading the judicious spectator to feel and to think "This is a human being, with the basic equipment to lead a productive life; [for we] see how not only the external circumstances of action, but also anger, fear, and desire have been deformed by racial hatred and its institutional expression. The unlikeness that repels identification becomes the chief object of our concern" (94).

But Nussbaum's rich analysis of the difficulties whites feel in relating to Bigger makes that unlikeness more problematic than her theory lets her grant. It is clear that Wright's text deepens our capacity to understand Bigger in his unlikeness. Yet the deeper whites come to appreciate how wounded Bigger is by his upbringing in a racist society, the more difficult it is to link that knowledge to unequivocal sympathy. He raises a complex set of emotions in whites, and perhaps not only in whites, involving fear and self-preservation and the resulting need to evade self-contempt. And once those emotions enter it is not possible simply to translate what sympathy Bigger elicits from the judicious spectator into a moral orientation toward specific actions.

Nussbaum is confident that "the reader, while judging Bigger culpable (the degree of his culpability is certainly debatable), is likely to be, other things being equal, inclined to mercy in the imposition of punishment, seeing how much of his character was the product of circumstances created by others" (95). Yet I am not sure that the emotions he raises produce that judgment, nor that Wright even wanted that judgment.[8] The sympathy Wright calls for engages us with a seriously wounded psyche that for many readers will not elicit mercy, at least in relation to what they expect of the legal system. It is perfectly possible to respect Bigger's independence so much that one wants him kept away from the white world at all costs. Once sympathy aligns us with his character, and not just with his actions, we have very good reason to think that nothing so merely institutional as a relatively short jail sentence is likely to produce any change in Bigger. Instrumental reason then may well find itself using this sympathy to seek ways of eliminating the threat rather than improving the condition of the one found threatening.

Almost anyone reading this essay is likely to share a desire that mercy temper punishment in cases like Bigger's. But I suspect we cannot arrive at this judgment because of anything our emotions for him tell us. In fact, the motivating force here has very little to do with our emotional relation to Bigger's specific condition. Rather, what moves us to that mercy for Bigger is our affective investment in certain images of ourselves based on our overall political commitments. These investments do seem to me crucial to politics and are certainly modified by literary experience, but not quite by the experience of sympathy, or any other pathos-oriented attitude, and certainly not by what Nussbaum celebrates as the emotions of a judicious spectator who manages to control the impulses of the empirical self. For what in part leads us to go against what we know from our sympathy with Bigger is an intensely personal commitment to aligning ourselves with the politics of hope rather than the politics of despair and with a willingness to take political risks rather than to insist on safe order. These impulses are strengthened not by sympathy per se but by developing investments in positive identifications, if not with specific role models then with imaginary worlds that literary texts help us envision and populate with possible judges whom we want to please by acting as nobly as we can. Nussbaum's cognitive model of emotions can neither handle the dangers attendant on what we do come to know in passionate ways nor address the role of noncognitive fantasized identifications as fundamental to morality and to the impact literary experience can have in affecting morality by influencing identifications.[9]

If I am right, the limitations of Nussbaum's cognitive theory of emotions provide a superb contrastive stage on which to put our spotlight back on Yeats's poem. It seems clear that her position cannot adequately address either of the fundamental lyrical states in the poem—the dependency by which the speaker understands what power is and the assertiveness by which she explores her own access to it. Both are extreme states that require the spectator to suspend impersonal judiciousness. What matters is not what we come to know about the world but what our participation in the poem makes available as concrete, elemental abstraction. So from Yeats's point of view it is reason that must learn to accommodate states like those that the poem can make so intensely real and so appealing as representations of what the desire for desire might look like in its pure form. Yeats's poem sets ethos against pathos, insisting that while rationality may require Nussbaum's view of cognitive emotions, there are strong features of literary experience that sharply oppose it, features such as Wright's desire to leave his audience in despairing awe at Bigger's life. Where cognition might have been, there Yeats wants fascination to reign, since fascination opens the reader to what we might call pure lyrical power and its capacities to produce modes of satisfying self-reflection. And where Yeats is, there too we might find writers as diverse as James and Shakespeare and perhaps even Dante in his effort to characterize a loving intellect whose reason is far beyond any representations we might produce for it.

My praise of these states does not mean that we as agents can survive without heeding the claims of reason. It does mean that we as agents are not likely to thrive until we recognize how much that is in our possible interest is in conflict with reason as we understand its imperatives, or at least with how philosophers like Nussbaum understand its imperatives. Reason has its claims because we have to act in a world where accurate information is crucial, where laws of all kinds need to be honored, and where society needs shareable principles for assessing actions and agendas. But these claims have to take precedence for us only when we actually need to justify actions (and non-actions) or when we have to make analogous judgments about actions or agendas. Then we need disciplinary ethics, and disciplinary ethics always needs the background provided by discussions in moral philosophy. But much of our lives takes place on quite different planes where justifications can be assumed or where they are clearly after the fact and hence not fundamental. In these domains the worry about what is right is less pressing than the need to discover what is possible for us to feel and to project and even to speculate upon.[10] And in these domains the social impact of our actions proves less central than the possible impact on our private lives produced by specific imaginative states and related energy fields.

VI

And so I come to the last positive point that I think is sharpened by dwelling on what is problematic within ethical criticism. I want to show how an emphasis on ethos helps clarify the kinds of willing that are fundamental to literary experience, and I want to suggest the possibility that many of the values by which these experiences affect our actions emerge in the modes of challenge and provocation, and not simply in exemplary cognitive judgments. That in turn means we have to establish ideals of judgment capable of clarifying how simply the establishing of challenges can be an accomplishment central to the development of moral values. By examining how we are motivated to action and how aspects of will are brought to the fore in literary experience we can develop a fresh perspective on just how important ethos is to ethics.

Nussbaum's cognitive theory of emotions seems to rest in part on an assumption that the fit between philosophical reasoning and discriminating, sympathetic literary experience is matched by a direct fit between what we come to think is right, how we reach out to social identifications, and how we go on to act. Therefore, if one can specify the fit between concepts and perceptions and the appropriate emotions, one has the appropriate terms for handling those psychological dimensions enabling ethical reading to carry over into influencing ethical practice. Booth, on the other hand, introduces what seems a crucial third term for this psychology. In his scheme one has to move beyond the complex of percept, concept, and elicited spectatorial emotion to attribute some motivating factor specific to the complexity of individual situations.[11] Establishing those motivations is one important role played by the figure of the company we keep. That company is not merely something constructed by our judgments about texts. It also takes on the quality to judge us, to influence what desires we desire and consequently to provide both a measure of failure and a penalty for not keeping our will in alignment with our ideals. Failing those ideals is failing membership within this community.

Booth, however, sets unnecessary constraints on what might constitute the relevant community, and he severely limits the range of motives and interests by which literary experience influences both the decisions we make and the self-representations or modes of awareness that shape our understanding of those decisions. The image of texts as friends simply does not capture the many different kinds of intimate relations that texts enter in our lives, nor does it quite address the variety of productive energies brought into play by those intimate relations. Our affective lives can be strongly touched by pleasures, fascinations, and challenges that have their power because they refuse the domesticating ideal of friendship for other less stable and less comforting modes of presence. Moreover, these pleasures, fascinations, and challenges are not as easy as to subsume under criteria compatible with moral discourse as are appeals to friendship.

These different lines of relation affect the will in two basic ways. Even when we do affirm them or grant their importance to our lives, we may not base that determination on any specific categories or idealizing languages under which they fit. Texts appeal as particulars with their own distinctive promise of a relation that allows us to feel ourselves endowed with specific powers or capable of maintaining certain images of ourselves—by identification or by active struggle against domination. Indeed, the more identity issues seem directly at stake, the more we find it impossible to interpret the specific affirmations as relying on concepts or to specifiable criteria. In such cases we often experience the assertion of will simply as an extension of where we find our energies satisfyingly disposed. Consider again how iden-tification is invited by Yeats's poem—not because the poem somehow pro-vides us an idea affording a specific image for the self but because we find ourselves taking on the poem's own work of gathering an intensity of pro-ductive self-consciousness as its response to the utter loss of personal power represented in the initial situation. In our experiences of the lyrical at least, the will often emerges less through an interpretation of what is true or good about the text than as an attachment to what is powerful within it.

This claim about the will is not incompatible with the capacity of liter-ary texts to state the truth or to represent the good. The willing elicited by imaginative power simply occupies a different plane: it can accompany a range of judgments or perceptions because it simply determines the degree to which the person places stakes upon the particular state. So even when we do stress the truth value of an intense literary experience, our affirmation of it as an experience may depend less on the truth it offers than on our finding ourselves intensely identified with how its specific efforts at articu-lation provide a sense of discovery or sharpen what we thought we knew. We may affirm a text for how it represents moral situations, or we may affirm ourselves in relation to that text for how we find ourselves becoming moved in its presence. And, analogously, when we are moved to pity, we may respond directly to the object of pity or to the states of subjective intensity that the text offers us as agents capable of developing this specific intensity and scope of pity in relation to the world evoked.

Here, then, we enter another possibility for appreciating why Wittgen-stein thought ethics and aesthetics were one. There is a deep connection between how we affirm our own relation to the states or actions we inhabit and how we ultimately come to affirm the sense of completeness and of intense participation afforded us by works of art. From the point of view of ethics, the comparison to aesthetics foregrounds how closely our awareness of various exemplary states, of what carries force as ethos, becomes funda-mental to our own senses of identity. We are what we will most intensely, whether that be our investment in reason or our investments in what pro-vides material for reason to work upon. In both cases one important mea-sure of who we are as persons consists in the range of passions that we can occupy self-reflexively so that we take responsibility for the roles they play in our lives and in our representations of our lives. Conversely, what we call aesthetic emotion is trivialized if we take it as only a reaction to the power of form. I think aesthetic emotion is a condition of will that accompanies our regarding the work as offering a distinctive and powerful state of mind.

Aesthetic emotion may even be considered a strange kind of affect because it tends not to be focused on any particulars within the work but to characterize the force by which we respond to the piece as a whole, as if we were willing to take responsibility for who we became by virtue of our participation in it.[12] When we make such affirmative judgments it seems as if we cannot but want this text to be part of our world and we cannot but want ourselves to make this text part of how we see possibilities for affirming our own capacities within that world. On some occasions we could give ethical reasons for such judgments, but we also often find the emotions themselves capable of modifying the quality or degree of investments once relegated only to moral categories.

VII

Even those texts that tempt us by contrast and challenge to explore what such willing against the moral might feel like become part of the company we keep. But they can do so less as friends than as imaginative presences not only defining the most powerful and fascinating states of consciousness we know but also holding out the promise that by identifying provisionally with them we are likely to encounter ourselves at our most vital and most capacious. Where ethical criticism is forced, often against its best instincts, to treat texts as ultimately examples of something that philosophy can clarify and help assess, the ethos-based criticism that I am proposing deals directly with the examples as manifestations of qualities and powers that establish what is possible within certain ways of engaging the world. When we reflect on these examples we may decide we have to reject their long-term claims upon our loyalties because what they offer us in moments of intensity simply will not fit with the economies we work out as ways of directing our lives. But if we have experienced the works fully, we are hard-pressed to dismiss them as simply behavior we can judge or mistaken identifications we can easily dispel. Think of the continuing impact Shelley and Milton have had on poets who think they should know better. So these presences remain with us as challenges and as measures of the levels of intensity and commitment that we can continue to offer those texts with which we continue to identify.

Ethical criticism usually has little to say about this kind of struggle, or indeed about any kind of struggle between competing forces. For example, in Nussbaum there is substantial struggle against other philosophical positions, but her representation of reading makes it seem that all we need do is let the emotions compatible with judicious spectatorship have their way with us, while all writers need do is to learn the role of judicious spectators. And both deconstructive and Heideggerean versions of letting be put the burden of error simply on whether or not we succumb to categorical thinking and hence submit to some fantasy of the law. Gone is the psychomachia that classical literature loved, I think, because it so matched the authors' senses of what happened to them as they read and as they struggled to formulate desires for desires that neither made them ashamed before their chosen company nor left them passive followers of the moon in any of its social manifestations.

Perhaps ethical criticism has surrendered that view of the psyche's activity so that it could at least secure for literary experience the possibility of helping us dwell imaginatively within the sense of the self promised by our moral theories. If we are to feel we have any moral control over ourselves at all, we may be tempted to renounce visions of imaginative activity as a constant challenge to the will. But yielding to such suspicions seems to me to pay too high a price. Minimally, we risk rejecting the demand made by many literary texts that we be worthy of them by bringing to bear a self-consciousness so intensely invested that questions of how a will stands toward the material become inescapable. And we may risk settling for too passive or self-satisfied a morality that either comes to substitute for will or to lose its imaginative hold on us to become a mere wardrobe we reuse for social purposes because we have surrendered any fantasy that we can dress so as to turn an eye and engage a mind. These are reasons enough to make me wary of letting ethical criticism be a significant participant in the company our major texts invite us to keep.

Notes

1. Philosophers have long been aware of the need for some such distinction between ethics as concerned specifically with processes of justification and more general questions about values and ends. Perhaps the most useful contemporary formulation can be found in Nussbaum's *Love's Knowledge* (169), where she distinguishes between ethical theory as "the study of substantive ethical positions" and "moral philosophy" as a "general and inclusive rubric covering . . . many different types of ethical investigations." This is certainly preferable to the popular distinction between "ethics" as somehow the domain of high principle and "morals" as the mere social coding of those principles in different circumstances because it gets at the distinctive roles played by theorizing within professional philosophical discourse and more general speculations on "how should human beings live" (15). Yet the very generality she wins for the rubric "moral philosophy" runs the risk of bringing literature's general concern with how values are pursued within a discourse that turns out to look very much like "ethics" because assessing those values turns out to require the specific terms of moral philosophy: we are to

seek "reasons" for the kinds of action that are beggared by assuming that we arrive at them by moral calculi. Moreover, these philosophical assumptions are probably not sufficiently attuned to the deep conflicts in how even to talk about values that emerge among different cultural practices.

2. Martha Nussbaum's account of her shifting attitudes toward tensions between passionate love and "the ethical viewpoint" provides a good example of an ethical theorist acknowledging these challenges (see 50–53 of *Love's Knowledge* and her essay "Steerforth's Arm, 335–64). But her resolution of the problem by insisting on a "deep link between erotic attachment and a new, more yielding sort of moral rightness" (53) seems also to be a good example of how the challenge is usually ultimately resolved in terms that merely restore the ethical, with more chastened but also more imperious interpretive authority.

3. Several of my recent essays explore various aspects of this Nietzschean contrast, especially "Poetics as 'Untruth': Revising Modern Claims for Literary Truth."

4. Moral realism puts a somewhat different ontological spin on the ideals of judgment since it treats literary texts less as interpreting values than as instances of value claims to be treated as we treat other facts in the world. However, moral realism does preserve the same underlying hegemony of philosophical reasoning as do more hermeneutic and perfectionist approaches to texts. I attempt a more elaborate criticism of the relation between moral realism and literary studies in my *Subjective Agency* (139–50), where I respond to Terry Eagleton's recent work.

5. I have to admit that Derrida has gone a long way in addressing this problem within his general ethics by developing complex interrelations between response, responsiveness, and responsibility. Yet while Derrida certainly does not invoke traditional moral values, I think that he manages to evoke them in the background as his way of dignifying his focus on text as singular working signature. Without Western morality there would be no reason to care about this singularity, yet Derrida presupposes that this can stand as an ultimate value (or as close as his thinking comes to an ultimate value).

6. I misspeak. There is one much preferable perfectionist model for talking about the ethical in literary works, namely the treatment of poiesis developed by Richard Eldridge in *Leading a Human Life*. However, Eldridge's actual applications of this model to literary texts via literary criticism seem to me still hampered by the effort to make his dramatic situations correlate with stateable principles for what constitutes human flourishing.

7. Let me support this claim with specific quotations. This is the literary Nussbaum: "Certain truths about human life can only be fittingly and accurately stated in the language and forms characteristic of the narrative artist" (*Love's Knowledge* 5). Repeated acts of complex sympathy and empathy in relation to these narrative situations help forge a "distinctive ethical conception" (26) in their own right because they help us envision what constitutes a good life for human beings and what values make that life shareable. But then on the very next page she is content to argue that we should "*add* the study of certain novels to the study" of classical works in philosophical ethics, "on the grounds that without them we will not have a fully adequate statement of a powerful ethical conception" that we "ought to investigate." I find the claim that only "certain novels" should be studied especially difficult to reconcile with any argument that

there is a distinctive contribution made to ethics by literary experience. At best one can argue that these certain novels support or enrich her enlightened Aristotelianism.

8. In conversation, Bryan Glaser pointed out to me that Wright himself uses the courtroom parts of his novel to raise questions about judgment that seem to lead away from any possible institutional response to Bigger: to sympathize is patronizing; to execute utterly inhumane. Wright can do this because his larger ambition is to make us see the forces producing our impasse, and to do that we cannot just sympathize—we have to make our sympathy one feature of a complex political judgment suspicious of all dreams that moral identities matter very much at all in relation to what needs to be done.

9. In conversation, Richard Wollheim has made it clear to me the cost involved in linking emotions only to perceptions, as cognitive theory does, and hence denying all the fantasy dimensions that give the emotions their intensity and their hold on our lives. For a good example of problems that arise when this fantasy dimension is overlooked see *Poetic Justice* (64).

10. In the book I am writing I argue that the cognitive theory of the emotions makes a perfect fit with ethical criticism's emphasis on narrative fiction because the kinds of emotion stressed are those that can be negotiated by the *phronesis* providing the basic mode of judgment in that domain. But the realm of affects contains much more than the emotions that enter this fit. If one comes to the affects through the experience of lyric states, two other affective domains become at least equally important. These are the feelings, which I take to be the range of ways that our affective being spreads out into the world in particular moments without relying on narrative frames, and the passions, which I take to be those emotions in which the identity of the agent is overtly and intensely at stake.

11. One could argue that Nussbaum's judicious spectator creates the same problems of moving between ethical reason and empirical personal situations that one finds in Kant and in Rawls. I find Bernard Williams's *Ethics and the Limits of Philosophy* the most useful treatment of this topic, but I should also mention Michael Sandel's influential critique of Rawls along these lines. In Kant, will is not an issue because will is inseparable from reason: if one can enter the impersonal domain of reason one will have to will—reason is active and self-defining.

12. This is what Wittgenstein probably was referring to when he said that ethics and aesthetics are one.

Works Cited

Altieri, Charles. "Poetics as 'Untruth': Revising Modern Claims for Literary Truth." *New Literary History* 29 (1998): 305–28.

———. *Subjective Agency: A Theory of First-Person Expressivity and Its Social Implications*. New York: Blackwell, 1994.

Booth, Wayne C. *The Company We Keep: An Ethics of Fiction*. Berkeley: U of California P, 1988.

Eldridge, Richard. *Leading a Human Life: Wittgenstein, Intentionality, and Romanticism*. Chicago: U of Chicago P, 1997.

Nussbaum, Martha C. *Love's Knowledge: Essays on Philosophy and Literature*. New York: Oxford UP, 1990.

———. *Poetic Justice: The Literary Imagination and Public Life*. Boston: Beacon, 1995.

Sandel, Michael. *Liberalism and the Limits of Justice*. Cambridge: Cambridge UP, 1982.

Williams, Bernard. *Ethics and the Limits of Philosophy*. Cambridge: Harvard UP, 1985.

Wittgenstein, Ludwig. *Tractatus Logico-Philosophicus*. Trans. D. F. Pears and B. F. McGuinness. London: Routledge and Kegan Paul, 1961.

Yeats, William Butler. *The Poems of William Butler Yeats*. Ed. Richard Finneran. New York: Macmillan, 1983.

EXACTLY AND RESPONSIBLY
A Defense of Ethical Criticism

Martha C. Nussbaum

> To "put" things is very exactly and responsibly and interminably to do them. Our expression of them, and the terms on which we understand that, belong as nearly to our conduct and our life as every other feature of our freedom. . . . All of this means for [the artist] conduct with a vengeance, since it is conduct minutely and publicly attested. . . . Art is nothing if not exemplary, care nothing if not active.
>
> —Henry James, preface to *The Golden Bowl*

IN THE PREFACE to *The Golden Bowl,* as in many other writings, Henry James expresses the view that the novelist qua novelist is an ethical and political being whose conduct, as he "puts" things in prose in a certain way, is a form of exemplary moral conduct, expressing, out of the "soil" of his sensibility, a "projected morality."[1] It is also a form of political conduct, an example of the "high and the helpful public and, as it were, civic use of the imagination" (223–24). We need novelists in society, James argues, because the novelist is well-equipped to lead the attack against a culture characterized by the "rule of the cheap and easy" (223). He calls our imaginations to more exacting demarcations, our emotions to a more honest confrontation with our own selves and the real impact our conduct has on the lives of others. Because human beings do great damage to themselves and others through obtuseness and refusal of vision, "the effort really to see and really to represent is no idle business in face of the constant force that makes for muddlement" (149). The artist can assist us by cutting through the blur of habit and the self-deceptions habit abets; his conduct is ethical conduct because it strives to come to terms with reality in a world that shrinks from reality. When we follow him as attentive readers, we engage in ethical conduct, and our readings are assessable ethical acts.

James thus describes the artist's social function in terms that recall Socrates' characterization of his function in the sluggish Athenian democracy. Like a

59

"gadfly" on the back of a "noble but sluggish horse," Socrates said, he was attempting to wake up democracy so that it could conduct its deliberations in a more responsible and less habit-ridden manner. James agrees with Socrates that we need to be aroused from our ethical torpor; unlike Socrates, however, he insists that responsible ethical thought demands the prose of the artist and the acts of responsible readers. The terms of the novelist can help us to discover ourselves precisely because they are not the shopworn terms of ordinary discourse, all too often relied on by abstract philosophizing—terms that James calls "the standing terms" in order to indicate both their habitual character and their inertness. Instead, the novelist uses "the immense array of terms, perceptional and expressional, that . . . simply looked over the heads of the standing terms—or perhaps rather, like alert winged creatures, perched on those diminished summits and aspired to a clearer air" (339). For James, then, the aesthetic is ethical and political. It is precisely in virtue of the mastery of craft that enables the novelist to deploy "perceptional and expressional" terms with skill that he can make a contribution to a public victory over obtuseness and emotional deadness.

In his article "Against Ethical Criticism," Richard Posner appears to attack James's idea. With Oscar Wilde (or at least invoking the name of Wilde), he holds that literary works of art are not "moral or immoral," they are only "well or badly written." Any critic who brings ethical categories to the reading of works of art is thus bound to neglect the real aesthetic values the work contains and to impose on the text an alien set of concerns. In this essay I argue, against Posner, that James is correct in thinking that literary art can be ethical, and that responsible criticism of literary artworks can legitimately invoke ethical categories. I also argue that Posner's assault on ethical criticism is, at bottom, an assault on political egalitarianism, and that his defense of aesthetic detachment is best understood as an anti-egalitarian political stance.

Posner's attack is difficult to pin down, for three reasons. The first source of difficulty is Posner's failure to provide any extensive description or analysis of the arguments of the two ethical critics, Booth and Nussbaum, who are his targets. Thus, what aspects of our positions he actually opposes remain to some extent obscure. To make progress on this issue I therefore need to recapitulate the main claims I have actually made about the literary and the ethical, asking which of them Posner is really assailing.

The second source of difficulty is the fact that Posner advances two very different theses in the article, oscillating unclearly between them. The strong thesis is that literature has no ethical dimension and that the aesthetic values proper to the criticism of literature are altogether disjunct from ethical values. The weaker thesis is that literature frequently subverts simplistic and reductive forms of moralism; thus, ethical readers miss its distinctive contribution if they read in terms of simple and schematic moral categories. The strong thesis does entail the rejection of much that Booth and I do; but it is highly implausible, as I argue. The weaker thesis is much more plausible; it is also the one that is borne out by Posner's own literary examples— even the Wilde example, since Wilde was a highly ethical writer, profoundly concerned with compassion and the progress of the soul, albeit in an anti-Victorian way. But the weaker thesis could lead to no attack on my own use of ethical criticism, since it is precisely the thesis that I, along with James, have been asserting in order to make the case that moral philosophy needs literature.

The third source of difficulty, finally, is Posner's use of his examples. My own project focuses on realist novels of the nineteenth and early twentieth centuries. My method involves detailed analyses of these novels, and the whole point of my argument is that what we learn there could not be replaced by a simple paraphrase. Posner does mention quite a few novels, but he never engages in the sort of detailed analysis that would be needed to show to what extent his readings of those texts would differ from mine. In his book as well, his standard approach to novels is to offer a simple plot summary. He is somewhat more detailed in his treatment of lyric poetry, showing considerable sensitivity to poets' use of metaphor, rhythm, and language— as, for example, in the passage in the article in which he offers stanzas from Keats and T. S. Eliot as "touchstones of literary greatness."[2] His failure to engage with novels in a similarly detailed and linguistically attentive way makes it very difficult to say what the nature of our disagreement is. Posner's readers, moreover, may suspect that it is Posner, not Booth and I, who ignores the aesthetic values proper to the novel as genre, whereas Booth and I each spend a lot of time on details of structure, viewpoint, metaphor, sentence rhythm, and so on.[3]

II

To assess Posner's attack I must first describe its intended target, since Posner minimally does so. I say nothing about Booth, since Booth's paper speaks for itself; I discuss only my own writings, which Posner attacks at length throughout his article. I confine my remarks to the two books Posner actually discusses, since he does not discuss my treatments of literary works in other writings, such as *The Fragility of Goodness, The Therapy of Desire,* and recent articles on Emily Brontë, Marcel Proust, and James Joyce. I believe, however, that consultation with those other works would make the points I raise here even clearer.

Posner's attack is directed at two very different works: *Love's Knowledge,* where my primary concern is with moral philosophy and with the claim that moral philosophy needs certain carefully selected works of narrative literature in order to pursue its own tasks in a complete way; and *Poetic Justice,* where my concern is with the conduct of public deliberations in democracy, and where my claim is that literature of a carefully specified sort can offer valuable assistance to such deliberations by both cultivating and reinforcing valuable moral abilities. In neither work do I make any general claims about "literature" as such; indeed, I explicitly eschew such claims in both works, and I insist that my argument is confined to a narrow group of pre-selected works, all of them novels, and some of which (the novels of James and Proust, for example) are frankly very critical of their predecessors and contemporaries in the genre. I also make it very clear that even in terms of the general line of inquiry I map out, I have chosen to focus rather narrowly on certain questions about how to live, and to leave other equally interesting questions to one side.[4] Thus, no claim I make could be refuted by pointing out that novel A or B does not fit my description, since I all along insist only that my claims are applicable to certain writers discussed by me and to others who resemble them in relevant respects.

Nor do I claim in either work to offer an exhaustive account of the purposes of literature. I make it plain, in fact, that I believe literature has many purposes, and that formalistic criticism of literature has made an extremely valuable contribution. This point is even clearer when one considers the full range of my publications on literature, which focus on nonpolitical themes such as the relationship between love and anger, the incompatibility of romantic passion with social concern, the desperate agony of grief.[5]

It is, of course, true that ethical and political considerations have played, and continue to play, a central role in my own literary projects. But one should not infer from this that I believe this is the only legitimate way of approaching literature—any more than one would rightly infer from the fact that a person makes a career of playing the clarinet that this person thinks the flute an instrument not worth playing. I do believe that ethical and political issues are non-optional, in the sense that every human being ought to reflect about them in some manner. I also hold that the ethical and political criticism of literature is potentially helpful to most human beings in this reflective activity. But I certainly do not hold that there are no other issues worth worrying about, in connection with which literature may make a contribution; nor do I hold that it is always mistaken to consider literature for form alone, apart from consideration of any human issue. That sort of engagement probably would be mistaken for some authors and texts; but it may be suitable for others. In short: just as I am a pluralist about politics, holding that there are many reasonable comprehensive conceptions of the good that deserve our respect, so, too, I am a pluralist about literary approaches, holding that there are many that deserve to be respected and fostered. It is Posner, it seems to me, who is illiberal, holding that the approach I have chosen is utterly to be scorned. Why can he not accept it as one of the reasonable ones, which just happens to be different from his own?

But let us now return to the theses of the books Posner attacks. The two books have some common concerns. Both explore the implications of a pair of Jamesian ideas: that there is an intimate connection between form and content, and that some types of content can be completely and fully expressed only by including works that are conventionally called literary. Both, furthermore, focus on the role of literary art in fulfilling the Jamesian aim of making us fully responsible to the complexity of our experience "as social creatures."[6] They criticize excessively simplistic and reductive approaches to human experience that can be found in some parts of philosophy and the social sciences; both stress the cognitive role of the imagination and the emotions in bringing us into contact with the complexity of our own lives and the lives of others; both stress the importance of grasping complex and frequently fine-tuned qualitative distinctions, insisting that obtuseness results from a premature reduction of these to quantitative distinctions. In all those areas, both books see literary works as guides to what is mysterious and messy and dark in our experience, and both argue that social science has frequently been obtuse in its effacement of those features of life.[7]

At this point, however, the two books diverge, taking on substantially different opponents. The opponent in *Love's Knowledge* is the philosopher who, while granting that moral philosophy requires the full and fair consideration of all the major ethical views, denies that literature need play any role in that process. Notice that my argument could do no work against someone who holds that we need only study Kantianism or Utilitarianism in order to know all we need to know about ethics. It works only against someone who is committed to an overall procedure (which has its roots in Aristotle) that requires the theorist to work through all the major views, even and especially those that differ from her own. Utilitarian Henry Sidgwick, for example, held such a view of the methods of ethics; more recently, John

Rawls, while himself a Kantian, has defended a similar view. It would not be misleading to think of my project as addressed to Sidgwick, Rawls, and whoever follows them.

With Henry James and against this opponent, I assert that there is a distinctive type of ethical view—we may call it, with James, "the projected morality" (45)—that requires literary works of a very specific type, primarily exemplified by the late novels of James, for its complete investigation. This view is one that I associate with Aristotle, and it is characterized by four salient features: (1) an insistence on the plurality and noncommensurability of the valuable elements of a well-lived life; (2) an insistence on the importance of contextual complexity and particularized judgment in good deliberation; (3) an insistence on the cognitive role of the emotions; and (4) an insistence on human vulnerability and the vulnerability of the good. Much of the book is occupied with a discussion of the roots of these ideas in Plato and Aristotle and the complex connections of each of the four elements with the others. My claim is that in order to investigate this Aristotelian ethical view fully and fairly, we need to turn to texts in which the case for that sort of rationality is made out in a powerful and convincing way—and this cannot be done if we confine ourselves to works written in the abstract style characteristic of most contemporary moral theory. Utilitarian and Kantian ethics can probably be well and completely studied in abstract philosophical texts, I claim, but Aristotle's conception is much more dependent on "allies" who will make out the force of such obscure claims as the claim that "the discernment rests with perception," and that correct action "lies in a mean." Because Aristotle's conception leaves so much to particularized contextual judgment, one cannot well assess the conception without studying complex examples of such particularized judgment; and, of course, Aristotle's text does not supply such material. I claim that Henry James is a powerful ally of Aristotle, and one whom Aristotle badly needs if he is to convince us of his claims.

So far as I can see, Posner does not engage with this project at all. He never discusses the issues of ethical method and ethical theory on which my argument is based, and he seems to have no interest in them. Elsewhere, in fact, he has expressed a very contemptuous attitude to all ethical theorizing, so it is not surprising that he shows no interest in the question whether James is or is not a valuable ally of Aristotle, and even less in the question whether even a Utilitarian or a Kantian therefore has reasons to take James seriously. Posner does take issue with my reading of *The Golden Bowl,* or at least he appears to do so. But since his remarks are so brief and incomplete, I am unable to discover whether he really differs with my ideas regarding the role of particularity, emotion, and vulnerability, or whether he agrees with those ideas and simply doubts that Maggie Verver is a good exemplar of them. (He appears to think that I read the novel as offering some rather simple lessons about how to maintain a marriage: but really, the whole purpose of my reading was to argue that good choice is so highly particularized that one cannot say what choice is correct, in advance of knowing all the parties and their tangled history.)[8] So all in all I conclude that I simply do not know what Posner thinks about the project undertaken in *Love's Knowledge*. If I had to guess, I would guess that he thinks the entire idea of appealing to great novels for illumination regarding ethical theory is a perverse project, since these novels are important and the ethical theories of Aristotle and his fellow philosophers are entirely unimportant. But I see no argument on that question in "Against Ethical Criticism."

In *Poetic Justice* I attempt a related but different task: commending certain works of literature to citizens and public officials as a valuable source of deliberative enrichment. Focusing on the analysis of compassion and on the role of the imagination in promoting compassion, I argue that certain specific literary works develop those imaginative abilities in a valuable way and are therefore helpful to citizens—although they need, here again, to be closely allied to arguments in ethical theory that will make their contribution plain. But I begin further back, with an analysis of the very basic human ability that Charles Dickens calls "fancy": the ability to see one thing as another and one thing in another. I argue, following Dickens, that this ability lies at the heart of the ethical life. The kind of thinking a small child does when she asks, "Twinkle twinkle, little star, how I wonder what you are," has a crucial role to play in the life of a citizen. We see personlike shapes all around us: but how do we relate to them? All too often, we see them as just shapes, or physical objects in motion. What storytelling in childhood teaches us to do is to ask questions about the life behind the mask, the inner world concealed by the shape. It gets us into the habit of conjecturing that this shape, so similar to our own, is a house for emotions and wishes and projects that are also in some ways similar to our own; but it also gets us into the habit of understanding that that inner world is differently shaped by different social circumstances. These abilities, I argue, must be acquired in early childhood, by the early practice of storytelling. But they get an especially sophisticated and valuable development in novels such as those of Dickens, which take us into the lives of those who are different in circumstance from ourselves and enable us to understand how similar hopes and fears are differently realized in different social circumstances.

In order to establish that these novels really could make a valuable contribution to citizenship, I confront three closely related opponents. The first opponent is a reductionist social scientist who claims that no text that does not reduce qualitative distinctions to quantitative distinctions could possibly offer understanding. Against this opponent I argue (using the example of development economics) that social science needs to take account of the qualitative information novels such as those of Dickens make available, and that science can do so without ceasing to be science. The second opponent argues that because literary works arouse emotions, and emotions are always irrational, therefore they can never offer good guidance to public deliberation. Against this opponent I argue at length that emotions involve evaluative judgments that can be true or false, and that at least some of them are true and illuminating; emotions are not always good guides, but sometimes they can be very good guides. The third opponent says that whatever may be the case with social science more generally, narrative understanding is of no use in the law. Against this opponent I argue that it is frequently of great use; I focus on cases from criminal and constitutional law that involve understanding and astutely evaluating the situation of a person very different from oneself, and I argue that the type of understanding a judge or juror requires here is very similar to the type certain novels promote.

I do not, of course, claim that these arguments give us an exhaustive account of the roles literature may play in human life. I begin from the assumption that we are thinking about good citizenship in connection with the situation of the poor and excluded, and I intend simply to convince people already interested in these same issues that they can get some assistance from literature, even though many views of rationality in the academy will have suggested to them that they cannot.

Nowhere in *Poetic Justice* do I face an opponent who holds that we should not try to understand the experience of poor people, prisoners, racial minorities, and other excluded people, with a view to improving their lot and ameliorating their suffering. Nor, therefore, do I offer a substantive argument that this is a worthwhile endeavor. I assume for the purposes of argument that it is, and I hope to convince people who agree with that idea to turn to literature for illumination. I suspect that Posner's real target is this tacit premise of my entire argument. He suggests as much when he says that the reason *Hard Times* is a good novel is simply that it has one great comic character, Mr. Bounderby. The struggle of the poor, to which the novel is mainly devoted, plays no part in constituting, for Posner, its literary interest. I return to this issue shortly.

III

Posner offers four arguments against the type of ethical criticism I advocate. I call these the *empathetic-torturer argument,* the *bad-litterati argument,* the *evil-literature argument,* and the *aesthetic-autonomy argument.* I focus on the relationship of his arguments to my theses in *Poetic Justice,* although I occasionally refer as well to relevant portions of *Love's Knowledge.*

The *empathetic-torturer argument* is easily answered. Posner states, plausibly enough, that the ability to understand what another person is thinking and feeling does not automatically conduce to compassionate action. Sadists frequently have this ability and use it to torture those in their grasp. But Posner apparently has neglected chapter 3 of *Poetic Justice,* where I define the emotion of compassion, following Aristotle, as a painful emotion that requires three evaluative judgments: that what is happening to the person whom one contemplates is seriously bad, that it is not the person's own fault (or beyond the fault, if fault there is), and that the spectator has similar possibilities and vulnerabilities. This is not an unconventional analysis of compassion: one can find it in most of the major texts on that emotion in the philosophical tradition, from Aristotle to the present day. (Nor is it a new element in my work, as Posner suggests: I have spelled out this point repeatedly, in works dating back to 1986, most recently in the article "Compassion: The Basic Social Emotion.") Most philosophers who attack this emotion as pernicious do so while granting that this analysis is correct. What they usually object to, as I record, is an alleged overvaluation of the misfortune: following Socrates, they hold that "a good man cannot be harmed." It is this complex emotion, including all its evaluative judgments, that I hold to be linked to beneficial social action.

In short, I am fully in agreement with Posner that the phenomenon he designates as "empathy" is not sufficient to motivate good action; I never suggest that it is, and early in *Poetic Justice* I insist that empathy is likely to be hooked up to compassion only in someone who has had a good early education in childhood, one who teaches concern for others. I think more people have that sort of upbringing than the reverse and thus do not develop a general desire to torture humans (though, of course, they also often do not extend the recognition of humanity to all humans). But that evil torturers exist is obvious, and nothing in my argument casts doubt on this.[9]

The real question for Posner, then, is whether one could have compassion as I define it, while still wanting to torture the person. The torturer surely finds the other person's suffering a good thing and takes delight in it; moreover, the torturer often thinks that the person deserves to suffer, and she typically denies that her own possibilities and vulnerabilities are similar to those of the sufferer. I argue in *Poetic Justice* that the works of literature I consider promote compassion, not just the thinner empathy. (In "Compassion: The Basic Social Emotion," I make a related argument about ancient Athenian tragedy.) These works ask us to see what is happening to the central characters as bad in important ways. The importance of these novels, as I repeatedly stress, is cognitive: they shape, in their reader, certain evaluative judgments that lie at the heart of certain emotions. We may, of course, refuse the invitation to be so shaped, but if we fulfill responsively the role of the "implied reader," we will form those evaluative judgments. (Oscar Wilde's reading of *The Old Curiosity Shop*—"One would have to have a heart of stone to read the death of Little Nell without laughing"—was not a responsive reading of Dickens's text, whether or not we agree with Wilde that some literary failures on Dickens's part explain that response.)

The *bad-litterati argument* is equally easily answered. Posner, like many opponents of ethical criticism, thinks that it is a good objection to what Booth and I do to point out (a) that Nazis have read a lot of novels and been moved by them, and (b) that professors of literature are not better people than other people. But Posner's approach to the issue is entirely ad hoc and unscientific. Booth and I are talking about the interaction between novel and mind during the time of reading. We do not claim that this part of one's life inevitably dominates, although we do think that if the novels are ethically good it will have a good influence, other things being equal; nor do we claim that spending more time reading novels will make it more likely that this part will dominate. Moreover, reading can have the good effects we claim for it only if one reads with immersion, not just as a painful duty. Professors of literature are often jaded and detached; they do not read with the freshness and responsiveness of ordinary readers. Finally, we never draw from our claim that literature promotes ethical abilities the conclusion that the more time one spends reading, the better. All good things have to be integrated appropriately into the structure of one's whole life; excess along any dimension could jeopardize the good that a good thing can contribute.

As for the Nazis, in addition to pointing out that their society contained many very strong influences that militated against the good influence of the good literary works, we can also point out that not all the literary works they admired were the ones likely to promote compassion for human suffering. I am not aware that Nazis were great readers of Dickens, nor yet of Henry James. And they certainly were great readers of Nietzsche and listeners to Wagner, figures whose bad influence might well have undermined the good influence of Dickens even had there been such influence.

One further point must now be mentioned. When I spoke about compassion in *Poetic Justice,* I pointed out that compassion required us to judge that our possibilities were similar to those of the suffering person we contemplate. And, following Rousseau, I insisted that where our society has created sharp hierarchical separations we may well fail to have compassion for those on the other side of the barrier. Just as Rousseau's kings found it difficult to see their lot in the suffering of a peasant, so too we should expect Nazis to experience great difficulty in seeing their own possibilities in the sufferings of a Jew. I argue that literary works can help us cross these barriers, if they display the person on the other side of the barrier in a certain way, as a human being worthy of sympathy. But to do this they will need to address, and undermine, the very specific stereotypes that block us from seeing the humanity of specific groups with which we interact. This was my argument, in both *Poetic Justice* and *Cultivating Humanity,* for including works dealing with race in the curricula of universities and law schools. Even though many works promote a generalized compassion for suffering, if our society has impeded our vision of the lives of a specific group, we will need works dealing with that specific group in order to remove the barriers. Thus, following Ralph Ellison, I hold that novels dealing with race may "be fashioned as a raft of hope, perception, and entertainment that might help keep us afloat as we tried to negotiate the snags and whirlpools that mark our nation's vacillating course toward and away from the democratic idea." It will do so by defeating this "national tendency to deny the common humanity shared by my character and those who might happen to read of his experience."[10] Obviously, Ellison did not think that just any work of literature could perform this very specific task: it had to be a work dealing with race, one that would put the "common humanity" of a member of the racial minority unavoidably in the reader's mind.

So Posner's Nazi question should really be: What works did the Nazis read about Jews, and how were Jews portrayed in those works? The answer is clear. Jews were invariably portrayed in Nazi-era fiction as either totally nonhuman (insects or vermin, in many children's books),[11] or else as evil and threatening, parasites who prey on the social fabric of Germany.[12]

Many novels of this era are considered so dangerous, in today's Germany, that they can be accessed in research collections only by special academic arrangements and may never be copied.[13] So obviously Germans do not think that people are going to read them simply for aesthetic pleasure, and they do not think that literature is inert in political affairs. If Nazis had been brought up on compassionate portrayals of Jews, Posner would have at least the beginning of a question, though we would still need to insist on the complex relation between the time of reading and the rest of one's life. Since they obviously were brought up, instead, on works that powerfully and deliberately impeded such compassion, his objection has no weight.

We can add a final, more subtle point. Our thesis about the effects of literature is only in part a causal thesis, a thesis about what reading literature does to the personality. It is also, clearly, a conceptual thesis. We claim that the activities of imagination and emotion that the involved reader performs during the time of reading are not just instrumental to moral conduct; they are also examples of moral conduct, in the sense that they are examples of the type of emotional and imaginative activity that good ethical conduct involves.[14] It is by being examples of moral conduct that they strengthen the propensity so to conduct oneself in other instances.

The *evil-literature argument* is more complicated, and more interesting. Posner points to the obvious fact that literature is full of evil and frequently invites the reader's collaboration with evil, or at least with many things that today we regard as evil. Literature has great seductive power: it can get us to sympathize with class privilege, the oppression of women, war and pillage, and, finally, as my previous discussion records, hideous racism. So what can I possibly mean by suggesting that literature as such is a valuable aid to the civic imagination?

The first and simplest answer is that I do not claim that literature itself has such power. In fact, like Booth, I insist throughout *Poetic Justice* and the related chapter of *Cultivating Humanity* that literature needs ethical assessment and that not all works will prove valuable in my imaginary curriculum for citizenship. "Ethical assessment of the novels themselves, in conversation both with other readers and with the arguments of moral and political theory, is therefore necessary if the contribution of novels is to be politically fruitful" (*Poetic Justice* 10). Such assessment ought to be complex, focusing on the "implied author" of the literary work or, to put it another way, on the sense of life embodied in the work as a whole. The astute reader will not rush to reject a work because it contains a single episode or character giving evidence of a repugnant social prejudice. If that were the case, we would have to reject both James and Dickens, since their portrayals of Jews and blacks are by no means acceptable. Booth's metaphor of friendship is useful here: just as we may criticize our friends while still remaining friends, so too we may criticize James for having prejudices that were a little retrograde in his time, without utterly condemning him—although we might well not want a contemporary friend who exhibited similar prejudices. But the question will always be, what are we offered that makes us want to maintain the friendship despite what we criticize? If the criticized element lies too deep, too close to the roots of literary interest in the work, we may not be able to overlook it. Thus, Booth records that he now finds it impossible to laugh at Rabelais, since he is too keenly aware of the way in which the springs of humor in that author's work depend upon a vicious conception of women. If we do not react this way to Dickens and James, it is because there is deep insight, precision, and illumination offered by their works, along with the lesser and more localized patches of obtuseness. The same is certainly true of Homer, Shakespeare, and most of the other authors cited by Posner as bad influences. They are so, but only in a limited way; what they offer survives ethical criticism. I would add that the same is even true of an artist—Wagner, for example—who might be in some respects quite evil and a major bad influence. Wagner's art is of lasting value even to one who, like myself, abhors its smug images of civic homogeneity, because it offers deep insight into the nature of envy, hatred, and love, in ways that are not entirely bound up with the works' endorsement of an abhorrent social vision.

Thus, my reply is ultimately threefold: first, we need not read ethically or, as Booth puts it, "for life"; we may always decide to read for historical interest or for rhetorical and grammatical interest; in that case the ethical deficiencies of a work will not trouble us. Second, as Booth's idea of coduction implies, ethical reading is dialogical and conversational, and not all readers will have the same ethical view or project; thus a work that bores or offends one reader ethically may be exactly what the other is looking for, and we should applaud and investigate these differences. Third, works that we agree in condemning on one front may still offer us a great deal on another.

But I now arrive at a final point that qualifies my response. I have said that I make no claims about the moral properties of literature as such. But in a very limited and partial way, I suggest one such claim: that the sort of wondering and fancying encouraged by many distinguished works of narrative literature "nourishes the ascription of humanity, and the prospect of friendship" (*Poetic Justice* 39). This is so only of certain works, and only in a context already prepared for their impact. But I believe that the connection of early storytelling with the child's developing sense of compassion probably helps to explain the fact that there is a very general connection between our aesthetic and our moral evaluations of novels, in the following sense. We do not tend to rate highly, from the aesthetic viewpoint, novels in which all the characters are treated by the implied author simply as objects, without any inner world for which one cares. Consider Booth's marvelous critique of Peter Benchley's novel *Jaws* in *The Company We Keep*. Booth shows that the novel offers us a very restricted range of sentiments and that it portrays its main characters as cardboard cutouts, without any rich inner world. The female characters, especially, are portrayed as bodies ripe for slaughter. Booth records his critique as a moral evaluation of Benchley. But isn't it just these features of the text—its superficiality, its human barrenness, its formulaic use of persons as objects—that one would mention in an aesthetic critique? In general, exploitation makes bad art.

Take the case of pornography. There may occasionally be a pornographic novel that has aesthetic interest: this may be true, for example, of Sade. But I think this is so, insofar as it is, only because the novels of Sade challenge and rebut our usual expectations about compassion in a highly disturbing way: they do not just fail to exhibit compassion; they carry on an argument with the reader that this is a world in which compassion cannot be found. We might say that *Justine* is to Rousseau what *Candide* is to Leibniz: the graphic depiction of realities that cast doubt on a form of theoretical optimism. This project inspires our interest because of its intellectual seriousness. But we do not read *Justine* with delight or find it aesthetically pleasing. We read it as a test of our perhaps too complacent ethical sensibilities. Most garden-variety pornography lacks Sade's intellectual depth and thus lacks the limited aesthetic interest his novels possess. I suggest that in general and for the most part, and only where novels are concerned, we find aesthetically pleasing only those works that treat human beings as humans and not just animals or objects, that contain what I have called respect before the soul. But this quality is also moral, so we might say that in the novel aesthetic interest and moral interest are not altogether unrelated.[15]

Most difficult to answer is the *aesthetic-autonomy argument*. Here, Posner makes a claim that has a long and distinguished history, and that must therefore be taken very seriously by anyone who engages with that history. The claim is that aesthetic values are entirely distinct from ethical values, and people inquire in an improper way when they bring ethical questions to the assessment of a literary work. We see the idea of aesthetic autonomy in Posnerian sentences such as, "She does not deny the importance of aesthetic values, but she is prepared to trade them off against the moral" (3), and "Particularly remote from morality is the disinterested, 'art for art's sake' pleasure that much literature affords. . . . It is the pleasure that comes from being in the presence of beauty" (22).

I have no interest in denying that there may be some aesthetic properties of the literary works I discuss that have no ethical relevance. But James would ask us not to assume this without careful reflection. If to "put" is to "do," then we cannot assume that even the shape and cadence of a novelist's sentences, his choice of metaphors, his use of sound and rhythm, are altogether disjunct from his search for an understanding of the complexities of human life. Since my account of the ethical role of literature, in both books, stresses centrally the importance of showing the presence of complexity and particularity, I would, with James, be especially slow to concede that the ways in which a great literary artist "exactly and interminably and responsibly" makes us see the particular are lacking in ethical relevance. However, to rebut Posner I do not need to defend the thesis that most or all properties of a literary work have ethical significance. I only need defend the thesis that the works I write about are reasonably read with attention to ethical properties as among their salient properties.

One can think of works of art that can be contemplated reasonably well without asking any urgent questions about how one should live. Abstract formalist paintings are sometimes of this character, and some intricate but nonprogrammatic works of music (though by no means all). But it seems highly unlikely that a responsive reading of any complex literary work is utterly detached from concerns about time and death, about pain and the transcendence of pain, and so on—all the material of the "how one should live" question as I have conceived it. Thus, even with regard to works I do not discuss at all—poetic dramas, lyric poems, novels by novelists very different from Dickens and James—the aesthetic-detachment thesis is implausible if we use "ethical" and "moral" in the broad sense that I have consistently and explicitly given them.[16]

Another way of approaching this issue is to say that Posner frequently appeals to the idea of a true lover of literature, an idea of what that true lover looks to or values. Would Posner look to literature for an answer to that sort of question, a question about value or appreciation? If the answer to that is yes, as I believe, for Posner, it surely is, then Posner already sees literature as offering illumination in the evaluative domain. But why should he suppose that literature should offer illumination concerning aesthetic valuing, and not about ethical and political valuing, especially in cases where its subject matter is not aesthetic, but ethical or political (as is the case with many realist novels)?[17]

Nor, it turns out, does Posner himself consistently hold the aesthetic-detachment position. Indeed, the role he imputes to literature in human life is clearly a moral one in my sense, and one not far afield from the Aristotelian purpose I discuss in both books. Literature, he says, "helps us make sense of our lives, helps us to fashion an identity for ourselves." Reading a poem of Donne, he continues, will not persuade someone who never thought about love that love is the most important thing in the world. But it may "make you realize that this *is* what you think, and so may serve to clarify yourself to yourself" (20). That, of course, is exactly what I have been saying all along.

Posner's real target, it would seem, is not at all my general claim about the role that novels of Dickens and James might play in dispelling obtuseness and awakening us to a range of ethical possibilities. It is the more specific claim I make in regard to Dickens and related social novelists, namely that these novels awaken compassion for the suffering of the poor. No, says Posner, to read Dickens this way is to neglect the "aesthetic values" that great art affords. All great art should be read with detachment from such political purposes. Interesting that where the subject is old age or self-knowledge, Posner is happy to concede that literature pursues these ethical issues; but where the subject is helping out the poor, he pulls back into a stronger version of the aesthetic-detachment thesis.

I believe that Posner's claims simply fail as claims about the novels I am actually discussing. It seems to me impossible to conceive of an attentive and responsive reader of Dickens who did not pose the question "How should we live?" and who did not connect this reflection with thought about the social condition of the poor. Indeed, at the end of *Hard Times* Dickens addresses the reader in just these terms: "Dear reader! It rests with you and me, whether, in our two fields of action, similar things shall be or not. Let them be! We shall sit with lighter bosoms on the hearth, to see the ashes of our fires turn gray and cold." Dickens here charges the reader with a moral task, referring as he does so to the image of the fire that has played such a central role in the novel's reflections about the literary imagination. "You are on your way to death," he tells the reader—"like me, like Louisa Gradgrind. When she looked into the fire she saw dim shapes, but because she lacked a narrative training of her imagination she saw nothing that led to the amelioration of human life in Coketown. Now, reader of my novel, what will you imagine? It is up to you to make society better, and if you do so you will end your life more happily than my unhappy heroine. My story of Coketown has shown you some things that can be. But if they are to be, you must take action."

To this speech we can imagine Posner's likely reply: "I care nothing for the improvement of society; I care only for the amusement you have offered me by your pleasing character Mr. Bounderby. In general, I turn to art for the thrill of being in the presence of beauty, not for any extraneous ethical values. You, Charles Dickens, offer me that thrill on occasion, although you also offer much high-minded sentimentality that bores me, and many poor and stupid characters who are extremely taxing."

But Dickens would not be at a loss for words either. "Well, Judge Posner," we might imagine him saying, "it seems, then, that you are not a very valuable member of society, and before you die you may regret this fact. I never had a very high view of the legal profession, and my conversation with you has confirmed my view of its emotional aridity. But since you are a fascinating character, with your strange combination of intelligence and denial, quick formal perception and shallowness of feeling, I may possibly put you into my next short novel, which is due for the Christmas issue of one of the larger magazines. I shall not reveal the plot, except to say that it concerns ghosts."

What this imaginary dialogue brings out is that Posner's aesthetic-detachment view is not an alternative way of approaching Dickens's text; it is a repudiation of a great part of Dickens's text. Dickens is an author who demands to be read ethically, and ethically in a very specific sense, with attention to the equal worth of all human beings and the misery caused human beings by unjust social institutions. These ethical and political values are not "extraneous" but are absolutely central to his works. Posner, by repudiating the novel's ethical demand, repudiates Dickens and the Christian/ethical view of life to which Dickens is profoundly committed. He is criticizing my choice of authors, not offering new ways of reading the same authors.

And in the end I believe that this is what our debate is all about. Posner detests the compassionate/egalitarian vision of the world that I find deeply attractive. He goes for works that seem far removed from those material and social issues—the poetry of W. B. Yeats and T. S. Eliot, for example. I go for works that seem to me to advance our thinking about these material and social issues: the novels of Dickens and, in today's world, of authors such as V. S. Naipaul and Rohinton Mistry. I claim that all citizens need to ponder the issues to which these novelists direct us, since all live in a society in which circumstances of birth, social class, race, gender, and sexuality construct people's life chances as unequal in a pervasive way. For that reason, I commend Dickens and Naipaul to all citizens. Posner refuses the recommendation, insisting on taking his stand with works that keep him at a distance from the demand of the poor and the weak.

At bottom, then, the appeal to aesthetic detachment is not innocent of politics. To read Dickens in a detached way is to refuse his invitation to reflect. To cling to authors who can more plausibly be read in that detached and apolitical way is also to refuse the invitation of Dickens and other social authors to reflect. To be willing to reflect about old age and death, but not about the social condition of the poor and racially oppressed, is to permit reflection to enter one portion of one's life but to exclude it from another. (For what we see in Posner is clearly exclusion, not reflective anti-egalitarian argument.) Posner's choices as a reader and critic are, in short, the sort of choice that Henry James describes as "conduct with a vengeance . . . conduct minutely and publicly attested." As conduct, they invite our ethical scrutiny and assessment. Posner's acts as critic are the acts of someone who "puts" things in a way that shelters him from the claim of a painful reality. Notice that the avoidance is not in the practice of aesthetic detachment itself, which can be fine and delightful in its way, but in the dogmatic refusal to admit that any other relation to literature could possibly have any value.

Posner ends his new essay by claiming that I am "missing out" on something that could make me "happier and stronger," namely the possibility of an escape from our daily world, with its political obsessions, "into a world of morally and politically indifferent enchantment." This seems, first, just false: everyone derives such joy from reading.[18] But notice the way Posner characterizes the relationship between the moral and the aesthetic. Here, as so often, he represents the aesthetic as a joyful escape from confinement, the moral as something that encloses and constrains. But can he not imagine the joy that a person might feel when she thinks of human beings escaping from a world of injustice into a world of justice? In my childhood, the novels of Dickens provided just such a joyful sense of escape, from a world in which rich people ignored the claims of the poor into a world where those claims were acknowledged. This really was a source of great joy: it felt like a release from a stifling confinement into a space of human possibility. I could therefore also say that Posner is missing a great joy that could make him happier.

It is possible that neither of us will ever agree about who is missing what. But there is one significant asymmetry between Posner's position and my own. I say nothing against Posner's pleasure, nor do I wish to take it from him. I do think that all citizens ought to think about justice, and it seems to me that reading certain novels offers assistance in that task. But this involves no denigration of Posner's literary choices, provided he thinks about social justice in some way during some part of his life—as, in his judicial career, he plainly does. Why, then, should a hard-working judge not escape, at the end of the day, into a world of morally indifferent enchantment? I am also happy to grant that detached and formalistic criticism of literature is a valuable academic endeavor, and one that a great university should support. Posner, by contrast, insists that my type of literary experience and my type of criticism have no value at all. Because he finds the moral confining, he does not want anybody to learn to love it. It therefore seems to me that Posner, who claims to be the defender of liberal freedoms against their dogmatic political assailants—and who frequently is so—has written a most illiberal article. He should ask himself why.

Notes

1. See Henry James's *Art of the Novel* (45). I am very grateful to Wayne Booth and Richard Posner for their comments at our joint APA session where this essay was first presented and to Hibi Pendleton, Laurie Shrage, and Cass Sunstein for helpful comments on an earlier draft.

2. Posner has since made clear that he does not mean to claim that these works are touchstones for every kind of literary greatness—only for a particular sort, in which considerations of rhythm and sound play an especially central role.

3. For just one example, see the article "'Finely Aware and Richly Responsible': Literature and the Moral Imagination" (148–67) in *Love's Knowledge,* where the extended analysis of a metaphor provides the core of my ethical reading. The reading of *Hard Times* in *Poetic Justice: The Literary Imagination and Public Life* makes the character of the novelist's metaphorical imagination the center of its argument on behalf of literature.

4. See *Love's Knowledge:* "Here we must insist again that what we have on our hands is a family of inquiries; and not all our questions, even about how to live, will be well pursued in exactly the same texts. If, for example, we should want to think about the role of religious belief in certain lives that we might lead, none of the novels chosen here will help us much—except Beckett's, and that only in a somewhat parochial way. If we want to think about class distinctions, or about racism, or about our relationships with other societies different from our own—again, these particular novels will not be sufficient. . . . My choices of texts express my preoccupation with certain questions, and do not pretend to address all salient questions" (45).

5. For the first, see the treatment of Seneca's *Medea* in *The Therapy of Desire;* for the second, see my essay on Brontë's *Wuthering Heights* in *Philosophy and Literature;* for the last, see "Love and the Individual" in *Love's Knowledge* and "Emotions as Judgments of Value: A Philosophical Dialogue" in *Comparative Criticism.*

6. See James in his preface to *The Princess Casamassima,* where he describes the function of his art as the production of "an intelligent report" of "our apprehension and our measure of what happens to us as social creatures" (64–65).

7. See, for example, *Poetic Justice:* "One may be told many things about people in one's own society and yet keep that knowledge at a distance. Literary works that promote identification and emotional reaction cut through those self-protective stratagems, requiring us to see and to respond to many things that may be difficult to confront—and they make this process palatable by giving us pleasure in the very act of confrontation" (5–6).

8. Posner says nothing about my readings of *The Ambassadors* and *The Princess Casamassima,* both linchpins of my project, nor does he address my readings of Proust, the other central literary author in *Love's Knowledge.* In his new article, Posner now addresses *The Princess,* but in a peculiar way. Readers of his description, in his article, would have no idea that the main purpose of my essay on *The Princess* was to defend liberal reformist gradualism against the violent revolutionary tactics of the Marxist left; and no idea, either, that the core of my argument was that the revolution most worth working for is the one that consists in the awakening of the mind to a more accurate confrontation with particular human realities.

9. Joyce Carol Oates's fascinating novel *Zombie* is a portrait of such an evil torturer: the serial killer Quentin, who kills people in an effort to produce a lobotomized "companion" with whom he could have a relationship that does not require the recognition of humanity. In conversation, Oates has told me that her aim was to show how strange the world looks through the eyes of someone who has empathy but not compassion: that is, he can figure out what other people are thinking and feeling, and thereby do a good imitation of human behavior, but he just does not have the judgments that compassion requires. Oates, like Rousseau, thinks that compassion has an innate basis in normal human beings. I make no comment on that here.

10. See Ralph Ellison's *Invisible Man* (xxiv–xxvi).

11. See, for example, the display of children's literature in the Historisches Museum in Berlin, where the typical Jew is an ogre with an insect-like body (spindly legs were a staple of Jewish caricature) and a huge proboscis like that of a particularly dangerous wasp.

12. I am grateful to Rachel Nussbaum for conversation on this point.

13. Rachel Nussbaum did research on anti-Semitic novels about Jewish women at the University of Potsdam, as the result of such an arrangement. The novels were not permitted to circulate, and one had to read them in a special supervised room, rather like the Room X of Harvard's Widener Library that houses pornography. I would not support such restrictions on the circulation of politically ugly literature for the United States, but the history of Germany is different, and I would not presume to say that the Germans are wrong in adopting them.

14. For an argument on behalf of this conceptual thesis, see chapter 5 of *Love's Knowledge.*

15. How different is the case of lyric poetry? Obviously, there are features of rhythm and sound that play a large role here, and these are to some degree separable from the representation of human beings and human life—though how far? (We really do not admire Edgar Allan Poe today, because that is all he offers us.) Beyond this, I am

inclined to say that great lyric poetry usually is found great because it offers us something to think about in the area of human life and how it might be lived, and thus it has
a moral element in the broad sense of "moral" that I use throughout my writings. Posner
does not disagree, I believe. But I choose not to pursue that issue here, since I have not
written about lyric poetry.

16. Posner persistently fails to note that sense and equates having a moral interest
in the literary work with "extract[ing] a moral" from it ("Against Ethical Criticism" 23).

17. I am grateful to Laurie Shrage for this point.

18. See, for example, my defense of escape literature in my review of Booth's *Company* in *Love's Knowledge,* focusing on mystery novels. (I express my own enthusiasm
for Dick Francis.) One could also mention that many people (including myself) derive
the sort of pleasure Posner describes from other arts as well, such as music and dance.

Works Cited

Ellison, Ralph. *Invisible Man.* New York: Random House, 1992.

James, Henry. *Art of the Novel: Critical Prefaces.* 1934. New York: Scribner's, 1970.

Nussbaum, Martha C. "Compassion: The Basic Social Emotion." *Social Philosophy
and Policy* 13 (1996): 27–58.

———. *Cultivating Humanity: A Classical Defense of Reform in Liberal Education.*
Cambridge: Harvard UP, 1997.

———. "Emotions as Judgments of Value: A Philosophical Dialogue." *Comparative
Criticism* 20 (1998): 33–62.

———. *The Fragility of Goodness: Luck and Ethics in Greek Tragedy and Philosophy.*
Cambridge: Cambridge UP, 1986.

———. *Love's Knowledge: Essays on Philosophy and Literature.* New York: Oxford UP,
1990.

———. *Poetic Justice: The Literary Imagination and Public Life.* Boston: Beacon, 1995.

———. *The Therapy of Desire: Theory and Practice in Hellenistic Ethics.* Princeton:
Princeton UP, 1994.

———. "*Wuthering Heights:* The Romantic Ascent." *Philosophy and Literature* 20
(1996): 362–82.

Posner, Richard A. "Against Ethical Criticism." *Philosophy and Literature* 21 (1997): 1–27.

———. *Law and Literature: The Relationship Rethought.* Cambridge: Harvard UP,
1997.

II

CONFRONTING THE DIFFICULT

The Ethics of Race and Power

WHO HAS THE RIGHT TO FEEL?

The Ethics of Literary Empathy

KATHLEEN LUNDEEN

LIKE MOST golden rules, empathy is seen as more than a virtue; for many, it is a litmus test of one's humanity. In the political realm it is lobbied for in the form of social legislation and demanded of elected officials who must "relate" to their constituents. As privacy has become a public commodity and the talk show host the prototype of a leader, politically motivated empathy has on occasion escalated to the point of being maudlin. Though Bill Clinton is hardly ubiquitous, surprisingly few challenged him when he declared to a heterogeneous electorate, "I feel your pain." Although a show of empathy may enhance a person's profile in real-life encounters, it has of late raised suspicion when directed toward fictional subjects. Writers or readers who appear to empathize with another's life experiences are often accused of arrogating a cultural authority to which they have no natural claim.

Discourse of all kinds—poetic, fictional, critical—is taken at this time to be an artifact of social identity; the language of a particular text is thus treated as the secret code of those who share a designated mark of social identification. Moreover, since everyone is marked by society in a number of ways (through, for instance, ethnicity, class, sex, religion, age, physical mobility, and nationality), if we were to insist on shared identity in all areas, writers would only be fit to represent themselves, and readers, to understand representations of themselves. By this logic, autobiography would emerge as the sole legitimate creative genre, and it would be suitable only for a readership of one: its author.

Though no one proposes surrendering to such an extreme position, questions linger about the degree to which social identity insinuates itself into literary art. David Palumbo-Liu's musing on his experience as an assistant professor is worth noting since his account, which is hardly unique, reminds us that assumptions about literary empathy have real consequences:

> What do we do when called on (over and over again) to guest-teach *The Woman Warrior*? or *The Color Purple* or *Ceremony* and so on? Do we insist

that skin color has no bearing on the ability or right of anyone to teach a particular work and enter once again into the debates that inevitably follow regarding the politics of hiring faculty members of color? Is the request that I teach Maxine Hong Kingston a sign of the dreaded ethnic ghettoization or a sign of respect? (1078)

The question persists: to what extent is our literary engagement biologically or culturally determined?

Narrowing the authority of writers, readers, or teachers obviously reduces the scope of their literary activities, but it poses an even greater threat to culture: it debunks a fundamental assumption about cultural expression—namely, that representation presupposes a capacity for empathy. That particular assumption is so rooted in human consciousness that it has endured in the face of the shrewdest of arguments about the nature of representation. Notwithstanding postmodern pronouncements that all systems of representation are mechanisms of distortion (a claim that tacitly argues there is a truth to be distorted), the collective faith that representation is possible has not diminished. We might have expected in the wake of deconstruction to witness the long, withdrawing roar of verbal activity, but, of course, we have not. Though postmodern critique has not preempted representational acts, it has left many in a duplicitous relationship with culture, one in which they exercise their faith in language by speaking and writing but remain skeptical of others' verbal expression, always keeping an eye out for the ways they are being had.

In 1828, Felicia Hemans published a poem that, were it not for the problems it raises about literary empathy, might be dismissed as unmemorable. "Indian Woman's Death-Song" was inspired by an account of a woman who, distraught by the abandonment of her husband, drowned herself and her two young children in the Mississippi River. In the poem, Hemans romanticizes the mother's violence by presenting it as an act of courage. Preceding her sentimental rendering of the event, her several epigraphs to the poem—especially the quotation from James Fenimore Cooper's *The Prairie*: "Let not my child be a girl, for very sad is the life of a woman"—signal her editorial position. Hemans's refusal to question the woman poses an ethical dilemma for her readers, however: is her empathy with the woman a testament to her freedom from cultural hegemony, or is it evidence of a self-serving ploy by which she can exploit another culture for her own psychological gain?

Hemans learns of the drowning incident from William Keating's *Narrative of an Expedition to the Source of St. Peter's River*. Keating's retelling is telling. In the report, Keating makes the American Indians sound suspiciously English in sensibility:

> An Indian of the Dacota nation had united himself early in life to a youthful female, whose name was Ampota Sapa, which signifies *the dark day;* with her he lived happily for several years, apparently enjoying every comfort which the savage life can afford. Their union had been blessed with two children, on whom both parents doated with that depth of feeling which is unknown to such as have other treasures beside those that spring from nature. (310)

Keating goes on to explain that the husband, unbeknown to his spouse, acquires a second wife to increase his stature in the community. Once again, the word choice, syntax, and overall decorum of the prose reveal that Keating's narrative has been filtered through Anglo-American consciousness:

> Being desirous to introduce his bride into his lodge in the manner which should be least offensive to the mother of his children, for whom he still retained much regard, he introduced the subject in these words: "You know," said he, "that I love no woman so fondly as I doat upon you. With regret, have I seen you of late subjected to toils, which must be oppressive to you, and from which I would gladly relieve you, yet I know no other way of doing so than by associating to you in the household duties one, who shall relieve you from the trouble of entertaining the numerous guests, whom my growing importance in the nation collects around me. I have, therefore, resolved upon taking another wife, but she shall always be subject to your control, as she will always rank in my affections second to you." With the utmost anxiety, and the deepest concern, did his companion listen to this unexpected proposal. She expostulated in the kindest terms, entreated him with all the arguments which undisguised love and the purest conjugal affection could suggest. (311)

Throughout his account, even as Keating refers to the Natives as "savages," he portrays them as genteel folk who never miss an opportunity for felicitous phrasing. In the preface to the book, far from apologizing for editorial intrusions, he expresses regret for not being able to render all of his account in decorous language:

> The compiler has found it impossible, in the description of the scenery of the Mississippi, &c. to avoid the introduction of several words, which, although they are not sanctioned by the dictionaries, seem to be characteristic and essential in such descriptions: of this nature are the words—bluff, prairie, &c. The term creek, being used in different acceptations in England and America, has been avoided in all cases, though with some inconvenience.

> The word *run* will, it is believed, be found but once in the body of the
> work. Lest any false impression should be drawn from the introduction of
> the term *estuary,* it may be proper to state, that it has been inadvertently used
> in several cases to designate the outlets of streams where the tides do not
> reciprocate. In compiling from notes written by many persons under the
> disadvantages of fatigues, hardships, and privations, it is not easy, however
> it may be desirable, to avoid the use of all objectionable terms. (ix)

For nineteenth-century reporters, the rules of the game were clearly different from those for their twenty-first-century counterparts. In his account,
Keating appears to privilege propriety over authenticity. Though he never
suggests that he may have compromised the "facts" through his rhetorical
discretion, he, as a journalist, nevertheless, has a problem: if geographical
terms will make his readers blush, how can he possibly find a suitably delicate language to describe a mother murdering her children? Presumably,
he represents American Indian culture through European literary conventions to mitigate the horror of the infanticide and thus avoid offending his
refined readers.[1] Even more disturbing than his unfaithful rendering of the
American Indian's speech, however, is his implicit suggestion that the Native
woman's actions are sanctioned by her people. Not once in his account does
he suggest that the tragedy may have been a socially unsanctioned act of a
desperate woman. Rather, he presents it as data from which readers can
extrapolate the character of the Dakota tribe. At the end of this account, he
writes:

> It is stated by the Indians that often in the morning a voice has been heard to
> sing a doleful ditty along the edge of the fall, and that it ever dwells upon
> the inconstancy of her husband. Nay, some assert that her spirit has been seen
> wandering near the spot with her children wrapped to her bosom. Such are
> the tales or traditions which the Indians treasure up, and which they relate
> to the voyager, forcing a tear from the eyes of the most relentless. (312–13)

Keating's report that the tragedy achieved a mythological status within the
Dakota nation argues against its sociological relevance. Had it been a common event, it probably would not have been related to "voyagers" at all.

Unwittingly, Keating sends mixed signals to his readers. As mentioned
earlier, while he fashions the American Indians after Europeans in speech and
sensibility, he continually reminds his reader that these quasi-Europeans
are at some level "savage." The frontispiece to his book similarly offers a
mixed visual signal. Titled "Wanotan and his son," the engraving shows an
Indian adult posing, as it were, for a European portrait artist. Hand on hip
with one leg bent and Nordic facial features, he looks suspiciously like an

English gentleman in an Indian costume. A cursory glance at the engraving suggests that culture is little more than the cut of one's jib, but a closer look shows the son to be holding a spear. Keating's patronizing gestures are as transparent in his account as the artist's are in the engraving. Nowhere in his narrative does he wrestle with the contradiction in portraying the Indians as benign curiosities who are "just like us" (except, of course, for their barbaric nature), but rather implies that "noble savage" is not an oxymoron.

Like Keating, Hemans strains the story of the Native woman through a sieve of Western conventions. Her purpose is different, however. Whereas Keating sanitizes the murder and suicide so as not to offend his readers, Hemans celebrates it as a way of expressing, *without expressing,* her own death wish.

Hemans begins the poem by depicting the canoe as fragile and vulnerable and thus allows it to be seen as a metonym for the Indian woman:

> Down a broad river of the western wilds,
> Piercing thick forest glooms, a light canoe
> Swept with the current: fearful was the speed
> Of the frail bark, as by a tempest's wing
> Borne leaf-like on to where the mist of spray
> Rose with the cataract's thunder.

Like the canoe, which is simply a vessel, the earthly form of the woman, we infer, is but a temporary container for her immortal self. Moreover, we intimate from the metonym that the woman is as helpless and inculpable as "the frail bark" in which she rides. Hemans continues:

> —Yet within,
> Proudly, and dauntlessly, and all alone,
> Save that a babe lay sleeping at her breast,
> A woman stood.

Though it is highly improbable that an Olympic kayaker could stand in a canoe in a rushing river, Hemans shows the mother confronting death in full stature. In so doing, she manages to finesse an image of a woman who is both in control of her destiny and involuntarily swept away by circumstances.

She completes the opening of the poem by revealing the woman to be a poet:

> She press'd her child,
> In its bright slumber, to her beating heart,
> And lifted her sweet voice, that rose awhile

> Above the sound of waters, high and clear,
> Wafting a wild proud strain, her Song of Death.

The very notion of a "death-song" suggests Hemans's refusal to recognize the full implications of the woman's actions. As Anthony Harding notes, "Death, in [Hemans's] poems, is not so much the enemy of domestic affection as the necessary dark backdrop against which the affections show their true brightness. At times, death virtually becomes a kind of guarantee of the significance of a life, particularly of a woman's life" (138). In "Indian Woman's Death-Song," death appears to be little more than conveyance to a happier, safer place. Thus, the mother leaves the earth singing, as if art can transport her child and her into another world.

In her poem (which is Rousseauvian with a feminist twist), Hemans portrays the Native woman as having an affinity with the natural universe and implies that this enables her to express the universal grief of womanhood. It is no surprise that "Indian Woman's Death-Song" was published in Hemans's *Records of Woman* since ethnicity exists in the poem solely in the service of gender. Like Keating, Hemans has a double attitude toward race. Simultaneously accentuating and minimizing racial difference, she conceives of the Native woman in her own Western image. Not only does her Indian woman speak British English, she does so within the conventions of English lyrical verse:

> Will he not miss the bounding step that met him from the chase?
> The heart of love that made his home an ever sunny place?
> The hand that spread the hunter's board, and deck'd his couch of yore?—
> He will not!—roll, dark foaming stream, on to the better shore!

Through the rhymed iambic septameter, the epithets ("the bounding step," "dark foaming stream"), and the synecdoches (the heart, the hand), Hemans transplants American Indian experience from its own cultural ground to English soil. She even presents Native American religion in a Western form: the Indian woman, in what sounds like a prayer to the Christian God, clasps her child to her breast and implores the "Father of Ancient Waters" to "bear our lives with thee!" Toward the end of the poem she sings to her child, assuring her that she is taking her to

> the glorious bowers where none are heard to weep,
> And where th'unkind one *hath* no power again to trouble sleep;
> And where the soul shall find its youth, as wakening from a dream

—a place that closely resembles the orthodox Christian heaven.

The conventions Hemans uses were familiar to the readers of her day since at the time she wrote the poem, Anglo-American writers had appropriated the Indian death-song (as reported by those who had met Native Americans) and recast it as an English literary genre (see Goslee 246–47). From a twenty-first-century perspective, it might appear that Hemans commits an act of double jeopardy, first colonizing her subject and then placing her subject in a colonized genre. Hemans's representational act is complicated, however, by the fact that she and her subject are both women. She assumes an affinity with the Indian woman, who in the poem is Anglicized so that she is in all respects like Hemans. In all respects, that is, but one. The Indian woman has the courage to leave her mortal life and take her child with her.

By documenting the source of her poetic narrative in a prefatory note to the poem, Hemans lends authority to her rendering of the event. In stating that the Indian woman's voice "was heard from the shore singing a mournful death-song," she suggests that the song in the poem may be transcription rather than imaginative construction. But she neglects to say in the note that the poem is the product of a heavily mediated event. The drowning was witnessed by a woman of the Dakota nation who told it to her son. He, in turn, related it to Stephen Long (who led the expedition recorded by Keating); Long passed it on to Keating, and Keating (via his written account) to Hemans, who presents it to her readers as a poetic narrative. Thus, the prefatory note to the poem overauthorizes her account by omitting the fact that the event was filtered through several imaginations. Undoubtedly, in Hemans's day, many an unsuspecting reader assumed the song was more or less authentic.

In 1818, ten years before Hemans wrote the poem, her husband deserted her and their five children, one of whom was a newborn. Though Hemans's refusal to condemn, or even question, the Native woman's act might appear to argue in favor of cultural tolerance, her own domestic trials offer another explanation—that she ennobles an act of violence, a form of conduct unsanctioned by English society, in order to valorize by proxy her own unspeakable desire. Like Keating, Hemans intimates that the woman's actions are native to her culture. In the narrative blank verse that introduces the song itself, she writes:

> Upon her Indian brow
> Sat a strange gladness, and her dark hair wav'd
> As if triumphantly.

The smoothly orchestrated death, accompanied by a lyrical script (the woman's death-song), takes on the character of a tribal ritual. Since in the best of English families of the early nineteenth century mothers did not drown themselves and their children, Hemans, it appears, appropriates nonwhite culture as a filter for her own desperate voice. The poem is, thus, a cultural conundrum in that Hemans speaks on behalf of a Native woman so that the Native woman can speak for her. The apparent reciprocity between the women, however well Hemans intended it, is nevertheless little more than a rhetorical construction since to admire in hiding—to empathize in secret—is simultaneously to seek and shun identification with another. Like metaphor, empathy claims that something *is like,* but *is not,* something else, so that even when openly expressed, it is at once a condition of sympathy and alienation. Or, to put it another way, empathy manifests the apparent affinity one person has with another, but in so doing it magnifies the differences between them.

In several respects Hemans's poem resembles what Susan Ritchie has referred to as "ventriloquist folklore," literature that "presumes to speak on the behalf of some voiceless group or individual" (366–67). According to Ritchie, one of the features of this cultural expression is that it "ignores the ways in which context mediates presentation" (367). Further, it "establishes the folklorist as [a] kind of medium or channeler, who presents the true voices of those otherwise lost to an audience so eager for diverse articulations that they fail to note this 'diversity' . . . issues from folklore's single disciplinary throat" (367). Admittedly, situating "Indian Woman's Death-Song" in a matrix of present-day cultural issues is anachronistic, an empathic overstepping, since Hemans never intimates a political agenda, either in the poem itself or in her preface to the poem. Nowhere does she hint that the poem is designed to give a voice to a silenced member of an underrepresented class. Her sole desire appears to be to give herself a voice, something she can do only by proxy.

Just as Hemans may be more interested in hearing her own voice in the poem than in hearing the Indian woman's voice, many readers are more eager to hear their own voices in the poem than that of Hemans or the Indian woman. Demanding the empathy of literary writers, readers ask them to speak on their behalf, to validate their values, articulate their idealism. Derrida has argued: "What we call literature (not belles-lettres or poetry) implies that license is given to the writer to say everything he wants to or everything he can, while remaining shielded, safe from all censorship, be it religious or political" (37). License is also given, however, to readers of literature (*including* belles-lettres and poetry) who internalize such texts and make demands on the texts that they do not make on other kinds of writing. From a reader's perspective, literature does not denote that which is unreal so much as that which is hyperreal. Thus, readers want to hear literary voices as if they were their own in a clarified form. In "Indian Woman's Death-Song," the narrator's voice appears to merge with the Native woman's voice since there is no comment by the narrator after the Indian woman concludes her song. As a result, given the absence of an alternative view of the event, the reader is involuntarily implicated in this questionable empathy.

Occasionally, one reads in the newspaper about tragedies such as the one described in Hemans's poem. A few years ago, the following item appeared in American newspapers: "A woman who said she wanted to show her six-year-old daughter the view from the top of a twenty-two-story office building had planned a 'suicide ritual' that led to their death plunge" ("Police").[2] The brief report mentioned that the woman was "embroiled in a child-support case" with her former husband. Though this straightforward, unsentimental report undoubtedly elicited some sympathy for the obviously desperate woman, it also provoked outrage. Perhaps it is Hemans's lack of outrage that is most chilling in her poem. Perhaps, to paraphrase Keats, what is disturbing is not Hemans's envy of the Native woman's happy (fortunate) lot, but Hemans being too happy in her happiness, an affective state that reveals empathy to be potentially as dehumanizing as hatred or indifference.

The ethical dilemma inherent in empathy—forever finding oneself either too close or not close enough to the object of self-identification—is inherent in language itself, which embodies a self-contradictory dynamic. Every verbal act is essentially solitary in that it is initiated by an individual; it is recognized as language, however, only if it involves consensus—that is, only if it is already understood by the listener or reader. Though language is a means of individuation, its materials come from a communally owned source. Thus, in the act of articulation, a writer's voice is amplified so that the most confessional discourse resonates as if it were a collective utterance, spoken in unison. Wayne Booth articulates a reconciliation of the opposing impulses in language by deconstructing the binary of self and society:

> We talk about political actions as some kind of obligation that we owe, as individuals, to society, to others: we should be *altru*istic, not "self-centered." But if we are characters, social creatures by origin and definition, political and philanthropic actions are not performed out of duty to others but as acts of "self"- preservation; if the others are in me, "altruism"—the service

of alterity—and selfishness must either not be contrasted at all, or if they are contrasted the lines must be drawn in new ways. (243–44)

Because writers and readers can at some level make choices that circumvent the apparent conflict between self-expression and the accurate portrayal of others, Booth's argument informs the ethical issues surrounding representation. Nevertheless, at a deeper level writers and readers are often stymied between emotional autonomy and empathy. Since language is simultaneously a solitary and social phenomenon, the issue ceases to be whether writers and readers have the authority to show empathy but rather how they resolve the tension created by their joint impulses to individualize their response to something *and* to identify with another's response. Empathy, in essence, is an ideal of differentiated union with another, and that paradox should remind us that in literature, as in life, there are shared borders of identity that we are compelled to recognize but cannot cross.

Notes

1. Though Keating was a professor at the University of Pennsylvania, his book was published by a London press and thus enjoyed an English readership.

2. The incident, which was reported in the *Bellingham Herald,* occurred in Phoenix, Arizona.

Works Cited

Booth, Wayne C. *The Company We Keep: An Ethics of Fiction.* Berkeley: U of California P, 1988.

Derrida, Jacques. *Acts of Literature.* Ed. Derek Attridge. New York: Routledge, 1992.

Goslee, Nancy Moore. "Hemans's 'Red Indians': Reading Stereotypes." *Romanticism, Race, and Imperial Culture, 1780–1834.* Ed. Alan Richardson and Sonia Hofkosh. Bloomington: Indiana UP, 1996. 237–61.

Harding, Anthony John. "Felicia Hemans and the Effacement of Woman." *Romantic Women Writers: Voices and Countervoices.* Ed. Paula R. Feldman and Theresa M. Kelley. Hanover: UP of New England, 1995. 138–49.

Keating, William H., A. M., &c. *Narrative of an Expedition to the Source of St. Peter's River, Lake Winnepeek, Lake of the Woods, &c., performed in the year 1823, by order of the Hon. J. C. Calhoun, Secretary of War, under the command of Stephen H. Long, U.S.T.E.* Vol. 1. London: Whittaker/Ave-Maria-Lane, 1825.

Palumbo-Liu, David. "Historical Permutations of the Place of Race." *PMLA* 111 (1996): 1075–78.

"Police Say Mother Planned 'Suicide Ritual.'" *Bellingham (Washington) Herald* 4 February 1996: A3.

Ritchie, Susan. "Ventriloquist Folklore: Who Speaks for Representation?" *Western Folklore* 52 (1993): 365–78.

SETHE'S CHOICE
Beloved and the Ethics of Reading

JAMES PHELAN

> Now, too late, [Stamp Paid] understood [Baby Suggs]. The heart that pumped out love, the mouth that spoke the Word, didn't count. They came in her yard anyway and she could not approve or condemn Sethe's rough choice.
>
> —Toni Morrison, *Beloved*

Morrison's Unusual Guidance

"SETHE'S ROUGH CHOICE," her decision to kill her daughter rather than have the girl become a slave at the plantation they called Sweet Home, is at once the most stunning and most important event in Morrison's novel. Stunning for obvious reasons: how can the love of a mother for her child lead her to murder the child? Important not only because the temporal, psychological, structural, and thematic logic of the novel flows from that event but also because Morrison's treatment of it presents her audience with a difficult and unusual ethical problem. In order to appreciate the events of the present time of the narrative—1873—we need to know what happened in the woodshed behind 124 Bluestone Road on an August afternoon in 1855. In order to understand the characters of Sethe, Denver, and Beloved in 1873, we need to know that on that afternoon Sethe reached for the handsaw before schoolteacher could reach for her or her children. In order to come to terms with the novel's progression, its affective power, and thematic import, we need to come to ethical terms with Sethe's choice to pull the handsaw across the neck of her daughter.[1] The problem arises because Morrison stops short of taking any clear ethical stand on Sethe's rough choice but instead presents it as something that she, like Baby Suggs, can neither approve nor condemn. This essay seeks to explore the ethics of reading Sethe's choice by (1) contextualizing Morrison's treatment of it in relation to the typical relation between implied author and audience in ethically complex texts; (2) analyzing the narrative strategies Morrison uses to offer some limited guidance to our ethical judgment without clearly signaling her own assessment; (3) examining the consequences of that treatment for our relation to Sethe and, ultimately, to Morrison herself; and (4) considering the implications of Morrison's treatment for any larger conclusions we might draw about the ethical dimension of reading narrative. Let me begin by sketching my approach to the ethics of reading.

I regard the ethical dimension of reading as an inextricable part of approaching narrative as rhetoric. To approach narrative as rhetoric is to understand narrative as a rhetorical act: somebody telling somebody else on some occasion and for some purpose that something happened. This rhetorical act involves a multileveled communication from author to audience, one that involves the audience's intellect, emotions, psyche, and values. Furthermore, these levels interact with each other. Our values and those set forth by the implied author affect our judgments of characters, and our judgments affect our emotions, and the trajectory of our feelings is linked to the psychological and thematic effects of the narrative. Furthermore, the communicative situation of narrative—somebody telling somebody else that something happened—is itself an ethical situation. The teller's treatment of the events will inevitably convey certain attitudes toward the audience, attitudes that indicate his or her sense of responsibility to and regard for the audience. Similarly, the audience's response to the narrative will indicate their commitments to the teller, the narrative situation, and the values expressed in the narrative.[2]

Among the many approaches to ethics now being developed, this one is most closely related to those of Wayne C. Booth and of Adam Zachary Newton.[3] Each of them, like me, wants to root narrative ethics in narrative itself rather than in some abstract ethical system. Indeed, Booth emphasizes the pervasiveness of ethics in critical responses to literature, and Newton says that he wants to conceive of "narrative *as* ethics." Each of them moves, in his own way, from narrative to theoretical treatments of narrative and then back to narrative. In Booth's case, those theoretical treatments can be found in his own earlier work on the rhetoric of literature. His title, *The Company We Keep,* and his main metaphor, books as friends, grow out of his earlier exploration of the way that writing and reading make possible a meeting of minds between author and reader. *The Company We Keep* moves beyond Booth's earlier major emphasis on how such meetings occur to the contemplation of how our values are engaged as we read, especially the ethical consequences of desiring as the text invites us to desire. *The Company We Keep* also gives greater emphasis to the communal nature of ethical response, suggesting that the activity of discussing the values of texts, what Booth calls *co-ducing,* is ethically more important than getting the text "right."

Newton investigates the "ethical consequences of narrating story and fictionalizing person, and the reciprocal claims binding teller, listener, witness, and reader in that process" (11), an investigation that leads him to describe three kinds of ethical structure in narrative: the narrational, the representational, and the hermeneutic. Narrational ethics are those associated with the telling; they occur along the line of narrative transmission from author to narrator to narratee to reader. Representational ethics are those associated with "fictionalizing person" or creating character. Hermeneutic ethics are those associated with reading and interpreting, the obligations readers and critics have to the text. Newton synthesizes the work of Mikhail Bakhtin, Stanley Cavell, and Emmanuel Levinas as he does his analyses, borrowing especially Bakhtin's concept of *vhzivanie,* or live-entering (empathy with the Other without loss of self), Cavell's concept of acknowledging (being in a position of having to respond), and Levinas's concepts of Saying (performing a telling) and Facing (looking at or looking away).

Although I share much with Booth and with Newton, I do not want to adopt Booth's overarching metaphor of books as friends because it seems too limiting, or Newton's idea that narrative is equivalent to ethics because that seems not to recognize all the other things narrative is as well. Furthermore, although I find Bakhtin, Cavell, and Levinas all to be strong theorists, I am less inclined than Newton to look to theory for recurrent ethical concerns and more inclined to let individual narratives develop their own sets of ethical topoi. Like both Booth and Newton, my focus is on how the very act of reading entails ethical engagement and response, but I focus more than either of them do on the links among technique (the signals offered by the text) and the reader's cognitive understanding, emotional response, and ethical positioning. Indeed, the central construct in my approach to the ethics of reading is *position,* a concept that combines *acting from* and *being placed* in an ethical location. Our ethical position at any point in a narrative results from the dynamic interaction of four ethical situations:

that of the characters within the story world
that of the narrator in relation to the telling and to the audience; unreliable
    narration, for example, constitutes a different ethical position from re-
    liable narration; different kinds of focalization also position the audi-
    ence differently

that of the implied author in relation to the authorial audience; the implied
author's choices to adopt one narrative strategy rather than another will
affect the audience's ethical response to the characters; each choice will
also convey the author's attitudes toward the audience
that of the flesh and blood reader in relation to the set of values, beliefs, and
locations that the narrative invites one to occupy

Although the ethical dimension of reading engages our values and judgments, it is deeply intertwined with cognition, emotion, and desire: our
understanding influences our sense of which values the text is calling forth,
the activation of those values influences our judgments, our judgments influence our feelings, and our feelings influence our desires. And the other
way around.

As this sketch indicates, I assume that authors will attempt to guide us
toward particular ethical positions on their characters' actions, and it is easy
to show that authorial practice provides a strong warrant for the assumption.
In some cases, the guidance is very clear and the position easy to occupy:
Henry Fielding, for example, guides us to recognize that Tom Jones's actions
are always ethically superior to those of Blifil. In some cases, the key to the
narrative progression is the evolution of the protagonists' own ethical understanding and corresponding behavior: Jane Austen, for example, positions
us to recognize the initial ethical deficiencies of both Elizabeth Bennett and
Fitzwilliam Darcy and then represents the amelioration of those deficiencies,
an amelioration that in turn prepares the way for their happy union. In
some cases, authors will present us with characters who face difficult ethical
decisions and then guide us to see both the difficulty and their own judgment of the situation: Joseph Conrad, for example, allows Jim to tell the
story of how he jumped from the *Patna* but uses characters such as Brierly,
who commits suicide because he sees himself in Jim, and the French lieu-
tenant, who clearly states that the sailor's duty is to stay with the ship, to
indicate both the depth of Jim's temptation and the unequivocal negative
judgment of his action. In some cases, authors will show characters who
transgress standard societal and legal norms but nevertheless follow an ethically superior path: Ken Kesey, for example, represents Chief Bromden's
killing of the lobotomized McMurphy not as a horrible murder but rather
as an act of both mercy and courage. Even in situations where authors have
written famously ambiguous narratives, the ethical positions within each
side of the ambiguity are likely to be clearly delineated: Henry James in *The
Turn of the Screw*, for example, has sketched a portrait either of a heroic

governess who risks her own safety in order to protect the children in her care against evil ghosts or of a psychotic woman whose delusions constitute a serious threat to those children.

In short, providing ethical guidance to their audiences is one of the chief things that implied authors do: writing narrative involves taking ethical stands and communicating those stands explicitly or implicitly, heavy-handedly or subtly—or anything in between—to one's audience. Indeed, recognizing this communication helps us understand that the default ethical relation between implied author and authorial audience in narrative is one of reciprocity. Each party both gives and receives. Authors give, among other things, guidance through ethical complexity and expect to receive in return their audiences' interest and attention. Audiences give that interest and attention and expect to receive in return authorial guidance. The default assumption, of course, need not always be in place, but deviating from it necessarily entails certain risks. Audiences that place their own interests (ideologies, politics, ethics) at the center of their reading risk turning read-ing into a repetitious activity that misses the ways in which authors can extend their vision of human possibility and experience. Authors who do not provide guidance or who take aggressive stances toward their audiences risk alienating those audiences to the point of losing them. Implied authors who stop short of conveying their own ethical judgment of an action that is central to the narrative are doing something extraordinarily unusual—and extraordinarily risky. The narrative may fall apart because the center will not hold, or the narrative will become an inscrutable black hole, which absorbs every element of the work into its inscrutability. That *Beloved* escapes both risks is one sign of Morrison's remarkable achievement.

Establishing Ethical Position

As we turn to look at the interaction in *Beloved* among the four ethical sit-uations I identify above, the third one—the relation of the implied author to the telling and to the authorial audience—stands out as the key to the ethical problem of the novel. If we can work through the ethical implica-tions of Morrison's narrative strategies, we should be able to come to terms with her decision not to take a final stand on Sethe's choice. That working through means attending to the ethical consequences of several key authorial decisions: (1) about where in the progression of the narrative to disclose the information about Sethe's choice—at the end of part 1 rather than earlier or later, after some hints about the event before it is revealed; (2) about how to disclose the information—through three different tellings, one focalized through the white men who come to reclaim Sethe and her children for Sweet Home; one focalized through Stamp Paid; and one from Sethe's own perspective; (3) about how to link those tellings to other key moments in the narrative where her ethical stances are clearer.

Morrison's now famous opening focuses on the ghostly presence of a baby in the female space of 124 Bluestone Road: "124 was spiteful. Full of baby's venom" (3). Shortly after that, Morrison has the narrator add a cryptic reference to the baby's dying as part of a summary of Sethe's situation: "not only did she have to live out her years in a house palsied by the baby's fury at having its throat cut, but those ten minutes she spent pressed up against dawn-colored stone studded with star chips, her knees wide open as the grave, were longer than life, more alive, *more pulsating than the baby blood that soaked her fingers like oil*" (5; emphasis added). In one of Sethe's early conversations with Paul D about Denver, she makes reference to the events of August 1855 without telling the whole story:

> "And when the schoolteacher found us and came busting in here with the law and a shotgun—"
> "Schoolteacher found you?"
> "Took a while, but he did. Finally."
> "And he didn't take you back?"
> "Oh, no, I wasn't going back there. I don't care who found who. Any life but that one. I went to jail instead. . . ."
> Paul D turned away. He wanted to know more about it, but jail put him back in Alfred, Georgia. (42)

The first half of the novel is, in fact, filled with such incomplete, indirect, or cryptic allusions and references to Sethe's rough choice.[4] Consequently, Morrison establishes a significant tension between the implied author (and the narrator), who know about Sethe's rough choice, and the authorial audience, which receives only these partial, indirect, and cryptic references. This tension creates an aura not just of mystery but also of privilege around the mystery; each reference increases the audience's sense of its importance and the audience's desire to resolve the tension. The strategy of deferral establishes an ethical obligation on Morrison's part to provide some resolution to the tension, even as it compliments the audience on its abilities to register the various hints and to wait for the resolution. In the meantime, Morrison is providing careful ethical guidance through her complex narrative.

Although that guidance is carefully nuanced, its broad outlines are clear. First, by employing a protean narrator who exercises the privilege of giving us inside views of the major characters—Sethe, Paul D, Denver, and Baby Suggs—and who also comments directly on the action and the characters, Morrison seeks to multiply the number of valorized ethical perspectives. For example, Sethe, Paul D, and Denver all have very different feelings and judgments about Paul D's entering the house at 124 Bluestone Road. Rather than privileging any one character's view and the values upon which it is based, Morrison asks us to enter into each character's consciousness and to recognize the validity of his or her feelings and judgments.[5] Second, Morrison establishes slavery not just as an abstract evil but as one that even in 1873 has continuing and profound negative effects on Sethe and Paul D —and thus, on Denver and every one else in their circle. Indeed, Morrison's representation of slavery guides us to recognize the historical validity of Baby Suggs's conclusion that "there is no bad luck in the world but white-folks" (89). This ethical position is all the more compelling because slavery at the Garners' Sweet Home plantation was *relatively* benevolent. Third, Morrison identifies Sethe's habit of "beating back the past," her efforts to repress the events of 1855, as both impossible and dangerous; the consequence of this move is to increase the pressure on the revelation of those events—Sethe's future will be determined by what happens when she faces rather than beats back that past.

While establishing this context, Morrison builds toward the revelation of Sethe's choice both by providing enough information about 1855 for us to understand what is at stake for Sethe when schoolteacher arrives at 124 and by taking the events of 1873 forward to the point where Paul D asks her to have his child. The resolution of the tension, then, not only provides the audience with crucial information that makes the situation in 1873 intelligible, but it also provides a major turning point in the development of that situation. Each of the three tellings—and the triangulation of all three—contributes to the resolution and especially to the ethical guidance Morrison does and does not provide. As noted above, the first telling is focalized through the white men who come to return Sethe and her children to slavery; the following passage, in which the focalization begins with the slave catcher and then shifts to schoolteacher, is a representative example:[6]

> Inside, two boys bled in the sawdust and dirt at the feet of a nigger woman holding a blood-soaked child to her chest with one hand and an infant by the heels in the other. She did not look at them; she simply swung the baby toward the wall planks, missed and tried to connect a second time, when out of nowhere—in the ticking time the men spent staring at what there was

to stare at—the old nigger boy, still mewing, ran through the door behind them and snatched the baby from the arch of its mother's swing.

Right off, it was clear, to schoolteacher especially, that there was nothing there to claim. . . . [S]he'd gone wild, due to the mishandling of the nephew who'd overbeat her and made her cut and run. Schoolteacher had chastised that nephew, telling him to think—just think—what would his own horse do if you beat it to beyond the point of education. Or Chipper, or Samson. Suppose you beat the hounds past that point thataway. Never again could you trust them in the woods or anywhere else. You'd be feeding them maybe, holding out a piece of rabbit in your hand and the animal would revert— bite your hand clean off. . . . The whole lot was lost now. Five. He could claim the baby struggling in the arms of the mewing old man, but who'd tend her? Because the woman—something was wrong with her. She was looking at him now, and if his other nephew could see that look he would learn the lesson for sure: you just can't mishandle creatures and expect suc- cess. (149–50)

By unraveling the mystery this way, Morrison provides a highly unsettling experience for the audience. After seeing Sethe from the inside for so long, we feel emotionally, psychologically, and *ethically* jarred by seeing her from what is such an alien perspective, one that thinks of her as "a nigger woman" and as a "creature" equivalent to a horse or a hound. Indeed, Morrison has chosen to narrate this first telling from an ethical perspective that we easily repudiate. Not only does schoolteacher regard Sethe as a dog who no longer trusts its master, his concern is ultimately with himself and his loss, not at all with Sethe or her children. Strikingly, however, Morrison's strategy of moving away from Sethe's perspective and describing her actions from the outside highlights both the inadequacy of schoolteacher's racist perspective and the horror of what Sethe is doing: "holding a blood-soaked child to her chest with one hand and an infant by the heels in the other . . . she simply swung the baby toward the wall planks, missed and tried to connect a second time." If the shift in perspective is jarring, the revelation of Sethe's action is shocking. The physical description is not pretty, and it is not possible to find a way to make it pretty. At the same time, the physical description is not loaded with any ethical evaluation from Morrison. Instead, she just leaves it out there uncorrected—the description may be from the slave catcher's angle of vision, but there is no sign that the angle distorts his view of the physical action—and asks us to come to terms with it on our own.

Morrison does, however, leave space for us to defer that coming to terms. Since this first telling picks up the story after the white men have entered the shed, it does not explain how or why Sethe went there with her children. In the second telling, Morrison addresses that aspect of the story. The perspective here belongs to Stamp Paid; the telling occurs as part of a recollection he is prepared to share with Paul D but does not because Paul insists that the woman in the newspaper story Stamp gives him cannot be Sethe:

> So Stamp Paid did not tell him how she flew, snatching up her children like a hawk on the wing; how her face beaked, how her hands worked like claws, how she collected them every which way; one on her shoulder, one under her arm, one by the hand, the other shouted forward into the wood-shed filled with just sunlight and shavings now because there wasn't any wood. The party had used it all, which is why he was chopping some. Nothing was in that shed, he knew, having been there early that morning. Nothing but sunlight. Sunlight, shavings, a shovel. The ax he himself took out. Nothing was in there except the shovel—and of course the saw. (157)

Because Paul D holds fast to his belief that the woman in the story was not Sethe, Stamp wonders "if it had happened at all, eighteen years ago, that while he and Baby Suggs were looking the wrong way, a pretty little slavegirl had recognized a hat, and split to the woodshed to kill her children" (158).

Stamp Paid, too, sees Sethe from the outside, and though he also compares her to an animal, he does not reduce her to one. Indeed, the comparison of Sethe with a hawk on the wing works to illuminate the how and why: because Sethe senses danger, she instinctively reacts, fiercely and swiftly gathering her children into the shed. Because the perspective remains outside of Sethe and because the emphasis is on her instinctive reaction, Morrison's technique again stops short of rendering any clear ethical judgment. But Stamp Paid's final thought once again foregrounds the horror of what Sethe is doing: "a pretty little slavegirl . . . split to the woodshed to kill her children." The contrast between the condescending description, "pretty little slavegirl," and the plain statement of her purpose, "to kill her children," has complex ethical effects. The plain statement, when juxtaposed to the description of Sethe swinging her baby toward the wall, may initially move us toward concluding that Sethe's instinctive reaction is ultimately wrong—however instinctive, it is a frightening overreaction. But the condescending description, in combination with the power of our previous sympathy for Sethe, gives us space to defer any final conclusion yet again. If Stamp Paid is wrong about who Sethe is, perhaps he is also wrong about her purpose. But even as we defer a final judgment, we continue to contemplate the almost unbelievable horror of what Sethe has done. We may wish to adopt Paul D's attitude of denial, but, with this second telling through a more sympathetic focalizer, Morrison has effectively eliminated that coping strategy from our repertoire.

Sethe's own telling to Paul D—with occasional further commentary by the narrator—is, not surprisingly, the longest version of the story. Sethe circles the room as she talks, much as the novel has circled the event up until these three tellings. Sethe begins not with the day that the four horsemen rode into the yard but rather with her arrival at 124 twenty days earlier and the pride and love she felt as a result of that accomplishment:

> "We was here. Each and every one of my babies and me too. I birthed them and I got em out and it wasn't no accident. I did that. . . . It felt good. Good and right. I was big, Paul D, and deep and wide and when I stretched out my arms all my children could get in between. I was *that* wide. Look like I loved em more after I got here. Or maybe I couldn't love em proper in Kentucky because they wasn't mine to love. But when I got here, when I jumped down off that wagon—there wasn't nobody in the world I couldn't love if I wanted to. . . ."
>
> "I couldn't let her nor any of em live under schoolteacher." (162–63)

With Sethe's words to Paul D as background, Morrison shifts to Sethe's thoughts:

> Sethe knew that . . . she could never close in, pin it down for anybody who had to ask. If they didn't get it right off—she could never explain. Because the truth was simple. . . . [W]hen she saw them coming and recognized schoolteacher's hat, she heard wings. Little hummingbirds stuck their needle beaks right through her headcloth into her hair and beat their wings. If she thought anything it was No. No. Nono. Nonono. Simple. She just flew. Collected every bit of life she had made, all the parts of her that were precious and fine and beautiful, and carried, pushed, dragged them through the veil, out, away, over there where no one could hurt them. Over there outside this place, where they would be safe. . . .
>
> "I stopped him," she said, staring at the place where the fence used to be. "I took and put my babies where they'd be safe." (163–64)

Sethe's version is obviously a strong counter to the earlier two: her purpose was not to kill but to protect, her motivation was love, and the action was a success. She does act instinctively, but the instincts are those of mother-love. The animal imagery here does not suggest anything about her agency but rather about an association between schoolteacher and a feeling in her head—a matter to which I return below.

Thus, the progression of the stories gives us a progression of possibilities for ethical judgment: Sethe has committed a subhuman action; Sethe has done the wrong thing but done it instinctively and understandably; Sethe has done something difficult but heroic because it is done for the best motives and it turns out to be a success. Since the progression of the narrative perspectives, from outside to inside, from the white men's to Stamp Paid's to Sethe's, is a progression toward increasingly sympathetic views, we might be inclined to conclude that Morrison is guiding us toward accepting Sethe's version. Furthermore, if we stay inside Sethe's perspective, her account is very compelling. But the triangulation of all three stories indicates that Morrison does not want Sethe's story to be the authoritative version by calling attention to what Sethe leaves out of her account: the handsaw, the slit throat, the blood, the swinging of the baby toward the wall. In short, Sethe's telling is not definitive because it erases the horror of her action under its talk of motivations (love) and purpose (safety).

Furthermore, before the third telling concludes, Morrison uses Paul D to provide an internal counter to Sethe's perspective. Paul D, of course, is the most sympathetic audience Sethe could find within the world of the novel, someone who knows firsthand the evils of slavery and who also loves her. But Paul D immediately rejects Sethe's judgments and imposes his own, much harsher ones. Morrison's narrator shows that he immediately thinks, "what she wanted for her children was exactly what was missing in 124: safety" (164). Morrison also has Paul D say to Sethe that "your love is too thick," that "what you did was wrong, Sethe," and that "you got two feet, Sethe, not four" (163–65).

Of these responses, the first resonates most with the authorial audience. Our own experience of the narrative to this point shows that 124 has not been a safe place—literally haunted by the ghost of the dead baby and her return as Beloved, metaphorically haunted by the consequences of Sethe's rough choice. Furthermore, Sethe's own constant work "of beating back the past" indicates that her narrative does not accurately capture the complexity of her choice. Part 2 gives further evidence, in Sethe's extreme efforts to expiate her guilt toward Beloved, that she herself does not fully believe that her choice was the right one.

But Morrison also gives us reason not to endorse the rest of Paul's negative judgments. His remark that Sethe has "two feet . . . not four" clearly links his assessment with schoolteacher's, and that link affects our response to each one's judgment. On the one hand, Paul D's seeing Sethe's action in the same terms as schoolteacher does remind us of the horror of the physical description of what schoolteacher saw. But on the other, if Paul D adopts schoolteacher's terms, his assessment clearly cannot be entirely right. Again,

Morrison's technique leads us to rule out certain ethical responses—school-teacher's racist one, Sethe's own heroic one—without leading us to a clear position.

Connections

If the three tellings do not themselves position us clearly, perhaps the connections between these tellings and other parts of the novel will. I would like to look at the two most significant connections, both of which give greater weight to Sethe's perspective on her choice. Consider, first, the retrospective light cast by Sethe's account to Beloved about what happened when she overheard one of schoolteacher's lessons:

> This is the first time I'm telling it and I'm telling it to you because it might help explain something to you although I know you don't need me to do it. To tell it or even think over it. You don't have to listen either, if you don't want to. But I couldn't help listening to what I heard that day. He was talking to his pupils and I heard him say, "Which one are you doing?" And one the boys said, "Sethe." That's when I stopped because I heard my name, and then I took a few steps to where I could see what they was doing. Schoolteacher was standing over one of them with one hand behind his back. He licked a forefinger a couple of times and turned a few pages. Slow. I was about to turn around and keep on my way to where the muslin was, when I heard him say, "No, no. That's not the way. I told you to put her human characteristics on the left; her animal ones on the right. And don't forget to line them up." I commenced to walk backward, didn't even look behind me to find out where I was headed. I just kept lifting my feet and pushing back. When I bumped up against a tree my scalp was prickly. One of the dogs was licking out a pan in the yard. I got to the grape arbor fast enough, but I didn't have the muslin. Flies settled all over your face, rubbing their hands. My head itched like the devil. Like somebody was sticking fine needles in my scalp. I never told Halle or nobody. (193)

The retrospective light of this passage illuminates Sethe's choice in the following ways: (1) It explains why the sight of schoolteacher at 124 Bluestone Road makes Sethe feel as if hummingbirds are sticking their "needle beaks" in her scalp. In so doing, it provides further motivation for her instinctive response; having tasted freedom for herself and her children, how can she desire anything other than to put them all somewhere safe? (2) It shows how deeply racist schoolteacher's response to Sethe's rough choice is: her horrible actions do not cause him to think of her as a horse or a hound, but those terms provide the only way in which he can process the scene he witnesses. For these reasons, the retrospective light shines most brightly and most favorably on Sethe's telling. I will discuss the significance of this effect after looking at the second connection.

This connection involves Sethe and Paul D. In the first chapter of the novel, Sethe tells Paul about how she came to get the "tree" on her back.

> "Men don't know nothing much," said Paul D, tucking his pouch back into his vest pocket, "but they do know a suckling can't be away from its mother for long."
>
> "Then they know what it's like to send your children off when your breasts are full."
>
> "We was talking 'bout a tree, Sethe."
>
> "After I left you, those boys came in there and took my milk. That's what they came in there for. Held me down and took it. I told Mrs. Garner on em. . . . Them boys found out I told on em. Schoolteacher made one open up my back, and when it closed it made a tree. It grows there still."
>
> "They used cowhide on you?"
>
> "And they took my milk."
>
> "They beat you and you was pregnant."
>
> "And they took my milk!" (16–17)

Paul D's failure to understand that Sethe felt more violated by the white men's taking her milk than by their whipping her back shows that he does not understand what motherhood means to Sethe. His judgment that her "love is too thick" can be seen as a similar failure of understanding. Although Paul D knows the evils of slavery, he does not know what it is like to be both parent and slave, let alone both mother and slave. Reading Paul D's judgment of Sethe's choice in light of this earlier scene, we see that Morrison wants us to suspect his quick and sure negative response. Paul D is once again thinking like a man without children rather than like a mother.[7]

Since each connection works in its own way to support Sethe's narrative, we may be inclined to conclude that the weight of evidence now suggests that Morrison is directing us to endorse Sethe's view of her actions. But since neither connection actually addresses the recalcitrance Sethe's narrative encounters—the horror of child murder, the lack of true safety in her life— the better conclusion is that Morrison assumes that her harder task will be to maintain sympathy for Sethe once the events of August 1855 are revealed.

Consequences

In sum, I have been arguing that Morrison clearly designates some positions that we ought not occupy—Sethe deserves Paul D's harsh judgment; Sethe's own account should be endorsed—without positively establishing her own ethical assessment. As we have seen in the epigraph, Morrison incorporates this attitude into the narrative through the character of Baby Suggs, a source of knowledge and wisdom throughout the novel, who is finally unable either to approve or condemn Sethe's choice. Unlike Baby Suggs, however, the responsible audience member cannot simply withdraw from the ethical demands of the narrative and give his or her days over to the contemplation of color. Instead, we need to deal with the way Morrison requires us to recognize that Sethe's choice is somehow beyond the reach of standard ethical judgment—an action at once instinctive and unnatural, motivated by love but destructive to life. Consequently, the ethically irresponsible thing to do is to resolve the problem by reaching a clear and fixed judgment of Sethe's action. If other flesh-and-blood readers are at all like me, they are likely to find their judgments of Sethe fluctuating—sometimes the horror of the murder will dominate our consciousness, while at other times Sethe's desperation, motivation, and purpose will make her choice seem, if not fully defensible, at least comprehensible.

This inability to fix a position on the central action complicates our relation to Sethe as the central actor without disrupting our sympathy for her. Sethe becomes a character who was once pushed beyond the limits of human endurance and reacted to that pushing in this extraordinary way. Consequently, we turn our judgment on the institution that pushed her beyond the limits: slavery. It is, of course, easy to say that slavery is evil, but it is another thing for readers in the late twentieth and early twenty-first centuries—especially white readers—to *feel* the force of that statement, to comprehend the effects of slavery on individual human lives. Morrison's treatment of Sethe's rough choice moves readers toward such comprehension: in the space where we wrestle with the ethical dilemma presented by Sethe's choice, we must imaginatively engage with Sethe's instinctive decision that, when faced with the prospect of slavery, loving her children means murdering them. Such engagement transforms slavery from an abstract evil to a palpable one. Such engagement is also crucial to Morrison's larger purpose of challenging her audience to come to terms with slavery's continuing effects on the United States.[8]

At the level of author-audience communication, Morrison's unusual treatment of Sethe's choice also creates an unusual ethical relationship with her audience. The treatment is simultaneously a challenge and a compliment. She challenges us to have the negative capability to refrain from any irritable reaching after ethical closure about Sethe's rough choice, even as that challenge implies her faith that we will be equal to the task. Morrison's treatment retains the basic reciprocal relation between author and audience that underlies the ethical dimension of their communication, but it gives a new twist to that reciprocity. By limiting her guidance, Morrison gives up some authorial responsibility and transfers it to the audience. By accepting that responsibility—and by attending to the parameters within which Morrison asks us to exercise it—we have a more difficult and demanding, but also richer, reading experience. By guiding us less, Morrison gives us more. By exercising the responsibility Morrison transfers to us, we get more out of what she offers. For this flesh-and-blood reader, this ethical relationship is a key reason *Beloved* is one of the most unsettling and most rewarding narratives I have ever read.

Notes

1. In the years since its publication, *Beloved* has attracted a great deal of critical attention, becoming the subject of over two hundred books and articles, yet no one, to my knowledge, has directly addressed the ethics of Sethe's choice. The existing criticism is especially strong on the novel's many thematic components from history and memory to motherhood and identity as well as on its relation to previous American narratives and its mingling of Western and African cultural values. For a sample of this work, see Christian; Handley (on Western and African culture); Armstrong; Moreland; Travis (on relation to previous traditions); Hirsch; Wilt; Wyatt (on motherhood and its related issues); Hartman; and Moglen (on history and memory). For essays that focus on issues of narrative theory and technique, see Homans; Rimmon-Kenan; and Phelan.

2. For further discussion of this approach see my *Narrative as Rhetoric,* especially the introduction.

3. The ethical turn in literary studies over the past decade or so is a phenomenon that should be seen in relation to other, larger developments in the institution. The ethical turn, I believe, is part of the general reaction against the formalism of Yale School deconstruction in the wake of the revelations of Paul de Man's wartime writings; it is also compatible with, though distinguishable from, the continuing power of feminist criticism and theory and the rising influence of African American, multicultural, and queer criticism and theory, all of which ground themselves in sets of ethico-political commitments. The ethical turn in narrative studies is also part of a growing attention to the uses of narrative across the disciplines and in "everyday life."

From this perspective, we can see J. Hillis Miller's work on ethics as an effort to address the connection between the formal concerns of Yale deconstruction and the turn toward ethics. That ethics becomes, for Miller, another way of doing deconstruction as testimony to both the power and limits of deconstruction's conception of language as undecidable. We can also see Martha Nussbaum's philosophical investigation into narrative's capacity to offer thick descriptions of moral problems and moral reasoning as a rich instance of interdisciplinary interest in narrative.

4. For other allusions, see pages 12, 14, 15, 19, 37, 38, 42, 45, 70, 73, and 96 of the novel.

5. I do not mean to suggest that Morrison never exposes the limits of some values and beliefs held by the main characters. For example, she asks us to recognize both the immaturity of Denver's view of Paul D as an unwelcome intruder and the reasons why she clings to it so strongly.

6. The passage is "representative" in the sense that it provides an appropriate focus for my discussion of the ethical dimension of the first telling but not "representative" in the sense that all sections of the telling work the way this one does.

7. There is one more very suggestive consequence of following the connections between schoolteacher's lesson and his and Paul D's judgment of Sethe. These connections, along with a few other moments in the text, suggest that Morrison wants to question the distinction—or at least to question the usual assumed hierarchy of the distinction—at the heart of schoolteacher's lesson, that between the human and the animal. The inversion of the hierarchy is, of course, very much a part of the passage describing the lesson: Sethe has a kind of self-consciousness that we do not usually attribute to animals, whereas schoolteacher has lost all sense of what we usually think of as humanity in his assumptions about Sethe as subhuman. But Morrison goes further than that in the way in which the distinction operates in the larger narrative. First, as A. S. Byatt points out in her review of the novel, Sethe's giving birth to Denver depends on her going on all fours, on her acting as if she has four legs not two. Indeed, the symbolic forest that springs up between Sethe and Paul D after he renders his judgment may very well be the forest through which Sethe crawled on the night of her flight from Sweet Home, the night before Denver was born. Indeed, if Paul D's comment applies to Sethe's murder of Beloved, it also applies to Sethe's most unambiguous demonstration of motherly love and devotion.

Paul D's remark also is complicated by his own past actions that might suggest that he has four legs, not two, particularly his finding sexual release by rutting with cows. Schoolteacher's lesson, Morrison's suggestions about inverting the usual hierarchies, Paul D's comment to Sethe about how many legs she has, the Sweet Home men's sexual practices: all these elements of the narrative suggest that Morrison is very much interested in questioning the boundaries of the human, very much trying to suggest that the lines between the human and the animal are not as clear and clean as someone such as schoolteacher would like his pupils to believe.

8. For a discussion of how Morrison incorporates this challenge into the ending of the novel, see my chapter "Toward a Rhetorical Reader-Response Criticism: The Difficult, the Stubborn, and the Ending of *Beloved*" in *Narrative as Rhetoric*.

Works Cited

Armstrong, Nancy. "Why Daughters Die: The Racial Logic of American Sentimentalism." *Yale Journal of Criticism* 7 (1994): 1–24.

Booth, Wayne C. *The Company We Keep: An Ethics of Fiction.* Berkeley: U of California P, 1988.

Byatt, A. S. *Passions of the Mind: Selected Writings.* New York: Vintage, 1993.

Christian, Barbara. "Beloved, She's Ours." *Narrative* 5 (1997): 36–49.

Handley, William R. "The House a Ghost Built: Nommo, Allegory, and the Ethics of Reading in Toni Morrison's *Beloved*." *Contemporary Literature* 36 (1995): 676–701.

Harpham, Geoffrey Galt. *Getting It Right: Language, Literature, and Ethics.* Chicago: U of Chicago P, 1992.

Hartman, Geoffrey H. "Public Memory and Its Discontents." *The Uses of Literary History.* Ed. Marshall Brown. Durham: Duke UP, 1995. 73–91.

Hirsch, Marianne. "Maternity and Rememory: Toni Morrison's *Beloved.*" *Representations of Motherhood.* Ed. Donna Bassin, Margaret Honey, and Meryle Mahrer Kaplan. New Haven: Yale UP, 1994. 92–110.

Homans, Margaret. "Feminist Fictions and Feminist Theories of Narrative." *Narrative* 2 (1994): 3–16.

Miller, J. Hillis. *The Ethics of Reading: Kant, de Man, Trollope, Eliot, James, Benjamin.* New York: Columbia UP, 1987.

Moglen, Helene. "Redeeming History: Toni Morrison's *Beloved.*" *Subjects in Black and White: Race, Psychoanalysis, Feminism.* Ed. Elizabeth Abel, Barbara Christian, and Helene Moglen. Berkeley: U of California P, 1997. 201–20.

Moreland, Richard C. "'He Wants to Put His Story Next to Hers': Putting Twain's Story Next to Hers in Morrison's *Beloved.*" *Modern Fiction Studies* 39 (1993): 501–25.

Newton, Adam Zachary. *Narrative Ethics.* Cambridge: Harvard UP, 1995.

Nussbaum, Martha C. *Love's Knowledge: Essays on Philosophy and Literature.* New York: Oxford UP, 1990.

Phelan, James. *Narrative as Rhetoric: Technique, Audiences, Ethics, Ideology.* Columbus: Ohio State UP, 1996.

Rigney, Barbara. *The Voices of Toni Morrison.* Columbus: Ohio State UP, 1994.

Rimmon-Kenan, Shlomith. *A Glance beyond Doubt: Narration, Representation, Subjectivity.* Columbus: Ohio State UP, 1996.

Travis, Molly. "Speaking from the Silence of the Slave Narrative: *Beloved* and African-American Women's History." *Texas Review* 13 (1992): 69–81.

Wilt, Judith. *Abortion, Choice, and Contemporary Fiction.* Chicago: U of Chicago P, 1989.

Wyatt, Jean. "Giving Body to the Word: The Maternal Symbolic in Toni Morrison's *Beloved.*" *PMLA* 108 (1993): 474–88.

MORAL REPAIR AND ITS LIMITS

MARGARET URBAN WALKER

IN TONI MORRISON's novel *Jazz,* one might want to say, a man gets away with a murder.[1] Joe Trace, fifty, dazed and driven by the rejection of his eighteen-year-old girlfriend, Dorcas, hunts her down at a party and shoots her. This is Harlem in the 1920s. No one wants to deal with "helpless lawyers or laughing cops" (*J* 4), and an ambulance called does not bother to speed to the scene, so Dorcas bleeds to death of her wound in front of her friend Felice. Joe's wife Violet invades Dorcas's funeral in a fury to try to cut her rival's young dead face, but finally she stands a picture of the murdered girl on the mantle of their apartment, poisoning the space with grief and reproach, yet joining herself and Joe in nighttime vigils of staring at the young face. Joe cries by the window incessantly for months, no longer the dapper and trusted salesman, while Violet stares into melting malteds in reveries of indignation, seared by Joe's betrayal.

Violet got the picture on the mantle from Alice Manfred, the aunt who raised Dorcas from a child. Alice was astonished when Violet—the wife of Dorcas's killer and the woman who ruined her funeral—appeared forlornly at her door, but after a month, Alice let Violet in and comes to wait for Violet's visits, in which "something opened up" (*J* 83) as they talk jaggedly about Alice's dead niece and Violet's husband who killed her. Alice, a seamstress, begins to mend Violet's ragged clothes; or Alice irons and Violet watches. When Alice tells Violet impatiently "You got anything left to you to love, anything at all, do it" (*J* 112) and puts her iron down hard, she burns a hole right through a shirtwaist, and suddenly they rock with laughter "More complicated, more serious than tears" (*J* 113).

Three months after the killing, Violet takes the picture of Dorcas down from the mantle, and Joe sobs more quietly. Dorcas's friend, Felice, comes around to find a ring Dorcas borrowed and instead cries for the first time about Dorcas's dying "like a fool" (*J* 205) when no one seemed to care except about the blood that soaked the mattress. Joe and Violet and Felice take to each other, although she is embarrassed to watch these old folks start to dance to music drifting through a window. In spring, Joe takes another job and life resumes. In the opening paragraph of the story, Violet, in a fury after assaulting the dead Dorcas, let all her pet birds out in the winter's cold to freeze, including the parrot that said, "I love you"; in the final pages, Violet nurtures a newly bought sickly bird by nourishing it with music from the rooftops. Joe and Violet sleep during the day, go for walks, tell each other stories, and huddle afternoons peacefully under a worn quilt they dream of replacing with a powder blue blanket with satin trim. Alice Manfred, furious at Joe Trace's impunity but shamed at her own inability to protect her niece Dorcas, found "clarity" unburdened with courtesy in Violet's uninvited visits; she moved back to Springfield, Massachusetts.

At the end of the novel, the narrator speaks about her surprise: she thought she knew these "people" she watched and waited to describe, but instead found that she had to follow them to a place she did not expect:

> So I missed it altogether. I was sure one would kill the other. I waited for it so I could describe it. I was so sure it would happen. That the past was an abused record with no choice but to repeat itself at the crack and no power on earth could lift the arm that held the needle. I was so sure, and they danced and walked all over me. Busy, they were, busy being original, complicated, changeable—human, I guess you'd say, while I was the predictable one. . . .
>
> It never occurred to me that they were thinking other thoughts, feeling other feelings, putting their lives together in ways I never dreamed of. (*J* 220–21)

The narrator seems to have waited for the fitting comeuppance, for the score to be settled, for justice, natural, human, or poetic, to exact retribution, or at least a steep price. A lot of us have been waiting for it, too.

This tale haunts and disturbs me in a particular way. It is about the aftermath of violence of many types that people survive. But it is not only Joe Trace's unavenged killing of Dorcas that unbalances the wishful equation that fits a crime to a punishment in the logic of a certain kind of justice, for I have left most of the novel out in this description. The histories Morrison unfolds for these people show how love, loss, and violence echo within lives and down generations, for these histories are knotted with the violence of racism from slavery times on. Joe was abandoned by an unknown father and a mother who ran and hid like a wild thing in the woods. Violet's mother was poor and alone with too many children when her husband was run out of the county by white landowners for joining a party that claimed voting rights for blacks. She committed suicide, leaving Violet to be raised by her grandmother, True Belle, who as a slave had been forced to leave her own children and husband behind to care for her young white mistress and the white woman's illegitimate son by a young black man. Dorcas's father was stomped to death and her mother burned in a St. Louis race riot. These histories do not explain the characters to us. Instead, they make them more vivid and yet more opaque to us, and to themselves, in the ways real people can be. But they show the terrifying incalculability of the wages of violent and englobing racism and of our inabilities or refusals to pay them. Where, and to whom, does the equation that fits a crime to a punishment apply here?

I find myself moved to wonder and hope as Morrison shows some very broken lives repaired, rather than ruined. Still, I feel anxious and ashamed that I am moved by this, because in the story Dorcas has been killed by Joe. In the end, no one seems to speak for her. No one undertakes to exact a payment from her killer. Instead, some lives of some of the living are repaired. They are, against the odds, replenished with abilities to value life, to trust once more, to give care and pleasure again. The story strikes me as a parable, but what is the parable about? Is it about another route to some resolution that ordinary justice also tries to achieve? Is it about the possibility that justice does not alone set the standards for repairing the fabric of lives torn by wrongdoing? Or does it force us to see that it is no accident who is apt to get justice and who is likely to be brought to it? The fuller story reminds us starkly that our sense of justice may fix insistently on some crimes and not others—on the murder of one girl by a lover, for example, but not on the terror and cruelty and unnumbered murders of Africans and their descendants in U.S. slavery and the continuing aftermath of racism that frames the lives and histories of Joe, Violet, and Alice, as it does the lives and histories of all Americans today. But it also follows the story of a handful of particular human beings, some of whose shattered relations are nursed and revived, as so often is not the case in the wake of violence. Is this *moral* repair? Is what happened to and among Joe, Violet, and Alice an example of an important moral possibility?

Varieties of Moral Repair

What is "moral repair"? I use this phrase to refer to a familiar and unavoidable task human beings face. We need, over and over, to decide how to respond to wrongdoing, whether to ourselves or to others, and whether by ourselves or by others. Moral philosophers in the twentieth century have often liked to characterize ethics as answering the question "What ought I to do?" which implies a set of choices on a fresh page. Yet one of our recurrent ethical tasks is better suggested by the question "What ought I (or we) to do *now?*" after the page is blotted or torn by our own or others' wrongdoing. I am interested here in understanding how responses to moral wrongs can be ways to repair and sustain morality itself.

This sounds strange: how can "morality" be damaged or broken? I do not think we need to converge on a metaphysics of morals in order to see just this: whether morality has its ultimate source and authority in a divine rule, a transcendent order, a natural law, or in the human mind or heart, the reality of morality in our lives—its importance and its grip, its mattering to us rather than seeming like just somebody else's rules—is something that we human beings must produce and sustain in the real times and spaces of human societies. People can lose their grip on even the most basic forms of decency if they are moved by lust, money, power, or fame; and we are reminded almost daily of what Sissela Bok has called the "vast and shamelessly organized hatreds" (44), the massacres, genocides, and terrors that have indelibly marked the century now just past. Less dramatically, our senses of value and responsibility can be dulled, eroded, disconnected. Fortunately, they can also be confirmed and revived, even extended to people or situations to which we have not applied them before. Many are now conscious to an unprecedented degree of discriminations and humiliations that limit or endanger lives, and the world-spanning discourse of human rights is heard more and more, even if it is largely unfulfilled. Old forms of responsibility can be eroded or strengthened, and new ones established and enforced. But senses of value and responsibility can only be shorn up, shifted, lost, or newly installed *by us,* that is, by many acts of many of us, or at least by enough of us at a particular place and time. We do this by doing what morality requires, by teaching our children and reminding each other of it. We also do this by the ways we respond to the doing of what is *not* morally acceptable. We show what we will "stand for."

So, whether moral standards are discovered or constructed, there is not much room for denying that it is up to *us* to give them body in social life. When moral standards are transgressed, the force and the strength of that body is tested. Our responses to wrongdoing place bets on how much wear and tear that body can take, and what will nourish and heal it, rather than sicken and weaken it. Deciding what to do *now* may involve discerning what damages require emergency responses, strong remedies, or subtle adjustments, and which are best left alone to fade away. Of course, I'm leaning on a metaphor here, the image of a living body with needs for maintenance and with points of vulnerability. Morality is not a physical organism. But morality as a living dimension of our social lives does not take care of itself, although we all rely enormously on it to take care of us—to be real and forceful enough to prevent a lot of harm from coming our way. And at many times, for many of us, in ways large or small, this fails.

Philosophical discussions of responding to wrongdoing have been largely absorbed with discussions of blame and punishment. Punishment is one indispensable response to wrongdoing: we inflict some measured and proportionate but unpleasant or painful treatment on the wrongdoer. Philosophers, politicians, jurists, reformers, and penologists continue to debate what punishment as a social practice is about. The familiar rationales, which are not mutually exclusive, are retribution, deterrence, or rehabilitation: retribution requires harm or malice to be answered with something proportionately unpleasant for the wrongdoer; incapacitation or deterrence makes it impossible or unappealing for the wrongdoer or others to try this again; rehabilitation aims to do something constructive with wrongdoers that renders them fitter for law-abidingness, a thought no longer much in vogue in some places but very much alive in others.[2] Parents, teachers, and all of us in many circumstances of daily life are faced all the time with questions about whether to punish and why.

Yet whatever is an occasion for punishment is just as much an occasion for other or additional responses to come into play.[3] Friends let us down or play us false; spouses and lovers are unfaithful; partners fail to respect each other's needs or feelings; employers are unfair; associates are cruel; there are slights, insults, lies, indifference, aggression, or violence among us. It is important that we do not always think of punishing people when these things happen, although sometimes we do; these different cases remind us of a lot of alternatives to punishment that in fact are always there. Some of these responses to wrongdoing exclude each other, while some can combine.

We can let it go by accepting or forgetting. We can blame or reproach those responsible. We can demand that they acknowledge responsibility and wrongdoing, confirming our negative judgment. We can resort to forms of public denunciation or censure. We can resort to direct retaliation and paybacks, tit for tat. We might embark on more or less formal exclusion, ostracism, pushing wrongdoers to the margins of our personal, social, or public lives. If we are in a position to do it, we might impose punishment in the usual sense, a measured and representative penalty or reprisal. We can also demand a show of remorse, repentance, or other reparative attitudes from those who have done wrong. And whether these are forthcoming, we might demand from them reparative acts, like apology or penance, or acts of restitution or compensation, material or symbolic. Sometimes we decide to pardon or excuse, to accept either that the offense does not require redress, or that it is better to forego redressing it. Or we may continue to see redress as in order but find reasons to be merciful in diminishing the response. Those who have been injured—and only those—have the option of forgiving. Often this means relinquishing the hostility or resentment they legitimately feel toward the one who has wronged them, and it always involves foregoing some entitlements of the injured that would go hard on their injurer. Forgiveness may serve ends of reconciliation, where a prior relation has been ruptured; but even when we forgive we may decline to restore connections, and we sometimes forgive precisely in order to let go the connection itself. Lack of acknowledgment of wrongdoing by wrongdoers and third parties is a torment for those who believe themselves wronged. In some cases, we feel a need to insist on a truth's being established "for the record," whether that record is the formal one of history books or the shared understanding of a friendship, an institution, or a marriage. Some wrongs call out for memorials or commemorations, which preserve the rebuke to wrongdoers, the dignity of victims, and a warning to others. Finally, we want, as we say, to prevent the wrong from being repeated; pathos lies in the fact that no actual wrong ever is repeated, any more than it can be undone.[4]

I want to use the term "moral repair" to encompass punishment by situating it in a broader field of ways to address and redress wrongdoing that may replace punishment or combine with it. What they have in common is that they are all ways of *responding* to wrongs, not merely reacting to them; that is, they are attitudes and courses of action that people take up when a wrong has been done, whatever the nature and intensity of their reactions. These responses address wrongs *as* wrongs, that is, as something that should not have happened, and for which someone is, more or less, responsible. And they are supposed to do something precisely about *that,* to "set it right." So they involve at least two kinds of "fixing": they fix responsibility, that is, place it on certain actors, and they try to address damage or harm done culpably by actors in some restorative way. The damage done is always specific to the particular wrong; but all wrongdoings are occasions when trust in our moral understandings, and the hope that we are trustworthy in honoring them, are threatened or broken. Moral repair aims at reinstating moral terms and replenishing our trust and hope in them and in ourselves. But there are quite a lot of ways we can do this, or try to.

One of the aspects in Morrison's story that is beautiful *and* disturbing is that we see an ensemble of reactions to a murder, a paradigm of wrongdoing, and we see a reconstellation of fractured relationships and broken spirits, a course of rages and griefs that runs itself through to the reclaiming of a living present, and future, with some hope. And this is something, at least *one* thing, we would like to see responses to wrongdoing achieve, especially for victims and often for wrongdoers (even more so when wrongdoers are ourselves). Furthermore, Joe's killing of Dorcas is followed by his profound suffering and a virtually public exhibition of self-abasing remorse. Yet we are not sure we are seeing *responses* (rather than reactions) to the wrong that has been done in an attempt to set things right; or, we may wonder whether we are seeing the *right* responses. Nor are we sure how the tangled tragedies of family and racist violence Morrison weaves into the histories of these characters configure their sense of what wrongs can be righted and what crimes and betrayals are forgivable. More pointedly, what about our own senses of this? What wrongs do we, different readers, expect to be set right; what do we want forgiven, and what left alone?

This is the ambiguity for me in this parable. Ambiguities such as this, however, do not arise only in stories. I turn now to a political response to systemic wrongdoing that has fascinated people around the world. It is not a parable, but it has been a kind of pageant that has moved people deeply even as it sparked intense debate.

Truth and Reconciliation in South Africa

South Africa's Truth and Reconciliation Commission (TRC) arose from a strained and expedient political compromise. Yet it has evolved as a particularly ambitious and hopeful project of deliberate moral repair of a society moving from systematic race oppression and state violence to democracy. In using the South African example as a concrete reference point, I hope I honor the importance of South Africa's project, although I could not try here to do justice to the complexity of its problems nor to the details of its still unfolding story. The South African process reveals ambiguities in the concept of moral repair and conflicts in the practice of moral repair as a real social process.

Following South Africa's first all-race elections in 1994, a Truth and Reconciliation Commission was established to reveal the nature and extent of gross human rights violations (killing, abduction, torture, and severe ill-treatment) under apartheid during a prior thirty-four-year period (1 March 1960 to 10 May 1994), to grant amnesty upon application and full disclosure by perpetrators of such politically motivated crimes, and to restore the "human and civil dignity of victims" by allowing them to give their own accounts and to recommend measures of reparation for them.[5] While the adjudication of amnesty applications continues, on 29 October 1998, the TRC released its 3,500-page final report on human rights violations, which found the predominance of violations to have been committed by the state, but which also criticized conduct of almost every group involved in the liberation struggle, including the African National Congress, the party of the new society's first and now retired president, Nelson Mandela.[6]

The TRC is striking for the complexity of its design: the moving ceremony of public testimonies of both victims and wrongdoers, televised around the world; the commitment to naming and publishing names of wrongdoers on the "balance of probability" in light of evidence but without trial; and the right to confer individual amnesties that must be earned by wrongdoers' public admissions and full descriptions of their crimes. The TRC has power to subpoena people to give evidence, whether or not it incriminates them or exposes them to liability (although such evidence is not admissible against them in court), and there is a possibility of criminal prosecutions or civil actions against those who do not seek amnesty, or whose crimes are judged not political, or who do not tell enough of the truth. The TRC confirms the dignity of victims by inviting them with their stories into a public—in some cases global—space for validation and sympathy, while its reparation function recommends concrete compensation for the victimized, as well as measures to prevent future abuses.

In other words, significant power was vested in the TRC in order not only to find the truth—about the fates of individual victims as well as the actions of the South African government and its political opponents—but also to fix responsibility by informed judgment and moral standards (rather than legal proceedings), to prompt actors to take responsibility for their actions, and to impose accountability on them. At the same time, the process was designed to show respect to victims in several ways: it makes testimonies of injury an important public event; it credits testimonies without adversarial proceedings, thus affirming the credibility of testifiers; it allows victims and fellow sufferers to participate directly in constructing an official and historic record of South Africa's past; it makes a reparations scheme an integral part of the TRC's charge.

This clearly qualifies as a massive multipronged attempt at moral repair. It confirms the agency, responsibility, and dignity of the participants—victims, perpetrators, and bystanders. It asserts standards of human rights, while it publicly models compassion toward both perpetrators and victims, "humanizing" the former and consoling the latter.[7] It confirms that there are many and grave grounds for retribution but opts officially for reparation and conciliation, offering itself as a passage to a society of citizens, rather than victims and political criminals. Both the broad powers invested in the TRC and the wide scope of its aims suggest a great investment of trust and hope in this transitional creature of the new South African democracy. And trust and hope are the most fundamental bases for any moral order: trust in a set of shared understandings of what is right and good and in our common support of practices that express them; hope that these understandings and we who are responsible for supporting them will prove worthy of trust. At every stage of the TRC's work, however, almost every facet of this complex project has been questioned.

Since the TRC was established, accusations have recurred that its amnesty function subverts justice. "Justice" here means *retributive justice:* a moral imperative of giving people what they deserve for how they have acted, specifically, returning good for good and evil for evil. Amnesties simply suspend retributive justice. Amnesty may be understood to mean that a certain crime cannot be punished or is not worth punishing at the price of something else; for this reason, some people oppose amnesties for crimes against humanity even when finding them acceptable in some contexts for human rights violations. Perhaps most resoundingly, in cases where there have been extreme and attributable violations of human rights, amnesties are accused of creating a "culture of impunity," a social presumption that one can get away with anything as long as one has a certain kind or amount of power. This, in turn, not only fails to provide any deterrent to new or continuing abuses but also allows grave evils to pass unacknowledged or unattributed. Worse still, it permits lies and denials to stand or to stand up alongside the claims of victims. This humiliates victims and invalidates their experience; it ignores their suffering and rage or relegates it to a private problem.[8]

The TRC structure mindfully sought to avoid some of the worst features of amnesty with the novel idea of making *truth* the price of amnesty, as well as deciding to name names in an official document, honor victims with public acknowledgment and compensation, and clearly reiterate the moral line that separates victims from wrongdoers. Yet for all this, the fact remains that people who have committed brutal and indecent acts will in many cases be relieved of punishment or penalty, if not of official negative judgment. For its part the TRC can claim that only a little retributive justice could be practically achieved anyway, and that it would occur at a price of precious resources and political instability. But the TRC can also claim that its process offers kinds of justice that are not retributive. In particular, the TRC emphasizes attempts at *reparative justice,* where the new democratic government, hopefully with support from private money, will offer some kinds of compensation to victims, a gesture with symbolic as well as material force.[9] And the TRC ceremonial of public testimonies constituted a novel and riveting display of access to the realm of political authority to many wronged individuals or their families, whose credibility was honored and whose stories entered an official archive, in many cases resulting in public identification of wrongdoers and validation of the victims' injuries. This is *participatory justice,* giving opportunities for social participation and civil equality in the public sphere to many people who had been denied them.[10] In the TRC itself, architects and members used and progressively refined an ideal of *restorative justice,* a conception of healing broken relationships that focuses on concrete harms to human beings, accountability for wrongdoers, and involvement of victims, offenders, and communities together in the resolution of conflict and the restoration of harmony.[11] If the TRC may yet be said to offer some kind of *retributive* justice, it can only be on a collective scale: it collectively rebukes the white supremacist society whose record of human rights violations the TRC has produced.[12]

TRC justice debates raise issues of the role of justice compared to other values—truth, equality, dignity, peace, and well-being—and of the role of retributive justice in relation to restorative, reparative, participatory, or distributive justice. If the most primitive meaning of "justice" is a balance or equilibrium achieved by keeping things in the proper proportion, then we are reminded that moral repair—a process of restoring trust and hope in a clear sense of value and responsibility—is likely to involve multiple measures, both *of* justice and *other than* justice, that have to pull together in a particular case. They may, however, fail to do so even when intentions are for the best.

The TRC process seems designed with awareness both that different kinds of justice delimit each other, and that justice alone in any form is not enough. Justice alone—retributive or otherwise—is not adequate to nourish all the trust and hope that moral repair needs to create or restore. Beyond truth and justice, the TRC clearly aims to heal and to inspire, to uplift participants and observers and reconnect its citizens in the plane of equal dignity. And here there is another set of perplexing questions about moral repair. What repairs moral relations for one party may damage them for another; what provides bases for trust or hope for some may necessitate measures that inspire fear, resentment, or contempt in others. One way of reconnecting people may rule out another. And not everything that repairs people's feelings and relations is a moral repair, however desirable the healing may be.

Moral repair involves the restoration or reconstruction of confidence, trust, and hope in the reality of shared moral standards and of our reliability in meeting and enforcing them.

First, let us notice the problem of multiple parties. Most attempts at moral repair are bound to take account of, if not directly address, some number of people affected. While two is a minimum in personal cases, even there wrongs may afflict or concern others. In a case of social injustice or mass violence, of course, many are affected, if not directly by the wrongdoing, then often by its consequences, including the knowledge that something deeply wrong or evil has been done in their society. In fact, in both personal and social cases of moral repair one might need to address any of the following parties: wrongdoers; victims of wrongdoing; fellow sufferers of wrongdoing; accomplices in wrongdoing; beneficiaries of wrongdoing; bystanders to wrongdoing; a specific community housing wrongdoers, victims, or others; society as a whole; and in political cases a present or past state apparatus. Yet moral repair may not be able to address all of these effectively. Outcries against amnesties can be met with claims that the stability and future well-being of society require that individual victims and fellow sufferers forego retributive satisfactions. It may be argued in return that a state that does not show victims or communities that it will witness, if not punish, wrongdoing is discredited. Appeal to the good of society may be seen as threatening, rather than reassuring, to vulnerable communities within society that fear continuing exposure to humiliation or violence. Assurances or reparations to specific communities, on the other hand, often provoke hostility or indignation, especially if people who consider themselves bystanders feel a reparative process assigns them the role of accomplices or beneficiaries.

Mahmood Mamdani, head of African Studies at the University of Cape Town, suggests a problem of this kind in recent debates on the reconciliation process.[13] Mamdani notes that unlike in Rwanda, with shockingly many perpetrators but few beneficiaries of ethnic slaughter, in South Africa throughout apartheid there were relatively few perpetrators of the kinds of extreme human rights violations the TRC was created to document, but many beneficiaries, virtually all of white South Africa (*RD1*). The TRC focus on "perpetrators and victims" omits the "link between the perpetrator and the beneficiary" (*RD2*). The TRC thus leaves untouched the "experience of apartheid as a banal reality" (*RD2*) that affected every area of life crushingly for nonwhites to the benefit of the white minority. Worse, the TRC's proceedings allow white beneficiaries of apartheid who were not directly involved in gross human rights violations the role of an audience indignant at these crimes, thereby obscuring their own situation of having benefited from the regime the crimes supported. This aligns beneficiaries with the true victims, allowing the beneficiaries not to explore their social responsibility for receiving benefits through an unjust process supported by them. It further outrages the actual victims of both apartheid and other gross human rights violations because beneficiaries do not feel the need to be forgiven for anything. I am not in a position to know the extent to which Mamdani's analysis reflects the actual attitudes and reactions of segments of South Africa's population, yet U.S. news media have repeatedly reported significant resentment among white South Africans of the TRC proceedings as a kind of "witch hunt" designed to blame white people and make them look bad. This realistic example at least illustrates the problems of multiple parties and differing relations among them that tax the powers and foresight of schemes of moral repair. It is not only that not everything can be done; it is that some things can be done only at the price of others.

There are also questions of what kinds of repair are moral repair, and what kinds of moral repair it makes sense to attempt, especially in public and large-scale cases. The issues here include what ought to be attempted for victims and fellow sufferers, what forms of reconnection should be sought or urged, and how the affirmation of truths and moral judgments on what has occurred should proceed.

In *Between Vengeance and Forgiveness,* Martha Minow notes the "striking prevalence of therapeutic language in contemporary discussions of atrocities" and asks, "What is gained, and what is lost, through the attention to psychological healing, in contrast with gathering facts and securing punishments?" (22). Minow reveals how therapeutic and political goals sharply contrast, while in practice influencing one another. In a searching chapter on the power and limits of truth commissions, Minow, along with many others, recognizes that recounting, sharing, and confirming the veracity of painful memories of violence and indignity *can* be a cathartic and healing experience, but she recognizes the uncertainty of what a limited public process (or even moment) of avowal can provide for any victim and the possibility of exploitation of fragile people in a dramatic spectacle. She asserts that "reestablishing a moral framework, in which wrongs are correctly named and condemned, is usually crucial to restoring the mental health of survivors" (71). This may be true, but what about the reverse relationship: how does the goal of restoring the mental health of survivors bolster the project of moral repair?

Making services, including therapeutic and medical ones, available to victims of mass violence is certainly a humane and socially necessary response that might also be considered one kind of reparation, alongside material compensation and restoration of civil dignity. But I do not think that therapeutic measures *in themselves* constitute moral repair. Moral repair requires more than reviving capacities for trust and hope in wronged and seared souls: it requires good reasons to think that a society is once again *worthy* of trust and hope. This takes social and political transformations, with important symbolic aspects as well. From the point of view of moral repair, the testimony of those wronged in truth commissions, for example, should be viewed less in therapeutic terms than in terms of how it represents and respects their citizenship, civic dignity, credibility, and moral agency. For this is the "reestablishing of the moral framework" of which Minow speaks.

Nor should we be simply credulous about claims that it is always better to tell and to hear, to incorporate the story of your agony or indignity into the larger story of your life, even, if I dare say it, that truth and nothing but the truth can only set us free. These are things we really do not know for all purposes and situations about human beings. Many of us with respect to at least some situations of terrible violence, incompensable loss, and unrelievable anguish have thought what one student of regimes of torture, Lawrence Weschler, has stated: "We get the feeling that some places in the world could use a bit of forgetting."[14] Truth commissions have become a feature of the landscape of political transition. It will be increasingly important to distinguish and assess separately the political functions, the moral meanings, and the hopeful therapeutic views of them. It is unwise to accept easy analogies or parallels between individual traumas and episodes of political terror, even if the latter invariably give rise to the former.[15]

For related reasons it is reasonable to question generalized and orchestrated invitations to "reconciliation," or even "forgiveness." Notoriously, one cannot command forgiveness, nor can one extend it on behalf of someone else. A social process of validating injury and responsibility for injuring may produce acknowledgment in one sense, establishing the undeniability of certain truths. This is no small thing. But this kind of acknowledgment need not entail that violators, beneficiaries, or bystanders appreciate the suffering of those who have been wronged (Steiner, *Truth Commissions* 75). Those who concede that outrages such as genocide, disappearance, torture, or rape as terrorism are totally unacceptable need not, in fact, thereby fully acknowledge the dignity and equality of those who have been wronged (29).

One final crucial issue is a question of how truth, and *what* truth, is an appropriate vehicle for moral repair. Minow says: "A truth commission is charged to produce a public report that recounts the facts gathered, and render moral assessments. . . . In so doing, it helps to frame the events in a new national narrative of acknowledgment, accountability, and civic values" (78).[16] A truth commission must indeed establish relevant fact and identify wrongdoing clearly as such. Yet the scope and limits of this mandate are not completely defined. José Zalaquett argues that truth commissions should stick to revealing the facts about secret crimes and setting them in a coherent framework and should avoid engaging in more contentious historical interpretations; they should not name names in the absence of due process (Steiner, *Truth Commissions* 15, 19, 58). The TRC was empowered to reveal the names of human rights violators, as well as the details of violations. It is arguable that a truth commission that addresses the needs of individuals to know who ordered and who conducted their torment or the killing of those they loved provides a fuller form of moral repair than one that only provides the "big picture" of patterns of wrongdoing, especially those of a state apparatus of repression. It runs the risk of confirming to victims the identities of torturers and murderers who may not be punishable, for lack of evidence or reasons of amnesty; but at the same time it opens possibilities for other kinds of social censure, exclusion, and reproach that might in some cases be powerful weapons.

Even so, facts in a big picture, including names named, do not necessarily equal a full-bodied, much less a unique, narrative, and it remains a point of contention whether this idea is tenable. A prominent participant in the process leading to the TRC, Andre du Toit of the University of Cape Town, says that "it is not clear that a single narrative of reconciliation—a nation-building narrative—will emerge" (Steiner, *Truth Commissions* 19). Historian Charles Maier doubts that "victim and perpetrator could ever tell the same story." He suggests a "contrapuntal history," in which "voices move along side by side in relation to one another" (76). Philosopher Yael Tamir thinks that in conflicts such as that between Israelis and Palestinians a unified narrative is not a real possibility, and that "abstract acknowledgment of the injustice done by both sides" is the surer route to moving forward. She notes that the justification of arrangements like truth commissions is usually "very contingent on detailed contexts" (74–75). This we might take as our concluding theme.

A Coda on *Jazz*

I want to say now that the story of the sequel to the killing of Dorcas in Toni Morrison's *Jazz* can be seen as an example, indeed in some ways as exemplary, of moral repair: characteristically incomplete and imperfect; in which not all kinds of justice can be done; in which truths burn to be remembered but cannot always be fully told; and when told such truths need not by themselves account for the mysterious, at times seemingly miraculous, abilities of human beings again to trust and be worthy of trust. But *Jazz* is also a parable about moral repair. Lee Quinby calls *Jazz* a "genealogical fiction," one that opens closed doors on the past and in the present, acknowledging inconsistencies and surprises in the histories that make people, relationships, and societies what they are. In doing so, she says, it refutes claims to "possess *the* beautiful theory as a guide toward a reign of piece and harmony" (56). It resists closure under illusions that everything can—or has already—come out as it must and should be. At the same time, it tests our very selective senses of outrage, sadness, sympathy, and justice at others' grave injuries. Quinby says *Jazz* constructs "countermemories" that challenge the "concealments of the official, white-supremacist narrative," such as "the descriptions recorded in the 'family tree' histories of white U. S. slaveowners" (55). These family trees suggest the inevitability of a kind of equation, in which two, and only these two, make more. *Jazz* reminds us how little justice is ever done, or even attempted, where lives have been torn and scorched over generations of systemic oppression, with its opportunistic cruelty, its deliberately measured negligence, and its tightly managed "truths." Even so, Violet and Joe, and Alice and Felice, have their own lives to lead and to mend, their own truths to make and face. They, as we all, face their own specific tasks of moral repair and will seek justice, revenge, reparation, forgiveness, peace, reconnection, or lonely solace in such ways as their situations allow them, when they allow them, to renew hope and trust.

That is my point about moral repair. We should not think of moral repair as something for which there could be such a thing as *the*—one—beautiful theory that specifies always when and whether to punish or pardon or forgive or forget. It is not an equation in which crime plus correction yields right order restored, although we have powerful and not unreasonable needs to see things that way. What serves better are detailed understandings—practical, historical, political, and moral—of the many facets of moral repair as they apply to concrete situations. We need to understand kinds of moral repair as such within a common perspective that links them to the basic task of replenishing the trust and hope on which moral relations depend. It will always be the case that the trust and trustworthiness that need replenishing in the wake of wrongdoing are those of some number of particular people whose truths and histories, crimes and injuries, are never actually repeatable, even as they beg to be told. And we are never in positions to begin at the very beginning with utterly fresh pages or perfectly balanced scales. We need lively imaginations but also realism and humility about the powers and limits of moral repair.[17]

Notes

1. Toni Morrison's *Jazz* is cited herein as *J*.

2. A good discussion of the deserved ill fate of "rehabilitation" in the United States in the 1960s and 1970s, an approach sunk in psychological speculation, manipulation, and arbitrariness, is found in Kathleen Dean Moore's *Pardons: Justice, Mercy, and the Public Interest*. For an analysis of community conferencing as a productive consensual alternative to trial in working with juvenile offenders, see John Braithwaite and Stephen Mugford's "Conditions of Successful Reintegration Ceremonies: Dealing with Juvenile Offenders."

3. Interestingly, some cross-cultural research on apology suggests that people in the United States and Japan more often choose "responsibility-accepting accounts," that is, apologies, for their interpersonal breaches, and that even when excuses are made in order to mitigate responsibility there is a strong tendency where damages are not severe to accept excuses that are recognizably "standard" in type, regardless of believability. This suggests what we all know: if the stakes are not terribly high, and even sometimes when they are, we are willing to bypass punishing or even punitive responses. See Ken-ichi Ohbuchi's "A Social Psychological Analysis of Accounts: Toward a Universal Model of Giving and Receiving Accounts."

4. A singular discussion of the problem of the irreversibility and unpredictability, the "endlessness" of human action in the world of human affairs, is Hannah Arendt's chapter titled "Action" in *The Human Condition*.

5. For founding documents related to the TRC, see "Legal Background to the TRC" and "Justice in Transition" booklet at <http://www.truth.org.za/legal/index.htm> (20 February 2001).

6. See the TRC Website, <http:/www.truth.org.za> (20 February 2001), for Executive Summary and Internet Version of the Final Report of 29 October 1998. The TRC continues its resolution of amnesty applications as of February 2001.

7. The "humanizing" phrase is Martha Minow's; see *Between Vengeance and Forgiveness: Facing History after Genocide and Mass Violence* (78).

8. A strong argument against amnesty in cases of mass violence and political terror is made in Aryeh Neier's *War Crimes: Brutality, Genocide, Terror, and the Struggle for Justice*.

9. Andrew Sharp provides a suggestive discussion of reparative justice in another context in *Justice and the Maori*.

10. In *Justice and the Politics of Difference*, Iris Young offers a full theory of participatory justice.

11. A version of the TRC Final Report (29 October 1998) is available online on the TRC official Website, <http://www.truth.org.za> (20 February 2001). Fuller analysis can be found in Robert I. Rotberg and Dennis Thompson's *Truth v. Justice: The Morality of Truth Commissions*. See especially the essays by Elizabeth Kiss, André du Toit, Alex Boraine, Dumisa B. Ntsebeza, and Martha Minow.

12. A collection of documents that represents facets of the debate over the justice of TRC's amnesty and other functions is found in Roy L. Brooks's *When Sorry Isn't Enough: The Controversy over Apologies and Reparations for Human Injustice.* The debate continues in Rotberg and Thompson's *Truth v. Justice.*

13. Professor Mamdani's comments are taken from the transcriptions that appeared on the TRC Website. The first debate was a TRC Panel Discussion held at the University of Cape Town, 24 January 1997, transcribed at <http://www.truth.org.za/debate/recon.htm> (14 February 2001). The second debate was a TRC Public Discussion, "Transforming Society through Reconciliation: Myth or Reality?" held at Cape Town, 12 March 1998, transcribed at <http://www.truth.org.za/-debate/recon2.htm> (14 February 1999). In the text, I cite these as *RD1* and *RD2,* respectively. Summaries of Mamdani's statements appear as of 20 February 2001 at <http://www.truth.org.za/media/1998/9804/s980421c.htm> and <http://www.truth.org.za/media/1998/9803/s980303c.htm>. See also Mahmood Mamdani, "Reconciliation without Justice," *Southern African Review of Books* (November/December 1996): 3–5, cited in Charles Villa Vicencio and Wilhelm Verwoerd, "Constructing a Report Writing Up the 'Truth,'" in Rotman and Thompson, *Truth v. Justice.*

14. Weschler, in Steiner, *Truth Commissions* 13; see also Tamir 73. In "Attempts to Amend Human Rights Violations Will Not Alleviate Suffering," Michael Ignatieff questions whether truth alone may not lock those who perceive themselves wronged into an infernal present.

15. For a useful (but no longer fully current) survey of truth commissions, which have become political institutions in the past quarter century, see Priscilla B. Hayner's "Fifteen Truth Commissions—1974 to 1994: A Comparative Study."

16. See also Fr. Brian Hehir, in Steiner, *Truth Commissions* 22.

17. Special thanks to David Alliano, Evan Ebe, Jonathan Hogan, and Julianne LoMacchio, who spent a semester in my 1999 honors seminar thinking with me about alternative responses to wrongdoing. An earlier version of this paper was written for the David Ringelheim Lecture at Florida Atlantic University in 1999; I thank the university, the Ringelheim family, a lively audience, and Robin Fiore, who encouraged me to pursue this topic for the lecture. Versions were also given as an Ezra A. Hale Lecture at Rochester Institute of Technology and as an Austin and Hempel Lecture at Dalhousie University. A special thank-you to Katherine Mayberry, in the audience at RIT, who disagreed strongly with my reading of *Jazz;* I believe she would still disagree, but I have revised my reading as a result and learned a great deal in doing so. Thanks also to Wilhelm Verwoerd for catching errors regarding the TRC mandate and its members and to Martha Minow for reminding me to note the political origins of the TRC.

Works Cited

Arendt, Hannah. *The Human Condition.* Chicago: U of Chicago P, 1958.

Bok, Sissela. *Common Values.* Columbia: U of Missouri P, 1995.

Braithwaite, John, and Stephen Mugford. "Conditions of Successful Reintegration Ceremonies: Dealing with Juvenile Offenders." *British Journal of Criminology* 34 (1994): 139–71.

Brooks, Roy L., ed. *When Sorry Isn't Enough: The Controversy over Apologies and Reparations for Human Injustice.* New York: New York UP, 1999.

Hayner, Priscilla B. "Fifteen Truth Commissions—1974 to 1994: A Comparative Study." *Human Rights Quarterly* 16 (1994): 597–655.

Ignatieff, Michael. "Attempts to Amend Human Rights Violations Will Not Alleviate Suffering." *Human Rights: Opposing Viewpoints.* Ed. Mary E. Williams. San Diego: Greenhaven, 1998. 181–86.

Minow, Martha. *Between Vengeance and Forgiveness: Facing History after Genocide and Mass Violence.* Boston: Beacon, 1998.

Moore, Kathleen Dean. *Pardons: Justice, Mercy, and the Public Interest.* New York: Oxford UP, 1989.

Morrison, Toni. *Jazz.* New York: Plume, 1992.

Neier, Aryeh. *War Crimes: Brutality, Genocide, Terror, and the Struggle for Justice.* New York: Random House, 1998.

Ohbuchi, Ken-ichi. "A Social Psychological Analysis of Accounts: Toward a Universal Model of Giving and Receiving Accounts." *Japanese Apology across the Disciplines.* Ed. Naomi Sugimoto. Commack: Nova Science, 1999. 9–46.

Quinby, Lee. *Millennial Seduction: A Skeptic Confronts Apocalyptic Culture.* Ithaca: Cornell UP, 1999.

Rotberg, Robert I., and Thompson, Dennis, eds. *Truth v. Justice: The Morality of Truth Commissions.* Princeton: Princeton UP, 2000.

Sharp, Andrew. *Justice and the Maori.* 2nd ed. Auckland: Oxford UP, 1997.

Steiner, Henry J., ed. *Truth Commissions: A Comparative Assessment.* Cambridge: World Peace Foundation, 1997.

Young, Iris. *Justice and the Politics of Difference.* Princeton: Princeton UP, 1990.

III

MAKING
DARKNESS VISIBLE

The Ethical Implications of
Narrative as Witness

ETHICS BEFORE POLITICS

J. M. Coetzee's *Disgrace*

James Meffan and Kim L. Worthington

The Collapse of Ethics and Politics:
Critical Responses to Coetzee

ETHICS, FOR many commentators on South African literature, is fundamentally political in conception. In much criticism on South African literature the terms "ethical" and "political" are frequently used interchangeably; alternatively, and even more problematically, "ethics" is assumed to be secondary to and consequent on politics. Frequently, in discussions of literature by white writers, "ethical writing" has referred to writing that has performed the *political* task of refusing the authority of the dominant minority during the apartheid era and, more recently, writing that refuses to maintain the cultural and epistemological divisions between (white) self and (nonwhite) Other that are the legacy of half a century of apartheid politics. Simply put, ethical writing in South Africa is that which engages with, and is responsible to, Otherness—where the self-Other binary is always understood in terms of the most visible markers of difference, those of skin color. It responds to a specific, contextualized political legacy of racism in liberal humanist terms that understands all selves to be equally deserving of opportunity, justice, and so on, regardless of difference. So, for example, in their recent introduction to *Writing South Africa,* Derek Attridge and Rosemary Jolly define ethics as "the continuing attempt to do justice to others, or, more precisely, 'the other'—the encountered person, group, or culture which does not conform to the set of beliefs, assumptions, and habits that make up the encountering self" (6). And for Michael Marais the ethical writer is one who complies with the "ethical imperative of responsibility for the other" ("Introduction" 4).

This is familiar territory to those acquainted with recent postcolonial debates, turning as they do on questions of reprimand, responsibility, and guilt. Appeals to ethical imperatives, indexed by the use of such terms as writerly "responsibility" and "duty," are common fare in such debates and come hand in hand with often simplistic assumptions about the political efficacy of "resistance writing." So conceived, ethical writing functions as political "counter-discourse"; it speaks—it *must* speak—to, of, and for the Other silenced by marginalization or exclusion in the violent appropriations and overwritings of colonial narration or the narratives of colonialism. The limitations of such thinking are apparent in reductive comments such as the following: "all writing in South Africa is by definition a form of protest or a form of acquiescence . . . since all writing in South Africa has obvious and immediate political consequences" (qtd. in Kossew 13). Protest or acquiescence is yet another inadequate binary imposed on a literature, culture, and country already riven by the prescriptions of binary thinking: black/white, aesthetics/politics, colonizer/colonized, guilt/blame. Understood in these terms, ethical (white) writing in South Africa is a literature constituted in and as the writer's political responsibility, indeed duty, to refuse racial authority, paradoxically (as we will argue) by speaking of and for the marginalized or silenced Other.

One white South African writer who has been accused of irresponsibility as a result of his refusal to *simply* repudiate the authority of the state in the period of apartheid rule, and its aftermath, is J. M. Coetzee. Most articles and books on this author at some time touch on and elaborate the terms of the ongoing debate about the political (ir)responsibility of Coetzee's writing, particularly in light of the postmodernist tendencies that characterize his narratives. It is not our purpose or intention to trace these familiar debates here.[1] What we are concerned to show is the extent to which such debates are informed by certain ethical assumptions and to suggest that it is by the prescriptions of these that Coetzee refuses to be bound.

Coetzee himself continually resists the simple collapse of ethics into politics, pointing again and again to the necessary distinction between what he calls the writer's social "obligation" and "transcendental [ethical] imperatives" that exceed politics (*Doubling* 339–40). In the discussion that follows we suggest, with particular reference to Coetzee's latest novel, *Disgrace,* the extent to which this is a distinction that, for the writer, must be upheld. Our interest lies less in the work of Coetzee, or in South African writing more generally, than in the extent to which unexamined assumptions about ethical responsibility pervade postcolonial discourse and render deeply problematic claims about the efficacy of "resistance writing" as a means of challenging imperial or racist constructions.

Ethics as "Responsibility for the Other"

In commenting on the "Politics of the Novel," Michael Marais argues that "some postcolonial efforts at recovering supposedly alterior histories are political and not ethical or, put differently, the political masked as the ethical." One of his concerns is with "the prospect of establishing an ethical relation between the novel and otherness . . . an ethical mode of novelistic representation, that is, a form of representation which evinces a responsibility for the other by asserting its irreducible difference. . . . [S]uch a representational mode would have to be deeply anti-representational" ("Introduction" 1). For Marais, the violence of narration operates not as analogous to but as parallel with colonial violence. It is a violence that can be seen to operate at the level of politics insofar as it is a violence that occurs as an effect of representation (in texts as in interpersonal and international relations). And representation, as Edward Said reminds us in *Orientalism,* is as reliant on exclusion as inclusion. Indeed, it is representation that objectifies the Other, reducing the Other to an object available to and constituted in the processes of colonial observation: "The visible, that which is seen, is a direct result of representation" (9). And seeing is, of course, synonymous here with knowing. Representation is a partial and exclusionary process by means of which one comes to "see," that is, to *know,* the Other. The products of this knowledge are, inescapably, constructed within the limits of one's own perception. The consequence is a violent reduction of the Other to the order of the same, regardless of the good will of the observer or representer.

Marais suggests that imperialist representational violence commonly finds expression in occlusion: effectively, it enacts an effacement or silencing of the Other in its processes of narration, even in the attempt to speak (of) the Other. Further, "such concealment reveals a nexus between the universalizing drive of European structures of knowledge, the representational procedures of the realist novel, and the history of European colonialism" (3). The problem for postcolonialism as it is established here is how to represent histories alterior to European colonialism without reenacting and reinscribing colonial representational violence. How does one write of and for the Other without representing the Other as an object knowable to and interpretable by the colonial gaze, the imperial eye/I? In the (guilty) discourse of postcolonialism terms such as "assimilation," "appropriation," and "silencing" feature again and again in formulations of this dilemma.

The attraction of Coetzee's work for discussion in these terms is immediately evident. For Coetzee is, above all else it seems, deeply concerned with the ethics, if not the politics, of relations between the self and its Others; indeed, he is deeply concerned with the representational relations of self and Other. In his analysis of Coetzee's work in "Writing with Their Eyes Shut," Marais suggests that Coetzee sidesteps this problem—assimilation-appropriation through representation—by refusing to represent the Other; instead, he "attempts to establish a relation with the other as outside history" (45). In this manner, Marais suggests, Coetzee enacts "the ethical imperative of responsibility for the other" (44). In developing his argument, Marais insists on maintaining the distinction between ethics and politics and suggests that Coetzee's work inverts the common assumption that ethics arises from politics: "I am not suggesting that Coetzee posits an ineluctable division between politics and ethics but simply that politics *begins* as ethics in his fiction" (45).

Marais's argument raises numerous problems, not least to do with the derivation of the "ethical imperative of responsibility for the other" or his failure to define adequately who or what "the other" is. With respect to the former, Marais notes the source of his understanding as the work of Levinas: "Emmanuel Levinas defines ethics as respect for alterity" ("Introduction" 16n). But a crucial elision must be noted in Marais's various formulations of this imperative: Levinas's conceptions of ethics as "respect for alterity" becomes, in Marais's formulation, "respect for the other."

In defense of the "imperative" that he proclaims, Marais argues that a lack of respect for the Other amounts to "totalizing violence" in the somewhat routine terms noted above. But this does little to establish the basis for a claim that acts of violence toward the Other are unethical, unless with recourse to the terms of an ethical framework that is here assumed to be unproblematically self-evident, indeed imperative. (Moreover, paradoxically, to hold such an understanding up as an imperative is to enact the same kind of epistemological violence that the imperative proscribes.)

Although a discussion of Levinas's work is entirely outside the scope of this essay, a brief survey of some of his major claims with respect to the ethics of self-Other relations is necessary. Levinas uses the term "adequation" to name the process by which the Other is rendered intelligible ("seen") through representation and hence is appropriated and constructed by and in the terms of the agent of observation or narration, resulting in what he calls the "imperialism of the same" ("Trace" 347). As Simon Critchley elaborates in his discussion of Levinas in *The Ethics of Deconstruction*, intelligibility involves a process by which Otherness is reduced to the order of the same ("the knowing ego"); it is "achieved through the full adequation or correspondence of the ego's representations with external reality: truth" (6). Epistemology, then, is a product of a "digestive" ontology: "ontology is the movement of comprehension which takes possession of entities through the activity of its labor; it is the movement of the hand, the organ grasping . . . which takes hold of (*prend*) and comprehends (*comprend*) entities in the virility of its acquisition and digestion of alterity" (6).

Alterity, for Levinas, is that which resists the totalizing violence of adequation, that which remains outside the bounds of intelligibility. How one might characterize such a quality is suggested in Levinas's discussion of infinitude as that which exceeds thinking and yet which is knowable as precisely that excession: "we can say that the alterity of the infinite is not canceled, is not extinguished in the thought that thinks it. In thinking infinity the I from the first thinks more than it thinks. Infinity does not enter into the idea of infinity, is not grasped; this idea is not a concept. The infinite is radically, absolutely, other" ("Philosophy" 54)." What might be drawn from this is a distinction between alterity (as a kind of "radical, absolute otherness" unthinkable within the order of the same) and what might be termed comparative Otherness (as difference known in the terms of, and hence reducible to, the order of the same). The former is representable, paradoxically, only as an excession of thinking and representation; the latter is representable in terms of differentiation that necessarily reinscribes it within binary logic (and hence epistemological violence).

Significantly, then, for Levinas alterity is to be understood as an experience rather than as a realizable quality. It is an experience that is entirely subject- and context-specific: alterity is that which exceeds the terms and bounds of the (individual) thinker's cognition, and hence varies with the limits of understanding for each percipient subject. Alterity does not ever equate with a singular embodied Other: the black, Third World, colonized Other so often evoked in postcolonial discourse. (Indeed, insofar as recognition is experienced, recognition of, say, a bodily form as human, the idea that alterity might be perceived as coextensive with the totality of another person must surely be implausible: the embodiment of Otherness as the Other involves a process more complex and, certainly, in part of the order of the same, than a simple experiencing of alterity.) The experience of alterity is, in Levinas's terms, nothing more than a subjective acknowledgment of the limits of the percipient's knowing, of his or her inability to contain all that is perceivable within the ambit of understanding.

Three points are crucial. First, the demands made by alterity are self-applied and not directed to the Other except as that Other effects the process of self-critique: "ethics occurs as the putting into question of the ego, the knowing subject, self-consciousness" (Critchley 5). As Levinas observes, "We name this calling into question of my spontaneity by the presence of the other, ethics" (*Totality and Infinity* 43). Second, ethics is the *ongoing process* of self-critique, in particular, of putting the knowing ego into question through the process of the exposure to and recognition of alterity, absolute Otherness. And third, ethics so conceived is not reducible, as Jill Robbins comments, to the "derivative and used up senses of right conduct, a set of moral precepts, or any particular morality" (5). As Robbins succinctly notes, "Prior to the elaboration of all moral precepts, the interruption [the calling into question of the ego by alterity] *opens* ethics, is its upsurge" (5–6).[2]

In his later work (notably *Otherwise than Being*), Levinas characterizes this experience of alterity in his formulation of "the Saying." Again, Critchley's gloss on Levinas is useful; he defines the Saying as "the performative stating, proposing, or expressive position of myself facing the Other. It is a verbal or non-verbal ethical performance, whose essence cannot be caught in constative propositions. It is a performative doing that cannot be reduced to constative description. By contrast, the Said is a statement, assertion, or proposition, . . . concerning which the truth or falsity can be ascertained" (7). Saying, in these terms, is performative, interlocutory; it is "the sheer radicality of . . . the event of being in relation with an Other; it is the non-thematizable ethical residue . . . of language that escapes comprehension, interrupts philosophy, and is the very enactment of the ethical movement of the same to the Other" (7). So characterized, the Saying is a relational process rather than a fixed relationship; it is movement, not stasis; it reaches toward an infinite future (of further Saying), rather than recording a past interaction or history (the Said). Violent adequation of the Other is precluded because the Other remains outside the limits of comprehension, outside of history, un-Said.

But how meaningful is an ongoing relational "event" that "escapes comprehension"? What scope is there for political agency in the "sheer radicality" of such an understanding of ethics? How can the Saying provide a foundation for politics without being reduced to the fixity, and potential totalitarianism, of the Said? As Critchley formulates the problem: "How is the Saying, my exposure to the Other, to be Said, or given a philosophical exposition that does not utterly betray this Saying?" (7).

The questions raised here, via this brief discussion of Levinas's notion of the Saying and the Said, offer a point of return to the debate about the ethics or politics of Coetzee's fiction, specifically as these are read within the terms of postcolonial criticism and theory. Coetzee's novels, as numerous critics have noted, are particularly concerned with the politics of representation or, put another way, with how not to reduce the Other to the "Said." The familiar vocabulary of postcolonial criticism, notably that which registers concern about authentic indigenous expression or the colonial assimilation and appropriation of the colonized (people, culture) with recourse to the metaphor of "voice," features strongly in such readings. In these terms Coetzee is concerned not only with the extent to which *characters* in his fictions are (or are not) culpable for speaking (for), and therefore silencing or denying voice to, the Other but also with the extent to which *he* is guilty of reinscribing or rearticulating appropriative or colonial violence in the novelistic representation of voice.[3] The writer's dilemma might be summed up thus: to speak or write (the Other) or not to speak or write (the Other)? Not to speak the Other might render one guilty of exclusion or omission; however, speaking the Other enacts another kind of betrayal: "any voice we hear is by that very fact purged of its uniqueness and alterity" (Attridge 226).[4]

As is often noted, Coetzee's fiction is full of marginalized, silent characters —those unable to speak, those who refrain from speech, or those disallowed speech (whether as a result of prescriptions within the ontological realm of the fiction or as a result of the author's refusal to give them voice within the narrative). It has been suggested that in these occlusions and absences Coetzee manages to evade the problematic inscription of Otherness, the appropriation of voice: the absences speak of an unviolated presence outside the realm of representation. Those supportive of his postmodernist tendencies suggest that Coetzee's utilization of a variety of disruptive narrative strategies and self-reflexive maneuvers undermines the authority of the writer (Coetzee) and the reader, thereby avoiding—or radically disarming—representational or interpretative violence.[5] Others, like Benita Parry, rebut such political recuperations of Coetzee's writing: "the consequences of writing the silence attributed to the other as a liberation from the constraints of subjectivity . . . can be read as reenacting the received disposal of narrative authority," an authority she understands to be "grounded in the cognitive systems of the West" (150).

One can see how readily a writer such as Coetzee is damned both ways in debates about the politics of voice: whether "speaking" or refusing to "speak" the Other he enacts a narrative mastery analogous to colonial operations. But, as we later argue, the untenability of the writer's position so conceived is a consequence of critical appraisals that prioritize the political over the ethical. A reconsideration of the ethical, rather than the political, nature of

Coetzee's representations of interpersonal interaction might suggest ways in which the circularity of such a debate could be short-circuited.

Levinas's "solution" to the problem of how to "Say" the Other without reducing it to an intelligible ("Said") object or history within the "cognitive systems" of the percipient or writerly subject is discussed at length by Critchley, who summarizes that "it is a question of exploring the ways in which the Said can be unsaid, or reduced, thereby letting the Saying reside as a residue, or interruption, within the Said" (8); "the Saying is a performative disruption of the Said that is instantly refuted by the language in which it appears" (164). Importantly, this interruption or disruption is never complete but is itself always subject to interruption: "*The reduction is never pure or complete*" (165; Critchley's emphasis). In short, "the ethical signifies through the oscillation, or alternation, of these orders [the Saying and the Said]" (165). Robbins describes this disruption "as a disturbance between world and that which exceeds world, a shaking up of the mundane, a collision . . . between two orders" (24).

In his final chapter, Critchley returns to the question, raised above, about what kind of politics might arise from such a conception of ethics. He asks "whether a politics that does not reduce transcendence is still possible" (217). And, further, "what meaning can community take on in difference without reducing difference?" (219); "what conception of politics would be necessary in order to maintain" the thought of community as "an open, interrupted community that is respectful of difference and resists the closure implicit within totalitarianism and immanentism?" (219). For Critchley, the answer lies in Levinas's notion of "ethical transcendence," which "enters into politics in the relation to the singular Other, the being who interrupts any synoptic vision of the totality of social life and *places me radically in question*" (219; Critchley's emphasis).

This is crucial because the political effect of the ethical relationship with the irreducible Other (alterity), for Levinas, is self-critique on the part of the percipient subject, a critique that is necessarily subject- and context-specific and yet despite (or because) of this results in "a shaking up of the mundane," a challenge to one's everyday understandings and knowledge. This is wholly different from the assumptions that Marais derives from his reading of Levinas: responsibility for the embodied Other *known* as different because it is represented or conceived within the order of the same. In the slide from radical alterity to specific, embodied Otherness, Marais's (mis)appropriation of the conception of "responsibility for the other" is in danger of becoming the paternalistic gesture implicit in the relational preposition "for."

Respecting Alterity: *Disgrace*

Coetzee's latest novel, *Disgrace,* presents a departure from many of his earlier novels in a number of ways, although it is still fundamentally concerned, as we argue, with the ethical nature of the relationship of the self with its Other(s). Strikingly, contra his early novels, *Disgrace* is set in a clearly delineated place and time: contemporary, post-apartheid South Africa. As such it immediately signals an overt engagement with the "real material conditions" of South Africa—although the political nature of this engagement will be less than satisfactory to many critics. Further, the novel differs with respect to the narrative mode(s) employed by Coetzee. In many of the earlier works the denial of voice to certain characters is, at least in part, an effect of Coetzee's choice to write in inherently restricted narrative modes, notably the first-person narrative voice.[6] In these novels, the failure to represent the viewpoints of others is thus explainable in terms of the limitations of the narrators themselves and quite naturally points up questions about perspectival limitations or narrow-mindedness and hence the tenuous and exclusionary authority of those who speak or write stories.

Disgrace, however, is narrated in the limited third person.[7] The story is that of David Lurie, a (white) South African university professor, and his fall into disgrace: expulsion from the institution for sexual misdemeanor. It is also the story of Lurie's attainment of some measure of secular grace[8]— although the restricted nature of this is disturbing for those seeking simple answers to questions of culpability and redemption. Superficially, the choice of third-person narration seems odd in a novel that, with few exceptions, offers little beyond the protagonist's point of view—an effect achieved, in large part, through the persistent use of free indirect discourse that is, it seems, exclusively attributable to Lurie. The effect of the close alignment of narrator and protagonist is in this respect not unlike that of a first-person narrative in its limitation of perspective. But there is one important exception: in a first-person narrative we accept, as part of the convention, the limitation to the narrator's point of view; here we ask *why* we are denied access to and knowledge of the thoughts and motivations of other characters. And it is a question we reflect back on the protagonist: why does Lurie disregard or fail to recognize the thoughts and motivations of the others with whom he interacts?

In many ways the novel can be read as an account of Lurie's interactions with Others. Initially, these interactions, particularly with women, seem readily open to reader critique: they are narrowly selfish (as with his ex-wife), even deluded (as with Soraya, the prostitute), but nonetheless within the bounds of acceptability. However, the (moral and legal) consequences of such self-circumscribed interactions with Others are pushed to their furthest extreme (as is the reader's sympathy) in the account of Lurie's seduction of Melanie Isaacs, his young student. Following one minimally consensual sexual encounter, Lurie again forces himself on Melanie, an act described as follows: "She does not resist. All she does is avert herself: avert her hips, avert her eyes. She lets him lay her out on the bed and undress her: she even helps him, raising her arms and then her hips. . . . Not rape, not quite that, but undesired nevertheless, undesired to the core. As though she had decided to go slack, die within herself for the duration, like a rabbit when the jaws of the fox close on its neck" (2).

Whose voice is evoked here? Who speaks the simile inviting comparison between Melanie and the victim of a predatory animal, and hence of Lurie as predator? If it is Lurie—attributable to him in terms of free indirect discourse—then the self-condemnation implied in the image suggests an admission of guilt that cuts against the qualifier "not quite." But if the partially exonerating distinction claimed here—between rape and "not quite [rape]"—is offered by the narrator, and not the protagonist, this refuses any simple alignment of reader sympathy with either protagonist or narrator. This passage, in part because of the inflammatory nature of the justification of the act described, exemplifies the disturbing quality of Coetzee's narrative voice in the novel and suggests the extent of the unease that characterizes the relationship between narrator and protagonist—an uneasiness in which the reader is also implicated. Melanie's motivations are implied (her passivity might suggest fear of violent force; she helps him to undress her, perhaps, to bring the encounter to a speedier end) but never stated—not by her, her seducer, or the narrator. In the absence of what might be called her "voice," in the terms established above, the reader is left to interpret her actions and is thus as open to charges of (mis)appropriation of her motives and desires as is the protagonist. The lesson is one familiar to Coetzee's readers: how readily the narrative of another, particularly a silent Other, can be conscripted to meet the requirements of one's own story, one's own interpretation.

What is most disturbing, perhaps, is the extent to which the reader is unable to gauge the sincerity of Lurie's interpretation of the event: for him to remain sympathetic, or at least not utterly despicable, we need some indication of his sincere evaluation of his actions (i.e., that he really believes this is not rape; or that he really does and is contrite), even if we do not share this evaluation. But judgments of sincerity, and so contrition, inevitably turn on the compatibility of our moral understandings with those of the speaker. Despite the clear evidence given of Lurie's ability to rationalize his behavior (here and throughout), what is disallowed is any comfortable (or comforting) degree of fit between our moral evaluations and those of Lurie. And how might one judge, how might one apportion blame or guilt, in the face of such incommensurability?

In the account of the institutional apparatus that is brought to bear on Lurie as a result of this encounter (or rather, Melanie's official complaint regarding it), Coetzee begins to drive home the extent to which the failures of Lurie's personal relationships—that is, the failure or inability of the self to comprehend alterity or Otherness (or to attempt to ameliorate this inability by appeal to a principle of "reciprocity")—might be failures that apply in the political and judicial arenas as well. The parallels between the university tribunal that seeks an official apology from Lurie and the Truth and Reconciliation Committee established in South Africa following the dismantling of the apartheid regime are pointed and ultimately condemnatory. The point Coetzee seems to be making in his portrayal of Lurie's appearance before the tribunal is that an evaluation of one's sincerity is unavailable to another percipient subject and can be measured only by external expressions, all of which can be faked. Moreover, Lurie is invited to either fake contrition, to merely *appear* sincerely apologetic to comply with the formal requirements of the institution (this from the male members of the tribunal), or to expose for their assessment his "sincere feelings," to speak "from [his] heart" (4; this from the women). But, Coetzee seems to ask, what scope is there for assessment of the sincerity of an apologist whose terms of reference do not coincide with those who judge it? Sincerity, or the lack of it, is not an adequate measure of contrition or culpability in the face of incommensurable difference.

As a result of his refusal to apologize sincerely, or bare his "heart," in the terms demanded by the tribunal and the institution it serves, Lurie is expelled and leaves his home to live, for a time, with his daughter Lucy on her smallholding in the Eastern Cape. Lurie seeks a friendship with his daughter that is premised on his paternal role as guide and protector; one in which the appearance of respect for Lucy's significant ideological, generational, and gender differences masks an inability to regard her in any but his own terms,[9] or to treat her as a fully responsible, equivalent adult male agent. That such paternalism—Lurie's assumption of an agential authority that refuses its equivalent to the Other—is characteristic of liberal colonial interactions with the colonized is not, of course, coincidental given the wider political context of the novel.

In his engagements with his daughter Lurie clearly attempts to assert the primacy of the paternal bond: he is her *father* after all. Initially, in the face of this rather benign assertion of paternal authority, Lucy seems willing, and able, to extend to her father precisely what he seems unable to grant her: a pragmatic, even generous, acceptance of his difference. That is, until an event occurs that forces her beliefs and values into direct conflict with Lurie's: in a brutal attack at the smallholding she is raped by three black men, Lurie is beaten and set alight, and the dogs she is kenneling are shot. Lurie's response to the attack is to seek retribution, the first step of which he sees as reporting the event to the police. Lucy's adamant refusal to do so, her rejection of the other alternatives he proposes (a holiday, travel to relatives in Holland, leaving her house and land), and her decision to carry the child conceived as a result of the rape are choices he—and perhaps the reader—cannot understand.[10] So, too, with her decision to accept her (black) "neighbor" Petrus's offer that she become his (third) wife (116). It is an arrangement of ostensibly mutual benefit, yet one in which she seems to lose far more than Petrus gains: he offers her familial and paternal protection, enabling her to remain without fear of further attack, in return for his acquisition of her land. To the reader this seems an untenable choice, not least because the autonomy Lucy seeks to preserve in this arrangement is so minimal (she will be allowed privacy within the four walls of her house).

Here, Coetzee seems to drive home the harsh reality of conditions in the new South Africa: not only the prevalence of unchecked sexual violence, but also the cruel truth of the extent to which "independence" from one system of authority invariably signifies the repopulation of existing power structures, rather than their abolition. In his representation of Lurie's relationship with Petrus, Coetzee seems to invite his readers to consider the dangers of a notion of self-Other engagement founded on the paternalistic idea of *respect for* an Other whose difference—understood as a difference in kind, in skin color—is conceived as inferiority. Clearly, Lurie understands that Petrus is no "old-style kaffir" (140), that he is not a "boy" in the telling lingo of former South African master-servant relationships. Moreover, Lurie recognizes that he, too, is a representative of the "the old days" (116), only one whose paternal authority has lost or is losing its purchase. But he nonetheless continues to regard himself, and Petrus (as Other), in terms of the simplistic and essentialist identificatory categories of race. That Petrus, now in a position of power accorded on the basis of similar race identifications, seeks simply to invert the previous dynamic and claim, or assert, paternalistic power seems a particularly resolute and unidealistic portrayal by Coetzee of (post)colonial self-Other race relations in South Africa and elsewhere. "Fatherly Petrus" (162) seems hardly an improvement on the fatherly missionaries and founding fathers of colonial construction.

Even more disturbing is Coetzee's implication of the effect, in such a binaristic economy of power, of such relationships for those who are doubly or multiply oppressed in terms of, say, race and gender. As a (white) woman whose value is determined according to male ownership, Lucy is merely another object of exchange, no less than "a car, a pair of shoes, a packet of cigarettes" (98). She can assert minimal agency only as a choice between unpalatable alternatives; and her selection of ("Fatherly") Petrus—whose authority is now more legitimate than that of Lurie, who is representative of what has been disempowered, even emasculated—suggests the persistence in the new economy of paternal self-Other relationships no less than it forces us to realize her inescapable subjection in the terms of such a dynamic. Moreover, what seems to be insisted upon, against Lurie's Romantic idealism, is the extent to which human subjects are inescapably embedded in historical contexts that may, indeed do, severely restrict their expression of agency.

Significantly, Lucy's refusal of her father's paternalistic protection is illustrated in terms of her desire to speak her own story in a passage that clearly highlights the relationship between narration and subjection:

> "David, I can't run my life according to whether or not you like what I do. Not any more. You can't behave as if everything I do is part of the story of your life. You are the main character, I am a minor character who doesn't make an appearance until halfway through. Well, contrary to what you think, people are not divided into major and minor. I am not minor. I have a life of my own, just as important to me as yours is to you, and in my life I am the one who makes the decisions." (198)

The irony of the passage is glaringly evident—Lucy *is* a minor character in the novel, one who does not make an appearance until halfway through; also, until quite recently, she has been a minor in the care and charge of her father, who would continue to see her in this light. But what Lucy's assertion seems to highlight, particularly in drawing attention to the narrational aspect of the text, is the extent to which the assertion of her agency might interact with another's (Lurie's); how he might attempt to "hear [his story] through another's ears" (66).

In discussing the attack with her father, it is his gender difference that Lucy asserts: she challenges his sense of being "on the same side":

> "When it comes to men and sex, David, nothing surprises me anymore. Maybe, for men, hating the woman makes sex more exciting. You are a man, you ought to know. When you have sex with someone strange—when you trap her, hold her down, get her under you, put all your weight on her—isn't it a bit like killing? Pushing the knife in, exiting. Afterwards, leaving the body behind covered in blood—doesn't it feel like murder, like getting away with murder?"
>
> *You are a man, you ought to know:* does one speak to one's father like that? Are she and he on the same side? (18–19)

The narrator's (Lurie's?) question here highlights the provisionality of identity configured in terms of group membership and, by extension, political allegiance. Here, Lucy asserts a difference between herself and Lurie—"You are a man"—that to her appears much greater than the identifications that could be claimed between him and the attackers. She is a woman, the victim of male sexual violence; he is a man and, in all but the letter of the law, a rapist. But the essentialism claimed in such a gender identification seems precisely what must be contested if one is to argue for the ethical possibilities of relational difference.

How is Lurie and Lucy's relationship to survive this crisis of difference? In political terms, how does one avoid factionalism—oppositional identification in exclusionary terms, the taking of "sides"—in the face of difference? Only, it seems, by Lurie's acknowledgment of and respect for Lucy's alterity and, crucially, in his attempt, however limited, to *imagine* a way across the divide of apparent incommensurability—an imaginative act that is enabled, if at all, by the identifications that he perceives them both to share (they are both victims; they are both white). Such an imaginative act proves difficult: Lurie, who was not in the room in which the rapes occurred, finds he can quite readily reconstruct the scene from the perspective of the assailants, but his similar attempt to reconstruct the event from Lucy's perspective lacks conviction—to himself and to readers. As he himself realizes (assuming that the narrative's free indirect discourse is attributable to him), "The question is, does he have it in him to be the woman?" (160). In any "real" sense the answer is, of course, no; but what is crucial is that he has asked this pointedly self-directed question.

Lurie—in formulating a question whose very terms recognize another's perhaps insurmountable alterity—can be seen to have made a substantial, indeed ethical, step toward respect for the Other (Lucy), not as specified, embodied Other, but as bearer of alterity. Not only does he recognize that the Other's (Lucy's) understanding may be constructed in the terms of experience he does not, perhaps cannot, share; he also recognizes that respect for this alterity entails the attempt to imagine himself as her, while aware of the impossibility of realizing the attempt. Arguably such an attempt *must* fail if one is not to reduce alterity to the domain of the Same, to the terms of one's own knowing, the Said: Lurie, a man, cannot "be the woman," unless by imagining her in his gendered terms. But it is precisely this failure, the necessary failure of the imaginative attempt, that may be ethically productive, for it issues in self-critique a recognition of the limitations of his own perceptions. Moreover, where he can imagine himself as "the woman" is in the terms of those identifications that he and Lucy do share: being the woman must be *like* being a victim, an experience they have in common.

And if the effects of such self-critique—the recognition of one's limited percipience—are not to be immediately foreclosed on by the reduction of alterity to the status of a *known,* embodied Other, then such imagining is an activity that must be ongoing and forever incomplete. It is an ongoing act of self-questioning ("Saying"), of attempting to imagine an alterity that cannot be imagined completely—for such completion can only be realized in the terms of simplistic identifications: what it might be "like," which is never quite the same. The best to be hoped for is an ongoing recognition of the limits of one's own ego, the boundaries of one's knowing, a recognition that ensures respect for, albeit not a complete understanding of, alterity.

Emphatically, we would argue, what is not being offered here is any narrow account of gender essentialism, the conception of selves and Others as fixed within impermeable and exclusionary categories. Indeed, as we have suggested, if anything mitigates against the potential factionalism of essentialist conceptions of identity it is the plurality of an individual's identifications. Rather, what is offered in *Disgrace* is an account of the ethical as self-directed evaluative process, not extra-personal imperative: in the face of the alterity asserted by Lucy, Lurie attempts to imagine himself as Other and, recognizing the failure of that attempt, continues to try.

What we are suggesting in the terms of the discussion of Levinas offered above is that Lurie "places [himself] . . . in question" as a result of Lucy's assertion of difference and, crucially, his respect for that assertion. The consequences, for him, are far from startling; he is a man unwilling to change (indeed, one who is characterized and characterizes himself in precisely these terms) and makes very little of what might be called "personal progress" in the novel. If there is some indication that Lurie gains some new understandings of himself—or rather himself in relation to Others—these are relatively small insights. Such a change might be traced in his relationship with Bev Shaw subsequent to the attack, a relationship based on what appears to be mutual empathy rather than on the satisfaction of personal desire and in which talking, ultimately, replaces sex.

We might similarly see Lurie's apology to Melanie Isaacs's father as an indication of further change, particularly in light of his adamant refusal to apologize to the university tribunal over the affair. And yet here, too, Coetzee denies the reader any idealistic interpretation of the protagonist's actions, or any simple means of assessing his sincerity. In fact, the extent to which Lurie has not changed seems to be foregrounded throughout the scene in the representation of his lustful appraisals of Melanie's twelve-year-old sister, Desiree.

In the final scene in the novel, Lurie agrees to the killing of a lame dog who has adopted him as master: an act at once compassionate and deeply pragmatic (there are simply "too many" dogs in a country starved for resources for its human occupants), which might also be read as a renunciation of paternalism, or an act of humility: Lurie acknowledges that he is without the authority or credibility to act as protector to the dog, let alone his daughter.

For many, Coetzee's "answer," continual self-questioning, in a debate that is concerned with how we relate to Others is entirely too self-directed to count as ethical. That Coetzee, as we have argued, proposes further self-questioning may well not be enough for those who, in the face of gender (or race or class) inequity, seek solutions that will enable us to speak with our Others without speaking for them, without appropriating their voices. Indeed, the self-questioning proposes cuts to the heart of a certain brand of liberal multiculturalism that is prevalent in postcolonial discourse: the idea that we must simply learn to speak *with* our Others on equal terms. Yet as the novel asks: speak on whose terms? whose equality?

What will gall the reader, and probably incite new criticism of Coetzee's quietism, is his refusal in *Disgrace* to do more than suggest the need to ask new questions of the self. What of *politics,* the reader might ask? In the face of the urgent political context of violent race and gender relations in which Coetzee has chosen to set his novel, Lurie's small gestures of personal renunciation, his minimal realizations, seem woefully inadequate. The novel does little to suggest how Lurie begins to engage *better*, or more equally, with people such as Petrus, unless in the terms of an imaginative act by which the reader is left to extrapolate out from an ethics figured as intimately personal to the realm of the political.

What Coetzee seems to resolutely refuse his reader is any simply *moral* identification with Lurie—indeed, one of the many risks taken in this novel is the portrayal of what will be, in the eyes of many readers, a distasteful protagonist. But this portrayal is instructive in precisely the terms suggested above: in the absence of sympathetic identification, and the failure of the reader's attempts to ascertain Lurie's sincerity, the reader is invited to enter into a respectful relation with a perhaps morally repugnant alterity, an ongoing process of imagining Lurie's difference that might cause us to question our own understandings.

In short, Coetzee does not seek to speak with his readers; nor does he offer comforting, Said moral certainties. Instead, perhaps, he seeks to encourage the reader to self-critique in the performative process of the act of imagination that is reading and from this basis to suggest the political possibilities of an ethical respect for alterity.

Notes

1. Coetzee's writing is routinely judged, by critics on the Marxist left, as morally deficient for its failure of adequate representation of material reality in apartheid South Africa (see Neville Alexander, Paul B. Rich, and Michael Vaughan). Anti-intellectual liberal critics find his nonrealist narrative strategies to be irresponsibly self-pleasuring: "masturbatory" in Michael Chapman's condemnation (33). Even as astute a critic as Coetzee's fellow South African writer Nadine Gordimer has questioned the political efficacy of what she deems his "allegorical" writing ("Idea of Gardening") and his failure to perform what she elsewhere terms the "essential gesture," an expression of social responsibility demanded of writers in repressive regimes (*Essential Gesture*). For a discussion of these critical responses, see, for example, Kelly Hewson's "Making the 'Revolutionary Gesture.'"

2. Maintaining a distinction between the terms "moral" and "ethical" is important here. The terms might be distinguished (in terms familiar to philosophical discourse) as first- and second-order modes of conception. Accordingly, first-order moral consideration is that which applies a particular evaluative framework to assess actions or character; second-order moral consideration is that which applies to the status of evaluative frameworks themselves.

3. Such readings are plentiful with *Foe* and *Life and Times of Michael K,* which are most commonly read in these terms. Derek Wright offers a succinct formulation: in *Foe,* Coetzee "has demonstrated the oppressive structures—in this case colonial narratives —that render blacks [Others] voiceless" (118). Sue Kossew concludes her discussion of the *Life and Times of Michael K* with the assertion that in "problematizing both the

narrative voice . . . and the silence [of Michael] itself, Coetzee reveals his awareness of the problems of narrative (story), silence, and voice that exist for both the colonized Other and for the settler writer" (11).

4. Attridge's words are taken somewhat out of context here, as he is discussing canon formation and Coetzee's place in the literary canon; however, they are true to his concerns with Coetzee's work more generally as suggested by the following comment on *Foe:* "the novel refuses to endorse a simple call for the granting of a voice within the existing sociocultural discourses; such a gesture would leave the silencing mechanisms, and their repressive human effects, untouched" (228).

5. Recently, Rosemary Jolly, Sue Kossew, and Dominic Head, among others, have argued for the political efficacy of Coetzee's choice of postmodern narrative strategies. Similarly, Michael Marais reads *Foe* as a "critique of interpretative authoritarianism," suggesting that the novel "depicts strategies of reading as a will to (interpretative) power, a struggle between dominant and dominated" ("Interpretative Authoritarianism" 9–10, 13). David Attwell suggests that Coetzee uses "the subject of *writing*" to explore political issues of power, legitimacy, and authority (26).

6. Or variants thereof—epistolary address, journal writing, and so on.

7. And it is narrated in the present tense, suggesting a refusal of history and insistence on the performative act of Saying.

8. Coetzee's concern with the problematics of secular confession and redemption —that is, with the desire to attain grace through confession to an authority that is not transcendental, not God—is given full expression in "Confession and Double Thoughts" (*Doubling* 193–232).

9. A striking example of this phenomenon is the extent to which his understanding of her lesbian sexuality is entirely conceived in terms of his male, heterosexual, and, explicitly, Romantic conceptions of desire and "passion": "Perhaps they sleep together more as children do, cuddling, touching, giggling, reliving girlhood—sisters more than lovers. Sharing a bed, sharing a bathtub, baking gingerbread cookies, trying on each other's clothes. Sapphic love: an excuse for putting on weight" (86).

10. The implication is that such choices are no longer tenable in the new South Africa: the privilege of going on holiday is something that white South Africa may well have to forgo if they are to do the work that stakes their claim to belonging; and a return to the colonial center (the Dutch, of course, first settled South Africa) is an impossible dream, as countless settler narratives suggest. Lucy's insistence on staying on the land suggests perhaps her desire to claim the right to occupancy in the land in which she (and her forebears) have settled, to exchange settler status for a sense of belonging.

Works Cited

Alexander, Neville. "A Plea for a New World." *Die SuidAfrikaan* 10 (1987): 38.

Attridge, Derek. "Oppressive Silence: J. M. Coetzee's *Foe* and the Politics of the Canon." *Decolonizing Tradition: New Voices of Twentieth-Century "British" Literary Canons.* Ed. Karen R. Lawrence. Urbana: U of Illinois P, 1992. 212–38.

Attridge, Derek, and Rosemary Jolly, eds. *Writing South Africa: Literature, Apartheid, and Democracy, 1970–1995.* Cambridge: Cambridge UP, 1998.

Attwell, David. *J. M. Coetzee: South Africa and the Politics of Writing.* Berkeley: U of California P, 1993.

Chapman, Michael. "The Writing of Politics and the Politics of Writing: On Reading Dovey on Reading Lacan on Reading Coetzee on Reading." *Journal of Literary Studies* 4 (1988): 327–41.

Coetzee, J. M. *Disgrace.* London: Secker and Warburg, 1999.

———. *Doubling the Point: Essays and Interviews.* Ed. David Attwell. Cambridge: Harvard UP, 1992.

Critchley, Simon. *The Ethics of Deconstruction: Derrida and Levinas.* Oxford: Blackwell, 1992.

Gordimer, Nadine. *The Essential Gesture: Writing, Politics and Places.* Ed. Stephen Clingman. London: Jonathan Cape, 1988.

———. "The Idea of Gardening." *New York Review of Books* 1 February 1984: 3, 6.

Greenfield, Matthew. "Coetzee's *Foe* and Wittgenstein's *Philosophical Investigations:* Confession, Authority, and Private Languages." *Journal of Narrative Technique* 25 (1995): 223–37.

Head, Dominic. *J. M. Coetzee.* Cambridge: Cambridge UP, 1997.

Hewson, Kelly. "Making the 'Revolutionary Gesture': Nadine Gordimer, J. M. Coetzee, and Some Variations on the Writer's Responsibility." *Ariel* 9 (1988): 55–72.

Jolly, Rosemary. *Colonization, Violence, and Narration in White South-African Fiction: André Brink, Breyten Breytenbach, and J. M. Coetzee.* Athens: Ohio UP, 1996.

Kossew, Sue. *Pen and Power: A Postcolonial Reading of J. M. Coetzee and André Brink.* Amsterdam: Rodopi, 1996.

Levinas, Emmanuel. *Otherwise than Being or Beyond Essence.* Trans. Alphonso Lingis. The Hague: Martinus Nijhoff, 1987.

———. "Philosophy and the Idea of Infinity." *Collected Philosophical Papers.* Trans. Alphonso Lingis. The Hague: Martinus Nijhoff, 1987. 47–59.

———. *Totality and Infinity: An Essay on Exteriority.* Trans. Alphonso Lingis. Pittsburgh: Duquesne UP, 1969.

———. "The Trace of the Other." Trans. Alphonso Lingis. *Deconstruction in Context: Literature and Philosophy.* Ed. Mark C. Taylor. Chicago: U of Chicago P, 1986. 345–59.

Marais, Michael. "Interpretative Authoritarianism: Reading/Colonizing Coetzee's *Foe.*" *English in Africa* 16 (1989): 9–16.

———. "Introduction: The Novel and the Question of Responsibility for the Other." *Journal of Literary Studies* 13 (1997): 1–20.

———. "Writing with Eyes Shut: Ethics, Politics, and the Problem of the Other in the Fiction of J. M. Coetzee." *English in Africa* 25 (1998): 43–60.

Parry, Benita. "Resistance Theory: Theorizing Resistance, or Two Cheers for Nativism." *Colonial Discourse/Postcolonial Theory.* Ed. Francis Barker, Peter Hulme, and Margaret Iverson. Manchester: Manchester UP, 1996. 172–96.

Rich, Paul B. "Apartheid and the Decline of the Civilisation Idea: An Essay on Nadine Gordimer's *July's People* and J. M. Coetzee's *Waiting for the Barbarians.*" *Research in African Literatures* 15 (1984): 356–94.

Robbins, Jill. *Altered Reading: Levinas and Literature.* Chicago: U of Chicago P, 1999.

Said, Edward W. *Orientalism: Western Conceptions of the Orient.* London: Penguin, 1991.

Vaughan, Michael. "Literature and Politics: Currents in South-African Writing in the Seventies." *Journal of Southern African Studies* 9 (1982): 118–38.

Wright, Derek. "Fiction as Foe: The Novels of J. M. Coetzee." *The International Fiction Review* 16 (1989): 112–18.

THE LIST IS LIFE

Schindler's List as Ethical Construct

Todd F. Davis and Kenneth Womack

He who saves a single life saves the world entire.

—The Talmud

DESPITE ITS tremendous acclaim in the popular press and its significant role in revisiting the Holocaust for a contemporary global audience, Steven Spielberg's film adaptation of Thomas Keneally's *Schindler's Ark* has received a generally unfavorable response from the intelligentsia.[1] Critics of *Schindler's List* often denounce Spielberg's film because of his violation of the Jewish notion of *Bilderverbot*—the Jewish taboo against visually representing the Holocaust—his ostensibly didactic pretensions, his failure to adapt Keneally's novel in an authentic and responsible fashion, and his brash sentimentality as both storyteller and director. Yet Spielberg's many detractors neglect to account for his desire to tell Oskar Schindler's remarkable narrative of altruism within the larger context of the Holocaust. "*Schindler's List* must never be looked upon as *the* Holocaust story," Spielberg himself remarks. "It is only *a* Holocaust story" (qtd. in Nagorski 77). Fearing that *Schindler's List* will become the master text of the Shoah—a reasonable concern, given the popular success of Spielberg's film and the director's considerable reputation as a populist filmmaker—a number of critics in the academy question Spielberg's depiction of the Holocaust and essentially overlook his substantial ethical intentions for bringing Schindler's story to bear on the lives of an audience many decades removed from the atrocities of the Second World War and Nazi genocide. A reading of *Schindler's List* using recent insights in moral philosophy and ethical criticism provides us with a mechanism for understanding the moral and pedagogic motives that undergird Spielberg's narrative. In addition to addressing the director's struggles in the film with such philosophically vexing issues as truth, responsibility, and altruism, interpreting *Schindler's List* as an overtly ethical construct allows us to examine Spielberg's narrative in terms of the historical moment for which it was produced and the popular audience for whom it was explicitly intended.

The form and content of Keneally's novel and Spielberg's film entreat us to explore the ethical imperatives inherent in each narrative.[2] While other schools of literary criticism might prove revelatory regarding the investigation of such issues as gender, aesthetics, and language, such theoretical approaches invariably direct our attention away from the ethical conflicts that confront us within the fabric of all narratives, particularly in those stories that ask difficult questions about our human capacities for good and evil. Ethical criticism, with its express reliance on the insights of contemporary moral philosophy, challenges us as readers—and, indeed, as viewers—to reflect inwardly upon our own ethical choices in relation to the moral dilemmas that literary characters encounter in a given text. The act of telling Schindler's story necessarily confronts Spielberg with the difficulty of presenting a compromised hero, a protagonist of ambiguous moral character whose most problematic traits serve him well in his ultimate quest to save the lives of more than eleven hundred Jews. A member of the Nazi party, a womanizer, and a shameless wartime profiteer, Schindler makes an unlikely hero by any standards. As Schindler's wife, Emilie, admits, "Oskar had done nothing astounding before the war and had been unexceptional since. He was fortunate, therefore, that in that short fierce era between 1939 and 1945 he had met people who summoned forth his deeper talents" (Keneally 396–97). Schindler's unremarkable life before and after the war makes his wartime accomplishments seem even more poignant. Quite obviously, no one would question a popular narrative in which the protagonist saves numerous lives while simultaneously resisting the Nazi party, remaining faithful to his wife, and never profiting from the easy spoils of war. Yet those are the clichéd trappings of melodrama, not the conflicted stuff of real life.

Schindler's wartime experiences clearly confronted him with special ethical challenges, many of which he simply refused to contemplate. As Keneally's novel makes clear, Schindler scarcely considered, if at all, the ethics of his numerous marital infidelities, his questionable dealings with various officers of the Third Reich, or his staggering financial success during a race-driven war. Keneally freely admits that we do not know the "condition" of Schindler's soul (190). Yet the vivid memories of the Jews that he saved—the *Schindlerjuden,* as the survivors affectionately refer to themselves—offer convincing testimony to the veracity of Schindler's deeds and to the unwavering conviction with which he ultimately carried them out. In his introduction to *Schindler's Ark,* Keneally acknowledges availing himself of the novel as a literary mode, yet attempting at the same time to "avoid all fiction, since fiction would debase the record" of the ambiguities of Schindler's life (10). Spielberg recognizes a similar dilemma in his appropriation of the feature film as the means of telling Schindler's story. The conventions of the silver screen encourage any director of popular films to entertain, to simplify the often convoluted storylines of history, and to maintain the audience's interest at all costs. In an interview with Franciszek Palowski, Spielberg contends that with *Schindler's List* "I feel like more of a journalist than a director of this movie. I feel like I'm reporting more than creating. These events," he adds, "this character of Oskar Schindler, and the good deeds he did at a terrible time weren't created by me, they were created by history" (172).

Despite the director's claims of journalistic impartiality and the necessity of historical distance, the film adaptation of Schindler's story confronts Spielberg with a variety of philosophical and narrative quandaries concerning the nature of such concepts as truth, responsibility, and altruism. Contemporary moral philosophers continue to engage in debate over these very issues because their adherence to temporality and the historical moment never truly diminishes. The notion of truth—particularly when considered in terms of biographical and historical representation—calls into question the problematic aspects of creating a genuinely factual depiction of Schindler's story in specific and of the Holocaust in general. Although Spielberg seeks to don the guise of journalist in his film, he ultimately shuns the requirements of facticity in *Schindler's List* in order to establish the larger truths that dominate his narrative.[3] Terrence Des Pres reminds us that such narratives essentially function as the testimony of survivors and are "rooted in a strong need to make the truth known" (30). The eyewitness accounts of the *Schindlerjuden* in Keneally's novel, then, imbue Spielberg's adaptation with a profound sense of responsibility to represent the truth about their experiences during the Holocaust. In *Moral Prejudices: Essays on Ethics,* Annette C. Baier observes that "great and influential moral theorists have in the modern era taken *obligation* as the key and the problematic concept, and have asked what justifies treating a person as morally bound or obliged to do a particular thing" (4). In addition to obliging Spielberg to offer an accurate representation of the Holocaust, faithfully narrating Schindler's act of altruism demands that Spielberg resist the temptation to sanctify his protagonist, to render Schindler into an uncompromised figure of mythological proportions.

Schindler's List finds many of its most compelling aspects in Spielberg's ability to portray Schindler as an imperfect and often unseemly character.

The success that Spielberg achieves in underscoring the depths of Schindler's flawed persona in the film's early stages ultimately serves, moreover, to enhance the intensity of his later ethical transformation. By primarily focusing the film upon Schindler's act of altruism—rather than allowing the atrocities of genocide to overwhelm his narrative—Spielberg invites us to ponder the individual human stories that bring the larger catastrophe of the Holocaust into relief. "Moral knowledge," Martha C. Nussbaum writes in *Love's Knowledge: Essays on Philosophy and Literature,* "is not simply intellectual grasp of propositions; it is not even simply intellectual grasp of particular facts; it is perception" (152). It is this sense of moral recognition that most eludes the many critics of *Schindler's List.* For them, the tragedy of the Holocaust often looms too large to merit anything but cinematic silence in the face of an ostensibly unknowable, possibly unredeemable event. For this reason, Spielberg opts to tell his story using the stark reality of black-and-white images:

> I think black and white stands for reality. . . . I don't think color is real. I think certainly color is real to the people who survived the Holocaust, but to people who are going to watch the story for the first time, I think black and white is going to be the real experience for them. My only experience with the Holocaust has been through black-and-white documentaries. I've never seen the Holocaust in color. I don't know what Auschwitz looks like in color. Even though I was there, it's still black and white in my eyes. I think color would have added a veneer of almost farce. (qtd. in Schleier 12)

By forcing his audience to confront the awfulness of the Holocaust, Spielberg creates an ethical forum in which a contemporary audience hopefully might perceive the reality inherent in Schindler's improbable act of altruism.

The notion that *Schindler's List* violates *Bilderverbot* functions as a significant moral dilemma for many of the film's critics. Claude Lanzmann, the director of the celebrated documentary *Shoah* and one of Spielberg's most vocal detractors, describes the Holocaust as "unique in that it erects a ring of fire around itself, a borderline that cannot be crossed because there is a certain ultimate degree of horror that cannot be transmitted. To claim it is possible to do so is to be guilty of the most serious transgression" (14).[4] Other critics such as Simon Louvish fear that Spielberg, the director of such fantasy- and adventure-driven films as *E.T.: The Extra-Terrestrial* and *Jurassic Park,* will construct a cinematic "Holocaust theme park": "At the end of the day, the most Spielberg can do is to draw his spectators, for the three hours the film runs, into his Holocaust theme park," Louvish writes.

"See the amazing Schindler factory. Quake at the imminent departure of the train transports. Shiver as you pass beneath the Dantesque archway with snow falling" over Auschwitz (15). Louvish's damning remarks about *Schindler's List* underscore the deep emotional response that many in the intelligentsia feel regarding what they perceive to be Spielberg's blatant violation of *Bilderverbot*.[5] The mere existence of *Schindler's List* obviously infringes upon the taboo against visual representation.

Yet Spielberg's motives for re-creating the horrors of the Kraków ghetto, the Plaszów labor camp, and Auschwitz clearly do not find their origins in any desire to transgress the strictures of *Bilderverbot* or to offend his audience. The story of Schindler's redemptive act compels Spielberg—as with Keneally in *Schindler's Ark*—to employ these infamous locales as his setting. Rather than remaining silent in the face of Schindler's singular and moving act of heroism, Spielberg chooses to reproduce Keneally's novel for the screen in spite of the fact that such an adaptation forces him to stage acts of human devastation of which Lanzmann's *Shoah* merely speaks. While he often struggles himself with the issue of narrating the Holocaust, Nobel laureate Elie Wiesel asks, "Is silence the answer? It never was. And that is why we try to tell the tale" (19). Simply put, Spielberg *must* tell Schindler's story. As with other works of Holocaust literature, Spielberg's film recognizes that mere silence hardly begins to account for the all-encompassing, banal forms that evil takes on in such moments of human cataclysm.[6] From the horrors of an SS *Aktion* in the Kraków ghetto during which two German soldiers pause to discuss classical music with Jewish children frolicking on a playground amid the starvation and human ruin of Plaszów, *Schindler's List* demonstrates the seemingly incomprehensible ways in which an abiding sense of evil intermingles with workaday human existence. In such moments, the course of life and death seems both more *and* less arbitrary.

Critics of the film often malign Spielberg for engaging in a form of unrestrained didacticism in *Schindler's List*. According to Bryan Cheyette, "*Schindler's List* maneuvers restlessly between clichéd pieties and a more neutral documentary realism. It is," he adds, "finally unable to contain the uncertain certainties of its didactic pretensions" (237). There is little question that some of Spielberg's motives in *Schindler's List* are didactic in nature. To describe his philosophy in the film as mere pretense, however, defies the ethical strength of *Schindler's List*'s formal structure. In his adaptation of *Schindler's Ark*, Spielberg draws upon the series of character binaries that undergird Keneally's novel. In the film, Spielberg emphasizes in particular the peculiar relationship between Schindler (Liam Neeson) and Amon Goeth (Ralph Fiennes), as well as the more ethically productive liaison between Schindler and his Jewish accountant Itzhak Stern (Ben Kingsley). The filmmaker clearly utilizes the former relationship as a means for highlighting the power of Schindler's transformation and for underscoring the evil that permeates the human soul as embodied by Goeth, Plaszów's demented commandant. The currency of their relationship finds its roots in the notion of "gratitude," as they each define it in a significant early encounter. Schindler's gratitude often manifests itself in the form of bribes, elaborate parties, and black-market gifts. "Among men like Goeth and Oskar," Keneally writes, "the word 'gratitude' did not have an abstract meaning. Gratitude was a payoff. Gratitude was liquor and diamonds" (172).

Armed with this knowledge, Goeth extracts numerous "gratuities" from Schindler throughout the film in exchange for a variety of "favors." Such instances include Goeth's provision of Jewish slave labor for Schindler's Kraków factory, his eloquent testimony in Schindler's defense after Schindler impulsively kisses a Jewish girl, an illuminating moment in which he acquiesces to Schindler's pleas to provide water for a group of Jewish prisoners awaiting transport to the Mauthausen concentration camp in sweltering boxcars, and, ultimately, when he accepts payment for the liberation of the *Schindlerjuden* from Plaszów. As with the film, Keneally's novel establishes Goeth as Schindler's "dark brother," his unethical doppelgänger. Keneally makes clear that "Oskar abominated Goeth as a man who went to the work of murder as calmly as a clerk goes to his office. Oskar could speak to Amon the administrator, Amon the speculator," Keneally writes, "but knew at the same time that nine-tenths of the Commandant's being lay beyond the normal rational processes of humans." Yet at the same time, Keneally reminds us that Goeth "was the berserk and fanatic executioner Oskar might, by some unhappy reversal of his appetites, have become" (171). Both Keneally and Spielberg underscore the precarious fraternity that marks Schindler and Goeth's relationship in the revelatory scene in which Schindler cajoles the commandant into allowing him to hose down the cattle cars destined for Mauthausen. Initially amused by his friend's seemingly impetuous behavior, Goeth evinces concern as he recognizes a perceptible change in Schindler's demeanor: Schindler is "not so much reckless anymore but possessed," Keneally writes. "Even Amon can tell that his friend has shifted into a new gear" (267). Terrified by Schindler's dangerous, public, and illegal efforts on behalf of a group of Jewish prisoners bound for certain death, Goeth demonstrates an unlikely compassion for Schindler, whose behavior, he fears, will land him in Poland's notorious Montelupich prison, or perhaps even worse, at Auschwitz.

Goeth's fully realized character—skillfully developed as Schindler's violent other in Keneally's novel and deftly replicated in Spielberg's film—continues to confound *Schindler's List's* detractors. Anticipating a flat, one-dimensional cipher, critics such as Cheyette deride Goeth's onscreen representation as "reminiscent of B-movie Nazis" (236); Sara R. Horowitz similarly describes him as the "outrageously evil Goeth" (137). Such adventure-driven fare as Spielberg's own *Raiders of the Lost Ark* often exploits caricatures of SS officers and German soldiers in their narratives, providing us with little detail, if any, regarding the characters' particularity. Surely, the same cannot be said for Goeth's appearance in *Schindler's Ark* or in his later characterization in *Schindler's List.* In the novel, Keneally provides us with a careful and expansive rendering of Goeth's convoluted persona:

> He was sentimental about his children, the children of his second marriage whom, because of his foreign service, he had not seen often in the past three years. As a substitute, he was sometimes attentive to the children of brother officers. . . . He considered himself a sensitive man . . . a *Literat*: a man of letters. And, though, at this moment, he would have told you that he looked forward to his taking of control of the liquidation operation, . . . his service in Special Actions seemed to have altered the flow of his nervous energies. (160)

Although he, too, refuses to placate Goeth's homicidal tendencies, Spielberg also demonstrates the more complicated dimensions of the commandant's character in a number of instances.

While Spielberg never allows us to consider Goeth's behavior as anything other than deplorable—the commandant of Plaszów in fact spends much of his screen time engaged in the random persecution and murder of his prisoners—the filmmaker also makes us privy to Goeth's own struggles with his attraction to his Jewish maid. In one of the film's more dynamic sequences, Spielberg shifts between scenes of a buoyant Schindler at a glamorous social event, a surreptitious Jewish wedding in the Plaszów prison barracks, and a deeply conflicted Goeth fighting against the temptation of his infatuation for his servant Helen Hirsch (Embeth Davidtz). In a lengthy monologue, a tormented Goeth questions his attraction to Helen—"Hath not a Jew eyes?" he asks, in a mock-Shakespearean tone—before ultimately denying his feelings and unleashing his wrath upon her. When Schindler later attempts to win Helen's liberation from Goeth's villa in a card game,

Goeth initially balks at the possibility of her departure. In the film, Goeth fantasizes about returning to Austria with Helen and "growing old" with his maid. After Schindler convinces the commandant that his twisted affection for Helen can result in nothing but her death, Goeth agrees to gamble his servant's destiny. Such moments demonstrate the great lengths to which Spielberg goes to flesh out Goeth's character. The filmmaker leaves the issue of Goeth's affections intentionally unresolved—is he gambling her future out of greed or affection?—and in so doing provides us with a more nuanced and richly textured image of unregenerate evil.[7]

In dramatic contrast with his crassly mercantile relationship with Goeth, Schindler's more meaningful association with Stern likewise finds its roots in a purely business relationship. Originally the accountant at Deutsche Emailwaren Fabrik (DEF), Schindler's Kraków factory, Stern provides the ethical companionship necessary for Schindler's unlikely moral transformation.[8] In the film, Stern functions as Schindler's de facto moral guide, offering the kind of redemptive fraternity unavailable to Schindler through his relationship with Goeth. Stern initially wins Schindler's favor through his abilities as an accountant, as well as through his capacity for understanding and manipulating the slippery commerce of a wartime economy. For Schindler, Stern at first represents an essential cog in the machinery of his business. He performs a variety of integral functions for Schindler, including assembling DEF's labor force, arranging Schindler's schedule, managing the factory's accounts, and assisting Schindler with the many bribes and black-market negotiations that ensure DEF's profitable existence. Yet the evolution of their unexpected friendship also allows Stern to influence the gradual shift in Schindler's ethical consciousness.

Spielberg highlights two telling scenes that demonstrate Schindler's moral transformation under Stern's tutelage. In the first scene, Stern arranges a meeting in which a one-armed, elderly Jewish machinist wishes to thank Schindler for his employment at DEF and for the refuge that Schindler's factory provides. "You're a good man," he tells an angry and embarrassed Schindler. "You saved my life. God bless you." Although he initially fumes at Stern for placing him in an awkward situation, Schindler later demands reparations from the German government after two SS guards murder the machinist in a random *Aktion*. A later scene with Stern confirms what the audience already rightly suspects—that Schindler's purely mercantile approach to the welfare of his workers merely functions as a facade. In an intense moment of reflection, Schindler struggles with his own transformation from a strictly self-driven egotist to a more selfless being on the verge of tremendous personal sacrifice. In an angry outburst, Schindler bellows at Stern because of the anxiety that characterizes his agonizing shift in inter- personal values: "People die. It's a fact of life. . . . What am I supposed to do about it? Bring everybody over? Is that what you think? Send them over to Schindler. Send them all. His place is a haven, didn't you know? It's not a factory. It's not an enterprise of any kind. It's a haven for rabbis, and orphans, and people with no skills whatsoever." No longer able to perceive his workers as mere gears in his financial engine, Schindler recognizes the individual humanity of his Jewish staff at DEF. For Schindler, they now exist as essen- tial members of his ethical community.

Facilitated by Stern's moral agency, Schindler finds the origins of his eth- ical redemption in an epiphany of sorts. As with Keneally's novel, Spielberg accomplishes this end through an event that moral philosophers describe as a "cataleptic impression"—a cognitive, philosophical phenomenon that, according to Nussbaum, "has the power, just through its own felt quality, to drag us to assent, to convince us that things could not be otherwise. It is defined as a mark or impress upon the soul" (265). Schindler experiences precisely such a moment while horseback riding in the hills above the Kraków ghetto with Ingrid (Béatrice Macola), his secretary and lover. "They were impeccably turned out," Keneally writes, "in long hacking jackets, riding breeches, and dazzling boots" (127). Below them, SS guards violently liquidate the ghetto. Moving from building to building, they round up the Jews for transport to Plaszów, pausing only to commit summary executions and beat their prisoners into mind-numbing submission. "Schindler felt an intolerable fear for them," Keneally writes, "a terror in his blood which loosened his thighs from the saddle and threatened to unhorse him" (129). His horror at the brutal destruction of the ghetto becomes personified by the figure of a toddler in a scarlet coat. Spielberg's colorization of her clothing succeeds in highlighting the toddler's particularity, an essence of unique- ness that might otherwise be lost against the black-and-white tableau created by the ghetto's doomed citizenry and their indifferent tormentors. After witnessing the ghetto liquidation and its dehumanizing savagery, Schindler can simply no longer ignore the evil that threatens to engulf, and ultimately erase, a community that he has come to value. "Beyond this day," Schindler would later claim, "no thinking person could fail to see what would hap- pen. I was now resolved to do everything in my power to defeat the system" (Keneally 133).⁹

Spielberg's overarching desire to capture the impact of Schindler's ethical transformation occasionally leads him beyond the cold confines of historical authenticity and into the brash theater of sentimentality. It is in such moments that Spielberg's film most dramatically diverges from the strictly biographical intentions of *Schindler's Ark*. As a number of critics have astutely observed, the inherent visual power of film often becomes dangerous when audiences receive film as literal truth without the benefit of critical distance. In such instances, a given film's historical representations become concretized, whether it may be fictional, nonfictional, or otherwise. "Verisimilitude," Horowitz argues, "is not reality but artifice posing as reality. When this 'as if' posture goes on uninterrupted by a self-conscious moment, the film presses its claim for historical truth simply by virtue of being film" (122). In this way, the pseudo-historical representation of reality in films such as Oliver Stone's *JFK* and *Nixon*, as well as in John Madden's *Shakespeare in Love*, may come to be seen as the "truth" by an uncritical audience. Clearly guilty of fabricating scenes of historical and biographical import without factual antecedent—most notably, in the critically maligned shower scene in which the *Schindlerfrauen* are bathed in water rather than the expected lethal dose of Zyklon B, as well as in Schindler's emotional parting with the *Schindler-juden* in Czechoslovakia—Spielberg sometimes abuses the notion of historical authenticity in order to fashion moments of sentimental power that may lead his audience to comprehend larger ethical truths.[10]

Spielberg's affinity for sentimentality—for the filmic construction of a grandiose gesture—distresses many of the film's most vocal critics. David C. Toole, for example, argues that "where Keneally avoids the sentimentalism that he knows will drain his story of its earth-shaking power, Spielberg delivers pure sap" (288). Spielberg's decision to embellish Schindler's farewell scene in Czechoslovakia offers a useful case in point regarding his penchant for sentimentality. In Keneally's novel, Schindler's departure seems understated. His Mercedes quietly rolls out of the compound's gates because "everyone was too unnerved to make formal goodbyes" (375). For Spielberg, such an ending fails to satisfy his theatrical desires for underscoring once more the epic and moral proportions that he perceives in Schindler's story. During his tearful departure in the film, an emotional Schindler becomes awestruck by the enormity of the Holocaust, wishing that he had purchased freedom for even more Jewish prisoners. "I could have gotten more out," he laments. "I threw away so much money." Such a sentimentalized gesture, of course, runs counter to the sensibilities of many contemporary critics. As Paul Lauter explains in *Canons and Contexts*, "The dominant view, certainly since the modernist revolution against nineteenth-century gentility and emotionalism, has been suspicion of literary sentiment; indeed,

among the most damning terms in a critic's arsenal has been 'sentimental.'
We have much preferred the detachment and aesthetic distance of irony"
(106). Rather than maintain a sense of artistic distance in *Schindler's List,*
Spielberg not only wishes to draw the characters in his film into close proximity with one another by virtue of a group embrace but also to dissolve
the emotional distance between audience and story.

Remarkably cognizant about the "presentness" of his film, Spielberg
explicitly collapses conventional notions of aesthetic distance in *Schindler's
List* in an effort to celebrate Schindler's exemplary act of selflessness with
generations of moviegoers. "Let us not forget," Judith E. Doneson astutely
observes, "that a historical film is as much about the present as it is about
the past" (149). Spielberg highlights *Schindler's List*'s presentness through
the colorized sequence that concludes the film. In this moving scene, the
director unites the past with the present as the surviving *Schindlerjuden* and
their film counterparts place ceremonial stones upon Schindler's grave-
stone to the hopeful strains of "Jerusalem of Gold." Clearly, *Schindler's List*
fulfills a range of important purposes for a contemporary audience. In a
world in which Holocaust "revisionists" absurdly dispute the catastrophic
proportions of the Shoah, *Schindler's List* forces viewers to contemplate the
enormous scope and devastation of genocide.[11] Spielberg's film also performs
a useful memorial function for a culture that accesses much of its knowledge
and history through visual media. "As a contribution to popular culture,
[*Schindler's List*] can only do good," John Gross writes. "Holocaust denial
may or may not be a major problem in the future, but Holocaust ignorance,
Holocaust forgetfulness, and Holocaust indifference are bound to be, and
Schindler's List is likely to do as much as any single work to dispel them"
(16).[12] By participating in numerous educational seminars and subsidizing
the commercial-free broadcast of *Schindler's List* on national television,
Spielberg has ensured the film's didactic function for future generations. In
the end, it seems that Schindler's singular act of altruism will share in humankind's most significant obligation. Plainly and simply, it will teach.

Notes

1. Published as *Schindler's List* in the United States, Keneally's novel was awarded
the coveted Booker Prize in 1983. For a useful discussion regarding the textual differences between the American and British versions of the novel, see Tim O'Hearn's
"*Schindler's Ark* and *Schindler's List:* One for the Price of Two."

2. For purposes of this essay, Spielberg will be referred to as the de facto author of
the film version of *Schindler's Ark.* While Steven Zaillian wrote the screenplay for
Schindler's List, Spielberg is clearly the target of the film's numerous detractors in the

intelligentsia. As Jeffrey Shandler observes, "Much of the attention, both positive and negative, focuses on Spielberg. This contrasts with discussions of the miniseries [*Holocaust*], in which, as a rule, critics directed their comments at its medium rather than its producer, director, or scenarist," Shandler adds. "But whereas the most common epithet hurled at *Holocaust* was that it was a 'soap opera,' critics of *Schindler's List* assail its *auteur*" (160).

3. The considerable artistic freedom and space inherent in the novel as literary form afford Keneally with the means for telling Schindler's story and the corresponding narratives of the *Schindlerjuden* in their entirety. The conventions of the novel allow Keneally to adhere to the facticity that necessarily eludes Spielberg in *Schindler's List* because of the generic and temporal constraints endemic to filmic narrative. In his introduction, Keneally reminds us that all events in the novel "are based on the detailed recollections of the *Schindlerjuden,* of Schindler himself, and of other witnesses to Oskar's acts of outrageous rescue" (10). Spielberg enjoys no such freedom in *Schindler's List.* For the filmmaker, condensing Keneally's novel and reducing the text's scope—with its multitudinous details and its wide-ranging forays into the lives of the *Schindlerjuden*—demands the conflation of scenes and characters, the diminution of events, and the collapse of temporality.

4. Jean-François Lyotard similarly compares Auschwitz to "an earthquake [that] destroys not only lives, buildings, and objects but also the instruments used to measure earthquakes directly or indirectly" (57). For Lyotard, then, the Holocaust becomes unrepresentable.

5. For Michael André Bernstein, Spielberg's violation of *Bilderverbot* seems perhaps even more egregious and foreboding because of what he describes as the "*Schindler's List* effect," or the "way the Holocaust is currently at risk of being presented, if only in people's first exposure to the subject, chiefly as the factual 'basis' for Steven Spielberg's movie" (431).

6. Hannah Arendt describes the "banality of evil" as "the phenomenon of evil deeds, committed on a gigantic scale, which could not be traced to any particularity of wickedness, pathology, or ideological conviction in the doer. . . . However monstrous the deeds were, the doer was neither monstrous nor demonic," she writes. Evil "can spread over the whole world like a fungus and lay waste precisely because it is not rooted anywhere" (qtd. in Novick 135). In her memoirs, Emilie Schindler confirms Arendt's formulation of evil in the concentration camps. For her, the evil of Nazism found its origins in "the most infamous and brutal corners of the human soul" (153).

7. In both the novel and the film, Keneally and Spielberg contrast Goeth's uncertain feelings for Helen with his tremendous and unwavering affection for Schindler. "Oskar had the characteristic salesman's gift of treating men he abhorred as if they were spiritual brothers," Keneally writes, "and it would deceive the Herr Commandant so completely that Amon would always believe Oskar a friend" (170).

8. For purposes of streamlining Keneally's plot, Spielberg's film conflates Schindler's three business advisers—Stern, Abraham Bankier, and Mietek Pemper—into a single character. For example, it is actually Bankier, rather than Stern, whom Schindler rescues from the deportation train in Keneally's novel.

9. In his rave review of the film, Roger Ebert praises Spielberg for not attempting to explain Schindler's transformation from a "victimizer into a humanitarian." "Any possi-

ble answer," Ebert writes, "would be too simple, an insult to the mystery of Schindler's life" (179). While Spielberg hardly attempts to account for every facet of Schindler's ethical renewal, he nevertheless offers compelling evidence in the film that events such as the liquidation of the ghetto helped set Schindler's moral conversion into motion.

10. Cheyette, for example, argues that after the shower scene the film's "documentary realism begins to unravel disastrously" (232). Terrence Rafferty, however, valorizes Spielberg's inclusion of the scene and his attempts to educate viewers about many aspects of the Holocaust. *Schindler's List*, he writes, takes us "even further, straight into the heart of darkness: we follow the women who wound up at Auschwitz-Birkenau into the showers" (132). It is worth noting that the shower scene—in sharp contrast with the scene depicting Schindler's emotional farewell in Czechoslovakia—has a legitimate, albeit vague antecedent in Keneally's text.

11. Obviously, films such as *Schindler's List* and *Shoah* offer powerful refutations to the outrageous claims of such figures as Arthur R. Butz, whose *The Hoax of the Twentieth Century: The Case against the Presumed Extermination of European Jewry* suggests that the Nazis never systematically murdered millions of Jews in the concentration camps. While such academic and religious texts as Pierre Vidal-Naquet's *Assassins of Memory: Essays on the Denial of the Holocaust* and Kenneth S. Stern's *Holocaust Denial* provide an enlightened response to Holocaust skeptics, a film such as *Schindler's List* clearly has the potential for educating a larger audience about the vastness and brutality of the Holocaust.

12. Historian Elazar Barkan concurs with Gross's remarks about the educational function of *Schindler's List*. "Spielberg's success normalizes the Holocaust beyond Lanzmann," Barkan writes. "He brings it down from the sophisticated and inaccessible pedestal and makes it into human-sized—horrific as it was—experience. For Lanzmann's admirers, Spielberg may be a sacrilege. Yet, for the millions who have seen *Schindler's List* but have never heard of *Shoah,* Spielberg has represented the Holocaust in a way that can and will be comprehended. For most of us who recognize that multiple perspectives are better than a pure single view, Spielberg has added much to our understanding of the production of memory" (1250).

Works Cited

Baier, Annette C. *Moral Prejudices: Essays on Ethics.* Cambridge: Harvard UP, 1994.

Barkan, Elazar. Rev. of *Tango of Slaves,* dir. by Ilan Ziv; *Korczac,* dir. by Andrzej Wajda; and *Schindler's List,* dir. by Steven Spielberg. *American Historical Review* 99.4 (1994): 1244–50.

Bernstein, Michael André. "The *Schindler's List* Effect." *American Scholar* 63 (1994): 429–32.

Butz, Arthur R. *The Hoax of the Twentieth Century: The Case against the Presumed Extermination of European Jewry.* Torrance, CA: Institute for Historical Review, 1976.

Cheyette, Bryan. "The Uncertain Certainty of *Schindler's List*." Loshitzky 226–38.

Des Pres, Terrence. *The Survivor: An Anatomy of Life in the Death Camps.* New York: Oxford UP, 1976.

Doneson, Judith E. "The Image Lingers: The Feminization of the Jew in *Schindler's List*." Loshitzky 140–52.

Ebert, Roger. "Spielberg Masters Subtlety in Film: *Schindler's List* Follows a Man's Trek to Heroism." *Oskar Schindler and His List: The Man, the Book, the Film, the Holocaust, and Its Survivors.* Ed. Thomas Fensch. Forest Dale, VT: Eriksson, 1995. 179–81.

Gross, John. "Hollywood and the Holocaust." *New York Review of Books* 3 February 1994: 14–16.

Horowitz, Sara R. "But Is It Good for the Jews? Spielberg's Aesthetics of Atrocity." Loshitzky 119–39.

Keneally, Thomas. *Schindler's Ark.* London: Hodder and Stoughton, 1982.

Lanzmann, Claude. "Why Spielberg Has Distorted the Truth." *Guardian Weekly* 3 April 1994: 14.

Lauter, Paul. *Canons and Contexts.* New York: Oxford UP, 1991.

Loshitzky, Yosefa, ed. *Spielberg's Holocaust: Critical Perspectives on Schindler's List.* Bloomington: Indiana UP, 1997.

Louvish, Simon. "Witness." *Sight and Sound* 4 (1994): 12–15.

Lyotard, Jean-François. *The Differend: Phrases in Dispute.* Trans. Georges Van Den Abbeele. Minneapolis: U of Minnesota P, 1988.

Nagorski, Andrew. "*Schindler's List* Hits Home." *Newsweek* 123 (14 March 1994): 77.

Novick, Peter. *The Holocaust in American Life.* Boston: Houghton Mifflin, 1999.

Nussbaum, Martha C. *Love's Knowledge: Essays on Philosophy and Literature.* New York: Oxford UP, 1990.

O'Hearn, Tim. "*Schindler's Ark* and *Schindler's List:* One for the Price of Two." *Commonwealth Novel in English* 5 (1992): 9–15.

Palowski, Franciszek. *The Making of Schindler's List: Behind the Scenes of an Epic Film.* Trans. Anna Ware and Robert G. Ware. Secaucus, NJ: Birch Lane, 1998.

Rafferty, Terrence. "A Man of Transactions." *New Yorker* 20 December 1993: 129–32.

Schindler, Emilie. *Where Light and Shadow Meet: A Memoir.* Trans. Dolores M. Koch. New York: Norton, 1996.

Schleier, Curt. "Steven Spielberg's New Direction." *International Jewish Monthly* 108 (1994): 8–14.

Shandler, Jeffrey. "Schindler's Discourse: America Discusses the Holocaust and Its Mediation, from NBC's Miniseries to Spielberg's Film." Loshitzky 153–68.

Spielberg, Steven, dir. *Schindler's List.* With Liam Neeson, Ben Kingsley, Ralph Fiennes, and Embeth Davidtz. Universal Pictures, 1993.

Stern, Kenneth S. *Holocaust Denial.* New York: American Jewish Committee, 1993.

Toole, David C. "Witnesses and Voyeurs: The Perils of Remembrance in *Orbit of Darkness* and *Schindler's List.*" *Soundings* 77 (1994): 271–93.

Vidal-Naquet, Pierre. *Assassins of Memory: Essays on the Denial of the Holocaust.* 1987. Trans. Jeffrey Mehlman. New York: Columbia UP, 1992.

Wiesel, Elie. "The Holocaust as Literary Inspiration." *Dimensions of the Holocaust: Lectures at Northwestern University.* By Elie Wiesel, Lucy S. Dawidowicz, Dorothy Rabinowitz, and Robert McAfee Brown. Evanston, IL: Northwestern UP, 1977. 4–19.

POETS OF TESTIMONY

C. K. Williams and Jacqueline Osherow as Proxy Witnesses of the Shoah

SUSAN GUBAR

ONE OF THE most frequently anthologized Holocaust poems in English elaborates upon a passage from *The Theory and Practice of Hell* by Eugen Kogon, a survivor of the Buchenwald concentration camp who used his training in sociology to write the book in 1945. That Anthony Hecht's "'More Light! More Light!'" glosses a survivor's testimony—isolating one passage, framing it, substantially revising it—illustrates the importance of factual references in documentary verse that implicitly heeds but ultimately rejects Theodor Adorno's injunction against the barbarism of writing poetry after Auschwitz.[1] The term "documentary verse" remains necessarily elastic, of course, for some contemporary writers reproduce the exact words of survivors, while many others edit, analyze, or partly create the European sources they invoke to ground their work in historical specificity. "The more narrowly we look into the perplexing lens of Auschwitz, the more painful will the perception be," Cynthia Ozick has explained, adding, "It is moral ease to slide from the particular to the abstract" (153). American authors of documentary verse about the Holocaust eschew moral ease by connecting poetic utterance decades after the Shoah with the particular suffering it inflicted on its individual victims. By testifying to the testimonials of the victims of calamity, poets deploying archival material serve as proxy witnesses.[2]

But if, for poet-witnesses of witnesses, documentary sources enable verse to guard against sliding into the moral ease of abstraction, what does such verse lend documentary material? The practices of poetry remove an event from the chronicles that preceded and followed it, facilitate meditation on its significance even when traditional devices for meaning making are baffled, and thereby wrest it for retention from the overwhelming flood of the past. In addition, verse can pry new insights out of history by retrieving arresting memories not yet assimilated into banal or clichéd reconstructions

in public memorials and popular forms. In other words, poets who exca-
vate eccentric or even trivial details from the calamity can deploy their own
struggle to understand so as to counter not only cultural amnesia but also
collective memories that lose their potency when they get recycled as pack-
aged commodities totalizing the Holocaust. As in much documentary verse,
the narrowness of the aesthetic lens in "'More Light! More Light!'" entails a
withholding of some circumstances, a fragmenting that paradoxically clarifies the moral significance of one of the disaster's many disasters, indicting
the traditions of Western civilization that make the poem possible but that
failed to prevent or perhaps even enabled the calamity twice remembered
(once by the witness, once again by the pondering poet). The humility with
which Hecht repeats a flagrantly *un*poetic incident in the Shoah refutes
facile theories about its causes and consequences, while generating an attentiveness to the inexplicable contortions and ellipses in eyewitness accounts
of trauma, thereby placing the poem in a tradition that constitutes a poetics
of anamnesis.

In its fourth through seventh stanzas, Hecht's poem condenses Kogon's
testimony about a group of prisoners on quarry detail in the spring of 1944
when an SS detail leader ordered a Polish man named Strzaska to bury alive
two Jews.[3] After the Pole refused, he was himself sentenced to their fate—
"He was ordered to change places with the Jews"—but then exhumed in the
last minute by Jews forced "To dig him out again and to get back in" the
ditch themselves. By repeating an eyewitness account (rather than inventing
a narrative of his own devising), Hecht acknowledges that personal testimonials rival imaginative work in their approach to the Shoah. Yet the dissonance between Hecht's formalism—his rhyming of "hole" and "Pole,"
his four-line stanzas with lines of five beats, his imagery of "no light"—and
Kogon's horrific narrative charges the documentary text with allegorical
resonance, in the process resisting mere transcription, as do Hecht's exci-
sions. Just as Kogon's Buchenwald becomes Hecht's more generic "German
wood," just as Kogon's Strzaska becomes a nameless Pole (as anonymous as
the two Jews in Hecht's poem), the SS man degenerates into a disembodied
Luger, glove, riding boot. In several places in his narrative, Kogon provides
explanations for the episode that are omitted or amended in Hecht's poem
to heighten the scene's enigmatic depravity. First, whereas Kogon supplies a
motivation for the Nazi command (exhaustion presumably made the Jews
worthless as workers), Hecht presents the abhorrent scenario as nothing
more than a whim. Second, after Kogon's Strzaska refuses to bury the Jews
alive, he lies down in one of several ditches because he is threatened by a

"pick handle," but in Hecht's poem no belaboring or physical threatening of the man seems to be necessary. Third, although Kogon explains that the Jews then submitted to the order to bury the Pole "in the hope of escaping the ghastly fate themselves," Hecht implies instead that all empathy had been destroyed in the Jews before the time of the poem and that they therefore resemble the living dead, even before they are interred alive.

Taken together, all of Hecht's revisions give the episode the hallucinogenic generality of an illogical fable that investigates the meaning of what Kogon faced, namely what differentiates torture before the Third Reich from the genocide of the Third Reich. Kogon's sentence, "The two Jews now had to lie down in the ditch, while Strzaska was ordered to cover them up," contains the same information as Hecht's "the order came / To dig him out again and to get back in." But the parallelism of this last line, with its repetition compulsion, emphasizes the sadistic game, the nonsensical taking of turns, imposed by "the order" of things on exchangeable beings devoid of any identity except that conferred by a typology that translates adjectival racial terms into nouns to dislodge personhood. Although Kogon describes many prisoners madly working so as not to attract attention to themselves, relieved to be ordered to dig up the buried men, and at least minimally palliated (like Strzaska and Kogon himself) by their own survival as witnesses, the crisis of Hecht's isolated trio contains no possibility of rescuing efforts or firsthand recounting—the poem's Pole is shot on top of the grave of the Jews—as if to dramatize Dori Laub's reflection on the Holocaust as a unique historical occurrence that "*produced no witnesses*" (Felman and Laub 80). Burial alive is Hecht's trope for the fate of the Jews not only because so many Jewish people were literally buried alive during the Holocaust, but also, as Shoshana Felman has explained, because the "essence of the Nazi scheme" was to make the Jews "essentially invisible" by confining them to hidden death camps, by diminishing their materiality through starvation, and by reducing their dead bodies to smoke and ashes (95). That the buried are alive, while the dying lie bleeding unburied: this misrule governs not the original prose but the poetic conclusion of "'More Light! More Light!'"— a title that repeatedly echoes throughout the account of the episode and is used to encapsulate it as well.

Hecht places quotation marks around his title to reiterate what are reputed to be the last words of Goethe, the revered sage who lived in Weimar, only a few miles from Buchenwald. But, of course, the exclamation could also be the final cry of the buried-alive Jews at the end of the poem or, for that matter, the last thoughts during the three hours it takes the shot Pole to have his vision put out. That at the end of the poem "No prayers or incense rose up" around the Pole's body—visited only by the "black soot" of "Ghosts from the ovens" (65)—serves to differentiate him from the Protestant martyrs with whom the poem begins, a frame that definitely moves beyond Kogon's testimony. The sixteenth-century English context that opens "'More Light! More Light!'" informs readers that torture of the innocent always existed, but that historically it occurred in a setting of religious persecution where suffering attests to the dignity, fidelity, courage, even transcendence of an individual soul calling out to his God, not to the utter senselessness of forced labor, starvation, mass murder:

> Composed in the Tower before his execution
> These moving verses, and being brought at that time
> Painfully to the stake, submitted, declaring thus:
> "I implore my God to witness that I have made no crime."

The first word of the poem marks the contrast between grotesque yet spiritually significant Protestant martyrdom in the Tower of London and the torment of the Shoah, for it signals an act of introspection in, for instance, the composing of a spiritual statement that will make the event meaningful for the martyr's followers and will thereby compose *him,* lend him some metaphysical recompense for his suffering.

Although "the death was horrible," those crucified or burned alive were nevertheless permitted a "pitiful dignity" as they "howled for the Kindly Light." After the rhyming of "dignity" with "tranquility," Hecht's abrupt shift to Kogon's episode juxtaposes, on the one hand, the meaningfulness of death within the "Kindly Light" of the Protestant martyrs' spirituality as well as within the rationality of the Enlightenment that Goethe's literary work denotes and, on the other hand, the absence of any ethical illumination in the Holocaust. Indeed, motivated by a quest for knowledge, Goethe's Faust trades salvation for wisdom in a swap that seems far more reasonable than the pointlessness of the Nazi pact with the devil documented in Kogon's *Theory and Practice of Hell.* Did Hecht know that a poem by Goethe about the beauty of death by fire hung over some of the ovens?[4] Both the repentance of Goethe's Faust and the truth telling of the Protestant martyrs have been abrogated by a text implicitly about the bankruptcy of traditional paradigms for comprehending evil and suffering. Murdered, not martyred, the Pole in Hecht's parable undergoes two deaths—what Alvin Rosenfeld calls "the double dying" of the Shoah: first when he becomes nothing but the instrument of the Nazi instrument, when he understands himself to have been robbed (like the Jews) of any moral agency, and the light dies in "the blue Polish eye"; second when he is physically killed.[5]

Both in his reliance on factual commentary and in his manipulation of it, Hecht typifies a group of writers who use testimonials in verse to emphasize the dependency of poetic articulation after the Shoah on the personal witnessing of the survivors. Many American poets (one thinks especially of Charles Reznikoff in *Holocaust,* but also of Barbara Helfgott Hyett in *In Evidence* and Julie Heifetz in *Oral History and the Holocaust*) produced reports more journalistic than Hecht's by editing legal depositions or by recording interviews with soldiers and survivors. Their affidavits attempt to bring verisimilitude to what no one wanted to believe at the time, to what inspired in so many Americans during and after the war—even though they had been given a substantial amount of eyewitness information on the atrocities—an "overwhelming incredulity" and "skepticism" about an "enormity" that seemed more like a "wild nightmarish imagining" or mere "propaganda" than an actual event (Lipstadt 272–73). Perhaps for this reason, the literary framing of testimonials often paradoxically questions and simultaneously stresses the efficacy of documentary evidence as a mechanism for conveying literal truth and fostering empathy. What poetic forms achieve over unadulterated documentation (even in work that most carefully reiterates the testimonial upon which it draws) is the charging of words with their utmost meaning, even as verse configurations foreground the poet's reliance on (and at times incomplete understanding of) such testimonial.[6] The shortness of verse; its deliberate placement of words in visual lines that do not necessarily accord with syntactic breaks; the use of rhythm or rhyme; the compression of a plethora of details into fewer and therefore more galvanized terms and images; the reaching for metaphorical comparisons, albeit inadequate ones; the suppression of logical, narrative links: these allow creative writers to take factual material often dubbed "nightmarish imagining" or "propaganda" and use the imagination to make it more palpably real and yet also paradoxically more palpably constructed in place of the real. By stressing their dependency upon recalcitrantly alien eyewitness accounts, documentary poets do not set out to improve their sources, but instead return readers to such testimonies, even as their poems make a case for a rehumanizing verse that resists the barbarism of Auschwitz.

Foregoing unmediated reportage, quite a few contemporary poets swerve from accurate transcriptions of depositions to accentuate what is implicit in "'More Light! More Light!'"—namely an acknowledgment that artistic representations of the world described in the survivors' words inescapably construct versions of it.[7] At some remove geographically and temporally from the European sources they deploy, C. K. Williams and Jacqueline Osherow draw upon written and verbal material as occasions for verse speculations about the ethical and psychological repercussions of the Shoah. In the process, these two writers stress the opacity of presumably factual accounts, the blurring of the line between analysis or recollection and fact, and the gender dynamics at work in their interpretive efforts as well as the bleak pointlessness of such speculations, given the suffering of Europe's Jews and the fracturing of those moral imperatives that made the most orthodox and the most secular of its populace a people. Scrupulously attentive to the specificity of particular and often eccentric experiences, Williams and Osherow want documentary verse to continue to do the work of other testimonial forms that, in the words of Geoffrey Hartman, "dispel the anonymity of victimage" (325). At the same time, however, they frame their evidence (much as Hecht did) with literary and philosophical allusions as well as formal techniques that constitute their active intellectual engagement with it. In their proxy witnessing, Williams and Osherow participate in a poetics of anamnesis. Anamnesis: a calling to mind; a concentrating on a life before this life; in the context of documentary verse, a reflection on the lives of victims and survivors before the time of witnessing, of the author's composing of the poem, and of the reader's confrontation with it. Since generations of Americans born during or after the Holocaust cannot remember what we never knew, authors dedicated to a poetics of anamnesis ask us *not to forget* what we can neither recall nor fully comprehend.

Two quite different but equally ambitious poems—C. K. Williams's "Spit" and Jacqueline Osherow's "Conversations with Survivors"—focus on maverick episodes in order to incarnate the shock of criminal violence emerging as an everyday occurrence in the lives of Jewish men and women during the calamity. Williams's abstract theological speculations about the fate of God within the crisis of the Shoah contrast strikingly with Osherow's personal musings on her friendship with a survivor of Auschwitz, a divergence that underscores how gender can play a role in proxy witnessing. "Spit" deploys biblical exegesis and philosophical modes of inquiry rooted in an overwhelmingly male intellectual history, whereas "Conversations with Survivors" puts on display the psychological intimacy and specificity of detail often labeled emotive and thus traditionally feminine.[8] With studied detachment, Williams reacts to his reading about secular and religious authorities in the Holocaust, whereas Osherow expresses an infectious affection fostered by personal interactions with a seamstress who established a new life as a wife and mother in the United States. Yet what in another context Saul Friedlander called the "total dissonance between the apocalypse that was and the normality that is" (*Memory* 51) makes the works of both Williams and Osherow eerily commemorative. Not simply documentary, "Spit" and "Conversations with Survivors" accentuate their authors' inconclusive efforts to grapple with the meaning of experiences definitively not their own, events endured by victims and survivors hindered by the catastrophe from testifying directly themselves and therefore urgently ratifying the proxy witnessing of successors.

C. K. Williams attributes his epigraph—". . . then the son of the 'superior race' began to spit into the Rabbi's mouth so that the Rabbi could continue to spit on the Torah . . ." (48)—to *The Black Book.* One of several postwar books that together comprise a virtual *Black Book* genre in the 1940s authenticates as documentary fact an aberrant form humiliation took during the Shoah, which Williams records in his disturbing poem. The approach of "Spit" to the complex subject of Nazi atrocities gains legitimacy through Williams's willingness to confront the difficulty of comprehending the perverse account he has perused, a quandary announced by his opening admission: "After this much time, it's still impossible." Then the writer attempts to imagine the impossible scene recounted in *The Black Book,* but in a language of "probablys" that underscores his distance from the temporal and geographical place inhabited by one Rabbi in a torn overcoat, clutched by a uniformed SS man, next to a Torah with its "letters blurring under the blended phlegm." The incident of the SS man spitting in the Rabbi's mouth so that the Rabbi can continue to spit on the Torah exemplifies reports of religious leaders made to dance and sing before being shot or tortured, Torahs and prayer shawls defiled, worshipers herded into synagogues first locked and then set ablaze: these deeds would be accompanied by Nazi declarations that "We are fighting against you and against your God! Death to all of you! Let your God show whether he can help you!" (Apenszlak 227).[9]

Just as aware as his readers of how "many years" have intervened since the occurrence of the event recounted in *The Black Book* and wondering "what is there to say" about it, Williams nevertheless hazards a closer glance at the lips of the two men brushing, the "eyelashes of both of them / shyly fluttering." While soldiers impatiently stand by, wanting to "Get it over with," the poet (like the SS man) lingers:

> . . . back there the lips of the Rabbi and the other would have brushed
> and if time had stopped you would have thought they were lovers,
> so lightly kissing, the sharp, luger hand over the dear chin,
> the eyes furled slightly and then when it started again the eyelashes of
>   both of them
> shyly fluttering as wonderfully as the pulse of a baby. (48)

Yet the audacity of words such as "lovers," "dear," "shyly fluttering," and "wonderfully" immediately plummets Williams into the glum concession, "Maybe we don't have to speak of it at all, it's still the same." In this first section of "Spit," the epigraph from *The Black Book* is dramatized, but to what end? Although obviously no intercession can change the course of the history that he is recounting, Williams investigates its meaning because, as he puts it in another poem about torture, "There will always be the victim; trembling, fainting, fearful, abducted, bound," and "there will always be the order, and the brutes, thugs, reptiles, scum, to carry out the order" ("Interrogation II" 269).

Yet what order would the SS officer be following? The particular form that Jew hatred takes in "Spit" stresses its primitive irrationality, suggesting that the Nazi commitment to genocide cannot be explained by recourse to modern economic or political motivations. For how is the Third Reich strengthened or protected during a debilitating war by the costly, time-consuming death industry of the concentration camps or, in this particular case, by an officer spitting in a Rabbi's mouth? Williams also abjures the idea that the Final Solution can be blamed on an authority-bound personality blindly following bureaucratic orders. Instead, he presents the bizarre doubling of Nazi, "the son of the 'superior race,'" and Jew, the Rabbi of the chosen people, to establish Nazism as a religion (or anti-religion) devoted to the higher power of a state that joins its adherents emotionally to each other and to the work of repairing a flawed world; a sect whose communal rites link duty to a greater good that can only be brought into being through the annihilation of a competing, false faith.[10] Instead of the efficient murder of the Jews, their forced compliance in defiling their own sacred symbols and their participation in self-pollution appear to be the point. Antithetical belief systems, Nazism and Judaism, enter the poem through the physical union of the SS man and the Rabbi, which hints either at homosexual desire or at its perversion into a pleasure at degradation that absorbs the SS man "obsessed with perfect humiliation."[11]

The Nazi, intoxicated with the power he wields over his victim and with the physical proximity such power admits, flaunts an amorous intimacy with his prey: "you would have thought they were lovers." Even the metaphor that likens fluttering eyelashes to "the pulse of a baby" connects the act of torment with lovemaking, just as spit glues the SS man to the Rabbi, wedding them face to face in what looks like a kiss.[12] However, given the "stained beard" clutched by "the sharp, luger hand," Williams's homosocial scene hardly corresponds to the sort of comradely embrace that often figures in poems and stories about *Blutbrüderschaft,* for instance, between boyish soldiers during World War I.[13] If what in a more innocent age John Addington Symonds called "the gospel of comradeship" later animated "the manly love" of fascism (3:485), Williams intimates that its spin-off constitutes a sadistic drama of dominance between the phallicized SS man "with his stiff hair and his uniform" and the feminized Jew with his "parched mouth" and "torn overcoat." Replete with a Bible, "Spit"'s marriage of heaven and hell, of sacred victim and civic tormentor, occurs inside a moment dedicated to the polluting of the Hebrew Bible. An ejaculation that looks like a kiss but functions as enforced oral sex pays the Jewish Judas back to punish him for his murder of God's son, to disgrace the Jewish people for their stubborn adherence to Mosaic Law, thus bringing to mind the loathing of Jews propagated by Paul's *Epistle to the Romans* (9–12), although the doubling ironically places the Nazi in the role of Judas, the Rabbi in the part of the Rabbi.

The widespread belief among Christians that Jewish people handed over the Messiah to torment and death meant, as George Steiner has explained, that "Judaism eradicated from within itself not only the act of divine election, the 'chosenness' by and for God's unique purpose; it tore up from within its own flesh and spirit *the very right to hope*" (58). In addition, by refusing to recognize Jesus as the Messiah, "the Jews have postponed the day of man's salvation, the apocalyptic enfranchisement of suffering humanity and the eternal justice and peace which are to attend the Second Coming" (58). Several repercussions from these anti-Semitic lines of reasoning are dramatized in the SS man's spitting so the Rabbi can expectorate on the Torah. First, the pollution of the book that represents the Jewish faith, the desecration of the Torah, signifies the discrediting of Jewish refusal to welcome the Messiah as God's son and thereby dramatizes contempt for a theological monotheism now identified with what Steiner calls "sterility and despair." Second, by using the Jewish mouth as a receptacle for waste, the SS man eliminates Jews from the human community and, by so doing, brings one degree closer the promised salvation that will free humankind from the nightmare of history. Yet how can the polluting Nazi not himself be corrupted by physical contact with the man designated a pariah? Since, ironically, the SS man plays the part of Judas treacherously kissing the holy Rabbi, does the Nazi's impassioned embrace attest to an admission of his own guilty desire for the Jew, for the Torah? That Paul, the author of *Epistle to the Romans,* defined himself as "an Israelite, a descendant of Abraham" (11:1), frames his convoluted, conflicted response to the Jews: "As regards the gospel they are enemies of God, for your sake; but as regards election they are beloved for the sake of their forefathers" (11:28–29). In any case, the central event in "Spit" seems "in excess of our frames of reference," to use the words Shoshana Felman employs to describe Holocaust testimony (5). Given the tension between a Nazi atavism charged with ancient resentments and the industry of death the fascists so efficiently manufactured out of decidedly modern technologies, the reader's mind *cannot* settle into understanding.

As the poem progresses, the perversity that occurred during the Holocaust no longer appears "out" or "over" there, but instead internalized, "twisting and hardening us." Despite his hesitations, the conclusion of Williams's first section turns toward a consideration of "every conceivable torment" that "we make of God," and why "we're almost ashamed to use" these "as metaphors for what goes on in us." However, the poet asserts, "we do anyway"; that is, we do utilize what happened in the war as an analogy for our own capacity for harming and being harmed. As if exonerating Sylvia Plath from charges that she profaned the Shoah by exploiting its images as symbols for her own psychic terrain, Williams adopts *The Black Book*'s account to illuminate the "terror and hatred" within all of us when facing the Otherness of another person. Although some readers will refuse to concur with the poet here, the SS man and the Rabbi locked in his embrace have something to do with "love," something to do with "battle," for "we watch ourselves in love / become maddened with pride and incompletion." When God and our souls turn against us, Williams explains, "there is so much terror and hatred" that we try to make the Other "defile his own meaning" in our "struggle to survive each other" (49). The seduction of Nazism, according to Williams, is related to a narcissistic fantasy of striving to tack mortality itself onto the Other so as to assert one's own omnipotence.[14] Whereas Plath's identification with the Jew led her to analyze the lure of a feminized masochism, Williams explores the disturbingly amorous SS man to consider the battle for preeminence he associates with masculinism and sadism.

But, in the second and concluding stanza of "Spit," Williams swerves from such sexual psychologizing, returning to the theological issues he had initially addressed by flatly introducing "another," seemingly quite different "legend" about Moses choosing a live coal over a diamond and popping the red ember into his mouth "so for the rest of his life he was tongue-tied and Aaron had to speak for him." In the third volume of *Midrash Rabbah, Exodus,* the tale is explained. Although Pharaoh used "to kiss and hug" Moses, the child's playing with Pharaoh's crown created suspicion and fear among the "magicians of Egypt," some of whom wanted "to slay him and others to burn him," but Jethro argued that the "boy has no sense" and should be tested (33). After a gold vessel and a live coal were placed before Moses, the angel Gabriel pushed the child's hand from the gold "so it seized the coal, and he thrust his hand with the live coal into his mouth, so that his tongue was burnt, with the result that he became slow of speech and of tongue" (34). In the Holocaust context, of course, not only the wish to slay and burn Moses but also the catch-22 of the "test"—either he burns himself or he is murdered—resonate with the persecution of the Jews of Europe. In the framework of the poem's opening, the kiss of Pharaoh, who becomes anxious that the child will displace him, replicates the SS man's embrace, establishing genocide in a long history of hostility against Jews. To be guarded by God's guardians against such violence means being marked in a peculiarly painful way by the anguish of tongue-tied utterance.

The scarred tongue of Moses—"it must have been like a thick embryo slowly coming alive, butting itself against the inner sides of his teeth and cheeks"—recalls the desecrated mouth of the parched Rabbi carrying the weight of the SS man's spit. That God burned in the bush and Moses in the mouth made them "cleave together," according to Williams, whose God lives in the "caves of the body, the gut cave, the speech cave." Although the SS man believes he is making the Rabbi foul the word of God, the SS man himself performs that task by sullying the Rabbi's mouth, where God resides. What Williams's conclusion foresees is the devolution of God into a slobbering, howling force, horrified and diminished by the senseless cruelty of humankind. How could Moses not know

> that all of us were on fire and that every word we said
>   would burn forever,
> in pain, unquenchably, and that God knew it, too, and would say
>   nothing Himself ever again beyond this,
> ever, but would only live in the flesh that we use like firewood,
> in all the caves of the body, the gut cave, the speech cave:
> He would slobber and howl like something just barely a man that beats
>   itself again and again onto the dark,

moist walls away from the light, away from whatever would be light for
this last eternity.
"Now therefore go," He said, "and I will be with thy mouth."

Like Paul Celan, Williams writes angrily about and against the nonspeaking
of God in the midst of Jewish suffering, not exactly a silence, according to
Williams, but a blaring gibberish that undermines the redemptive potential of poetic speech after Auschwitz. Moses' wounded tongue, the Rabbi's
dry mouth, the SS man's kiss, the turns of the poem itself: did the Shoah
occur because of our garbled, maimed expression of whatever possibility
God stood for? If we are all made in God's image, if the Rabbi and the SS
man wear the human countenance divine, God has been reduced by the
Holocaust to a dribbling, bawling replicant of what humanity has degener-
ated into.[15]

More audaciously still, the final line of "Spit" also asks, how could even
a slobbering, howling God—a spirit whose impotent immanence in the
physical world registers human pain and diminishment—take up residence
in the spiteful SS man's mouth? Perhaps the immanence of Divinity is precisely what remains at issue in "Spit," for the Torah insists through Moses'
commandments on the central importance not of the Second Coming, not
of a heavenly afterlife, but of human righteousness within the world in its
imperfect state. Perhaps the SS man seeking to defile the Rabbi in what
looks like a kiss finds himself locked in a love-hate struggle with Jews not as
God-killers but as God-creators.[16] Does the Mosaic Law of the Torah ask too
much so that its worshipers had to be destroyed to deny the validity of their
God's rigorous commandments? Repeating a sample of Hitler's table talk
—"The Jews invented conscience"—Steiner asks, "for this crime, what forgiveness?" (59). Moses' five books make God inseparable from each human
being's duty to act justly in the here and now of daily life: maybe this is
what the SS man so fears, hates, and passionately embraces in the Rabbi
and his creed.[17] Or, perhaps the transcendence of Divinity is precisely what
remains at issue in "Spit." Jewish monotheism, according to Maurice Blanchot, presents speech as the site where human beings "hold themselves in
relation with what excludes all relation: the infinitely Distant, the absolutely
Foreign" (127–28); language does not abolish distance from the Otherness
of Divinity but instead maintains it, "preserved in its purity by the rigor of
the speech that upholds the absoluteness of difference" (128). The SS man
who would spit on the Rabbi's mouth and on Moses' words metamorphoses
into a drooling, bellowing God—spit is conflated with spirit to suggest how

the proponents of National Socialism sought to annihilate with their own chosenness a faith based on the irreducible relation of human speech to the "absolutely Foreign." The SS man does not decimate but instead expresses God perversely, twisted in the chambers of his own flesh. Although the poem refrains from explaining why, what God has become in our embodied mouths is a sign of our impotent incapacity to articulate righteousness or reside with "the absoluteness of difference."

Like Williams, but in a form and lexicon quite different from his, Jacqueline Osherow turns her attention toward people unexpectedly caught up in a disaster never fully comprehended then or now. Although Williams's preoccupation with the long line of free verse and the theological issues that accrue from his reading differs from her fascination with stanzas of iambic pentameter and the domestic details of private conversations, although he concentrates on perpetrators and victims while she focuses on survivors, Osherow also wants to attend to exactly those memories that have not found their way into Holocaust museums and memorials so as to push against the reductive ways the Shoah has been remembered. Since, as Andreas Huyssen has observed, "the attempt to counteract allegedly frivolous trivializations such as the television series *Holocaust* by serious museal and monumental representations may just once again freeze memory in ritualistic images and discourses" (256), one potential antidote to the freezing of memory is close scrutiny of those accidental details that have gone thus far unnoted. For Osherow, these derive from "conversations with survivors" (the title of her volume) whose stories in their specificity and novelty jar us into a new awareness of what common people endured when the unthinkable occurred within an otherwise ordinary life.

The prizewinning title poem of Osherow's volume epitomizes her effort to chronicle the impact made upon her by the dialogues she sustained with a woman named Fany Hochmanova Brown, who had unpredictably fashioned hats at Auschwitz (out of whatever SS women brought her) and then manufactured cloth at a textile factory to which she had been transported (located in an ancestral mansion owned by one Baron Macholt). The hats are made with "Bijoux, dangling cherries, nesting birds / Whatever they'd picked over from the piles / left vacant just outside each crematorium" (22), and along with what she receives from doing the makeup and hair of her client-guards, she is paid with cigarettes that garner more than gold on the black market, as Fany learns "to *organize*." While Sam, who eventually would become her second husband, trades jewels (that he finds in the lining of the clothing he delouses) for more prized cabbages, she manages

> To find the stray undamaged seconds at Auschwitz
> And piece them into minutes, hours, days,
> Four decades in America, three sons,
> Two side-by-side refrigerators (22–23)

before she dies in a hospital. As the pun on "seconds" hints—both second-hand things and seconds of time—Fany's gift is stitching together a life despite the "hopeless odds" (23) of Hitler, of cancer.

Eschewing printed sources, Osherow captures Fany recalling her past in a present composed of pill and potion taking, visits to the hospital, betting in Atlantic City, and winning the Pennsylvania lottery when Sam's use of the number tattooed on her arm and the "lucky error" of a cashier who could not understand his Yiddish accent earn him more than a thousand dollars. Hats, cigarettes, jewels hidden in lined coats, cabbages, pills, potions, blood transfusions, gaming tables, lotteries—all the paraphernalia of currency and exchange at the beginning of this poem bespeak Fany's struggle to survive. She herself had been one such commodity "After Ray Brown, maker of banana splits / At an ice-cream parlor in Atlantic City," had paid her passage from Europe "And five hundred dollars to the government / To send her back in case they didn't marry" (24). But by that time she had herself become the wearer of a hat, a tartan tam-o'-shanter, as well as an expert in what Elizabeth Bishop calls "the natural madness of the hatter"; Bishop's allusion to Lewis Carroll's Mad Hatter in "Exchanging Hats" seems eminently suited to the antic inventiveness with which Osherow's concentration camp milliner faces adversity.

Unlike her sister Dora, Fany had a talent for "making do at Auschwitz," perhaps because she had been the wildest Jewish girl in her Slovak town. Maybe this extraordinary vitality, coupled with her attentiveness to physical details, is what adds such vibrancy to her italicized descriptions of labor in the camp—"*Making big rocks into smaller rocks*"—or to the miraculous train ride—sitting in a passenger train "*like people*"—when she was sent to the textile factory of Emmerich Macholt:

> Each station stop was like a visitation:
> *The women on the platforms wearing suits,*
> *With lipstick on, with suitcases and hats,*
> *I remember this like it was something wonderful.* (25)

Instead of registering horror at the normal life adjacent to the nightmare of the camps, Fany revels in rosebuds on a veil across a woman's forehead. Certainly her pragmatic optimism echoes Sam's when he

breaks in to praise the crematoria.
Before that they would make them dig a ditch
And throw them in, pour on kerosene
And light a match" (24)

though the slippage in his "*them*" (prisoners) and "*them*" (corpses) belies his buoyancy. It is evident, too, when an eerily empty factory informs the other girls at Emmerich Macholt that the war is over, and they proceed to go "crazy" while Fany stays behind cutting cloth for the "*schmates*" she would wear on her way out of Europe.

However, at this point in the narrative, the poet begins to equivocate about the relationship between her own stories and those of Fany. First, we are told in splendid anarchic detail about the looting and smashing in which the factory girls engaged while Fany stayed behind sewing:

> They hurled soup tureens at huge ancestral portraits,
> Plates, cups, teapots, creamers, gravy boats—
> An eighteenth-century trove of heirloom Meissen—
> Shattered on its maiden voyage in air.
> Kitchen knives attacked brocaded sofas,
> Embroidered footstools, bedsheets, goose-down quilts,
> Dinner jackets, evening gowns, fur coats,
> Belgian lace-trimmed hats on porcelain dolls.
> Whole rooms were lost in feathers, shards and tatters
> And others disappeared when gilt-edged pages
> Leapt from books to kindle piles of furniture
> And warm the cheering, gaunt, exhausted girls. (25–26)

The Nazis' preservation of delicate porcelain, ancestral paintings, ornate furniture, expensive toys, and libraries amid the trashing of human beings results in the girls "smashing glass" in a retaliatory mini-Kristallnacht and book burning that Fany did not witness. So evocative of the battle scenes in Pope's *Rape of the Lock,* the piling up of costly plunder turned into a hodge-podge of debris, like the piling up of nouns, issues in the perfect iambic pentameter of the last line, as the mock epic form itself makes a mockery of the heroic ideologies, pageants, and postures of German fascism.

"Fany tells me she was not among them"; however, Osherow chronicles the scene of disorder with obvious formal delight. Then, the poet wonders how Fany could possibly remember seeing a pair of Chinese vases crushed on the marble stairs from the vantage of her window. Next, Osherow explains, Fany "doesn't say she didn't join the others" when they hoisted bolts of fabric and flung them off the roof, but "Fany never actually described it," though the poet does:

Paisleys, tartans, pinstripes, spangles, flowers
Spreading out like momentary tablecloths
For elusive rows of victory-banquet tables
Frantically awaiting phantom guests. (26)

Yet Osherow subsequently admits, "It was probably the dull, gray twill of Nazi / Uniforms or stripes for prisoners." Though she could ask Fany's sister, she refrains because "I don't like the facts she tells me" (26). In a curious way, only at this point in the poem, when the poet considers going to a source like Dora to piece together the scenes of Fany's final illness, does it seem as if Fany may really be dead. Exceptionally uncanny, the simultaneous aliveness and deadness of Fany that Osherow achieves are heightened by a remembrance of a period when Fany called Sam and Dora to the hospital because she was convinced she was dead—"Death and being alive were just the same!" (27)—until later she laughs over a dream so vivid she had dragged them out at dawn. The same aliveness and deadness accrue to Vivien Leigh, the actress Fany liked to think she resembled, or to the reels of her life Osherow wants to believe Fany saw on the television screen, "Less unendurable from such a distance" (28). Even at her burial, when the Rabbi describes "how for years he'd lose his place / In his Rosh Hashanah or Yom Kippur sermon / When he caught sight of Fany, dressed to kill" (28), she seems more animate than her mourners.

In the last two pages, where Osherow begins to explore what it means to be a poet engaged in conversations with survivors, she appreciates Fany's desire to have a scribe, her "Saying *I could not forget this name*" but meaning "*I* should not forget it" (29), Fany's promise to tell all the facts she had never told the ghostwriter of a magazine story about her "Miracle Marriage." Understandably resistant to being turned into Fany's secretary, Osherow confronts precisely the self-effacement that the documentary tradition involves:

Not that I set out to be a ghostwriter.
I meant to be a poet, make connections;
All along I've had an end in mind
With Fany floating off the hospital roof
On a bolt of cloth that fleetingly bears wings. (29)

But facts intervene and Osherow must submit to them: "Fany was so sick" . . . "There's nothing I can do; facts are facts" . . . "And even if they aren't facts, I'm helpless / Against a woman . . . Who tells about a pair of man-sized vases, / Some fabric sailing off a roof, a train—" (29). Besides,

> What does it matter that she leaves things out?
> Who is it that doesn't leave things out?
> even I, writing now, haven't got the heart
> Not to leave out some of what I know. (29)

The omissions of Fany and the poet hardly qualify but instead foster affection, as Osherow does not conclude by winging her ghostly instructor away on bolts of fabric within a Chagallean landscape of resurrection because the incursion of the apocalyptic into the ordinary necessitates a new aesthetic:

> I'd rather marvel at you, Fany,
> In the kitchen, spelling MACHOLT, drinking tea,
> Defining *organize* as making hats.
> What I need is a revised mythology,
> A self-sufficient hybrid of Eurydice
> Who earns her own departure from the underworld
> Without the risk of lovers looking back. (29–30)

The mythology that Osherow finds at the end of the poem, when she dramatizes Fany's return to her hometown, is a trope of restitution not of the youth of which Fany was robbed, not of the suffering that she bore, not of the person she had been before the disaster struck or the person she might have become if it had not, but simply of those "best things" she had so providently packed away and placed with her most prized customer back in the Slovak town, the "*schmates*" of her youth. Instead of floating Fany off the hospital roof on a bolt of winged cloth, Osherow's last line depicts this former customer and friend returning from upstairs with the bat-winged jacket and scoop-necked blouse Fany had stored away: "To hand your ghost a chest of your best things" (30). The rhythms of Shakespeare's most beautiful love sonnets, of Pope's exquisitely balanced heroic couplets, do not recount the linear narrative of Fany's life so much as they capture moments of being, even (as at the end) when she has been reduced by history to a ghost of her own prior self. But if Fany was reduced to a ghost after the war when she was physically alive, she becomes animate after her death in Osherow's verse. In her poetic self-definition—a ghostwriter for this particular ghost—Osherow provides a paradigm for proxy witnessing of the Holocaust.[18] Because the apparition of a past robbed of its potentialities has haunted second-generation artists of the Holocaust, it has led them to devise methods to honor the spectral presence of its victims. By emphasizing how very little we can know about the subjectivity of their deceased subjects, American poets dedicated to a poetics of anamnesis simultaneously evade the charges of appropriation or plagiarism that have plagued their novelistic counterparts and question the mimetic as well as the expressive potency of art after Auschwitz, turning it toward a more modest, more historical undertaking[19]: neither the mirror nor the lamp can resurrect the dead or redeem the disaster.

In "Conversations with Survivors," Fany's visceral delight in beauty—the charm of a purplish gray umbrella, a turquoise turban, a velvet collar—makes her a model for the poet who nevertheless braves the consequences of her departure from the traditional aesthetic governing the lyric. As Osherow pays her respects in a verse "Letter to Rainer Maria Rilke," therefore, she clarifies her misgivings about the consummate lyricism he exemplifies: "The enormous thing that now divides us," she explains, is "so much larger that / To name it is to break the lyric's rules. / If I write *history*, will you stop reading?" (5). Convinced that she must take into poetic account the unpoetic history that "has had its way with us," Osherow counterpoints Fany's efforts to cling to the finery of femininity with Nazi determination to reduce Jews to "*schmates*" and "*stuck*."[20] Whereas starvation, tattooing, enforced shaving, even (paradoxically) nudity took away the marks of gender (hair, beards, breasts, names, menstruation, pregnancies, lactation disappeared, as skeletal bodies took on the neutered fragility of a childlike decrepitude), Fany's costumes when she is "dressed to kill" constitute precisely the flimsy yet compelling effort to maintain humanity that Osherow embraces as the source of her inspiration. As in "Spit," where the patrilineal genealogy Williams traces from the Rabbi back through Jesus to Moses confers a masculine authority quite distinct from the fetishized masculinism of Nazi ideology, Osherow looks upon Fany's ferociously feminine arts and crafts as a regendering process opposed to the dehumanization of anti-Semitism.

If Osherow as a ghostwriter supplies one resonant figure for proxy witnessing, Williams uses his fable of the "tongue-tied" Moses, his howling God, and the Rabbi with his spitting "parched mouth" to furnish another prototype that links the stammering negations, foreignisms, jolting breaks, admissions of failure, and repetitions of verbal art after Auschwitz to prophecy. Just as the unclean lips of Isaiah, the demurrals of Jeremiah, and the mutism of Ezekiel bespeak their defeated efforts to communicate what in its defiance of ordinary understanding retains a sublime "unattainability," the Holocaust poet expresses not only the wish to be infused but also the anxiety of being inundated by the Otherness of the dead as well as the incomprehensibility of the Final Solution.[21] Drawing upon documentary materials that call attention to the impossibility of creative invention, the incorporated testimonies of victims and survivors in verse composed in the English language can neither be thoroughly internalized (ingested) nor abjured (expectorated). This prophetic "impass" (66), which Herbert Marks links in the biblical tradition to Moses' efforts "to renounce his own prerogative in favor of an otherness he is still tempted to disavow" (72), informs verse about the Shoah that swerves from the documentary to convey the powerful resonances of testimony, to derive multiple meanings from it even when the difficulty of conveyance itself reflects its authors' ambivalence over a wish to address the material and a terror of misconstruing or, worse yet, blunting its meaning. Both the "ghostwriter" and the "tongue-tied," spitting prophet address the perplexing gaps between then and now, there and here, that attend the poetics of anamnesis.

Conspicuously dissimilar in their engendering of proxy testimony, Williams and Osherow stretch the poetic enterprise, goaded by the need to uncover events neither aesthetic nor histrionic and thus absent from literature as well as from Holocaust textbooks and museum displays. To Rilke, Osherow announces that "for those of us / Who, just like you, would rather speak of angels / There's a lasting streak of ash upon the tongue" (5–6). According to Williams, too, an ashy past waits "to receive us," accessible "not by imagination's nets, / but by the virtue of its being, simply being, waiting patiently for us like any other unattended, / any other hardly anticipated or not even anticipated—as much as any other fact rolling in . . ." (139; Williams's ellipses). From Gerald Stern in "The War against the Jews" to W. S. Merwin in "The Dachau Shoe" and Jane Shore in "Holocaust Museum," from John Berryman in three poems entitled "from *The Black Book*" to Denise Levertov, Michael Hamburger, and Jorie Graham in works about postwar Nazi trials, lyricists who allude to archival and scholarly material on the Holocaust deploy the partiality of the particular to protest against universalizing rhetoric.[22] In some of the more successful of these texts, writers sheer away from objects (like mounds of shoes, shorn hair, confiscated luggage, eyeglasses, extracted teeth) frequently exhibited in museums and from historically central events (like the Eichmann trial), focusing instead on quirky and seemingly odd data about people not accorded any public space. In doing so, these writers counter society's collective memory of the Holocaust, its public reconstructions of the past, and thereby question the idea of any transcendent or coherent memory. Renouncing the possibility of attaining a definitive, all-encompassing interpretation of an event as devastating as the Shoah, such proxy witnesses highlight anomalous experiences that in their very unexpectedness put the lie to any deceptive sense that the totality of the Holocaust can be captured.[23] A "clownish madness and sadness" accrues to documentary details that impart an uncertain solidity to what is reported.

Etty Hillesum's letter from Westerbork camp in Holland, dated 2 September 1943, describes as "clownish madness and sadness" scenes related to a revue that was "taking over the whole camp." Although inmates on duty had no overalls, everyone sewed overalls "with little puffed sleeves" for the dancers in the "overall ballet" until, that is, they were due to leave on the last transport. Saul Friedlander begins his introduction to a collection of essays entitled *Probing the Limits of Representation* with this excerpt and concludes with a speculation that seems pertinent to it and to the volume's title:

> Documentary material itself often carries the story of minute incidents which seem to escape the overwhelming dimension of the overall catastrophe but which nonetheless express the excess that cannot yet be put into phrases or, differently stated, that leaves an extraordinary uncertainty in the reader's mind, notwithstanding the ultimate significance and total "concreteness" of what is being reported. (20)

Since the detachment upon which reportorial venues depend had been so thoroughly put into question by the Nazis' manipulation of even the most realistic of media, a number of poets who investigate documentary sources abdicate the pretense of objectivity by emphasizing their struggle to apprehend exactly the "minute incidents" that "express the excess" Friedlander analyzes.

To break the lyric's rules, not with personal testimony but by recollecting a concrete, highly individualized past not experienced firsthand, Williams and Osherow formulate a poetics of anamnesis that remains in thrall of what Williams seeks to recover:

> Not "history" but scent, sound, sight, the sensual fact, the beings and
>   the doings, the heroes,
> unmediated now, the holy and the horrid, to be worked across not like a
>   wistful map, but land. ("The Past" 139)

More tentative, though just as astonishingly moving in her hesitations, Osherow poses a grammatically inconclusive set of questions that describes the anxieties attendant upon a linguistic excavation studiously willing to accept its liabilities, namely the possibility that proxy witnessing cannot possibly produce what one would ordinarily consider a poem:

If we do not find our way is it a poem?
If we not only do not make sense
But we also don't make beauty in the bargain,
So absorbed in excavating our details
That we momentarily forget our purposes
And then don't dare to make one alteration
For fear that we'll obliterate our lives?

("Above the Casa del Popolo" 58)

The ambiguous last pronoun here hints that the lives of the dead emanate the alterity of biographical subjects who have nevertheless been embraced as figures of the poets' own genealogies. Against the authoritative as well as the authoritarian uses to which rhetorically ambitious writing had been put by cultural institutions that either produced or did not derail the growth of fascism in Europe, an American writing practice composed of undigested and indigestible facts, inexplicable incidences, decidedly tentative speculations, and admitted omissions refuses to provide aesthetic recompense or explanatory interpretations for the brutality of the Shoah. To counter the numbing amnesia inflicted on its casualties by traumatic injury and on their descendants by our collective overexposure to widely circulated narratives of atrocity, contemporary poets adapt adopted testimonies composed about and by the victims to attest to the survival of their abiding significance.

Notes

This paper could not have been written without the support of a Rockefeller Fellowship and the staff as well as the other Fellows at the Virginia Foundation for the Humanities. I am indebted to the insights of Donald Gray, Anna Meek, and Alvin Rosenfeld.

1. Throughout this essay, I am referring to Adorno's famous statement, "After Auschwitz, it is barbaric to write poetry," a maxim in the minds of most poets who compose verse about the Shoah. Adorno himself returned to this sentence ("I have no wish to soften the saying that to write lyric poetry after Auschwitz is barbaric") in an essay that goes on to admit, "it is now virtually in art alone that suffering can still find its own voice, consolation, without immediately being betrayed by it" (312).

2. I am indebted in my thinking to Robert Jay Lifton's analysis of what he calls "survivors by proxy" (145) and to Dominick LaCapra's analysis of the "secondary witness" (267), though I would not use these terms for the poets I am discussing (and I suspect they would not either) because such terms could be misconstrued as a mode of appropriation. Aware of the geographical and temporal distance that separates them from those touched by the Shoah, the poets of testimony often haltingly and hesitantly testify as belated nonparticipants to the testimonies of survivors as well as victims.

3. Here is Kogon's original account: "The Detail Leader spied two Jews whose strength was ebbing. He ordered a Pole by the name of Strzaska to *bury* the two men, who were scarcely able to keep to their feet. The Pole froze in his tracks—and refused!

The sergeant took a pick handle, belabored the Pole and forced him to lie down in one of the ditches in place of the two Jews. Next he forced the Jews to cover the Pole with soil. They complied, in terror of their lives, and in the hope of escaping the ghastly fate themselves. When only the head of the Pole was still uncovered, the SS man called a halt and had the man dug out again. The two Jews now had to lie down in the ditch, while Strzaska was ordered to cover them up. Slowly the ditch was filled with soil. When the work was done, the Detail Leader personally trampled down the soil over his two victims. Meanwhile the rest of the prisoners kept on working at a mad pace, without a let-up, fearful only that they too might attract the attention of the brute. Five minutes later, two of them were called aside and ordered to dig up the two men who had been buried. The spades flew—perhaps it was still possible to save the comrades. In the dreadful haste, a spade cut open the face of one of the two Jews—but he was already dead. The other still gave feeble signs of life. The SS man ordered both to be taken to the crematory" (92).

4. "Ashes were still / in the room, / and in the far / corner, hanging / above the ovens, / a poem by Goethe, / in German, a poem / about the beauty of death by fire" (Hyett 95).

5. Langer puts it this way: "The Pole's initial error was to behave as if he were being taken from the Tower to a public execution in a traditional atmosphere of spiritual reality; 'casual death' had taught the Jews the futility of such an expectation. Recognizing his 'error,' the Pole has no recourse but to abandon his 'soul' too, as a commodity worthless in the context of his immediate experience—for without the possibility of honor, death loses its meaning" (6).

6. Of course, there can be no such thing as "pure" or "literal" documentation because, as many people have noted, even eyewitness testimonials have a shape that derives from literary structures. On the "utmost" charging of meaning in poetry, I am indebted to the writings of Gioia (20).

7. It is difficult to demarcate responses to the Shoah in terms of generations; however, Williams and Osherow write at a greater remove than Hecht, whose work appeared in the 1960s (whereas Williams's work appeared in the late 1970s and Osherow's in the 1990s). Unlike Hecht, who toured Europe as a soldier at the end of World War II, Williams and Osherow did not witness the atrocities firsthand.

8. Of course, the linking of the masculine with the head, the feminine with the heart, has a long and much vexed history, dating back most dramatically to the Victorian ideology of sexually separate spheres. Needless to say, I am not arguing that women have never produced philosophically abstract verse (one thinks of the work of Jorie Graham, for instance) or that men did not play an important role in the creation of confessional poetry (one thinks of Robert Lowell, of course). However, the personal, occasional voice has played a major role in the history of women's lyric production, whereas the prophetic role of the bard has had a long history in male-authored poetry. I also write that "gender *can* play a role," because it does not always. Instances of cross-gender proxy witnessing abound, most brilliantly in the photo-texts of Jeffrey Wolin, some of whose most moving works record the testimonial words of women of the Holocaust. See his *Written in Memory*.

9. In *The Black Book of Polish Jewry,* attacks on the Jewish religion are specified: "In many towns the *Sepher Torahs* (scrolls of the law) were defiled in the most shameful manner. On *Rosh Hashona,* 1939, in Plonsk, near Warsaw, the Nazis made the Jews assemble

in the town square and compelled them to set fire to the *Sepher Torahs* and other holy books. The Nazi officer who had issued the order fired his revolver into the heap before the flame was applied, shouting: 'I have shot the Jewish God!' . . . Rabbi Moshe Menachem Segal of Lodgz was compelled to tear up the *Sepher Torahs* in a synagogue. . . . In several towns the Nazis herded the Jews into the synagogues and set the buildings on fire, burning the Jews alive. . . . The rabbis were subjected to the most unrestrained abuses" (226–27). *The Black Book* about the Soviet Union states that "The German newspapers conducted an 'explanatory campaign,'" adding that "'The Jews have long planned to rule the world.' To provide substance for this foolish thought, quotations were juggled from the Talmud and the Bible" (Ehrenburg and Grossman 119). *The German Invasion of Poland: Polish Black Book* is typical in its insistence that the brutality recounted in its pages cannot be communicated: "The methods of warfare employed by the Germans, and their cruelty, are so horrifying that it is not possible to conceive what has happened in Poland unless one has seen it with one's own eyes" (64).

10. I am indebted to Wayne Booth's lecture on the "common grounds" of all creeds called religions, a lecture at the University of Virginia on 13 March 1999. According to Booth's definition, Nazism should be considered a religion. In his discussion of the concept of "redemptive anti-Semitism," Friedlander explains that "Germanhood and the Aryan world were on the path to perdition if the struggle against the Jews was not joined; this was to be a struggle to the death. Redemption would come as liberation from the Jews—as their expulsion, possibly their annihilation" (*Memory* 87).

11. In his discussion of homosexuality and German fascism, Theweleit points out the absence of homosexuality, for what "becomes imperative . . . for survival" is the prevalence of "the pleasure of object degradation in the homosexual act" (318). Speculating on why this occurs "in existing societies based on compulsory heterosexuality," he considers such pleasure as "a persecution of desire in general" (319). In other words, "homosexual acts 'committed' as acts of maintenance are not necessarily attributable to what we know as homosexuality; indeed it is far more likely that acts of maintenance and devivification will be heterosexual" (320).

12. For readers of Levinas, who sees in the "being-face-to- face" the "impossibility of negation," this poem will be especially disturbing. Although Levinas believes that "The commandment 'Thou shalt not commit murder' is inscribed in the face of the other," Williams would obviously disagree (Peukert 24).

13. Consider, for instance, D. H. Lawrence's brilliant story "The Prussian Officer" in this regard or Wilfred Owen's poem "Strange Meeting": like many others, Lawrence and Owen dramatize how the enemy and the soldier, or the officer and the enlisted man, enter into a kind of murderous love affair in their power struggles with each other. See the discussion of *Blutbrüderschaft* in Gilbert and Gubar's *Sexchanges* (309–13). Eve Kosofsky Sedgwick sees in Lawrence "one ramification of Whitman's influence [which] is toward an authoritarian realm steeled to conquest by sexual repression and compulsion" (216). It is "this hating homophobic recasting of the male homosocial spectrum— a recasting that recognizes and names as central the nameless love, only in order to cast it out—that has been most descriptive of the fateful twentieth-century societies, notoriously but by no means exclusively the Fascist" (216). While many critics have studied the homosocial bonding at work between and among Nazi men, Williams seems more interested in how this comradely allegiance shapes the dynamics of anti-Semitism.

14. As in "Combat," a poem in which Williams describes his youthful physical intimacies with a German mother and daughter by admitting that he "might have been their Jew, . . . an implement for them, not of atonement" but "of absolution" (98), "Spit" situates the dynamics of fascism within a psychosexual scenario.

15. Williams discusses his evolving attitude toward divinity in an interview with Ed Hirsch: "The god I was talking to became, in his imperfections, simply malevolent, or indifferent, which was worse. A sort of laissez-faire conservative, who was letting everything go to pot, for the sake of some dubious economic equations, some absurd political idealizations. He wanted to have it both ways: to be loved as a loving god, and to deal with us as an indifferent one" (Williams, "Written Interview" 152–53). In another interview, conducted by Lynn Keller, Williams explains the God in some of his poems, "the God of theodicy, the allower or even perpetrator of evil. I think that God had a lot to do with my becoming aware of what the Holocaust had been. In the best sense, the God I conceived of was descended from some of Buber's ideas. God as something the collective human soul experiences, God as what happens between our psyches" (Williams, "Interview" 172). In an essay entitled "Beginnings," he recalls being slapped in his face "until I'd admit that I'd killed God" and goes on to consider the prejudice incorporated into "one's personality where it wouldn't obtrude onto active reflection. ('Spit in my face, you Jewes,' says Donne, me hardly blinking)" (274).

16. This line of thinking is part of Steiner's meditation on Gentile anxiety about "an almighty, all-seeing, all-demanding Deity" that makes enormous ethnical demands on people, though Steiner reminds us (much as Williams does) that "the Judaic invention and 'killing' of God (the two are, psychologically, twinned) turned murderous" in a period when Christianity was receding from spiritual centrality in an "anti- or post-Christian society" (59).

17. The Jewish Black Book Committee's *The Black Book: The Nazi Crime against the Jewish People* includes an excerpt from Rosenberg's *Myth of the Twentieth Century* in which the author argues: "It is impossible for a genuine German to accept a God of the Jews. As a book of religion, the Old Testament must be done away with once and for all. In this way we shall bring to an end the vain effort of the last fifteen-hundred years to transform us mentally into Jews—an effort to which we owe, among other things, our present material Jewish domination" (36).

18. Especially in the metaphotography of Shimon Attie's *The Writing on the Wall* and Aharon Gluska's *Identity Pending*, visual methods are devised to honor the spectral presence of victims. On Attie, see Hirsch (264–68). On Gluska, see Liss (113–14) and Baigell (87–88). Christian Boltanski also experiments with photographs of photographs of the victims.

19. I am thinking specifically about the charges brought against such prose writers as Jerzy Kosinski, D. M. Thomas, and (most recently) Binjamin Wilkomirski.

20. A painting entitled *Human Laundry Belsen 1945*, by Doris Clare Zinkeisen (exhibited at the British War Museum), helps to explain the poignancy of Osherow's proxy testimony. Skeletal frames as limp as the rags that hang from them and as brittle from wear lie heaped on hospital beds, much as documentary photographs at the liberation of the camps featured piles of uniforms more visible than the starved corpses they covered. Shoshana Felman has pointed out the relationship between "*schmates*" and the victims in Nazi terms. "*Wieviel Stuck?*" the German officer asks during the first roll

call Primo Levi endured at the bus station that took him to Auschwitz: "How many pieces?" (16).

21. See Herbert Marks's essay relating Kant's definition of the sublime object as one "whose representation determines the mind to think the unattainability of nature as a presentation of [reason's] ideas" to the biblical prophets' efforts to convey "nothing more than the fact of conveyance itself" through "negation and tautology" (61, 62). One of Williams's finest poems deals with his mother's effort to bring him out of silence, to lift him "from those blank caverns of namelessness" by mouthing his words a second after he said them ("My Mother's Lips" 84).

22. Charles Bernstein, who sees the Shoah as a "crisis of representation" because "the Real is not representable," points out that "the detail rather than the overview" works "*against* the idea of poetry as an imperializing or world-synthesizing agency (of the zeitgeist)" (201).

23. My thinking here has been shaped by Geoffrey Hartman's point that the idea that a "memorial book will emerge with something of Biblical strength" could actually "produce a deceptive sense of totality, throwing into the shadows, even into oblivion, stories, details and unexpected points of view that keep the intellect active and the memory digging" (319). See also Andreas Huyssen (253).

Works Cited

Adorno, Theodor W. "Commitment." *The Essential Frankfurt School Reader*. Ed. Andrew Arato and Eike Gebhardt. New York: Continuum, 1998. 300–18.

Apenszlak, Jacob, Jacob Kenner, Isaac Lewsin, and Moses Polakiewicz, eds. *The Black Book of Polish Jewry: An Account of the Martyrdom of Polish Jewry under the Nazi Occupation*. New York: Howard Fertig, 1982.

Baigell, Matthew. *Jewish-American Artists and the Holocaust*. New Brunswick: Rutgers UP, 1997.

Bernstein, Charles. "The Second War and Postmodern Memory." *A Poetics*. Cambridge: Harvard UP, 1992. 193–217.

Bishop, Elizabeth. "Exchanging Hats." *The Complete Poems, 1927–1979*. New York: Farrar, Straus and Giroux, 1983. 200–201.

Blanchot, Maurice. *The Infinite Conversation*. Trans. Susan Hanson. Minneapolis: U of Minnesota P, 1993.

Booth, Wayne C. Lecture on the "Common Grounds" of Religion. U of Virginia, Charlottesville, 12 March 1999.

Celan, Paul. *Speech-Grille and Selected Poems*. Trans. Joachim Neugroschel. New York: E. P. Dutton, 1971.

Ehrenburg, Ilya, and Vasily Grossman, eds. *The Black Book: The Ruthless Murder of Jews by German-Fascist Invaders throughout the Temporarily Occupied Regions of the Soviet Union and in the Death Camps of Poland during the War of 1941–1945*. Trans. John Glad and James S. Levine. New York: Holocaust Library, 1980.

Felman, Shoshana, and Dori Laub. *Testimony: Crises of Witnessing in Literature, Psychoanalysis, and History*. New York: Routledge, 1992.

Friedlander, Saul. Introduction. *Probing the Limits of Representations: Nazism and the "Final Solution."* Ed. Friedlander. 1–21.

————. *Memory, History, and the Extermination of the Jews of Europe.* Bloomington: Indiana UP, 1993.

————, ed. *Probing the Limits of Representations: Nazism and the "Final Solution."* Cambridge: Harvard UP, 1992.

The German Invasion of Poland: Polish Black Book. Preface by His Grace the Archbishop of York. Authority of the Polish Ministry of Information. London: Hutchinson, 1940.

Gilbert, Sandra M., and Susan Gubar. *Sexchanges.* Vol. 2 of *No Man's Land: The Place of the Woman Writer in the Twentieth Century.* New Haven: Yale UP, 1989.

Gioia, Dana. *Can Poetry Matter? Essays on Poetry and American Culture.* St. Paul: Graywolf, 1992.

Hartman, Geoffrey. "The Book of the Destruction." *Probing the Limits of Representations: Nazism and the "Final Solution."* Ed. Saul Friedlander. 317–34.

Hecht, Anthony. *Collected Earlier Poems.* New York: Knopf, 1990.

Heifetz, Julie. *Oral History and the Holocaust: A Collection of Poems from Interviews with Survivors of the Holocaust.* New York: Pergamon, 1985.

Hirsch, Marianne. *Family Frames: Photography, Narrative, Postmemory.* Cambridge: Harvard UP, 1997.

Huyssen, Andreas. "Monument and Memory in a Postmodern Age." *Yale Journal of Criticism* 6 (1993): 249–61.

Hyett, Barbara Helfgott. *In Evidence: Poems of the Liberation of Nazi Concentration Camps.* Pittsburgh: U of Pittsburgh P, 1986.

Jewish Black Book Committee. *The Black Book: The Nazi Crime against the Jewish People.* New York: Duell, Sloan, and Pearce, 1946.

Kogon, Eugen. *The Theory and Practice of Hell: The German Concentration Camps and the System behind Them.* Trans. Heinz Norden. New York: Octagon, 1973.

LaCapra, Dominick. "Lanzmann's *Shoah:* 'Here There Is Not Why.'" *Critical Inquiry* 23 (1997): 231–69.

Langer, Lawrence. *The Holocaust and the Literary Imagination.* New Haven: Yale UP, 1975.

Levi, Primo. *Survival in Auschwitz and The Reawakening.* Trans. Raymond Rosenthall. New York: Vintage, 1989.

Lifton, Robert Jay. Interview by Cathy Caruth. *Trauma: Explorations in Memory.* Ed. Cathy Caruth. Baltimore: Johns Hopkins UP, 1995. 128–50.

Lipstadt, Deborah E. *Beyond Belief: The American Press and the Coming of the Holocaust, 1933–1945.* New York: Free P, 1986.

Liss, Andrea. *Trespassing through Shadows: Memory, Photography, and the Holocaust.* Minneapolis: U of Minnesota P, 1998.

Marks, Herbert. "On Prophetic Stammering." *The Book and the Text: The Bible and Literary Theory.* Ed. Regina Schwartz. Oxford: Blackwell, 1990. 60–80.

Midrash Rabbah. Trans. Rabbi Dr. H. Freedman and Maurice Simon. Vol. 3 of *Exodus.* Trans. Rabbi Dr. S. M. Lehrman. London: Soncino, 1939.

Osherow, Jacqueline. *Conversations with Survivors.* Athens: U of Georgia P, 1994.

Ozick, Cynthia. "A Liberal's Auschwitz." *The Pushcart Prize: The Best of the Small Presses.* Ed. Bill Henderson. Yonkers: Pushcart, 1976–77. 149–53.

Peukert, Helmut. "Unconditional Responsibility for the Other: The Holocaust and the Thinking of Emmanuel Levinas." *Never Again! The Holocaust's Challenge for Educators.* Ed. Helmut Schreier and Matthais Heyl. Hamburg: Kramer, 1997. 21–28.

Rosenfeld, Alvin. *A Double Dying: Reflections on Holocaust Literature.* Bloomington: Indiana UP, 1980.

Sedgwick, Eve Kosofsky. *Between Men: English Literature and Male Homosocial Desire.* New York: Columbia UP, 1985.

Steiner, George. "The Long Life of Metaphor." *Encounter* 68 (1987): 55–61.

Symonds, John Addington. *The Letters.* Ed. Herbert M. Schueller and Robert L. Peters. 3 vols. Detroit: Wayne State UP, 1969.

Theweleit, Klaus. *Male Bodies: Psychoanalyzing the White Terror.* Vol. 2 of *Male Fantasies.* Trans. Erica Carter and Chris Turner in Collaboration with Stephen Conway. Minneapolis: U of Minnesota P, 1989.

Williams, C. K. "Beginnings." *In Praise of What Persists.* Ed. Stephen Berg. New York: Harper, 1983. 267–80.

———. "An Interview with C. K. Williams." By Lynn Keller. *Contemporary Literature* 29 (1988): 157–76.

———. *New and Selected Poems.* Newcastle-upon-Tyne: Bloodaxe, 1995.

———. "A Written Interview with C. K. Williams." By Ed Hirsch. *Missouri Review* 9 (1985–86): 151–62.

Wolin, Jeffrey A. *Written in Memory: Portraits of the Holocaust.* San Francisco: Chronicle, 1997.

IV

WAYS OF SEEING

The Diversity of
Applied Ethical Criticism

FORGET THE PHALLIC SYMBOLISM, CONSIDER THE SNAKE

Biocentrism and Language in Margaret Atwood's "Snake Poems"

Ian Marshall

In one of Gary Larson's "Far Side" cartoons, a goofy-looking male adolescent, bug-eyed, pin-headed, and pear-shaped, chases after an equally goofy-looking girl. She's wearing pointy-rimmed eyeglasses and a ballooning purple dress with black polka-dots, and she's screaming. As the boy pursues her, his long tongue dangling excitedly from his mouth, he's brandishing a snake. The caption reads: "And for the rest of his life, the young reptile suffered deep emotional scars." Like many of Larson's cartoons, this one allows us—or forces us—to see life from the point of view of other creatures. But implicit in the cartoon are assumptions about gender and about our usual conceptions of snakes—as something both frightening and phallic.

Larson's cartoon provides a useful introduction to Margaret Atwood's "Snake Poems," first published in a limited edition in 1983 and later included as a section of her *Interlunar* collection. She seems as fascinated by snakes as are people in folk legends who are hypnotized by their unblinking gaze, and her "Snake Poems" constitute her attempt to "consider the snake," to comprehend and describe their nature, to explore and challenge human conceptions of their "meaning" and value. Atwood re-examines the usual symbolic associations and mythic roles of snakes, and she creates, with impressive virtuosity, new metaphors by which she tries to capture the essence of snake. Ultimately, though her progress is as sinuous as the path of a sidewinder, she works toward a biocentric (or at least herpetocentric) appreciation of and understanding for the snake. Along the way she considers the difficulty of entering the consciousness of another species through the human medium of language, exploring not just what language can say about snakes, but what snakes can reveal about language.

The first poem, "Snake Woman," reverses the roles in Larson's cartoon, as Atwood remembers herself as a girl frightening men by carrying snakes, "limp and terrorized," into the dining room. "What fun I had!" she exults —but then she concludes, "Now, I don't know. / Now I'd consider the snake" (8). She does just that in the subsequent poems, exploring the role of the snake in human myth and in the human psyche, considering its appeal and its terrors from our perspective, but also trying to understand it on its own terms. In doing so, Atwood models the environmental ethic that ecocritics and deep ecologists call "biocentrism"—the attempt to view the world from a nonhuman perspective, to see it from the perspective of the biotic community, the assemblage of living things in an area. Some critics call that shift in perspective "ecocentrism," referring to the ecosystem. Call it biocentrism or ecocentrism, the idea is to move beyond anthropocentrism to a view that takes into account all the living things in an area, a view that is in truth not centered at all.

There are literary precedents for this ecologically inspired ethical move, of course. Lawrence Buell in *The Environmental Imagination* shows that Henry Thoreau made the shift to ecocentrism over a decade before the word *ecology* was even coined (in 1866, by Ernst Haeckel). In reading *Walden*, Buell sees the shift indicated by the gradual decrease in Thoreau's use of "I" and the increase in references to "Walden," "the Pond," and the "wild" (122). The pattern repeats itself in Thoreau's life's work, as he became less interested in going to nature so as to discover spiritual lessons about the self, and more and more interested in writing natural history that is less about himself and more about other living things. In the twentieth century, poet Robinson Jeffers called that move *inhumanism,* which he defined as "a shifting of emphasis and significance from man to not-man" (*Double Axe* xxi), and which he dramatized in poems such as "Hurt Hawks," where he claimed that he had "sooner, except the penalties, kill a man than a hawk" (*Selected Poems* 45). Most famously, proto-biocentric ideas formed the basis for Aldo Leopold's land ethic. "A thing is right," said Leopold, "when it tends to preserve the integrity, stability, and beauty of the biotic community. It is wrong when it tends otherwise" (224–25). Leopold's ecocentric epiphany came when he watched the "fierce green fire" fade in a dying wolf's eyes and then learned to "think like a mountain," seeing wolves not just as evil killers depriving human hunters of their deer quota but as essential players in a mountain's ecosystem and as a species serving as an indicator of the health of the mountain's wilderness habitat (129–33).

Atwood, then, follows a tradition of nature writing grappling with the problem of how we humans can move outside ourselves to see the world through lenses that filter out reflections of ourselves.[1] She has taken on the interesting test case of the snake—perhaps of all life forms the one most loaded with associations in human culture, mostly negative, and a long history of bad human press. What could be more Other than the snake, seminal, we might say, in one of our culture's key stories as *the* antagonist, loaded with symbolic associations, from the phallus to the wilderness.

So how does Atwood go about trying to see the snake clearly? First, she gives factual information, much of it based on close observation. She points out that all snakes are carnivores, and she seems to have watched them eat:

> There are no leaf-eating snakes.
> All are fanged and gorge on blood.
> Each one is a hunter's hunter,
> nothing more than an endless gullet
> pulling itself on over the still-alive prey. (11)

She knows the different methods snakes employ in dispatching their prey —the constrictor able "to squeeze the voice out of anything edible," and the pit viper, with its "teeth like syringes" and "nasty radar / homing in on the deep red shadow / nothing else knows it casts" (11). Clearly, she knows how viper fangs operate, and she is familiar with the heat-seeking properties of the Jacobson's organ. She is familiar, too, with the camouflaging effect of snakes' coloring, describing one that "dissolves / and flows into the rock," and she is knowledgeable enough about snake anatomy to describe "the spine / with its many pairs of delicate ribs / unrolling like a feather" (23). She knows of "their live births and squirming nests" (12)—in her native Canada, garter snakes winter together by the thousands. And she has looked at snakes up close. It must be a garter that she depicts as "green and yellow / striped like a moose maple" (9). In "Lesson on Snakes," she describes one with

> . . . a throat
> like the view down a pink lily,
> double tongue curved out like stamens. (9)

She is familiar with the smell of a snake ("part skunk, part inside / of a torn stomach" [8]), and the taste of a rattler ("a little oily" [13]). Her taste test leads to some of the wittiest lines of the sequence:

(Forget the phallic symbolism:
two differences:
snake tastes like chicken,
and who ever credited the prick with wisdom?) (13)

Her quip about the phallic symbolism of snakes, her debunking of the usual symbolic association, indicates another of her methods for trying to "consider the snake." It is not enough to describe what she sees or knows; she also must challenge the myths, legends, and false "facts" that color our perceptions of snakes and in essence conceal the real thing from us. Forget the phallic symbolism, and forget Eden: a snake is "hardly / the devil in your garden / but a handy antidote to mice" (9). Most of her debunking project comes in "Lies about Snakes." Among the lies:

that they cause thunder,
that they won't cross ropes,
that they travel in pairs (10)

Regarding the supposed cobra dance elicited by snake charmers, Atwood points out that "snakes cannot hear music." Contrary to legend, the glass snake does not "break when stepped on. . . . nor is it transparent" (10). In fact, she adds, "Nothing / could be more opaque," the pun suggesting the difficulty of trying to see through all the myths, stories, lies, and associations in order to perceive her subject clearly.

What is most striking about the poems is the sheer verbal energy Atwood expends trying to define and describe the snake, often through metaphor and simile. The snake is, to quote from a number of the poems, a "green light blessing your house," a "vein of cool green metal / which would run through my fingers like mercury," "a raw bracelet / gripping my wrist." It eats "like a sock gone ravenous, like an evil glove / like sheer greed, lithe and devious." It is something "for whom killing is easy and careless / as war, as digestion," a "sinuous ribbon of true darkness, / one long muscle with eyes and an anus, / looping like thick tar out of the trees." It has, in addition to the "teeth like syringes" and "nasty radar," an "alien / chainmail skin, straight out / of science fiction." It is "a snarled puzzle / only gasoline and a match can untangle," it is a "god," a "divinity," "mere lunch: / metaphysics with onions," "somebody's grandmother . . . / in widow's black and graceful / and sharp as ever," "a dancer who is now / a green streamer waved by its own breeze," and "the breath / that shivers in the yellow grass, / a papery finger, half of a noose." It speaks with "an old voice, like the blue stars," or "that voice of a husk rasping in the wind," and its mating is "barely sexual, /

a romance between two lengths / of cyanide-colored string." It "proclaims resurrection / to all believers," it is "an argument / for poetry," "a shift among dry leaves / when there is no wind, / a thin line moving through / that which is not time," "a movement / from left to right, / a vanishing. Prophet under a stone," a "long word, cold-blooded and perfect," it is "itself a tongue, looping its earthy hieroglyphs," it is "one name of God," and it is "the nameless one / giving itself a name" (8–22).

Atwood's creativity in the art of simile and metaphor is impressive, but there is an obvious paradox here. For someone who is trying to "consider the snake," Atwood seems to see the snake mostly in terms of something else, mainly human artifacts (a bracelet, a sock, a ribbon, string, a word, something wearing chain mail, with syringe teeth, and the radar of heat sensors) or body parts (gullet, muscle, tongue). In part those descriptions might tend to domesticate the snake, render it familiar and comprehensible. Somehow, though, the effect is to highlight the snake's strangeness—a living thing that looks like a sock wearing chain mail and brandishing a syringe? a body that is all gullet? It seems like something out of a Dalí nightmare. Such descriptions do not really make the snake seem more tame or familiar —rather, they expose the desperation with which we struggle to penetrate the mystery of the snake, to see it in terms that make sense to us, no matter how ill-fitting those terms. But the mystery persists, and for all the domestic images, Atwood puts just as much emphasis on the ophidiophobic awe with which we regard the snake. A hungry sock? Sure—but also part god.

Perhaps Atwood considers the snake's virtuosity as metaphoric vehicle as inherent in its propensity for shape-shifting. It is the perfect symbol— imbued with a significance that is hard to pin down, reverberating with possibility. But do those possibilities bring us any closer to understanding the snake itself? Are we getting to know the snake as snake when we are encouraged to see it in such obviously human frames of reference? At times Atwood does move outside those frames of reference, pointing out that the snake is "only a snake after all" (13). But clearly, in considering the snake, she has not tried to obliterate human conceptions of the snake, or her own imaginative perceptions. We are, after all, human, with a history of acquaintance with the snake, with imaginations that render the snake hypnotic, often in very individualistic ways.

With all that we know of the snake, and all that Atwood has considered of the snake—the snake as snake, its beauty, its delicate ribs, the snake as legend, the snake as symbol, with deep affecting power, the snake as god— we react with a near-universal response, a response that Atwood bemoans in the last line of the penultimate of her snake poems: "You know this and still kill it." Rather than honor or admire or worship or even tolerate, rather than live and let live, we "go for the shovel, / old blood on the blade" (21).

What Atwood comes around to, then, is a not-so-subtle preservationist plea for snakes' rights. Precisely because the snake carries with it so many associations, because its shape is so suggestively shifty and hard to pin down, it makes an excellent test case for our environmental conscience. Sure, biocentrism sounds fine in theory—respect all living things and try to look at the world from the perspective of the whole ecosystem. But how far are we willing to go in practice? Are we willing to heed Atwood's SOS call for a . . . s-s-s-snake: Save Our Snakes?

That is exactly where biocentrism leads us—whirling outward in a widening spiral of rights. In his famous essay on the land ethic, Aldo Leopold begins with a description of Odysseus's response to his unfaithful slaves and servants upon his arrival back at Ithaca—he hanged them. Leopold points out that Odysseus was far from an unethical man—but his decision to dispose of his human property was not then considered a question of ethics. Since then, the definitions of ethical behavior have broadened considerably. In his description of what he calls "the ethical sequence," Leopold points out that the "first ethics dealt with the relation between individuals" —as in the Ten Commandments. Later ethical concerns dealt with the individual in relation to society—as in the Golden Rule. But that is as far as our ethics has gotten us. Leopold foresees as an "evolutionary possibility and an ecological necessity" the development of a further expansion in the ethical sequence, to account for our "relation to land and to the animals and plants which grow upon it" (202–3). Roderick Nash in *The Rights of Nature* offers a similar vision of "the expanding concept of rights," broadly defining "rights" not as a legal concept but as "intrinsic worth which humans ought to respect." In the "pre-ethical past," says Nash, morality involved consideration only of self-interest. In the "ethical past," morality expanded to include concern for family, tribe, and region. In the present, it has expanded to include nation, race, and humankind in general. At every stage, notes Nash, the expansion of rights is at first met with resistance, even incredulity —witness the slow progress of civil rights in America, legally guaranteed only as recently as 1964, with the passage of the Civil Rights Act. Nash also sees us now at the starting point of expanding rights to animals, as marked by the Endangered Species Act of 1973 and the rise of animal rights activists and deep ecologists (4–7). Deep ecologists believe that the extension of rights to the nonhuman world—or, as David Abram aptly puts it, the "more than human world"—will not take place until we can leave behind an anthropocentric view of the world. We should not act to conserve nature because it is useful to us or provides us with some advantage, even if it is a spiritual as opposed to an economic advantage, nor because we are God's appointed caretakers of Earth, but because we accept the right to life of all living things. In answer to the question of what rattlesnakes could possibly be good for, John Muir once said that they are "good for themselves, and we need not begrudge them their share of life" (57–58). Or as Atwood puts it in reference to snakes in general:

> The reason for them is the same
> as the reason for stars, and not human. (12)

Ultimately, it seems, snakes defy definition or capture by the human frame of reference.

And there arises another paradox. Atwood, like many contemporary nature writers, asks us, in Denise Levertov's words, to "come into animal presence." But the asking takes the form of the exclusively human means of written language. How do we come into animal presence, how do we leave behind a human frame of reference, how do we adopt the perspective of another living thing and try to convey that perspective to others while employing the human means of written language?

That question is central to David Abram's *The Spell of the Sensuous,* a philosophical inquiry into the role of language in separating modern civilization from the natural world. Abram finds it more than coincidental that oral cultures universally retain closer, more respectful relationships with nature than do "civilized" cultures with written languages. Written language, says Abram, is the prime agent of distancing us from nature. In a culture like ours, language is seen and employed no longer as something that grows from or participates in the world around us, each breath, each formation of the word, involving a taking in of the world and a gift of something back. Rather than adopting a mode of communication akin to the world of nature —the stream chatter of water, rock, and gravity or the hiss and kiss of wind's tempestuous relationship with pine—we employ a language that is almost entirely self-referential, of and by and for humans, partaking only of the human realm. Places no longer contain our stories, the air no longer carries them to us—texts do, and the words on the page are for our eyes and minds only. The marks on the page are no longer pictures of the world but an arbitrary representation of the sounds we make. It is a self-contained system, and even our spoken language now seems to hark back to the page, not the world. A quick example offered by Abram: the letter *M* comes from the Hebrew word *mem,* meaning water, and the shape has its origin as a drawing of waves. Originally, then, in the Semitic writing that preceded our alphabet, the ideogram *M* evoked a sensory image from nature. But now the letter *M* does not represent anything but a sound we make, one that is meaningful only to us. It is no longer associated with the word for water. True, "traces of sensible nature linger," but "only as vestigial holdovers . . . they are no longer necessary participants in the transfer of linguistic knowledge." We have moved a lengthy step "away from the sensible phenomenon that had previously called forth the spoken utterance, to the spoken utterance itself, now invoked directly by the written character." The written word now represents "the vocal gesture, completely bypassing the thing pictured" (100–101).

Written language, claims Abram, especially that relying on a phonetic as opposed to a pictographic alphabet, is the villain in our fall from grace. It is the wall we have built around ourselves, and nature, as we say, is outside. Here is the paradox—written language may be what has separated us from nature, says Abram—but to tell us this, he uses written language. And, in fact, he concludes by suggesting that this is the nature writer's task: "*taking up* the written word, with all of its potency, and patiently, carefully, writing language back into the land" (273).

A daunting challenge, surely. But impossible? Is that not akin to what literature always does—takes us outside of ourselves, allows us to try on other lives for a brief spell, to experience, almost as if we are on the inside, what another existence feels like? A twentieth-first-century white male can read, say, Toni Morrison's *Beloved* and come to know, or come to understand, or at least come to empathize with, the experience of a black slave woman in nineteenth-century America—and maybe even come to understand and accept, if not condone, an action (the murder of one's own baby) that previously seemed unthinkably hideous. That is the magic trick of literature, that art we make with language. In fact, the starting point for Abram's inquiry is his study of shamanism and magic in oral cultures. "The traditional magician," he says, "cultivates an ability to shift out of his or her common state of consciousness precisely in order to make contact with . . . other forms of sensitivity and awareness. . . . It is this, we might say, that defines a shaman: the ability to readily slip out of the perceptual boundaries that demarcate his or her particular culture" (9). Does a book not perform the same magic? In the past quarter century or so, we have relied on literature to perform that magic in fostering an appreciation for multicultural Others.

But in the field of literary studies, perhaps we have underestimated the magic. We have maintained a very high regard for literature's ability to make other human cultures come alive for us—but we have paid little attention to the work of our shaman-writers in tapping into the spirits of other species.

Of course, there is a key difference between entering into the consciousness of another human being and learning to think like a mountain, or a hemlock, or a snake. And there is an obvious difference in this new extension of the concept of rights from any that has gone before. Trees do not petition for their rights; snakes do not speak of the distress of oppression. But then again, perhaps the extension of rights to a previously excluded group is never the result of simply hearing their stories—it is a product of entering into dialogue. Consider the case of African Americans in nineteenth-century America. While many African Americans offered eloquent written testimony to the inhumanity of slavery, those testimonies alone did not rid the country of the peculiar institution. The stories initiated a dialogue. Truth be told, in our literary history, at least, it is the other half of the dialogue that first entered the perceived mainstream of American consciousness. Henry Thoreau's antislavery essays were in the literary anthologies when Frederick Douglass's *Narrative* was either absent or briefly excerpted, and Olaudah Equiano, Sojourner Truth, Harriet Wilson, and Frances Harper were consistently absent. This is a familiar story to us these days; we have witnessed a remarkable expansion of the literary canon in recent decades. My point is that social change comes not when some oppressed Other calls for the change, but when that call is responded to, at first by a minority portion of the mainstream. Then the dialogue broadens, controversy and debate ensue, and eventually the right wins out, and rights are expanded.

But how can nature participate in such a dialogue? In Bakhtin's conception of the dialogic, dialogue takes place even when a character is not directly quoted. A speaker's language takes on the inflections of another character when speaking of that character or coming into contact with that character. And it is not just a matter of language style, but of worldview. The speaker enters into the other character's world in order to communicate with that character, and the character enters our world and changes it to incorporate something of the character's world by his or her mere presence there. And, of course, says Bakhtin, we enter into dialogue whenever we address a subject that has inspired some previous dialogue.

What does it mean to enter into dialogue with nature? It means to look closely, to pay attention to fact, to see how a species is adapted to its life situation and environmental circumstances. It means to adopt a different rhythm—life lived at a pace not of the car and the coffee break, rush hour, quitting time, and the deadline, but life stretched motionlessly by a rock, awaiting prey; life tangled with many other lives in a winter nest; life striped like a moose maple. It means to attend to a language that is not written down, one that we have never wholly understood but that speaks to us nonetheless. We have on occasion caught the gist of it and have written on it—its recurring themes of beauty, peace, harmony, spirit, the sacred. It is a language amenable to meditation, one that speaks to us of the meaning of our lives and of ultimate meaning that goes beyond that. To enter into dialogue with nature is to continue that conversation. This really should not seem such a mysterious process. Abram makes the point that human language once involved a reciprocal interaction with the natural world— we imitated its sounds, we used the same medium of language, the air, that other species capable of vocalization use to communicate. The taking in of that raw material of language, and the giving it back with each spoken word, involved us in a process that was not exclusively human. Born of "reciprocity and participation," nourished by the "gestures, sounds, and rhythms" of other living things, the language of oral cultures "'belongs' to the animate landscape as much as it 'belongs' to ourselves," says Abram (82). It is only our fairly recent association of language with writing, he says, that led to our sense of separation from other living things. What we need now is a written language that reestablishes connections with other living things, that recognizes the possibility of dialogue.

And this is perhaps the most admirable quality of Atwood's "Snake Poems." In considering the snake, she also examines the means by which we consider the snake: language. Of all the metaphors Atwood tries out in attempting to capture the snake, the idea of the snake as a kind of language, or language user, is the most prominent and developed. "Psalm to Snake" celebrates the snake as an "argument for poetry." How is a snake suggestive of poetry? Let us count the ways. It is "a shift among dry leaves / when there is no wind," the "leaves," I take it, referring to pages, turning by some mechanism other than breeze, words slithering across them, leaving a trail "in the blank sand" of the page. It is "a thin line moving through / that which is not / time"—which I take to mean space, the blank space of the page, where it has the power of "creating time," just as a poem creates a world that references the past and will continue to speak in and to the future. It speaks in a "voice from the dead," just as the dead may continue to speak to us, in Shakespeare's words, "so long as men can breathe and eyes can see." But the snake's language, like the poetry for which it argues, is "oblique and silent." Silent, because it is alphabetic; oblique, because the truths it tells (it is, after all, a "Prophet under a stone") are told aslant—and a-curl, and a-whorling, as fluid as cursive. If a snake is a "long word," it is a word that shifts and moves and reforms itself, as indeterminate as the lay of a line of poetry. It moves—that is part of the fascination of both snake and poem.

"The White Snake" recounts a legend of an eyeless snake that "looks like water freezing" and "lays quartz eggs." As the legend has it:

> If you can find it and eat it
> then you will understand
> the language of the animals. (15)

One man has succeeded in devouring the white snake, and upon swallowing, the sudden rush of sound, "like a wall breaking," blinds him, the light within "filling his mouth like blood, / like earth in the mouth of a man buried." Is this a parabolic warning about the effect of achieving a biocentric perspective? To be able to enter animals' lives so as to understand their language would be disaster—maybe because we would be devastated by what they had to say about us. What a blow to our exalted image of ourselves, perhaps. And to have the earth in our mouth would render us speechless—would deprive us of the distinctively (as we typically see it) human act of speech, the utterance of word after word. The man could do nothing ever after "but listen / to the words, words around him everywhere like rain falling"—but words not of his making, words of those who before could not speak to us.

Atwood points out the apparent moral of the tale:

> Beware of the white snake, says the story.
> Choose ignorance. (16)

We are better off not hearing what the world has to say. Or so says the story. In the last line of the poem Atwood undercuts all that has preceded. "There are no white snakes in nature," she says, debunking the legend—and along with it, its moral. The story tells us we are better off not being able to hear what the world has to say—but it is based on a false premise and leads to a false conclusion. The ignorance we are encouraged to choose is based on an anthropocentric view of nature. Perhaps, suggests Atwood, we *should* put the earth in our mouths, should shut up (for once) and listen to the words falling like rain.

Or maybe we should look at the writing on the ground. The elusive and shifting quality of language evident in "Psalm to Snake" is referred to in "After Heraclitus" as well. I presume that the title refers to Heraclitus's claim that "you can't step in the same river twice," and language is the fluid element invoked. The snake is able to "talk with the body," forming "letter / after letter . . . / itself a tongue, looping its earthy hieroglyphs" (20). Again, the suggestion is that the snake is trying to tell us something, trying to spell it out for us. In part, what it has to tell us has to do with the regenerative power of nature, which is described as:

> . . . a fire
> we burn in and are
> renewed, one skin
> shed and then another.

As Atwood tells us in "Metempsychosis," the snake emerging from sloughed-off skin "proclaims resurrection"—the snake as son of God (14). If we respond to this messiah with fear, Atwood recommends that we grasp, in the body of the snake, "the darkness that you fear." Feeling a "cool power coiling into [our] wrists," we will see the darkness turn to "flesh and embers"—flesh and embers from that regenerative fire of nature that we call life. The snake has the creative power of language, or of a god. It is:

> . . . the nameless one
> giving itself a name,
> one among many
>
> and your own name as well. (21)

In the beginning, the story goes, was the word, and in Atwood's version of things it seems that the snake had the power and spinal agility to spell it out. Of course, in the story of creation as we know it, the process of assigning names was taken over, after God had the first word, by our human patriarch. In taking on that role, Atwood's snake, passing down sentence after sentence, is blurring the lines between God, human, reptile. To utter words, suggests Atwood, to string them together and use them to shape existence in the form of a story, is not just to take on the power of a god—it is to adopt the practice of nature. Perhaps more important, once alerted by the snake as nature's scribe to the presence of earth's language, we can begin to attend to its stories.

The final lines of the sequence suggest that the figure of the snake is just a starting point for our attempt to hear, or read, what nature has to say:

> On the plain below you is a river
> you know you must follow home. (22)

In the river's meandering we can see the shape of snake, speaking to us, leaving signs that allow us to find our way back to the world from which we have distanced ourselves. As Abram says, "The earthly terrain in which we find ourselves, and upon which we depend for all our nourishment, is shot through with suggestive scrawls and traces," among which, echoing Atwood, he includes "the sinuous calligraphy of rivers" (95). The language Atwood brandishes before our eyes, mimicking river and reptile, brings poetry back to earth.

It is precisely Atwood's focus on the snake's propensity for alphabetic maneuver that makes her "Snake Poems" something different in the realm of biocentric nature writing. Atwood suggests a resolution to the paradox that Abram describes—to use written language to cross the barrier erected by written language. Atwood shows that our alphabet, with its apparently arbitrary system of representation, also has its analogue, its model, maybe its source, in nature. We have seen these shapes before, spelled out for us in snakeskin, impressing us with their beauty and power, calling for acts of interpretation. Surely there must be some meaning being spelled out in the body of the snake. In its movements it has spelled out words and sentences and stories, and its fangs have left the decisive imprint of a colon, indicative of something to follow.

Atwood's "Snake Poems" illustrate the attempt to adopt a biocentric perspective and highlight the difficulties of doing so—difficult because our view of any species comes loaded with all kinds of preconceptions, and difficult because the attempt is conveyed in the human medium of language. Atwood's poems suggest that the way to move toward biocentrism is to grapple with those difficulties. To consider the snake means to consider not just the snake as snake, as living thing, but to explore its mythic status as well. In her "Snake Poems" Atwood is clearly aware of previous narrative conversation on her subject—conversation that has been bounded by anthropocentric considerations. But she also addresses the world view of the snake—she sees beauty, she sees evolutionary adaptations in evidence, she sees something that defies our conceptualizations. What makes her "Snake Poems" noteworthy, though, is not solely her move toward biocentrism—in that move she is part of a literary tradition that has gained enough momentum to become a recent trend. Rather, it is her attention to the problem presented by the use of language in doing so, and her suggestion that the act of writing can itself be regarded as a natural act.

Notes

1. Atwood's work, of course, is usually categorized as part of the feminist tradition, not the nature-writing tradition. But clearly the natural world has been a recurrent concern of Atwood's, from *Surfacing* to *The Journals of Susanna Moodie* to *Wilderness Tips*. The difference is that those works lent themselves to a feminist critique as well as an ecocritical critique, and the feminist slant is less apparent in the "Snake Poems." Perhaps that accounts for the lack of critical attention to "Snake Poems." Despite the high regard in which Atwood's work is held, not one article or book chapter has been devoted to "Snake Poems."

Works Cited

Abram, David. *The Spell of the Sensuous: Perception and Language in a More-than-Human World*. New York: Vintage, 1997.
Atwood, Margaret. *Interlunar*. London: Jonathan Cape, 1984.
Buell, Lawrence. *The Environmental Imagination: Thoreau, Nature Writing, and the Formation of American Culture*. Cambridge, MA: Belknap, 1995.
Jeffers, Robinson. *The Double Axe and Other Poems*. New York: Liveright, 1977.
————. *Selected Poems*. New York: Vintage, 1965.
Leopold, Aldo. *A Sand County Almanac and Sketches Here and There*. 1949. Special Commemorative ed. New York: Oxford UP, 1989.
Muir, John. *Our National Parks*. Boston, 1901.
Nash, Roderick. *The Rights of Nature: A History of Environmental Ethics*. Madison: U of Wisconsin P, 1989.

MAKING, TAKING, AND FAKING LIVES

Ethical Problems in Collaborative Life Writing

G. Thomas Couser

Whose book is this?

—Malcolm X

ALTHOUGH ISSUES of literary ethics may arise in any genre, ethical dilemmas seem to be built into collaborative life writing in ways peculiar to it.[1] With fiction, ethical criticism is usually concerned with issues of meaning and of reception: in the simplest terms, does the text have beneficial or harmful effects on its audience? But nonfiction generally and life writing specifically raise other concerns. Indeed, although Wayne Booth limits his scope to fiction in *The Company We Keep*, he asks key questions that are perhaps even more compelling for life writing than for fiction: "What Are the Author's Responsibilities to Those Whose Lives Are Used as 'Material'?" (130), "What Are the Author's Responsibilities to Others Whose Labor Is Exploited to Make the Work of Art Possible?" (131), and "What Are Responsibilities of the Author to Truth?" (132). With collaborative life writing especially, ethical concerns begin with the production of the narrative and extend to the relation of the text to the historical record of which it forms a part.

Ethical issues may be particularly acute in collaborative autobiography because it occupies an awkward niche between more established, more prestigious forms of life writing. On one side is solo autobiography, in which the writer, the narrator, and the subject (or protagonist) of the narrative are all the same person; at least, they share the same name.[2] On the other side is biography, in which the writer and narrator are one person, while the subject is someone else.[3] In the middle, combining features of the adjacent forms—and thus challenging the common-sense distinction between them—is as-told-to autobiography, in which the writer is one person, but the narrator and subject are someone else. The ethical difficulties of collaborative autobiography are rooted in its nearly oxymoronic status; the single narrative voice—a simulation by one person of the voice of another—is always in danger of breaking, exposing conflicts of interest that are not present in solo autobiography. Although the process by which the text is produced is dialogical, the product is monological; the two voices are permitted to engage in dialogue only in supplementary texts—forewords and afterwords—and even there, the dialogue is managed and presented by one party, the nominal author. Insofar as the process is admitted into the narrative, then, it is exclusively in supplementary texts, and generally as a chapter of the *writer's* life. Though critics are not in a position to mandate disclosure of the process, fuller disclosure is likely to reflect a more ethical collaboration; such disclosure is certainly rhetorically effective, insofar as it suggests that the nominal author has nothing to hide.

Autobiographical collaborations are rather like marriages and other domestic partnerships: partners enter into a relationship of some duration, they "make life" together, and they produce an offspring that will derive traits from each of them.[4] Each partner has a strong interest in the fate of that offspring, which will reflect on each in a different way. Much of this is true of any collaborative authorship, of course; with autobiography, however, the fact that the joint product is a life story raises the stakes—at least for the subject. It is easy enough to articulate ethical principles that should govern the production of collaborative autobiography. The fundamental one might be a variant of the Golden Rule: do unto your partner as you would have your partner do unto you. Thus, autobiographical collaborations should be egalitarian; neither partner should abuse or exploit the other. Given the subject's stake in the textual product, a corollary principle would be that the subject should always have the right to audit and edit the manuscript before publication. As we shall see, however, in some circumstances, this is easier said than done.

The vast majority of collaborative life stories result from partnerships that are voluntary, amicable, and mutually beneficial. Still, there is a thin and not always clear line between making, taking, and faking the life of another person in print. Coauthoring another's life can be a creative or a destructive act, a service or a disservice, an act of homage or of appropriation. The potential for abuse lies partly in something the term itself tends to elide: the process, though cooperative, is usually not in the literal sense a matter of collaborative *writing* (which has its own problems). Rather, some of the difficulty comes from the disparity between the contributions of the two partners. Obviously, there are different kinds and degrees of collaboration, but, in most cases, one member supplies the "life" while the other provides the "writing." The extent to which this is an oversimplification of the process depends on a number of things. I do not mean to endorse a model under which "writing" is taken too literally; as contemporary rhetorical theory insists, in some sense the entire process of composition, from initiation and invention to copyediting, is "writing." Nor do I mean to imply that the "writer" is entirely dependent on the subject for the "story"; most writers are drawn to their subjects by previous knowledge of them, and most supplement interviews with independent research. Nor do I mean to identify "form" exclusively with "writing" and "content" with "life," or to imply that the "writing" does not affect the content; any mediation carries its own message(s). Indeed, as we shall see, mediation can be a source of ethical problems, especially in cases of cross-cultural collaboration; for example, when the implications of the form are unavailable to the subject, there is the danger of misrepresentation that will go undetected by him or her. Ultimately, however, no matter how involved the subject is at each stage of the project, the partners bring different skills and contributions to the final project; their labor is of different kinds, and most of the wording of the final text is attributable to the "writer." In the final analysis, then, the partners' contributions are not only different, but incommensurate, entities —on the one hand, lived experience mediated by memory; on the other, the labor of eliciting, recording, transcribing, organizing, and revising this material.

The inherent imbalance between the partners' contributions may be complicated by a *political* imbalance between them; often, collaborations involve partners whose relation is hierarchized by some difference—in race, culture, gender, class, age, or (in the case of narratives of illness or disability) somatic condition. Having power or rank over someone is not the same as overpowering that person, of course; the latter is a pitfall that may be evaded. In the scenario typical of ethnographic autobiography, however, the subject may indeed be subject to the writer's domination, in part because the subject is likely to be one of "those who do not write"—in Philippe Lejeune's phrase. This has historically been the case with American racial minorities —African Americans in the case of slave narrative and Native Americans in the case of what Arnold Krupat calls Indian autobiography (30), and much recent criticism has been devoted to recuperating the point of view of subjects who are people of color. My own recent work on narratives of illness and disability suggests that, like other marginalized groups, people who are ill or disabled may therefore also be at a disadvantage with respect to their collaborators. The political imbalance latent in narratives of illness and disability is perhaps most obvious and most problematic in those cases in which the completion and publication of the narrative devolve upon a survivor who narrates another's terminal illness. For example, I have found that relational (particularly parental) narratives of gay men who die of AIDS are often unwittingly heterosexist to some degree; because they are generally written and published posthumously, the subject has no opportunity to audit them.[5] But there are other circumstances in which disability or illness may compromise the ethics of the collaboration; for example, disabilities that make solo autobiography impossible may also make it difficult for the subject to review the manuscript and mandate changes.

Even where such review is possible, the process may involve unintentional misrepresentation. A case in point is that of *I Raise My Eyes to Say Yes,* by Ruth Sienkiewicz-Mercer and Steven B. Kaplan. Sienkiewicz-Mercer has been severely disabled from birth by cerebral palsy, so that she can neither speak nor write; unable to keep her at home, her family sent her to a state facility where she was misdiagnosed as mentally retarded and in effect "warehoused"—supervised rather than educated. Eventually, she was able to make her abilities known, and partly in response to the disability rights movement, she has been able to move out of the state facility. Her story— which, as a story of liberation, is akin to a slave narrative—was written with the collaboration of a lawyer and advocate for people with disabilities through an extremely labor-intensive process. Sienkiewicz-Mercer would scan customized word-boards to select a category, and through a series of questions and answers she would sketch out a skeletal account of an incident; Kaplan would then flesh this out and read it back to her for any corrections.

I see no reason to doubt the accuracy of her narrative, which Sienkiewicz-Mercer had the opportunity to edit. And there is no question of exploitation: Kaplan serves deliberately and faithfully as her advocate. But there is a serious discrepancy between Sienkiewicz-Mercer's level of literacy—as Kaplan describes it, she reads "at best, at a first-grade level, recognizing only simple words placed before her in a familiar context" (vii)—and the voice of the narrative, which is that of a college graduate and fluent writer. Such discrepancies may be characteristic of many ghost-written or collaborative narratives, and they may not always be as problematic as academics make them out to be. One could argue that an account relying on Sienkiewicz-Mercer's diction and syntax might have been unpublishable (and virtually unreadable); is it not better to have a text written from her point of view than no story at all? Furthermore, a text reflecting her level of literacy might have given a misleading indication of her sensibility and intelligence: simple syntax may connote, even if it does not properly signify, simplemindedness. Still, when mediation is ignored, the resulting text may be (mis)taken for a transparent lens through which we have direct access to its subject (rather than to its author). And it is here that the veracity of the narrative as a first-person account of Sienkiewicz-Mercer's life may be called into question. On the one hand, Kaplan professes his concerns about possible distortions; on the other, he produces a text that Sienkiewicz-Mercer could never have produced even if some wondrous technology could transpose words directly from her mind to the page. Kaplan's claim that though "most of the words were not generated by Ruth . . . the thoughts and emotions, the impressions and observations expressed by these words, are Ruth's alone" (xii) assumes too much independence of content from form, message from medium. The liberties Kaplan takes with "translation" in effect hypernormalize Sienkiewicz-Mercer (if that is not an oxymoron). The problem is that the monological prose belies the very labor-intensive dialogical process by which it was produced; in fundamental ways, it masks or erases the disability that has so profoundly shaped its subject's life. Here, then, we have an odd ethical dilemma; the very mediation that seemingly empowers Sienkiewicz-Mercer is deceptive in some fundamental way. Representation in the political sense and representation in the mimetic sense seem fundamentally at odds: in his desire to speak *for* her, Kaplan speaks *as* her in a way that misspeaks her thoughts and feelings.

In the scenario typical of celebrity autobiography, the political dynamics are reversed: here, the subject typically outranks the writer in wealth and clout. The balance of power favors the better-known partner; there is only one Madonna, and she can presumably have her pick of partners.[6] We might schematize collaborative autobiography, then, by imagining examples as lying along a continuum from ethnographic autobiography, in which the writer outranks the subject, to celebrity autobiography, in which the subject outranks the writer. Although I would estimate that most collaborative narratives are situated at the ends of the continuum, significant numbers of texts can be found closer to the middle. At the very center, we would find texts produced by partners who are true peers—for example, dual autobiographies—in which each partner contributes a separate narrative, and truly coauthored (rather than as-told-to) autobiographies.[7] Close to the center, but toward the ethnographic end of the continuum, would be found those single-author texts that Paul John Eakin calls relational lives—

such as Spiegelman's *Maus*—and that I call "auto/biographies," for memoirs of proximate others, such as close relatives or partners, are often collaborative in some sense or degree. In these texts there is more than one subject, and the act of collaboration may itself be part of the narrative rather than treated in supplementary texts, as is the case at the ends of the continuum.

Wherever we are on the continuum, it makes little sense to discuss the "ethics" of collaborative autobiography in isolation from the politics of collaboration—or, for that matter, the economics of collaboration—for ethical problems are most likely to occur where there is a substantial political or economic differential between partners. Furthermore, different ethical issues tend to arise depending upon where the texts are located on this continuum. For example, violation of privacy tends to be more of an issue in relational lives, where the partners know each other intimately, than in most other forms of collaborative autobiography.

Ethical violations—inequities—occur mainly in two distinct but interrelated aspects of the project—the portrayal and the partnership. The justice of the portrayal has to do with whether the text represents its subject the way the subject would like to be represented, whether that portrayal is in the subject's best interests, the extent to which the subject has determined it, and the degree and kind of harm done by any misrepresentation. Harm can be done to the subject's privacy, to his or her reputation, even to his or her integrity as an individual.[8] Problems in the portrayal may be manifest in the text—or in its relation to other texts—and thus relatively easy for critics to detect. (Of course, as critics, we cannot correct these problems but only correct *for* them.) Problems with portrayal are most likely to crop up when the subject's ability to audit and edit the manuscript is limited—that is, mainly in the ethnographic scenario. In cases like this, the critic may act, in effect, as the advocate of the subject, whose life may have been inaccurately portrayed or unfairly appropriated.

In many, perhaps most, cases of ethnographic collaboration, the subjects never confront their published alter egos; their "lives" appear in print elsewhere, among those who do write, and they are damaged neither by the process nor by its product (which is not to say that the process may not be in some way exploitative). *Black Elk Speaks,* by John G. Neihardt, however, offers an interesting case in which the subject of the narrative was discomfited by it in ways he could not have anticipated.[9] The production of this story involved not just translation from Black Elk's Lakota to Neihardt's English but a complex cross-cultural collaboration involving members of Black Elk's family and tribe and members of Neihardt's family. Despite

Neihardt's good intentions, it is now possible to tell, thanks to the recuperative work of Raymond J. DeMallie, that—and how—Neihardt imposed his own agenda on the resulting text. In particular, he was at pains to suppress evidence of Black Elk's acculturation. To this end, Neihardt ended the narrative with the massacre at Wounded Knee in 1890 and omitted any mention or acknowledgment of Black Elk's conversion to Roman Catholicism early in the twentieth century.

In theory, it would have been possible for Black Elk to have reviewed the text; it could have been translated back to him by the same collaborators who produced the transcripts. Such a process would have been difficult, however, and it would not necessarily have enabled him to assess the implications of publishing this account of his life. As it happened, he was not given the opportunity to audit the text. And, as DeMallie reveals, when the book was published, it became a source of some discomfort to him. The reservation clergy were upset that the book portrayed their model convert as an unreconstructed "longhair." Although we have no way of knowing Black Elk's full response to this, we do know that he felt impelled to "speak" again—in a document that reaffirmed his Christian faith. Indeed, he complained that he had wanted Neihardt to include a chapter narrating his conversion. Although it is tempting to read these complaints as induced by clerical pressure, it appears that Neihardt's representation of Black Elk did not completely conform to his self-image and the accepted image of him in his community. The aftermath of publication suggests that he felt that the book did him some injustice (DeMallie 60).[10]

The equity of the partnership has to do with the conditions and division of labor and the distribution of the proceeds. Since this aspect has more to do with the process than with the textual product of the collaboration, violations here may not be manifest in the text and are less easy for critics to detect. (Issues of ownership and distribution of the proceeds of the collaboration are generally least accessible to our inspection; assignment of copyright, though accessible, does not disclose division of proceeds.) In the case of Black Elk, the equity of the partnership, as well as of the portrayal, have come into question: DeMallie's research uncovered a letter in which Black Elk complained that he had not been compensated as promised for his contribution to the book (DeMallie 59–63).

A prime concern with any partnership is whether collaboration is truly voluntary or somehow coerced. Most of us would imagine inequities of partnership as occurring exclusively in the ethnographic scenario, as part of its presumably imperialistic nature, but they may occur in the celebrity scenario as well. There, the relationship between subject and writer is sometimes effectively that between employer and employee, with all the potential for abuse that lies in such relations. According to Andrew Szanton, a professional writer of autobiographies, writers have more at risk economically in these collaborations than subjects do, since such projects often represent the writers' livelihood but rarely that of the subjects, who are generally financially secure (interview).[11] That economic security may, of course, make them generous. In some instances, subjects in effect give away their life stories, but these are generally not the most marketable ones. In any case, there is some potential even in the celebrity scenario for economic exploitation.

A case of a writer claiming exploitation is that of William Novak, who agreed to a flat fee for writing his first celebrity autobiography, *Iacocca,* which then surprised him by becoming a best-seller. When his request for a share of the paperback royalties was turned down, Novak felt he had been cheated out of his fair share of the proceeds. He complained publicly, to no avail (Wyden). Despite any inequity in the distributions of proceeds, Novak had no legal recourse, having signed a contract that afforded him no royalties, and his ethical position was undermined by the fact that Iacocca donated his royalties to charity. In any case, to the extent that his career took off after (and as a result of) his writing of *Iacocca,* the inequity was at least partially redressed.

Another ethical dilemma characteristic of celebrity autobiography is the possible conflict between the writer's obligation to portray the subject as he or she would wish and the obligation to the historical record. Michael Korda has written instructively on the problem that Ronald Reagan's selective memory posed for his collaborator, Robert Lindsey. For example, Reagan remembered a tête à tête with Mikhail Gorbachev in a boathouse on Lake Geneva as a turning point in his negotiations with Gorbachev in November 1985; in fact, the two had not been alone together but rather had been surrounded by a number of translators and security people (Korda 92). More problematically, although Reagan spent the war years in Hollywood, he remembered having been present with the United States Signal Corps at the liberation of the German concentration camps—a memory appropriated from documentary film of that process (93). Such lapses in—or creations of—memory force collaborators to choose between serving as compliant corroborators and functioning as reality checks, between loyalty to their subjects and fidelity to historical truth. Collaborators need to decide how aggressively and extensively to check the accuracy of the record they are helping to create. The position of biographers is different: for them, there is a clear obligation to check the record and no necessary obligation to the subject—except in the case of the authorized biographer. Autobiographers, interestingly, are generally not viewed as obliged to research their own lives; the presumed subjectivity of the genre gains them a degree of latitude.

Professional autobiographers, like Andrew Szanton, may think of their role as analogous to that of defense attorneys, who may know more than they divulge and whose ethical obligations are to put the best possible face on their clients' behavior without outright deception. This may be the proper ethical stance for the professional collaborator; the professional critic, however, is justified in putting a higher value on historical truth. In cases, especially ethnographic ones, in which the subject, or source, is taken advantage of by the writer, the ethical duty of the critic may be to defend the disenfranchised subject; in the case of celebrity autobiography, the ethical duty of the critic may be to protect the historical record.

Collaborations, like these, with celebrities are always consensual; in any case, they also have built-in checks and balances that may deter or at least minimize exploitation. Each partner may use for leverage the indispensability of his or her contribution. Celebrity subjects would seem to have the upper hand, since presumably their stories are the sine qua non of the project;[12] they can threaten to cease cooperating and choose other partners. But lives are not copyrightable, and if celebrities cease cooperating, the collaborators may point out that, in order to protect their investment of time and labor, their only alternative is to turn what were to be autobiographies into *bio*graphies. Their leverage lies in the fact that biographies, though presumably not as marketable as collaborative autobiographies, do not have to be as flattering. (Biographers' ethical obligations to their subjects are quite different from those of collaborators; indeed, contemporary biography would suggest that biographers feel little or no ethical obligation to their subjects.[13]) In the case of collaborative celebrity autobiography, then, the dynamics of the collaboration serve to minimize the potential for inequity in both dimensions—that of the portrayal and that of the partnership; subjects unhappy with their portrayals can demand revisions; writers unhappy with the terms of the collaboration can try to renegotiate them.

Nevertheless, such checks and balances sometimes fail to prevent dissension; like the marriages to which they are often compared, collaborative partnerships sometimes come apart, sometimes acrimoniously. A pertinent case here is the story of the failed collaboration between Fay Vincent, the former commissioner of major league baseball, and David A. Kaplan.

Vincent withdrew from the collaboration on his memoir, *Baseball Breaks Your Heart,* as the manuscript was nearing completion in 1994, apparently because he was reluctant to publish a book that would revive the controversies in which he had been involved (Sandomir). Vincent did not challenge the accuracy of the manuscript but rather its tone; the real issue seemed to be hostile references to people with whom he was dealing at the time, such as New York Yankees owner George Steinbrenner. Implicitly, then, he was suggesting that publication of the book would do him harm by rekindling some of the antagonisms of his years in office. In the summer of 1997, Kaplan took Vincent to court, claiming the right, as coauthor and joint copyright owner, to publish the book on his own; his claim was, in effect, that Vincent had deprived him of the fruits of his labor.

Such a conflict between collaborators points up an issue close to the heart of collaborative autobiography: whose property is the collaboratively produced life story? Vincent's position was that, although he shared copyright with Kaplan, he retained control of the final manuscript; as his lawyer remarked: "How could it be any other way? Otherwise, it's giving your life story to someone else." The answer to the question "Whose life is it, anyway?" may not be as simple as Vincent's lawyer suggests, since the manuscript in question was in part the product of Kaplan's work—including independent research. The nonpartisan legal opinions cited in the *New York Times,* however, came down mostly on Vincent's side, on the principle that, unless he explicitly gave up control over the manuscript, he should still be assumed to have it. As one copyright lawyer put it, "people working on a collaboration about their own lives tend to control their stories, until they give up control." (This is not as tautological as it sounds.) But Vincent's case rested uneasily on "oral agreements" he claimed to have made with Kaplan; in a preliminary ruling, the judge "wrote that he was not persuaded that the co-authors were bound by an oral contract."

In ethnographic autobiography, where the balance of power favors the writer over the subject, the ethical pitfalls are quite different. Collaboration is supposedly a matter of give and take, but in the ethnographic scenario the most obvious danger is the taking of liberties—the appropriation of a life story for purposes not shared, understood, or consented to by the subject. This is a particular danger of the ethnographic scenario because—as was evidently the case with Black Elk—differences of culture may impede or prevent the obtaining of truly informed consent. The same may be true, as indicated above, of differences in age or somatic condition; indeed, I would put most parental memoirs of children and some disability narratives in the ethnographic category. For instance, Michael Dorris's *The Broken Cord*, his account of raising an adopted son whose development was affected by fetal alcohol syndrome, fits both categories: it is a parental memoir of a disabled child that conforms disturbingly to the ethnographic scenario. One consequence of Dorris's discovery of the source of Adam's problems—his birthmother's consumption of alcohol while pregnant—is the tendency to treat him as a type rather than as an individual. Although the early chapters focus on Adam's problems of development, he is portrayed there as a fully individualized character. As is the case in most parental narratives of impaired children, the emphasis is on efforts to maximize his potential, despite his limitations. Emphasis begins to shift to what Adam *cannot* do after Dorris adopts other children and especially after he and his wife, Louise Erdrich, have children who exemplify "norms" to which Adam does not measure up (see, for example, 120, 127–29). This tendency culminates in the book's peroration, which offers a litany of things Adam will never understand or appreciate (264).

After the moment of "diagnosis," Adam tends to become a type and his story a case history; emphasis shifts to his generic (genetic) traits and to larger cultural problems. And eventually, as *narrator*, Dorris abandons the role of advocate for his son and takes up the role of crusader against the use of alcohol by pregnant women. Indeed, insofar as Adam's problems are seen to result from cultural pathology in the Native American community, the book veers toward ethnographic life writing, or even ethnography proper. Dorris assumes the role of the outside expert or anthropological authority—usually a non-native—who enlists in a collaborative life-writing project a native subject not otherwise inclined to generate an autobiography. It is unusual, and troubling, that in this instance the role of the anthropologist is assumed by a parent and that the "informant" is his son. The crucial difference from most ethnography, however, is that here the disparity between the two parties is not a difference in race or culture; rather, that disparity is a function of Adam's congenital FAS-related cognitive disabilities, which, though related to patterns of Indian alcohol abuse, are not intrinsic to his cultural heritage. In practice, then, though for very different reasons than those operating in most earlier texts, this book's production involved the sort of asymmetrical collaboration typical of ethnographic autobiography, in which the editor tends to exercise cultural authority over his "subject."[14]

What is tendered as autonomous self-representation—the appended narrative by the son, "The Story of Adam Dorris by Adam Dorris"—is in effect mediated in ways the putative autobiographer cannot understand or control. Just as he was apparently incapable of adjusting his appearance in everyday life to the expectations of others, Adam could not fully imagine, and thus could not censor, the way he was being presented to a reading public. In this case, the subject is put at a disadvantage not so much by his culture as by his disability. Despite Dorris's noble intentions, then, he produced a book in which disability assumes the role of cultural difference in defining and subjugating the Other in anthropological discourse. Although Dorris did elicit Adam's testimony, that testimony serves mainly to corroborate Dorris's characterization of Adam in the narrative that precedes and introduces it. Adam's text is contained and defined by his father's. On the whole, then, Dorris seems to have arrogated authority in ways reminiscent of "colonial" ethnography.

Collaborative autobiography is inherently ventriloquistic. The dynamics of the ventriloquism, however—the direction in which the voice is "thrown" —may vary with the location of the collaboration on the continuum described earlier. In ethnographic autobiography, the danger tends to be that of attributing to the subject a voice and narrative not originating with him or her—and that he or she may not have edited. *Black Elk Speaks* is a classic example; indeed, the most frequently quoted paragraphs have turned out to be wholly Neihardt's invention. This danger exists, of course, in celebrity autobiography, as well; some celebrities—notably Darryl Strawberry and Ronald Reagan—have notoriously not *read,* much less written, their so-called "autobiographies." But, unlike Black Elk, they *could* have reviewed the prose ascribed to them. In celebrity autobiography, perhaps the greater danger is the reverse dynamic, in which the subject assumes or is given more credit for the writing than is legitimate. Although I am otherwise excluding ghostwritten autobiography from consideration here—that is, the use of an unacknowledged collaborator—I would point out that, by academic standards, ghostwritten autobiography is tantamount to plagiarism. If the ghostwriter consents to being anonymous, as is usually the case, the process is not plagiarism in the sense of appropriation of another's intellectual property without permission: the arrangement is that the writer's compensation takes the form of a paycheck and not a byline, so there's no violation of the partnership. And, of course, the wide acceptance of the practice—like that of presidential speech writing by ghosts—suggests that there is not considered to be any dishonesty involved because none but the most naive might be fooled. Here is a good example of a case where the ethics of trade publishing and those of academic publishing differ sharply.

But a ghostwritten autobiography does, I think, raise a minor ethical issue with regard to the truthfulness of the portrayal. The text implicitly falsifies both the history of its subject— who did not in fact labor single-handedly to produce it—and the subject's image: he or she may not be a person *capable* of writing such a text.

Looked at from another angle, the projection of the voice of the writer or interlocutor onto the subject is tantamount to forgery. This occurs mainly with ghostwritten celebrity autobiography, where the signature of the source may be worth more than the signature of the writer. As Philippe Lejeune points out, with ethnographic collaboration, the "story takes its value, in the eyes of the reader, from the fact that [the subjects] belong (that they *are perceived* as belonging) to a culture other than his own, a culture defined by the exclusion of writing" (196). A complex but relatively mild form of the forgery of celebrity autobiography seems to have occurred in the literary aftermath of the death of Diana Spencer. Andrew Morton, the author of a biography called *Diana, Her True Story,* claimed, after her death, that his title had been an understatement: the book was not merely a *true* story but *her* story in the sense that she was its principal source (Hoge). Accordingly, he rushed into print a new version with an amended title: *Diana, Her True Story—In Her Own Words.* In effect, then, Morton claimed that a book presented originally as "his" biography of her was in fact a covertly collaborative life-writing project—a sort of ghostwritten *bio*graphy, or pseudonymous autobiography in the third person. His claims raise ethical issues aside from the questionable propriety of his attempt to capitalize on Diana's death by reviving his "life" of her. If his claim is not true, then this case is an instance of one ethical violation, forgery—the false attribution of material to the "subject" of the book in order to heighten its apparent authenticity (and thus, not incidentally, its already considerable commercial value). If his claim is true, the act may be a violation of a pledge to keep her involvement in the production of the original book confidential.

Forged or ventriloquistic autobiography may take less benign forms than this—if we broaden our scope beyond those practices usually deemed literary or anthropological. As Margreta de Grazia has pointed out, a false confession obtained by means of torture might euphemistically be described as "collaborative autobiography"; such a text would obviously involve inequity in portrayal as well as of "partnership." In such cases, both the process and the product may be extremely harmful to the subject; indeed, here the faking of a life may quite literally involve the taking of a life. The extortion of a *true* confession—that is, a confession to a crime the confessor did commit

—could also be described only euphemistically as a collaborative autobiography. The dynamics of the "confessions" of condemned prisoners in England in the eighteenth century can illustrate how the ethnographic and the celebrity scenarios may complement one another. In-house confessions "dictated" to prison ordinaries and distributed at the time of execution—as if spontaneous and simultaneous with the execution—were sometimes supplemented by extramural accounts written by journalists for a popular audience. The in-house "confessions," which were coerced, sometimes by torture, reflected the authority of the state in more than one sense: they were scripted according to narrow conventions and reflected the apparent internalization of self-condemning social norms. (They were confessions in the religious and moral as well as the legal sense.) In contrast, convicts might arrange to produce, with the collaboration of an independent journalist like Daniel Defoe, a quite different sort of testimony—a kind of criminal's celebrity memoir. Prisoners would be treated more favorably in terms of both process and portrayal in the extramural confessions than in the intramural ones. Though they might be formulaic, these texts were more voluntarily produced, and the subjects were more in control of their own representation. While these accounts might be preferred on ethical grounds because of their less compulsory quality, they would, of course, be more at odds with the official ethos.

Further examples of subtly coercive—and thus unethical—collaborative life writing may be found in abuses of psychiatric practice. Most forms of psychotherapy involve—indeed, consist of—what might be seen as "collaborative autobiography." What is ideally a benign and therapeutic process, however, is liable to ethical misuse (like any collaboration with a professional, such as a physician or lawyer). Obvious examples may be found in the "recovering" of false memories of abuse or other trauma, except that here we have not coerced confession but coerced accusation—autobiography as character assassination.

Another relevant distinction between collaborative life-writing scenarios may be found in the degree of professionalization of the authors. Today, ethnography in the narrow sense is produced by professional anthropologists, who are currently haunted by the complicity of ethnography in imperialism, cultural or otherwise. Indeed, ethnography and ethnographic life writing have been so thoroughly theorized and analyzed as to have been virtually paralyzed. By a broader definition, of course, the ethnographic scenario includes amateur practices, such as Neihardt's collaboration with Black Elk, in which professional ethics are nonexistent or not highly developed. Similarly, those who write celebrity autobiography for a living are not organized professionally; they are a relatively small number of freelancers who function without an explicit or shared code of ethics (Szanton interview). Finally, those who collaborate in scenarios toward the middle of the continuum between ethnographic and celebrity collaboration—for example, parental biographers of children or those who collaborate with the ill and the disabled to write their lives—are generally even less conscious of being part of a professional group with ethical restraints.

Collaborative autobiography is practiced today with great frequency and openness. At least, this is one implication of a recent Steiner cartoon in the *New Yorker*. The scene is an elementary school classroom, complete with a globe on the teacher's desk and a flag in the corner. Two students, a boy and a girl, stand next to the teacher's desk, facing the rest of their class. The boy smiles smugly, hands clasped behind his back, while the girl reads from a paper she is holding: "'What I did last summer,' by Scott Sweningen, as told to Samantha Gerhart." The teacher's expression is impossible to read, but one wonders about the elementary ethics here; what would clearly be cheating, if done surreptitiously—the writing of one student's composition by another—is apparently acceptable when done openly. The joke is, I guess, that collaborative autobiography has trickled down to the level of the clichéd first assignment of the school year. If this cartoon is an indication, collaborative autobiography will only become more common; if that is so, we need to extend and intensify our consideration of the full range of ethical issues it raises.

We may apply ethical standards in two different scenarios. One is retrospective; we may investigate and stand in judgment of the ethics of published texts. The other is prospective; we may seek to head off ethical violations by setting forth guidelines to influence future life writing. Whichever scenario we operate within, our influence and power are indirect and diffuse. We need to remember that, as critics of life writing, we occupy a distinct and awkward position with respect to the practice of it; our ethics may be at odds with the ethics of those—professional as well as amateur—who practice collaborative life writing. And we need to be attentive to the benefits as well as the liabilities of collaboration. For example, it may be tempting to decry ethnographic autobiography insofar as it may seem inherently to reduce its subjects to types. But such an objection to ethnography may invoke values, such as that of the uniqueness of the individual, that are alien to some of the cultures it seeks to represent. It may be, too, that the recuperative benefits of ethnography outweigh its costs. For example, it could be argued that, despite Neihardt's taking of some liberties in his collaboration with Black Elk, the text they produced collaboratively has helped to preserve and to disseminate Lakota culture; Black Elk and his people have benefited from the collaboration in ways he may not have fully anticipated. In any case, it may be unwise for us to devise ethical principles that would effectively censor or censure whole genres of life writing. Literary critics may have an important role to play in the ongoing development of collaborative life writing, particularly if we extend our consideration beyond the texts traditionally considered literary, but we need to be careful of self-righteousness—of devising, in the isolation of the ivory tower, excessively fastidious principles.

Notes

1. Other forms of life writing also involve collaboration—more so than is sometimes acknowledged. Biography—even when not authorized—is never done single-handedly, at least when living sources are consulted. Autobiography is often, perhaps almost always, a relational enterprise. Even when it is not, it may require backstage consultation with others to fill in memory's gaps. I confine myself, however, to auto-biographical projects that involve *conscious* and *active* cooperation.

2. More technical terms for narrator and protagonist are "the subject speaking" and "the subject spoken," as used by de Grazia (290). While useful, these terms also seem clumsy to me.

3. "Subject" is today an ambiguous, multivalent term: grammatically, it suggests agency; politically, it suggests the opposite—passivity or subordination; in poststructuralism, it suggests constructedness and provisionality. Here, I use it in none of these senses, but rather in the everyday sense of "topic"—in this case, the person the book is about.

Some critics refer to the subject of collaborative autobiography as the "dictator," others as the "speaker." In the case of ethnographic autobiography, "dictator" seems too often ironic, in view of the political meaning of that term; that is, it implies a kind of dominance not characteristic of the usual speaker; in the cases of celebrity autobiography, it may be more apt, but even there it underestimates the agency of the collaborator.

The problem with using the term "speaker" for those Philippe Lejeune refers to as "those who do not write" is that some who do not write do not *speak* either. I am thinking here not so much of deaf people, who may use sign language to communicate their narratives and who generally can read the written narrative their collaborators produce, but rather those whose disability may prevent speech and sign language as well as writing—such as those with cerebral palsy or other such disorders. In any case, "speaker" implies the ability to speak, which is not universal, and cases of disability are extremely interesting and problematic in this regard. See my discussion of Sienkiewicz-Mercer later in this essay.

What to call the other partner is also problematic: "author" is sometimes technically correct, but sometimes the collaborators are coauthors. Even when they are not, "author" may ascribe the resulting text unfairly to one partner. Similarly, "writer" may overstate the interviewer's role, while "editor" usually understates it. Because in most cases one partner does most of what we usually mean by "write"—inscribe words by hand in lasting form—I use "writer" for the partner more responsible for the composition of the text.

4. As it happens, those in the publishing business sometimes use the marriage analogy for collaborative writing partnerships.

5. See my chapter "HIV/AIDS and Its Stories" in *Recovering Bodies: Illness, Disability, and Life Writing,* especially the section on "Family Plots: Relational AIDS Memoirs."

6. Rosemary J. Coombe has argued that celebrity identity is authored collaboratively and collectively, rather than individually. Nevertheless, in the marketplace, the celebrity has the advantage of licensing his or her own replication.

7. An example of a dual autobiography would be *Cancer in Two Voices,* by Sandra Butler and Barbara Rosenblum.

8. On violations of privacy and related issues, see Paul John Eakin, "The Unseemly Profession."

9. For a fuller account of this example, see my chapter "*Black Elk Speaks* with Forked Tongue" in *Altered Egos: Authority in American Autobiography* (189–209).

10. I do not want to portray Black Elk as merely a victim in this process. It is likely that the book reflected his shrewd use of an unfamiliar medium—autobiography—to convey his vision to a larger audience. Each partner may have used the other in ways of which the other was unaware.

11. Szanton has written the memoirs of Eugene Wigner, a Hungarian-born Manhattan Project physicist, and of Charles Evers, a civil rights leader and brother of Medgar Evers; he is currently writing the memoirs of former Massachusetts Senator Edward Brooke.

12. Such stories are not always worth what publishers pay for them. For example, according to Michael Korda of Simon and Schuster, although publishers love the glamour of having a former president as an "author," presidential memoirs usually lose money (88).

13. It is hard to imagine a contemporary biographer concluding, as M. O. W. Oliphant did one hundred years ago, that a biographer who discovers unexpected flaws in his or her subject "might well consider not writing the biography at all" (Bergmann 3).

14. For a full consideration of this book, see my essay "Raising Adam."

Works Cited

Bergmann, Linda S. "Widows, Hacks, and Biographers: The Voice of Professionalism in Elizabeth Agassiz's *Louis Agassiz: His Life and Correspondence.*" *a/b: Auto/Biography Studies* 12 (1997): 1–21.

Booth, Wayne C. *The Company We Keep: An Ethics of Fiction.* Berkeley: U of California P, 1988.

Butler, Sandra, and Barbara Rosenblum. *Cancer in Two Voices.* San Francisco: Spinsters Ink, 1991.

Coombe, Rosemary J. "Author/izing the Celebrity: Publicity Rights, Postmodern Politics, and Unauthorized Genders." Woodmansee 101–31.

Couser, G. Thomas. *Altered Egos: Authority in American Autobiography.* New York: Oxford UP, 1989.

———. "Raising Adam: Ethnicity, Disability, and the Ethics of Life Writing in Michael Dorris's *The Broken Cord.*" *Biography* 21 (1998): 421–44.

———. *Recovering Bodies: Illness, Disability, and Life Writing.* Madison: U of Wisconsin P, 1997.

de Grazia, Margreta. "Sanctioning Voice: Quotation Marks, the Abolition of Torture, and the Fifth Amendment." Woodmansee 281–302.

DeMallie, Raymond J. Introduction. *The Sixth Grandfather: Black Elk's Teachings as Given to John G. Neihardt.* Ed. Raymond J. DeMallie. Lincoln: U of Nebraska P, 1984.

Dorris, Michael. *The Broken Cord.* New York: Harper and Row, 1989.

Eakin, Paul John. "Relational Selves, Relational Lives: The Story of the Story." *True Relations: Essays on Autobiography and the Postmodern.* Ed. G. Thomas Couser and Joseph Fichtelberg. Westport, CT: Greenwood, 1998. 63–81.

———. "The Unseemly Profession: Privacy, Inviolate Personality, and the Ethics of Life Writing." *Renegotiating Ethics in Literature, Philosophy, and Theory.* Ed. Jane Adamson, Richard Freadman, and David Parker. Cambridge: Cambridge UP, 1998. 161–80.

Haley, Alex. Epilogue. *The Autobiography of Malcolm X,* by Malcolm X, with Alex Haley. New York: Grove, 1965. 383–456.

Hoge, Warren. "Now It Can Be Told: 1992 Tell-All Book's Source Was Diana." *New York Times* 30 September 1997: A7.

Korda, Michael. "Prompting the President." *New Yorker* 6 October 1997: 88–95.

Krupat, Arnold. *For Those Who Come After: A Study of Native American Autobiography.* Berkeley: U of California P, 1985.

Lejeune, Philippe. "The Autobiography of Those Who Do Not Write." *On Autobiography.* Ed. Paul John Eakin. Trans. Katherine Leary. Minneapolis: U of Minnesota P, 1989. 185–215.

Sandomir, Richard. "Co-Author Sues to Publish Vincent Book." *New York Times* 11 August 1997: 21+ (Sports).

Spiegelman, Art. *Maus I: A Survivor's Tale; My Father Bleeds History.* New York: Pantheon, 1986.

———. *Maus II: A Survivor's Tale; And Here My Troubles Began.* New York: Pantheon, 1991.

Steiner, P. Cartoon. *New Yorker* 15 September 1997: 72.

Szanton, Andrew. *The Recollections of Eugene P. Wigner as Told to Andrew Szanton.* New York: Plenum, 1992.

———. Telephone interview. 11 November 1997.

Szanton, Andrew, and Charles Evers. *Have No Fear: The Charles Evers Story.* New York: Wiley, 1997.

Woodmansee, Martha, and Peter Jaszi, eds. *The Construction of Authorship: Textual Appropriation in Law and Literature.* Durham: Duke UP, 1994.

Wyden, Peter. "The Blockbustering of Lee Iacocca." *New York Times Book Review* 13 September 1987: 1+.

THE SCANDAL OF
HUMAN COUNTENANCE

Witold Gombrowicz and Bruno Schulz in Exile
from the Country of Forms

ADAM ZACHARY NEWTON

Preface

IT OCCURRED to me, while fine-tuning this piece for its present appearance, to overhaul it entirely in light of a belated discovery. A recently published volume on Witold Gombrowicz contains an essay whose argument uncannily parallels my own, and—with perfect Gombrowiczian poetic justice—whose form does as well. The following piece begins and ends with face-offs between Gombrowicz and some cathected Other; so does the essay by Dorota Głowacka.[1] Głowacka proposes a scandal of mimesis, with appeals to the likes of Phillipe Lacoue-Labarthe and Derrida; I speak of the scandal of countenance, making the occasional nod in the direction of Levinas and Slavoj Žižek. I conclude by asking how readers regard a text that looks back at them; Głowacka ends by asking in what way readers can listen to the same text's silent laughter. In short, my essay about fiction obsessed with double and doubling had a doppelgänger—a reflected face to mirror my own, now "blemished by resemblance," as Głowacka herself might say. Perhaps, I thought, I should transpose this whole exercise to a prefatory face-off on the plane of criticism—a duel of critical interventions. And yet the very enterprise of critical intervention is something that Gombrowicz and Schulz, in different ways, sabotage in advance. And then I realized: of course, Gombrowicz had already anticipated me. "Another preface," he writes in *Ferdydurke,* "I must provide a preface, a preface is required of me, without a preface I cannot possibly go on. . . . Whether I like it or not, I cannot, no, I simply cannot, evade the iron laws of symmetry and analogy" (187). And so, begging your indulgence, let me briefly begin again.

Casting about for the most instructive way to place this presentation within the curvature of my work thus far, it occurs to me that it actually represents an arc of its own in a more restrictive sense—a camber hinging where I have been and where I am headed. Without meaning to appear facile, let me call this arc very simply the move from *face* to *place,* or from *face* as an ethical mediation between persons and also literary traditions, a kind of allegoresis, to *place* on that same model of interface or mediation—but for nationhood and ethno-cultural identity. I prefer a homelier word than *identity,* actually (homely, as in the Freudian etymology for the uncanny), and that is *belonging,* which neatly compacts the senses of reach or extension, appurtenance, and yearning. For my subject here is *belonging as something that has somehow already slipped*—more reach or want than appending or adhering. Like the diasporic adventure of being faced by another, the reach of place, the yearning *for* place, signifies not some experience of exile afflicting, say, the Jewish Other or any other Others, but rather the lack in every nation and nationally constituted self that becomes inevitable through its facing relationship with Others, those Others who alternately lay bare and constitute its national identity or *political* face. One belongs, but only, as Gombrowicz captures it oxymoronically, from or at a near distance. A small instance of such slippage can be identified in a recent discussion among Yiddishists on an e-mail list (Mendele) about a magazine article, "Guidebook to a Land of Ghosts," that treated what its author, Michael Chabon, called an "absurd and poignant artifact": the version, in Yiddish, of the "Say it in . . ." phrase book series for travelers to foreign countries. The article's point was itself poignant but ironic: there is no *Yiddishland,* no country, no nation where one might need the Yiddish equivalents of "What is the flight number?" or "I need something for a tourniquet" or "Can I go by boat/ferry to ——?" Of this last phrase, Chabon writes, "Whither could I sail on that boat-slash-ferry, and from what shore?" (Chabon 68). Yiddish—a fugitive, nonnormative, stateless language that for some is the very model for a certain kind of postmodernism, its own diaspora of commingled and deterritorialized tongues—where would its homeland lie? Some subscribers argued "nowhere"; others, "everywhere." Some cited parallel cases of surplus or lack between language and national boundaries. Others argued that whether the phrase book served as guide to an "imaginary Ashkenaz or Jewish Krypton" was beside the point: it serves as a language skills tool; or else, ideologically considered, it merely confirms the fact that Yiddish is a modern language among other modern languages. A commonsense response to the whole affair would be, "So much talking about talking in Yiddish!" (As the Yiddish saying goes, *a fresr iz nisht der vos est nor der vos ret fin esn* [a glutton is not the one who eats but the one who talks about eating].) But the lesson for my purposes is closer to something Alain Finkielkraut captures at the conclusion of his *The Imaginary Jew* when he zeroes in on "the word 'Jew'"—for which I would substitute *the language Yiddish*—as "no longer a mirror in which I seek my self portrait, but where I look for everything I'm not, everything I'll never be able to glimpse by taking myself as a point of reference" (219). In other words, Yiddishly speaking, my here is already an elsewhere: my face does not mirror back to me.

From "Yiddishly speaking" or "talking in Yiddish," let me pivot finally to something Jonathan Boyarin calls "thinking in Jewish," in his book by the same name, as one final signpost to this particular mapping of *my own* turn in thinking through "the ethical." In his preface, Boyarin says that the gerund *thinking in* can go in a couple of directions: intransitively, like the Yiddish reflexive construction *zikh arayntrakhtn*—*to think yourself into* something, to consider it in depth, but also transitively—where *thinking in* would resemble ushering in, welcoming in, piloting a different sense of identity through thought (Boyarin 3). This double-edged sense of thinking resonates for me in some compelling ways. On one hand, I have been "thinking myself into something" for a while now, which I have been calling *ethics,* and for which the face has served as overarching trope—an emblem for encounter and recognition drawn from Emmanuel Levinas; but it is also a *dugma,* an image, from within my own religious and textual tradition, where the word in Hebrew signifies a turning toward, a freeing or clearing, and specifically in regard to textual exegesis, interface, as in free for interpretation on two sides. In what follows the face is just such an *interface,* announcing and simultaneously undoing self-presence—it might even be said therefore to *diasporize,* in light of certain other inflections of face, in Hebrew, that connote vacating, turning aside, removing, and releasing. If selfhood is a face that has become vulnerable, national identity—or belongingness—is likewise a mug, a grimace, or a mask, a face stranded between its own self-determination and its collapse or refiguration under the glare of Others' faces, a mimeticism that always risks degenerating into mimicry or the migrancy of empty gestures and forms. If the human countenance is a scandal because of the ruptures it produces interpersonally, the nation is that countenance writ large, only *seemingly* whole and self-present. I might call this, in that same play on transitivity and intransitivity, "thinking-in Diaspora." And as something of a way station itself, this essay looks ahead, in fact, to a project entitled *The Elsewhere: On Belonging at a Distance,* whose epigraph might well read: "this 'being elsewhere' combined with the desperate wish to 'be at home' in a manner at once intense, fruitful, and destructive" (Scholem, qtd. in Kitaj 117). But for now, unless I wish to side-line myself on what Bruno Schulz calls a branch track of time—the temporal analogue to wandering in exile—I am overdue for the first of five brief tableaux in facing, Gombrowicz-style. To paraphrase a character in *Ferdydurke,* "to hell with more *pre*face; nothing but face!"

Scene One. Society; or, A Railway in Argentina

Sitting in an Argentine train compartment, seething at the press of Others, the twentieth-century Polish émigré writer Witold Gombrowicz begins his *Diary* entry for the year 1962 this way:

> That mug ten centimeters away. The teary, reddish pupils? Little hairs on this ear? I don't want this! Away! I will not go on about his chapped skin! By what right did this find itself so close that I practically have to breathe him in, yet at the same time feel his hot trickles on my ear and neck? We rest our unseeing gazes on each other from a very near distance . . . each person is curling up, rolling up, shutting, shrinking, limiting to a minimum his eyes, ears, lips, trying to *be* as little as possible. (3:17)

Although the entry makes it clear that its *ressentiment* is centered chiefly on the numbers of people compressed into the same car as Gombrowicz himself, "that mug ten centimeters away" does not exactly fade from readers' sight. It stays vivid (Gombrowicz has ensured as much), but partly because of the uncanny little scene that embeds it.

Literature, with criticism's help, has accustomed us by now to a whole scenic palette, diminutive theaters of figural enactment: Mirror Scenes, Scenes of Writing, Scenes of Reading, Scenes of Instruction, Scenes of Eating, even Scenes of Fasting (in Kafka's case). Gombrowicz offers, in their place, a Scene of Facing. Indeed, it is fair to assume that Gombrowicz expects readers of his *Diary* who are already familiar with his work—the 1937 novel *Ferdydurke,* in particular—to recognize such a scene as a lately added snapshot to a much larger portfolio of signature studies in the face-to-face.[2]

Thus, against the background of the author's abiding concern with the space *between* two persons, *that mug ten centimeters away* denotes not so much a countenance positioned opposite as an incitement to Opposition itself.[3] The gauntlet slap delivered to Gombrowicz's face is the fact that another faces him. The slap that answers it is his counter-face grimacing in return.

Przyprawienie geby ("fitting someone with a mug") describes the norm of human interaction in Gombrowicz, a relentless duel of face-making, face-wearing, face-imposing. One face creates the other; a grimace responds.

Both faces remain in dependent relation, face and grimace, mug and countenance, tracing a double helix of mutual deformation on into the negative
infinity.[4] There is no sublation or sublimation. Higher, theoretical operations merely repeat rather than resolve an almost chthonic drama.

"Nothing but the mug," says the aforementioned character in *Ferdydurke* who is looking for authentic countenance, "nothing sincere or natural,
everything copied, trashy, fake, bogus" (*Ferdydurke* [Borchardt] 206). Such
a search encompasses the face that looks at me and the face it imposes on
mine and the face I adopt in return and all the faces, mugs, grimaces, and
permutations of phiz that pass between us. Just as that definitive paradox of
Gombrowiczian space—"from a very near distance"—overrides any pro-
prietary ideas about autonomous identity, so face is synecdochic shorthand
for the face-to-face relation, for the scandal of one's own face forced into
self- consciousness and countermove by the face of another.[5] One *wears* or
shares a face; one does not own it.

My face is thus also my mask, not a site of saving and necessary heteroglossia in Bakhtin's sense, but a *heterophysiognomia,* a blend of my features
and the faces opposite mine. And if "it is impossible to detach from other
people" (*Diary* 3:77), it is no less impossible to free the face from its own
mugs and grimaces. The socializing stick shaken by parents at children—
"Don't make such faces or they'll get stuck"—has the ring of deepest ontological truth, face as *rictus.* Thus, sometimes in *Ferdydurke* face simply
signifies personhood; other times, it means "the agony of outward form."

Physiognomy—as counterintuitive but also deeply intuitive as it sounds
—is anything but private property. "How can one escape from what one is,
where is the leverage to come from?" Gombrowicz writes. "Our form permeates us, imprisons us, as much as from within as from without" (*Ferdydurke* [Borchardt] 47).[6] The sufficiency of my own private physiognomy
is always being interrupted or compromised by the intervening faces of
Others. Even if I seem finished to myself, a facing Other will make me
seem unfinished, de-shaped.

Moreover, any desire for self-sufficiency is ridiculed by the unruliness of
the face to begin with, by its enslavement not only to the faces of Others
but also to one's own body. I endure a ludicrous self-sabotage. Standing up
to the top of my height, I am still mocked by the very backside that joins
trunk to head.[7] The very fact of thighs calls consciousness down from its
lofty perch. Digits and toes conduct their own duel of grimaces in repeating each other, hand to foot. Human forms are not unified or consolidated;
they are composite, an aggregate of parts. Faces are their own mugs because

self-identity is self-parody. The face is a kind of double agent: the seat and sign of personal identity but also merely another composite body part. In short, we *wear* or *share* a face; we do not own it. Especially when it peers into the pages of a book.

The railway set piece, nested within *Diary* as a whole—itself the culminating work of Gombrowicz's oeuvre—can thus, without too much of a stretch, be understood to allegorize his own keen awareness of writing in the presence of reading Others, the aggregate mugs, reddish pupils, and tiny hairs of writerly/readerly nearness. *Diary* is where Gombrowicz achieves a Form possible only with readers' complicity. Unlike more "tactful" French diarists, he wants his own to be "more modern and more conscious, and let it be permeated by the idea that my talent can only arise in connection with you, that only you can excite me to talent, or what's more that only you can create it in me" (*Diary* 1:35). There are moments of uncanniness when reading that call one back to the phenomenal world, where a book suddenly stands in for a person speaking, where we become conscious of our hands holding a book and thus making contact through it with an author. The end of Toni Morrison's *Jazz,* for instance: "Say make me, remake me. You are free to do it and I am free to let you because look, look. Look where your hands are. Now." Or Whitman's lyric from *Calamus:* "Whoever you are holding me now in hand." Or Keats's posthumously published lyric "This living hand now warm and capable. . . . See, here it is—I hold it towards you." In Gombrowicz, those hands become a face. But *Diary* is also, as I have intimated, the backdrop for a gallery of faces, like this next one, a first cousin to the train-compartment scene, set against the backdrop of Argentina's *Museo Nacional de Bellas Artes.*

Scene Two. Art; or, Inside a Museum

> There were ten other people besides ourselves who walked up, looked, then walked away. The mechanical quality of their movements, their muteness, gave them the appearance of marionettes and their faces were nonexistent compared to the faces that peered out of the canvas. This is not the first time that the face of art has irritated me by extinguishing the faces of the living . . . Here in the museum, the paintings are crowded, the amount crowds the quality, masterpieces counted in the dozens stop being masterpieces. Who can look closely at a Murillo when the Tiepolo next to it demands attention and thirty other paintings shout: look at us! (*Diary* 1:22)

This kind of nausea is, in its way, profounder than Existentialist dread, because it draws a continuous line between the Sartrean *"L'enfer, c'est l'autres"* and the "hell which is other paintings or other books or even *this book* or *this painting* directly in front of me." While the image is obviously more dramatic for portraiture, Gombrowicz projects a face onto literature and philosophy, too: I don't just look at books, they hector me, shouting "look at us."

There is more to Gombrowicz, in other words, than just face. There is even philosophy. If the mini-opera in the train compartment may tap the figural marrow of Gombrowicz's work,[8] the scene in the art museum connects him, perhaps even more obviously, to a whole matrix of continental thought—though Poland's exact place on that continent is merely another way of putting Gombrowicz's central question: where is the leverage to come from? In the land of the minor (which is how Gombrowicz both expresses his Polishness and the meaning that modernism will therefore have for him), how should one keep company, share space with Heideggerians or French Existentialists? (Countries, as the fifth and last of these scenic vignettes will suggest, have faces, too.)

"*Ferdydurke* was published in 1937," Gombrowicz writes, "before Sartre formulated his theory of the *regard d'autrui*. But it is owing to the popularization of Sartrean concepts that this aspect of my book has been better understood and assimilated" (*Diary* 3:8).[9] In volume 3 of the *Diary*, he lays claim to having similarly presaged French structuralism. *Ferdydurke* predates Merleau-Ponty (*The Phenomenology of Perception*), Elias Canetti (*Crowds and Power*), Jacques Lacan (*Le Seminaire*), and, most relevant of all perhaps, the philosophical thought of Emmanuel Levinas, in which the figure of the face occupies an absolutely central position, the place where ethics is manifested and where the Other cuts across the grain of Self.[10]

But form such a gallery around Gombrowicz, and the philosophers become so many Murillos and Tiepolos, shouting "look at us! Look at our affinities, our tangencies! See the mugs we fit each other with!"[11] Along with the same character in *Ferdydurke* who exclaimed, "Nothing but the mug!" one wants to say, "To hell with philosophy!" The ruthlessly consistent vector of Gombrowicz's narrative poetics is itself a kind of face that will not stop irrevocably facing, staring, grimacing. To read him is to become intensely self-conscious that he forms the accusative case of your reading, as you, reciprocally, play direct or indirect object to his authorship. In other words, the scandal of human countenance is also a face-to-face mediated by the Book: the face-to-*book*-to-face. Is such glowering as thaumaturgic as, say, the imprecation signaled by the title of a Manuel Puig novel, *Cursed Be the Reader of These Pages*, or as collusive as Abbie Hoffman's *Steal This*

Book? It is certainly no less insistent about the gauntlets it flings down as a dueling character in *Ferdydurke* exclaims, "There are faces! There are slaps!"

Take the case of Sartre, whom Gombrowicz mentions frequently in *Diary.* A Sartrean reading of the chapped skin, little hairs on the ear, hot trickles, contraction of the self, and nearness of the Other in the train compartment scene would have *visage* held hostage to *regard, face* at the mercy of *gaze,* the For Itself haunted by an all-too-present staring Other. But perhaps the scene works the other way around, as a rejoinder to Sartre, a *face* to counter a *look,* an oblique way of acknowledging uneasily shared intellectual space.[12] That becomes a less figurative possibility when one comes upon another anecdote only pages later about the young Jean-Paul Sartre himself that bears for Gombrowicz a wholly Gombrowiczian stamp. (He even admits at the outset how much the anecdote resonates for him, for it is "not the first time that anecdotes add up like this" in his experience.)

Scene Three. Philosophy; or, A Street in Paris

Strolling in heavy traffic on l'avenue de l'Opéra one night, Sartre the prephilosopher is caught up by a surging crowd of pedestrians who suddenly appear to him paradoxically as both nonentities and sources of dread:

> It was especially hideous (as he confessed to friends later), when we experience a man a short distance away as an almost physical threat, yet if, at the same time, he is dehumanized by the mass, only the thousandth repetition of a man, a duplicate, an example, almost a monkey; when he is therefore, simultaneously, because of the numbers, very close and awfully far. Having found himself in this throng-crush, this people-nonpeople, our still young, nonauthor of Being and Nothingness takes to summoning loneliness with his whole soul: O! To stand out! Be apart! Break away! Escape! But people were standing on his feet. (Gombrowicz, *Diary* 3:40)

The experience becomes formative. Sartre decides to seek refuge in philosophy, mounting a defensive retreat into his consciousness and the concreteness of his personal existence—"a double wall with which he hermetically sealed himself from others, having slammed the doors of his 'I' after him." Gombrowicz then interrupts the flow of the story to tell us that evidently Sartre's existentialism began "in a crowd."

Sartre reluctantly admits that after immuring himself in his selfhood, he grew less happy with the idea of isolation as being sustained, existentially, in isolation. He notices, "in his peripheral vision, that it would find a glad repose in the thousands of [other] souls threatened by numbers." This confusion between "philosophy and numbers," between one's own thought and the press of Others, between a spot taken up in a museum and dozens of staring paintings, Sartre cannot seem to transcend: "Neither Consciousness nor the Concrete has the right to grow fat on such yeast."

Worse even than this resurfacing terror—"isolation fattened by numbers" —is the realization that this fear *itself* is not alone: "It immediately became magnified by the numbers of all those others whom he could identify himself with—and the burning of a tree became a conflagration of an entire forest in our philosopher." Sartre turns to himself one more time—"in being the Only One, I cannot be one of the many!"—and decides to resuscitate the Other whom he had previously annihilated philosophically—"rediscover, recognize, reinstitute, re-establish my bond with him!" He recognizes the Other's freedom, gives the Other the character of Subject, calls the Other into being. The horrifying consequence? "Our philosopher has found himself face-to-face with full numbers. He who took fright at the Parisian mob now saw himself facing all mobs, all individuals, everywhere and always."

Sartre presses on. *Being and Nothingness* is published. He throws himself into political causes, holds fast to the Sartrean pillars of responsibility and engagement, once again endeavors to "take humanity onto his shoulders":

> And he might have made it, if not for this, if not for the fact that numbers
> had again mixed into the whole, including everyone, overflowing in a way
> that was really indecent . . . the number of copies of his work . . . the number
> of editions . . . the number of readers . . . the number of commentaries . . .
> the number of thoughts that hatched out of his thoughts and the number
> of thoughts hatching out of these thoughts . . . and the number of all the
> different variants of these variants. (Gombrowicz, *Diary* 3:42)

Far worse now than any "throng-crush" of "people-nonpeople" who approach or surround one on the street is the infinitely greater upsurge of *readers,* being besieged by whom (as Gombrowicz puts it in *Ferdydurke*) "is like being born in a thousand narrow minds." To paraphrase Sartre's famous observation about Flaubert, *on est lu*—one is read.

The anecdote ends on a note of deflationary resignation. Sartre is distraught, wants to commit suicide, tries to commit suicide, but finally consoles himself with the thought that even though the swelling tide of readers is catastrophic because of the sheer numbers, at the end of the day it all comes to nothing "as a result of these same numbers," since dispersal actually hides a secret cushion: the more thought and language are disseminated, the less they are really understood: "people talk but no one knows about what, one about this, another about that, and somehow nothing comes of it" (Gombrowicz, *Diary* 3:42).

The end result is not so very different from that of the railway compartment: "each person is curling up, rolling up, shutting, shrinking, limiting to a minimum his eyes, ears, lips, trying to *be* as little as possible." Where the one is a duel, the other is a skirmish. As Gombrowicz puts it in *Diary,* "I am tumbling into publicism along with you and the rest of the world" (1:35). And it is face—textual and interpersonal—that drags me out of the amnion and clandestinity of "me" and pushes me into public view. Thus, faces not only "answer" backsides in Gombrowicz, but they deliver kicks to them and send their owners tumbling. The train compartment, the museum, and Sartre versus everybody; the face-to-face, the faces of art confronting faces of the living, and the book-as-face: Gombrowicz makes human countenance a scandal in all three—as in Derrida's essay on Levi-Strauss, that unthinkable something that both escapes and precedes a network of transparent significations. In the railway compartment it was the too-close Other, a foil or antagonist, a counter-face, a synecdoche for the crowd. In the museum, it was the tyranny of institutionalized mimesis. In the case of Sartre, it is a crowd that is finally only imagined but just as threatening—a virtual throng, the surplus of unseeable reading Others who lock eyes onto him through his book.[13] Medusa, the Muses, or the Maenads: stared at, framed, or dispersed into pieces. Hairs, sweat, and pupils, painted hairs, painted sweat, and painted pupils, or "those human opinions, the abyss of views and criticisms of your intelligence, your heart, every detail of your being, which opens up in front of you when you have incautiously clothed your thoughts in words, put them on paper and spread them among men!" (1:16–17).

I see these three scenes of Otherness, squared off against persons or paintings, or else cannibalized by other minds, as converging upon one more—a fourth, from a *Diary* entry that precedes the others by only pages, and that combines features of all of them. From scene one, the space of social commerce, through scenes two and three, the spaces of art and philosophy, I will call this scene the space of cultural politics.

Scene Four. Cultural Politics; or, Two Minor Modernists and a Polish Duel

Bruno.
I have long known about this edition prepared with such painstaking effort, yet when I finally saw the book [a recent French translation of Schulz's *Cinnamon Shops*] I winced. . . . He first showed up at my place, on Słuzewska, after the publication of *Cinnamon Shops*. He was small, strange, chimerical,

focused, intense, almost feverish—and this is how our conversations got started, usually on walks. That we needed one another is indisputable. We found ourselves in a vacuum, our literary situations were permeated with a void, our admirers were spectral. . . . After reading my first book, Bruno discovered a companion in me, for me to furnish him with the Outside without which an inner life is condemned to a monologue—and he wanted me to use him in the same way. . . . And here is where the "miss" or "dislocation," to use the language of our works, came in; for his extended hand did not meet my own. I did not return his regard, I gave him abysmally little, almost nothing, of myself, our relationship was a fiasco; but perhaps this secretly worked to our advantage? Perhaps he and I needed fiasco rather than happy symbiosis. Today I can speak of this openly because he has died. (Gombrowicz, *Diary* 3:3)

The rest of this extended reflection on Gombrowicz's fellow writer and Pole, Bruno Schulz, is forthright, unsparing, and often brutal, almost as though Gombrowicz and Schulz are positioned opposite one another in a railway compartment (as indeed they often are, figuratively speaking, when critics speak about them in the same breath).[14] Put another way, it is almost as if Gombrowicz's reading of Schulz summons up a face for him that he must deflect apotropaically, not merely by "wincing" or turning away "Bruno's regard," but by fitting him with a mug. Put a third way, Bruno is made to suffer Sartre's fate, a writer at the mercy of a reader's grimacing.

Schulz himself, in the last work of fiction published before his death, provides a kind of inadvertent confirmation of Gombrowicz's insight (though an author's fiction should never serve as affidavit for the life): "You rub against somebody, attach your homelessness and nothingness to someone alive and warm. The other person walks away and does not feel your burden, does not notice that he is carrying you on his shoulders, that like a parasite you cling momentarily to his life" (*Complete Fiction* 298).[15] Gombrowicz mounts a sustained diatribe against such symbiosis, the alternative to which—"fiasco"—etches into much sharper relief the rubbing, clinging, carrying, burdening of mutual need whose parasitism is also allergy.

The *fiasco* of the Other, of the self pressed against, subjected to, provoked by Otherness is what I have termed a "scandal"—the ordeal of intersubjectivity as physiognomy, as exteriority, but also as reading and narrative politics, in both cases what will not leave off inexorably facing. Gombrowicz's stand is the one of most resistance, since the integrity of one's own face is at stake: one has to stare back and dole out grimaces and mugs in the same measure that they are received. But the stand Gombrowicz takes against

Schulz exceeds the stuff of private discomfiture, since it takes place as a "tumbling into publicism" on the plane of *Diary* itself. Schulz and Gombrowicz are not alone in this particular compartment, the dominant to his submissive, for to witness the face-to-face is also to become a party to it.[16] The real scandal of countenance is that it is fully social, one gigantic train compartment of proliferous eyes, ears, and lips; and no one—not even readers—gets a free look.

Inasmuch as the Self is created or deformed from the outside, it wears a face. Inasmuch as the Self can lay claim to a latency or capacity for estrangement *within,* it wears a face. Inasmuch as the Other always enters unannounced, it wears a face. And at Gombrowicz's most authorially self-conscious, inasmuch as face looks out with a kind of narrative tic onto the space of reading, the bearing and imposing of faces is also something texts, authors, and writers can be said to exercise and undergo.

In the introduction to the Spanish edition of *Ferdydurke,* Gombrowicz addresses his readers in closing,

> I therefore beg you to keep silent. . . . For the time being—if you wish to let me know that the book pleased you—when you see me simply touch your right ear. If you touch your left ear, I shall know that you didn't like it, and if you touch your nose it will mean that you are not sure . . . thus we shall avoid uncomfortable and even ridiculous situations and understand each other in silence. My greetings to all. (*Ferdydurke* [Mosbacher] 9)

The *Diary,* his culminating and most personalized work in a flagrantly personalized *oeuvre,* transposes that virtual encounter onto the plane of reading itself. The figuration is less distinct—as in both the Schulz and the Sartre anecdotes, one has to "conjure" the face oneself—but the self-consciousness about being under the eyes of reading others is, if anything, even more profound. The Gombrowiczian face, one could say, is a kind of *symptom* (in Lacan's sense): summoned in the act of being warded off.[17]

What of the face in Schulz, the Schulzian face? It deserves more than a cameo appearance here, so I pivot to it by way of contrast and conclude. His relative obscurity, the frustration of a provincial fate, the ambient pathos of his personality, his Jewishness in a Catholic and prewar Poland— if anything, Schulz was even more conscious of the spell cast by the face, and his own need to conjure and ward it off. His fiction and his surviving correspondence show a writer in overdetermined relationship to readers— those whose faces he knew, as well as prospective ones he could only invoke or imply.[18]

Unlike its counterpart in Gombrowicz, however, the Schulzian face throws down no gauntlet. It does not believe in dueling. Nor does it proliferate, finding refuge in metonymy, safety in numbers. Instead, it lives a wholly metaphorical life. It is subject to the same forces that preside over everything else in Schulz's mythified fictional world: a fundamental principle of transmigrated form, objects turned into signs, persons collapsed into allegories of themselves, private space and time contracted into further depths of privacy or else dispersed into Otherness. The face appears, only to recede again, much as Gombrowicz says of Schulz himself in *Diary,* "extraneous," "superfluous." But perhaps there lies its significance, a minor element in a minor modernism that nonetheless reads the larger-in-scale as the fifth and final of these scenic vignettes will intimate.

The very first story of *Cinnamon Shops,* "August," describes a "half-wit girl," Touya, whose face "works like the bellows of an accordion. Every now and then a sorrowful grimace folds it into a thousand vertical pleats, but astonishment soon straightens it out again" (Schulz, *Complete Fiction* 6). The simile that conveys this figure (or her face) promises a kind of plenitude, the opposite pole to which—hollowed out or contracted space—is emblematized by Touya's mother, "white as a wafer and motionless like a glove from which a hand had been withdrawn" (7). The story ends with a face that is the empty glove to Touya's accordion:

> [Emil's] pale flabby face, seemed from day to day to lose its outline, to become a white blank with a pale network of veins, like lines on an old map. . . . He was sitting on a small, low sofa [and] it seemed as if it were only his clothes that had been thrown, crumpled and empty, over a chair. His face seemed like the breath of a face—a smudge which an unknown passer-by had left in the air. From the mist of his face, the protruding white of a pale eye emerged with difficulty, enticing me with a wink . . . but all fell away again and his face receded into indifference and became absent and finally faded away altogether. (10)

The pulse of Schulz's fiction oscillates between such fadings or diminishings, and corresponding pullulations of "immoderate fertility," as in the story "Pan":

> It was the face of a tramp or a drunkard. A tuft of filthy hair bristled over his broad forehead rounded like a stone washed by a stream. That forehead was now creased into deep furrows. I did not know whether it was the pain. The burning heat of the sun, or that superhuman effort that had eaten into his face and stretched those features near to cracking. His dark eyes bored

into me with a fixedness of supreme despair or suffering. He both looked
at me and did not, he saw me and did not see. His eyes were like bursting
shells, strained in a transport of pain or the wild delights of inspiration.
(*Complete Fiction* 47)

The face in Schulz folds in on its own metaphoricity, producing exquisite
similes that, in John Updike's trenchant description from his introduction
to the Penguin edition of Schulz's *Sanatorium under the Sign of the Hourglass,* evince both the prose's strenuous artifice and its harrowing effect
(xiii–xiv). The faces *are* their metaphors, wholly figural productions of
language. As there must be in Gombrowicz, there are thus neither counter-
faces nor mugs. "It is part of my existence," says a character in *Sanatorium
under the Sign of the Hourglass,* "to be the parasite of metaphors, so easily
am I carried away by the first simile that comes along" (*Complete Fiction*
309), a fate shared by the Schulzian face as well.[19] The counterpart in
Schulz to Gombrowicz's train compartment scene might therefore be this
incident:

> For a time I had the company of a man in a ragged railwayman's uniform
> —silent, engrossed in his thoughts. He pressed a handkerchief to his swol-
> len, aching face. Later even he disappeared, having slipped out unobserved
> at some stop. He left behind him the mark of his body in the straw that lay
> on the floor, and a shabby black suitcase he had forgotten. (242)

Only in the story "Tailor's Dummies" from *Cinnamon Shops,* where
Schulz lays claim to his most extravagant of pathetic fallacies, does he approximate Gombrowicz's notion of face as something imposed rather than
simply possessed, faces or expressions that "imprison" or coerce the simu-
lacra (waxwork figures, dummies) that wear them, but the seeming cruelty
here is merely the special case of a general principle: "a certain monism of
the life substance" for which "specific objects are nothing more than mask.
The life of the substance consists in the assuming and consuming of num-
berless masks. The migration of forms is the essence of life" (*Letters* 113).

How Schulz might have extended or complicated such mythopoesis is a
question that remains fixed in the grimace imposed upon it by a Gestapo
officer's bullet in 1942.[20] Schulz's death, as Gombrowicz coldly notes, licenses
a different kind of facing—something Gombrowicz had already prefigured
during Schulz's lifetime, when he drew him out in an exchange of open letters, exposing his face in public.

Gombrowicz, it seems, required foils and counter-faces to articulate the
features of his own. To this degree, his criticism and his demeanor as public

intellectual were of a piece with his art. Intersubjective space becomes an infinite regress of metonymy, the face that begets other faces as well as the face of human encounter that transposes into the face of reading. Schulz also sustains a consistency between life and art, but it is the more vulnerable and fixed consistency of metaphor. Faces fail to transpose but transubstantiate instead. Moreover, there is no face-*to*-face. The face is an object, a kind of pure passivity, held out by the fiction to be stared at (as to read Schulz's fiction, analogously, is typically the experience of languor and torpid assent, an almost postcoital feeling of abeyance).[21]

Even away from his fiction, when Schulz wrote correspondence to others, or answered Gombrowicz's open letter with one of his own, or produced critical essays on the subconscious or the mythologizing of reality or a Republic of Dreams, the face—as simply one metaphoric emblem among multiple others—is asked to do a different kind of work than in Gombrowicz. "A consecration by the ceremony of the spectacle": that is Sartre's description of the face-to-face instituted by reading, and it accurately conveys the ceremonial quality of Schulz's prose, its air of *nunc stans* that put Gombrowicz so ill at ease.[22] If a parallel Sartrean exemplification can be found for Schulz as for Gombrowicz, it might be the aesthetic first principle spelled out in Sartre's "Why Write?": "Kant believes that the work of art first exists as fact and that it is then seen. Whereas it exists only if one *looks* at it and if it is first appeal, pure exigence to exist. . . . The work of art is a value because it is an appeal" (Sartre, *"What"* 57). Consider this last scene.

Scene Five. Myth and History; or, The Face of Europe

> During his lifetime [Napoleon's] face may have been the face of an individual. Certainly, those near him knew that smile, that clouding brow, the flashes the moment lit up on his face. To us, from a distance, individual traits increasingly dim and blur, they seem to give out a radiance from within, as of larger, more massive features carrying in themselves hundreds of lost and irrecoverable faces. In the act of dying, merging with eternity, that face flickers with memories, roams through a series of faces, ever paler, more condensed, until out of the heaping of those faces there settles on it at last, and hardens into its final mask, the countenance of Poland—forever. (Schulz, *Letters* 62)

That is the conclusion of a critical essay, "The Formation of Legends," that Schulz wrote to commemorate the death of Jozef Piłsudski, marshal of Poland. It treats "greatness" in an abstract sense but also as the lasting effect —personified by Napoleon—that Western Europe has had over its Central and Eastern European Other. The receding of individual features that permits a heightening of more massive ones, the merging, condensation, and heaping of Faces into Mask, the expense of Others that silhouettes a Self: the scandal of (unifying) countenance here is the scandal of metaphor generally in Schulz.

Under *L'autre cap,* as Derrida might say[23]—the "other heading that is Form"—even the diminutions and grandiosities of Polish history and national identity—Poland's mimeticism, its "eternally unfinished, botched, patched up, and fragmented" quality—may be made to answer to the saving powers of myth and the artist's lyrical intensity. The face, one could say, is the condition of chiaroscuro and spatializes a similar notion from *Sanatorium under the Sign of the Hourglass* about time:

> What is to be done with events that have no place of their own in time; events that have occurred too late, after the whole of time has been distributed, divided, and allotted; events that have been left in the cold, unregistered, hanging in the air; homeless, and errant? Could it be that time is too narrow for all events? Could it be that all the seats within time might have been sold? (Schulz, *Complete Fiction* 131)

In fact, answers Schulz, an axis of substitution shunts branch lines of time or supernumerary faces into a zone of irrecoverability, where they are nevertheless preserved metaphorically. Perhaps this exorbitancy of metaphor, the transporting of contraband that cannot otherwise be registered (as Schulz puts it in *Sanatorium*), is what Gombrowicz meant when he charged Schulz with approaching art "as if it were a lake he intended to drown in" (*Diary* 3:6). Without my endorsing Gombrowicz's manichean distinctions between himself and Schulz as laid out in his *Diary*—"Bruno was a man denying himself. I was seeking myself. He wanted annihilation. I wanted realization. He was born to be a slave. I was born to be a master. He was of the Jewish race. I was from a family of Polish gentry" (3:6)—the Schulzian face does what the Gombrowiczian face cannot. Passively staring back or focused on an elsewhere—not grimacing or wincing or mugging—is how it stares back. And how perhaps it stares at Poland and makes Poland seem to stare back.

For Schulz, at least, literary transcendence seems possible if not through the writer's attempt to escape the economy of Forms, then through shapes that briefly assume a coherent physiognomy and solicit mere acknowledgment, the pathos of patch and fragment—an aching, swollen face. If Napoleon, the face of Europe, leaves in his place a greatness that bears the stamp of his feature forever, drawing the past behind him like a vast mantle carrying Poland in its train as well, Schulz will disclose that mantled Poland as itself a countenance, a mask mantling the land. And as with certain characters in his fiction, that mask-face becomes an occasion for transcendence, a liberating diasporism within the Country of Forms, a Europe *unbound.* Either borders and boundaries license a riotous overgrowth from within, or else they secure a no-man's land, as Schulz refers to a certain visage in *Sanatorium under the Hourglass,* a caesura in the general tumult:

> His face matured early, and strange to say while experience and the trials of living spared the empty inviolability, the strange marginality of his life, his features reflected experiences that had passed him by, elements in a biography never to be fulfilled; these experiences, although completely illusory, molded and sculpted his face into the mask of a great tragedian, which expressed the wisdom and sadness of his existence. (*Complete Fiction* 275)

And yet, Schulz tells us, that very same face, "under its mask of seriousness and sadness [consistently] broke into frivolous smiles that fought against its usually tragic expression." That is how Schultz can transform Poland's interwar Second Republic into what he called "The Republic of Dreams."[24]

If Schulz turns Polishness into exuberant diasporism, for Gombrowicz what lies at the core of Poland's history is "a debilitating mimeticism" instead. As Dorota Głowacka puts it, "having become a tyrannical and grotesque agent of history, the Polish tradition can only narcissistically exercise its own empty gestures, in a monstrous spectacle of self-parody" against which Gombrowicz "pitches a vision of history as a succession of forms which constantly mock each other and, in a pandemonium of universal mimicry, mutually expose their own artificiality" (Ziarek 72). As farce, history always repeats itself; and since it always repeats itself through a ceaseless massing of faces, History wears the mask of Comedy (or were there one, Irony).

In Gombrowicz, that master face is itself merely another duel of grimaces, but, as for Schulz, the face, strangely enough, can also sometimes offer a respite, perhaps even a lucky exile, from the economy of forms and its tyrannies. But only when it is *my* face. With perhaps his own nod to Napoleon, Gombrowicz succinctly puts such authorial and textual puissance this way: "*I* am a separate state." Otherwise put: I think—that is, I think best—in diaspora. Married forever to a town, in the poet Adam Zagajewski's words, Bruno Schulz escaped it—and Poland—by re-imagining them as forms to be disseminated, unmade and made up all over again.

Otherwise put, I "think-in," that is, I welcome or escort, Diaspora . . . like the Sabbath bride.

Witold Gombrowicz was born on an estate at Maloszyce in southeast Poland, lived in Warsaw as a child, became stranded in Argentina on the eve of World War II, and returned to Europe in 1963 an internationally recognized writer, four years before his death. Bruno Schulz lived, wrote, and died in the southeastern provincial town of Drohobycz off the north slope of the Carpathians in the Austro-Hungarian province called Galicia. Gombrowicz exchanged a European nation he regarded as minor, green, and subordinate for a Latin American nation in which he found only its mirror image. Schulz remained stuck and cramped in Jewish southeastern Poland in the 1930s and 1940s—the wrong place at the wrong time. Even in life, they seem to personify different rhetorical figures, a metonymic homelessness, on the one hand, and a metaphoric transmogrification of home, on the other.

And yet, as Dorota Głowacka observes, "each writer insists on the absolute condition of his exile: Gombrowicz, *persona non grata* among his compatriots in Argentina; and Schulz, self-exiled to the republic of dreams, a wanderer in foreign lands which open up in the heart of his hometown" (Ziarek 73). Between them is suspended the countenance of Poland in the middle decades of the twentieth century, Janus-faced and self-estranged, itself haunted by the death's head of National Socialism at one end and the grimace of Communism at the Other. For these two exiles, from within Poland and from without, metaphor and metonymy serve merely as different ways to map its features.

Using the trope of the face—an admittedly minor feature within a minor modernism—I wonder whether we might thus read the contrastingly larger-in-scale, linking the politics of nation with what seem to be the excesses or superfluities of narration. Europe at midcentury, nationalism as an always unstable fixture of identity, Otherness and "the minor" as vicissitudes and exigencies within Europe (or between Europes): Gombrowicz makes us see these features as a kind of rictus; Schulz, as a frivolous smile that fights against their usually tragic expression. Like the boundaries of human countenance, continents are similarly mutable at surface level, quietly but inexorably resisting the faces imposed on them by the masks of Nation and Hegemony:

> His pale flabby face seemed from day to day to lose its outline, to become a white blank with a pale network of veins, like lines on an old map. His face seemed like the breath of a face—a smudge which an unknown passer-by

had left in the air. From the mist of his face, the protruding white of a pale eye emerged with difficulty, enticing me with a wink, all but fell away again and his face receded into indifference and became absent and finally faded away altogether. (*Complete Fiction* 10)

To return full circle to my prologue, when the Other Europe, the Minor Europe, the Unbound Europe, seeks its face in the mirror, it discovers not a convincing self-portrait but rather, sometimes, everything it is not: a here on its way to becoming an elsewhere, a belonging that has already slipped. A face—resembling the lineaments of an old map whose features become increasingly more difficult to read. "A country of weakened forms," as Gombrowicz says of Poland, "where the East and West soften into each other"—resembling a face, with a pale network of veins—like a breath of a face—like a smudge—like a wink from within a mist.

Notes

1. See "The Heresiarchs of Form: Gombrowicz and Schulz" (Ziarek 65–88).

2. "Face" joins "Part," "Immaturity," and especially "Form" in Gombrowicz's specialized vocabulary for expressing the primacy of the interhuman. The following crucial explanation of the role played by Form in all of Gombrowicz's work comes from volume I of the *Diary:* "The most important, most extreme, and most incurable dispute is that waged in us by two of our most basic strivings: the one that desires form, shape, definition, and the other which protests against shape, and does not want form. . . . That entire philosophical and ethical dialectic of ours takes place against an immensity, which is called shapelessnesss, which is neither darkness nor light, but exactly a mixture of everything: ferment, disorder, purity, and accident" (93). See also the extended remarks on Form in volume 2 of the *Diary* (3–5 and 184–85); chapter 5 of *A Kind of Testament,* a short autobiographical work published shortly before Gombrowicz's death (69–82); and, of course, the fictive exploration of this construct in the novels *Ferdydurke, Cosmos,* and *Pornografia.* Jakób Liszka's "The Face: I and Other in Gombrowicz's *Ferdydurke,*" Ewa M. Thompson's *Witold Gombrowicz,* and Tomislav Z. Longinović's *Borderline Culture: The Politics of Identity in Four Twentieth-Century Slavic Novels* offer helpful secondary treatments, as does the recently published essay collection *Gombrowicz's Grimaces: Modernism, Gender, Nationality* (Ziarek).

3. Gombrowicz and Erving Goffman converge at more than just a shared place in the alphabet. See especially Goffman's *Interaction Ritual: Essay in Face-to-Face Behavior,* where the author describes the sociology of encounter in terms of "face-work," Goffman's *Stigma: Notes on the Management of Spoiled Identity,* and also William R. Cupach and Sandra Metts's *Facework.*

4. Compare, for example, this passage from Borchardt's translation of *Ferdydurke:* "Oh, give me one uncontorted face next to which I can feel the contortion of my own face, but instead—all around me were faces that were twisted, mangled, and turned inside out, faces that reflected my own like a distorting mirror—and this mirror image of reality truly held me down!" (47).

5. Later on in volume 3 of the *Diary,* Gombrowicz indulges in a "close scrutiny of bodies": "I drew physical defects out of the crowds, oh look, flat chest, anemia of the neck, hunchback, twisted trunk, the tragedy of those limbs. . . . I was persistent about seeking out a certain defect, a kind of very French inelegance dancing about their very lips, noses, not of all Frenchman but quite a few" (87).

6. In the introduction to *Pornografia,* Gombrowicz writes, "Man, tortured by his mask, fabricates secretly . . . a secondary domain of compensation" (8).

7. For the face is also made scandalous by the "backside" or "thigh," as Gombrowicz parcels out the body into various parts in *Ferdydurke.* An Otherness infiltrates the root of a person's metaphysical integrity quite independently of any human Other, a species of alienation Gombrowicz calls "the rump" to suggest that any Self Project is *already* undermined by the innate surrealism of the body. "I even imagined that my body was not entirely homogeneous . . . that my head was laughing at my leg and ridiculing it, that my leg was laughing at my head, that my finger was poking fun at my heart, my heart at my brain, that my nose was thumbing itself at my eye, my eye chuckling and bellowing at my eye—and all my parts were wildly raping each other in an all-encompassing and piercing state of pan-mockery" ([Borchardt] 2).

8. A parallel moment, for instance, occurs in volume 2 of the *Diary:* "I was walking along a eucalyptus-lined avenue when a cow sauntered out from behind a tree. I stopped and we looked each other in the eye. Her cowness shocked my humanness to such a degree—the moment our eyes met was so tense—I stopped dead in my tracks and lost my bearings *as a man,* that is, as a member of the human species. The strange feeling that I was apparently discovering for the first time was the shame of a man come face-to-face with an animal. I allowed her to look and see me—this made us equal— and resulted in my also becoming an animal—but a strange even forbidden one, I would say. I continued my walk, but I felt uncomfortable . . . in nature, surrounding me on all sides, as if it were . . . watching me" (24). The volume closes with an extended episode (231–39) that contains the following: "Face to face. Alone. Hand to hand. Foot to foot. Knee to knee. Face to face. Until this stupid identity begins to irritate me in the room, and I think, how is it that he repeats me, that I repeat him, face to face" (231).

9. See also volume 1 of the *Diary* (181–87). In *A Kind of Testament,* Gombrowicz makes similar claims about structuralism: "Yes I am a structuralist just as I am an existentialist. I am bound to structuralism by my approach to Form. Of course the human personality, which I believe is created 'between men,' in the human context which defines a system of dependencies by no means dissimilar to a 'structure.' In what I wrote before the war you will find expressions which have now been incorporated by the structuralists" (152). In volume 3 of the *Diary,* he says irascibly, "and please replace the word form with structuralism and you will see me at the center of today's French intellectual issues" (182).

10. The provenance of the face trope in Levinas is probably dual, appearing conspicuously at the end of Franz Rosenzweig's *The Star of Redemption,* a work that influenced Levinas deeply, but also saturating the biblical and rabbinical texts that undergird much of Levinas's philosophy. In Hebrew, "face" connotes turning toward and also means presence or selfhood, and it appears (as *mila maacha,* or leading word) in many scenes of encounter in the Torah. As Moses "hides his face" from God on Sinai in Exodus 10, for example, so God's answering threat of absence from the plane of human events

is called *hister panim*—the hiding of face—in Deuteronomy. Though not particularly Levinasian, perhaps most relevant in the light of Gombrowicz's fiction may be the verses in Genesis 31:2, "And Jacob saw that Laban's face was not with him, as it had been in the best," and 31:5, "Laban's face is not to me as it was previously." As Avivah Zornberg brilliantly reads them in her *The Beginning of Desire: Reflections on Genesis,* "Laban's face is part of Jacob's world; he carries its impress, its changing looks around with him." She adduces a homiletic gloss on a related Talmudic passage (*Berakhot* 6b) that centers on the self-consciousness induced by the gaze of others: "one who is too much affected by other's faces finds his own face turning all colors, blushing and paling in response to their changing expressions" (206).

11. The credible parallels Ewa M. Thompson draws between Gombrowicz and the work of Jacques Lacan and René Girard in *Witold Gombrowicz* (139–56) make the Levinasian resemblance, through French phenomenology, unsurprising by comparison. The most uncannily Levinasian moment in *Diary*—as though it came from *Totality and Infinity* itself—occurs in volume 3: "The point is (and I have noticed it for quite a while) that some sort of theory . . . imposes itself upon me in my relation to people: I know that essence powerfully . . . and I try to rouse the right reflex in myself. I know, I feel, the 'how' and 'whence' and 'why' of this other's 'approaching' or 'emerging' and what our 'disposition' is toward one another should not be a matter of indifference; I know that it should be more fundamental than one can express in words; and that it should be 'introductory,' or 'preceding' my other sensation constituting something like a background" (23). But perhaps the closest family ties can be tracked to Gogol's "The Nose," Pirandello's *Uno, Nessuno, e Centomila* [*One, No One, and a Hundred Thousand*] (published more than decade earlier), and *La Carne de René* [*René's Flesh*], by the Cuban writer Virgilio Piñero (whom Gombrowicz knew in Argentina, and to whom he delegated the responsibility of translating *Ferdydurke* into Spanish). Piñero's novel features a relentless body consciousness, the sadomasochism of pedagogy, and various scenes of grimacing and distorted face that all undoubtedly echo *Ferdydurke*. On the contemporary literary scene, one should also consult the preface to Gloria Anzaldúa's anthology of Chicana writing, *Making Face, Making Soul/Haciendo Caras,* in which she explains that *caras* [masks] denote the surface of the body inscribed by social structures, and *máscaras* [interface], a piece of material sewn between two pieces of fabric for support and stability, providing the space from which to crack the masks (2). I am very grateful to Joanna Brooks for this last reference.

12. Speaking of Sartre again, for instance, at the end of the entry for 1962, Gombrowicz chides him for his "cacophony of levels, tones, concepts," his "sudden tumbling from the peaks onto the flat plain," the switch from one voice expressive of "the spirit," to a second voice one associates with "a schoolmaster and moralist." He tells the following anecdote. "After going to bed with an elevator boy, the heroine of one of Thomas Mann's novels cries out in exaltation, 'What, I, Madame so-and-so, a poet, lady of society, in bed with a naked elevator boy!' I think this anecdote is right for Sartre not so much because of the dialectics of the 'base' which it contains as for the 'superstructure,' the elevator. For even in our time, one occasionally comes upon one of those scrupulous people who, panic-stricken that not his own substance but a mechanism is raising him aloft presses the button of the same machine to ride down as quickly as possible" (3:60–61). And in the entry for 1963, he opines, "Half of his deductions from

Being and Nothingness are unacceptable to me, they do not correspond to my truest experiences in life" (93). Later in the same volume, he tells us, perversely, that he only writes about Sartre anyway in order to distract himself from visiting Berlin on a Ford Foundation grant: "It is obvious—never write 'about Berlin,' 'Paris,' only about oneself . . . in Berlin and Paris" (110).

13. Or, in other words, a *regard de l'autrui* completely unimaginable within the pages of *Being and Nothingness*. In happier days—at least as recounted by an adult Sartre looking back on his childhood—a very different relationship to being read is imagined in a passage that describes with immense pleasure the prospect of becoming a "precipitate of language" disseminated through writing. "My bones are made of leather and cardboard, my parchment-skinned flesh smells of glue and mushrooms, I sit in state through a hundred thirty pounds of paper, thoroughly at ease. I am reborn, I at last become a whole man. . . . Hands take me down, open me, spread me flat on the table, smooth me, and sometimes make me creak. . . . My mind is in bits and pieces. All the better. People read *me*, I leap to the eye; they talk to *me*. I'm in everyone's mouth, a universal and individual language: I become a prospective curiosity in millions of gazes; to him who can love me, I step aside and disappear: I exist nowhere, at last I *am*, I'm everywhere. I'm a parasite on mankind, my blessings eat into it and force it to keep reviving my absence" (Sartre, *Words* 194–95).

14. Unfortunately, except for the recent *Gombrowicz's Grimaces*, most of this discussion is carried on in languages other than English. See, however, Russell E. Brown's *Myths and Relatives: Seven Essays on Bruno Schulz*, Diana Kuprel's "Errant Events on the Branch Tracks of Time: Bruno Schulz and Mythical Consciousness," and David Jarrett's "Bruno Schulz and the Map of Poland."

15. The passage comes from perhaps Schulz's most Gombrowicz-like story, "The Old Age Pensioner," which parallels *Ferdydurke* in its description of an adult's juvenilization.

16. The entry on Schulz is laced with the vocabulary of perversion and psychopathology, and the lineaments of Gombrowicz's own personality, not least his homosexuality, can be discerned between its lines—which is only fitting, since the face-to-face in Gombrowicz is, in this sense, always interlinear—a stretto or stichomythia.

17. In *The Sublime Object of Ideology*, Slavoj Žižek explains the dual meaning of "the symptom" in Lacan, an index to human personality as well as a semiotic choice: "The Lacanian answer to the question: From where does the repressed return? is . . . paradoxically: From the future. Symptoms are meaningless traces, their meaning is not discovered, excavated from the hidden depth of the past, but constructed retroactively —the analysis produces the truth; that is, the signifying frame which gives the symptoms their symbolic place and meaning. . . . What we must bear in mind here is the radical ontological status of symptom: symptom, conceived as *sinthome* [Lacan's coinage, meaning (among other things), a synthesis between symptom and fantasy], is literally our only substance, the positive support of our being, the only point that gives consistency to the subject" (Žižek 55, 75). The way in which it takes shape between analyst and analysand is analogous to the double bind of literary interpretation, chaining writer and reader in a complex exchange of cathexes. See in this context Hanjo Berressem's *The "Evil Eye" of Painting: Jacques Lacan and Witold Gombrowicz of the Gaze*.

18. One of Schulz's letters begins, "Dear Classmate, of course I remember you, and your face springs vividly before my eyes" (Schulz, *Letters* 89).

19. Compare also *Sanatorium under the Sign of the Hourglass* for the description of a man-dog: "How great is the power of prejudice! How powerful the hold of fear! How blind I had been! It was not a dog, it was a man. A chained man, whom by a simplifying metaphoric error, I had taken for a dog" (269).

20. In a letter to a publisher dated 10 October 1935, Schulz says that *The Messiah* (since lost) will be "the continuation of *Cinnamon Shops*" (103).

21. Which is to say of the sexual energies of Schulz's prose, that, unlike Gombrowicz's, there is no *friction*. It is worth pursuing the question of eros as a differentiating category for these two writers, say, along lines suggested by Barthes's distinction between texts of *plaisir* and those of *jouissance* in *The Pleasure of the Text*. If texts of pleasure can be linked to a "comfortable practice of reading," and texts of bliss to "a state of loss" or discomfort (14), Gombrowicz and Schulz might be thought of, likewise, in terms of the text that chafes or abrades on the one hand and the text that slides and slips away on the other.

22. "He was a fanatic of art, its slave. He entered this cloister and submitted to its rigors, carrying out its strictest injunctions with great humility in order to attain perfection. . . . Falling to his knees before the Spirit, he experienced sensual pleasure. He wanted to be a servant, nothing more. He craved nonexistence" (Gombrowicz, *Diary* 3:7). See also Głowacka's essay (73–75).

23. In *The Other Heading: Reflections on Today's Europe,* Derrida asks how a "European cultural identity can be responsible for itself, for the other, before the other" (16) in a pointed and punning critique of European centrality, exemplarity, and universality. Derrida's argument is itself wisely critiqued in an essay by Boyarin, "From Derrida to Fichte? The New Europe, the Same Europe, and the Place of the Jews," collected in *Thinking in Jewish* (109–39), but I cite it here especially in light of Derrida's various allusions to writings by Paul Valéry that correlate the continent of Europe, or its capitals, with human countenance; for example, "Valéry observes, looks at, and envisages Europe; he sees in it a face, a persona and he thinks of it as a leader, that is, as a head" (20); and, in reference to an essay entitled "Présence de Paris" written shortly before Gombrowicz emigrates to Latin America: "Just before this, the 'figure' of the face has guided the analysis of this capital of capitals. One actually looks the capital in the face. One distinguishes the face, the head, and the forehead" (119). Compare also Geoffrey Galt Harpham's suggestive analysis in *One of Us: The Mastery of Joseph Conrad,* of the figural place assigned to Poland in Joseph Conrad's fiction, on the model of the Lacanian "real"—"that which guarantees the consistency of the symbolic order, but cannot appear . . . except as disfigurement or 'stain.'" "Thus," says Harpham by way of example, "we can mark the appearance of Poland in such unlikely sites as the crushed face in the mud by the river in Conrad's first book, *Almayer's Folly*" (12).

24. The short fragment, "*Ojczyzna*" ["Fatherland"], concludes on just such a note of respite. Compare also "The Republic of Dreams" in which "nation" means nothing less than the artist-citizen's propensity for fictive narration.

Works Cited

Anzaldúa, Gloria. *Making Face, Making Soul/Haciendo Caras: Creative and Critical Perspectives by Women of Color.* San Francisco: Aunt Lute, 1990.

Barthes, Roland. *The Pleasure of the Text.* Trans. Richard Miller. New York: Hill and Wang, 1975.

Berressem, Hanjo. *The "Evil Eye" of Painting: Jacques Lacan and Witold Gombrowicz of the Gaze.* Albany: State U of New York P, 1995.

Boyarin, Jonathan. *Thinking in Jewish.* Chicago: U of Chicago P, 1996.

Brown, Russell E. *Myths and Relatives: Seven Essays on Bruno Schulz.* Munich: Verlag Otto Sagner, 1991.

Chabon, Michael. "Guidebook to a Land of Ghosts." *Civilization* June/July 1997: 67–69.

Cupach, William R., and Sandra Metts. *Facework.* Thousand Oaks, CA: Sage, 1994.

Derrida, Jacques. *The Other Heading: Reflections on Today's Europe.* Trans. Pascale-Anne Baruault and Michael B. Nass. Bloomington: Indiana UP, 1992.

Finkielkraut, Alain. *The Imaginary Jew.* Trans. Kevin O'Neill and David Suchoff. Lincoln: U of Nebraska P, 1997.

Goffman, Erving. *Interaction Ritual: Essay in Face-to-Face Behavior.* Chicago: Aldine, 1967.

———. *Stigma: Notes on the Management of Spoiled Identity.* Englewood Cliffs: Prentice-Hall, 1963.

Gombrowicz, Witold. *Diary.* Vol. 1: *1953–56.* Vol. 2: *1957–61.* Vol. 3: *1961–66.* Trans. Lillian Vallee. Evanston, IL: Northwestern UP, 1988, 1989, 1993.

———. *Ferdydurke.* Trans. Danuta Borchardt. New Haven: Yale UP, 2000.

———. *Ferdydurke.* Trans. Eric Mosbacher. London: MacGibbon and Kee, 1961.

———. *A Kind of Testament.* Trans. Alastair Hamilton. London: Calder and Boyars, 1973.

———. *Pornografia.* Trans. Alastair Hamilton. London: Calder and Boyars, 1966.

Harpham, Geoffrey Galt. *One of Us: The Mastery of Joseph Conrad.* Chicago: U of Chicago P, 1996.

Jarrett, David. "Bruno Schulz and the Map of Poland." *Chicago Review* 40 (1994): 73–84.

Kitaj, R. B. *First Diasporist Manifesto.* New York: Thames and Hudson, 1989.

Kuprel, Diana. "Errant Events on the Branch Tracks of Time: Bruno Schulz and Mythical Consciousness." *Slavic and East European Journal* 40 (1996): 100–117.

Levinas, Emmanuel. *Basic Philosophical Writings.* Bloomington: Indiana UP, 1996.

———. *Collected Philosophical Papers.* Trans. Alphonso Lingis. The Hague: Martinus Nijhoff, 1987.

———. *Totality and Infinity: An Essay on Exteriority.* Trans. Alphonso Lingis. Pittsburgh: Duquesne UP, 1969.

Liszka, Jakób. "The Face: I and Other in Gombrowicz's *Ferdydurke.*" *Philosophy and Literature* 5 (1981): 62–72.

Longinović, Tomislav Z. *Borderline Culture: The Politics of Identity in Four Twentieth-Century Slavic Novels.* Fayetteville: U of Arkansas P, 1993.

Mendele: Yiddish Language and Literature. Vol. 7. <http://shakti.cc.trincoll.edu-mendele.toc07.htm> (24 March 2001).

Morrison, Toni. *Jazz.* New York: Plume, 1992.

Newton, Adam Zachary. *Facing Black and Jew: Literature as Public Space in Twentieth-Century America.* Cambridge: Cambridge UP, 1999.

———. *The Fence and the Neighbor: Emmanuel Levinas, Yeshayahu Leibowitz, and Israel among the Nations.* Albany: State U of New York P, 2001.

———. *Narrative Ethics*. Cambridge: Harvard UP, 1995.

Piñero, Virgilio. *René's Flesh*. Trans. Mark Schafer. New York: Marsilio, 1989.

Pirandello, Luigi. *One, No One, and a Hundred Thousand*. Trans. William Weaver. New York: Marsilio, 1992.

Sandauer, Artur. "Gombrowicz and Politics." Trans. Edward Rothert. *Polish Perspectives* 29 (1986): 33–39.

Sartre, Jean-Paul. *"What Is Literature?" and Other Essays*. Cambridge: Harvard UP, 1988.

———. *The Words*. Trans. Bernard Frechtman. New York: George Braziller, 1964.

Schulz, Bruno. *The Complete Fiction of Bruno Schulz*. Trans. Celia Wieniewska. New York: Walker, 1989.

———. *Letters and Drawings of Bruno Schulz*. New York: Harper and Row, 1988.

Sloterdijk, Peter. *Critique of Cynical Reason*. Trans. Michael Elred. Minneapolis: U of Minnesota P, 1987.

Thompson, Ewa M. *Witold Gombrowicz*. Boston: Twayne, 1979.

Updike, John. Introduction. *Sanatorium under the Sign of the Hourglass*. By Bruno Schulz. Trans. Celia Wieniewska. New York: Penguin, 1979.

Ziarek, Ewa Plonowska, ed. *Gombrowicz's Grimaces: Modernism, Gender, Nationality*. Albany: State U of New York P, 1998.

Žižek, Slavoj. *The Sublime Object of Ideology*. London: Verso, 1989.

Zornberg, Avivah. *The Beginning of Desire: Reflections on Genesis*. New York: Doubleday, 1996.

HENRY JAMES, MORAL
PHILOSOPHERS, MORALISM

CORA DIAMOND

> The theorizing mind tends always to the oversimplification of its materials.
>
> —William James, *The Varieties of Religious Experience*

HENRY JAMES wrote no book called *The Varieties of Moral Experience,* but he was a great observer and painter of that variety, and philosophers, who often miss the variety, can learn much from him. In this essay, I am concerned with the variousness of moral disagreement and with the place of moralism in these forms of disagreement.

Philosophers tend to see ethics in terms of a background idea of the primary importance of judgment. Moral thinking is a type of evaluative thinking, and in evaluative thought one has in mind something or other—act, person, character trait—and considers the application to it of some evaluative term. The picture supports a philosophical conception of moral disagreement: moral disagreement will be disagreement whether a term of moral evaluation applies to such-and-such. We may also recognize a further possible kind of disagreement, over the acceptance or rejection of an evaluative concept (*blasphemous,* say, or *chaste*) or a set of such concepts.

For Henry James, the characterization of the distances there may be between human beings in their moral life and understanding proceeds altogether differently; judgment has not got the central position it has for philosophers. The immense difference between James and philosophers in approach to the description of moral life is tied to a difference in *which* concepts are salient. For philosophers: right and wrong, good and bad, duties, rights, and obligations, notions of virtue and of particular virtues. These hardly drop out of the picture for James: consider, for example, his interest in the very particular kind of courage shown by his cousin Minny Temple, and how he turns and returns to the representation of forms of courage like Minny's. James, though, is not interested in the judgment that someone or some action is courageous but in the exhibition and appreciation of this or that particular striking form. Among the concepts salient for James are some to which philosophers pay relatively little attention. Thus, for example, the opening of *The Tragic Muse,* which displays before us forms of philistinism, moralism, and aestheticism. We are indeed also warned that *responsibility* will count for something in this story, but we are warned, too, that what is to be understood as responsibility will itself not be separable from the very different lives we are just at that stage glimpsing. I focus on *moralism* as a notion that has or can have an interesting and deeply suggestive role in moral thought, too little reflected on by philosophers (Nietzsche being the most important exception) in large part because responsiveness to moralism is not so much a matter of judgment as of appreciation and of what we make the appreciation count for. In this essay I interweave discussion of what moralism is for James with discussion of some philosophical views of it.

Whatever the ambiguities and complexities of Henry James's relation to his father, one thing they share is an interest in moralism. In the case of Henry James Sr., the interest is entirely hostile; moralism, for him, is the spiritual evil. What he means by moralism is a kind of pride in the possession of moral goodness, but not only that. Moralism involves giving to the sphere of the moral a fundamental human importance that it lacks; it involves also a kind of fear of natural instincts and desires: "Leading me as it does to regard my inward self as corrupt, to distrust my heart's affections as the deadliest enmity to God, it logically prompts the crucifixion of those affections as especially well pleasing to Him" (James Sr., 160). His son was not given to theorizing about spiritual evil, and moralism as he saw it was not an unmitigated evil: it had its varieties, some of them even admirable. Although he does not theorize about moralism, James does think about it: characters and forms of living that one could describe as moralistic have, throughout his life, a conspicuous role in his fiction. Further, in his understanding of art—his own and its contrasts and similarities with that of his predecessors and contemporaries—the presence or absence of moralism is important. And a concern with moralism was, further, forced on him by the moralistic criticism of his day.

The term "moralism" is almost always used pejoratively—but not by James. Although he rejected from the start a moralistic conception of art, he could write this of Henry Fielding: "we see [Tom Jones] through the mellow air of Fielding's fine old moralism, fine old humor and fine old style, which somehow really enlarge, make every one and every thing important" (*Critical Muse* 503). The complexity of James's response to Fielding's moralism comes out in the contrast he drew between Walter Scott and Fielding. Fielding's novels, like those of Smollett and Richardson, aim, James says, to instruct and edify. Of *Tom Jones* in particular he writes, "The story is like a vast episode in a sermon preached by a grandly humorous divine; and however we may be entertained by the way, we must not forget that our ultimate duty is to be instructed. With the minister's week-day life we have no concern: for the present he is awful, impersonal Morality." James goes on to make clear the contrast with *Waverley,* the first "self-forgetful" novel. "It proposed simply to amuse the reader, as an old English ballad amused him. It undertook to prove nothing but facts. It was the novel irresponsible" (*Critical Muse* 21).

The term "irresponsible" is not used wholly ironically, but I am interested in what the passage suggests about James's view of moralism and how that view may be connected with some remarks of twentieth-century philosophers. D. A. J. Richards has argued that it is rational to accept a moral principle about mutual love, "requiring that people should not show personal affection and love to others on the basis of arbitrary physical characteristics alone, but rather on the basis of traits of personality and character related to acting on moral principles" (94). Bernard Williams refers to Richards's principle as "this righteous absurdity," and the account of which it is part as "richly moralistic" (16); Rai Gaita describes the same passage as involving the moralistic devaluing of what in human life makes possible our sense of the preciousness and irreplaceability of persons (156).[1]

What kind of criticism is made by the term "moralistic"? Williams suggests that the source of the "righteous absurdity" is "a feeling that love, even love based on 'arbitrary physical characteristics,' is something which has enough power and even authority to conflict badly with morality unless it can be brought within it from the beginning," and he adds that the feeling is a sound feeling (16). That is, the criticism that Richards's account is moralistic does not rest on a judgment that Richards is mistaken about the possibility of such conflict; the idea is rather that Richards's moralism, taken to be a disabling distortion of thought, lies in his way of conceiving the conflict as well as his response to it.

Williams's description of Richards's proposal as moralistic needs to be understood in the context of his more general criticism of the treatment by contemporary moral theories of a broadly Kantian type of the relation between the *moral* and the *nonmoral,* and especially their treatment of possible conflicts between morality and what lies outside it. When Williams describes as moralistic Richards's response to the possibility of conflict between love and morality, what he takes to be moralistic is not just Richards's proposal of a moral principle intended to prevent such conflict but also, and at least as significantly, his understanding of the character of the conflict, involving as it does a Kantian conception of human nature and of the role in our thought of the moral and the nonmoral. The moralism of Richards's *proposal* is inseparable from a moralistic understanding of the nature of the conflict that the proposal aims to head off. Although Williams uses the term "moralistic" only in his criticism of Richards, the term could have been used in expressing one of the essay's main criticisms of much contemporary moral theory, namely, that such theories are moralistic in their characteristic way of dealing with *all* the relations between the moral and the nonmoral: in their way of dealing with possible conflict and with what "morality" *allows* to go on outside its own realm—the realm of personal relations and personal projects.

What, then, is the connection between Williams's description of Richards's moralism and James's description of Fielding's? Williams describes Richards's feeling that love has power and authority enough to conflict badly with morality unless it is *brought within it from the beginning*. And James, in describing the eighteenth-century moralistic storyteller, tells us that he brings the entirety of the story into the sphere of the moral, from beginning to end. That is, Fielding's moralism is described by James as a mode of storytelling in which conflict of the sort Williams mentions cannot arise. The implied author, telling us of human love, human acts, human relations, does not allow us to enter sympathetically into these relations except insofar as that care is subject to the authority of awful, impersonal Morality. What is being thought of as "moralism" in the case of Fielding is not just the imposition of the authority of Morality but also Fielding's conception of the point of view of Morality. We may contrast James on Turgenev: the seriousness of a human subject is in what it reveals of human life to the caring mind. Turgenev's object is "that of finding an incident, a person, a situation, *morally* interesting," but finding a subject morally interesting is not a matter of finding in it what Morality would find. The eye for all of human passion, the "deeply sympathetic sense of the wonderful complexity of our souls," makes the moral interest; what can be of moral interest is discovered in the writing or in the reading (*Critical Muse* 82–84, 205). There is no idea here of a "moral point of view" *set over against* other sorts of attention to the human soul. If there is such a thing as a "moral point of view" exemplified by a writer like Turgenev, it is simply the point of view from which we see and attend with warmth and sympathy to the complex reality of human life: what is "moral" here emerges from the intelligence and fineness of the consciousness.

In remarking about Turgenev's "deeply sympathetic sense of the wonderful complexity of our souls," James expresses a view of the relation between morality and art that is in several interconnected ways offensive to moralism. It suggests that the sympathy and interest of the artist may appropriately go wherever they go, independently of any prior considerations of moral desert. But the description with sympathetic interest of someone whom morality condemns, someone who is taken not to deserve our sympathy, arouses moral outrage. The artist's sense of what is humanly interesting is like love in its capacity to conflict with and even to subvert morality, and it may seem thereby to constitute a possible threat to morality, if not subjected to its authority.

James's view further implies that no subject matter, no "sharp reality" (see *What Maisie Knew* 12), is out of bounds. Nor is an artist committed, in the treatment of a subject he or she finds of interest, either to making the judgments Morality would make or to inviting or inducing readers to make those judgments. Fielding's readers may be amused and entertained by the way, but their ultimate duty is to be instructed. James's rejection of a moralistic conception of the role of judgment is really the same point, seen from another angle, as the point about the artist's sympathy not being subjected to Morality: the stance of sympathetic interest and that of judgment are opposed, as is illustrated by the contrast in *The Ambassadors* between Lambert Strether and Mrs. Pocock in relation to the immoral but highly interesting couple in Paris.

The term "moralistic" frequently indicates an insistence on moral judging or the habit of moral judging, in contexts that only some would see as calling for such judgment. But the relation between moralism and the place and character of moral judging in human life is complex, as comes out in Annette Baier's discussion of Hume and Kant.

In "Moralism and Cruelty: Reflections on Hume and Kant," Baier several times describes Kant's account as "moralistic"[2] (443, 450–51) and explains why:

> Kant's is an overtly moralistic morality, holding us to account for all failures in which our faulty will has played a role, encouraging us to anticipate a just judgment by an all-seeing God. . . . Human conscience is to be a stand-in for the just divine judge, but not for the merciful pardoner, so forgiving ourselves is not encouraged. We are to demand moral perfection of ourselves, as God demands it of us. We are to be punctilious about leaving it to magistrates to punish people for breaches of their perfect obligations,

and leaving it to others to demand, each of herself, her own perfection. We are to show some concern for the happiness of our fellows, but only as far as the moral law allows room for that concern. . . . The Kantian conscience accuses, recognizes that punishment is deserved, but leaves it to God or the magistrate to inflict it. (443–44)

Here, what makes an account moralistic is not the idea that people should be forever acting as moral judges of *others;* it is rather the modeling of one's relation to one's own actions and character in terms of a kind of internal moral courtroom. Thus, Baier later makes the contrast with Hume's *non-moralistic* account by referring to Kant's as "moral law enforcement" (451).

Baier's contrast between Hume's nonmoralism and Kant's moralism turns also on the content of their accounts. She describes Humean morality as "[boasting] of its nonmoralistic avoidance of 'useless austerities, rigors and self denials' and [promising] 'nothing but gentleness, humanity, beneficence, affability; nay even, at proper intervals play, frolic and gaiety'"; the contrast between Hume and Kant is that between *epicureanism* and *moralism* (450–51). This contrast in content suggests something further. For a morality to be moralistic is not merely for it to prescribe what from a Humean point of view look like useless austerities, rigors, and self-denials. Such prescriptions have their source in a conception of human nature and of the significance in our lives of morality—and thus also of what needs to be strengthened in us, what we may need to be protected from. Any human good independent of morality, any interest or desire, might on occasion give rise to conflict with morality and hence (from the point of view we are characterizing as moralistic) should be brought under morality from the beginning; tendencies to indulge such interests or desires should be regarded with suspicion. That conception of human nature was a great theme of Henry James's (as it had been of his father's). For James it was associated in particular with New England. The New England character "takes things hard": it always wants to know what its duty is and is unwilling to *enjoy* unless it is certain it ought to. (See *The Bostonians,* chapter 2; *The Europeans,* chapter 3; cf. also *The Ambassadors,* chapter 1: "Woollett [the New England town] isn't sure it ought to enjoy. If it were it would" [13].) For James, what is to be contrasted with the New England subjection of life to "ought" is, most frequently, Europe; those of his characters who are New Englanders through and through hate Europe (Olive Chancellor, for example, in *The Bostonians* and Waymarsh in *The Ambassadors*). There are a number of reasons for their disliking Europe, and one is that Europe does not want to be improved. The New Englander feels the iniquity of the world and in Europe is painfully aware of iniquity ignored. Another thing hated in Europe is its "discrimination of types and tones," its interest in, tolerance of, shades and ambiguities.[3] Europe is seductive, something to be resisted, to be on one's guard against.[4] New England places under suspicion whatever might elude the authority of morality. That habit of suspicion (that form of the habit of judging) is an essential element in what James calls "taking things hard" (*Bostonians* 7; *Europeans* 33).

In discussing James on moralism and puritanism in *The Ambassadors,* Martha Nussbaum notes his portrayal of the moralistic character as "all moral pressure" (176): there is in that character an essential opposition to passivity and to (nonmoralized) emotion. This, I think, leads us back to the issues that lie just under the surface of James's remarks about Turgenev and the "deeply sympathetic sense of the wonderful complexity of our souls." What is objectionable there, from the point of view of moralism, is precisely that we may yield to sympathy, find ourselves enticed by it, when it is morally appropriate to resist. Nussbaum describes the hero of *The Ambassadors* as "yielding to the impressions of life as they unfold themselves before him—as allowing himself to be seduced" (187).

The level of specificity of content at which there is a tie between the content of a morality and the morality's being moralistic goes below the level alluded to by Baier in her quotation of Hume's "useless austerity" passage. Certain vices and virtues, certain principles, have particular significance in characterizing a morality as moralistic—lying, for example. Nussbaum mentions the importance James attaches to hatred of lying as a characteristic of New England moralism in *The Ambassadors.* The attitude toward lying also has great significance in his other treatments of moralism: in *The Europeans,* Europeans fib and lie (and are thus contrasted with New Englanders);[5] and again, in *The Bostonians,* Boston itself is "this unprevaricating city" (1), while Southerners and people from New York not only fib but (more significantly still) joke about it. The moral character of places is intensely felt by James. The contrast between America (or New England) and Europe is for James not just the contrast between moralism and aestheticism but often the more specific contrast between *rigor as to truth* and *enjoyment of appearance.* Another important connection between the content of a morality and its being moralistic concerns the significance attached to sexual morality and the particular character of the sexual morality itself;[6] yet another connection lies between the role given to retributive punishment and the morality's being moralistic. This latter tie is indeed central in Baier's account of Kant's morality as moralistic.

Some, at least, of the resentment occasioned by what is now labeled "political correctness" is a response to moralism on the left, moralism of a sort already present in the feminists and reformers sketched by James in *The Bostonians* and attacked by George Orwell in "The Art of Donald McGill" and other essays. No better example can be found of an element of human nature capable of clashing with morality, or what we take to be morality, than our sense of what is funny. Jokes, especially vulgar ones, depend heavily on stereotypes and on topics taken to be intrinsically funny, like sex and drunkenness; they thus have enormous potential for moral offensiveness and are frequently cruel. Hence, the familiar use of "That's not funny" to mean not that something is not funny but that we ought not to find it so. But how far should the jokey side of us, what Orwell called the Sancho Panza in us, be squashed into the space that morality (conceived in this or that particular way) is willing to allow it? If some answers to such questions are felt to be puritanical or moralistic, that feeling is a response to underlying ideas about human life and human good. Under cover, as it were, of "the authority of Morality," something with its own rights is being denied them: *that* is the feeling.[7]

These metaphors of territory, rights, authority, insubordination, and possible subversion are important; the figures of speech turn literal when poetry, the enemy of moral order, is banned from the territory of the Republic, as by Plato. I cannot here discuss Plato, but I want simply to note the connection between his treatment of art and what is being responded *to,* when someone's mode of thought is taken to be moralistic; namely, ideas about the distinctions between kinds of good and about possible conflicts between them, ideas within which the moral interests of the soul, which can be understood in a wide sense, are identified with one type of good or one group of goods (see Goldberg, esp. 27–29, 234–38). Perhaps it is worth noting here that Henry James was educated on principles very distant indeed from Plato's. Henry James Sr. believed, says Leon Edel, that "there was Divine Truth in the world and this the children were bound to discover for themselves under Divine Guidance" (115). In other words, the principles of the education to which the younger Henry James was subject involved the very opposite of the idea that morality dictates the exclusion from education of those elements of life that might subvert or conflict with morality.

I now want to look at the faults and failings to which those who reject moralism may be thought to be subject, starting with Hume as he might be seen by Kant. Baier states that "We know what Kantians should think about Hume's version of morality, since Kant more or less told us that" (436).

What she has in mind may include the opening section of part I of the *Ground-work of the Metaphysics of Morals*. Kant says there that a being endowed with all sorts of good qualities or with riches, power, and so on, but without a good will, will not give pleasure to a rational impartial observer, whereas Hume holds that what gives us pleasure has nothing to do with reason. There is no "ought" about it. A good will, in Kant's sense, is not, in Hume's view, a condition for some special sort of approval or pleasure significantly distinguishable from other sorts of response to people's qualities. This is not just a contradiction between two reflective accounts of morality. The contradiction at that level reflects a great difference in temperament and in the way temperament enters our conception of morality and of its place in our life.

The opening section of part I of the *Groundwork* also provides an account of what may be found troubling in the attitude toward art expressed by James not just in the remarks I have already discussed but also, for example, in his review of *Hedda Gabler* (*Critical Muse* 295–302). There is a strong current of life in Hedda, but there is (or so Kant would tell us) nothing good or admirable about such strength of life without a good will, which would direct that strength and make it conform to universal ends. Without the principle of a good will, the strength of life in Hedda makes her more dangerous and more abominable.[8] And what is the matter with *Hedda Gabler* from the Kantian point of view is that, in inviting us to view Hedda with sympathy and interest, to see her as complex and even attractive, the play corrupts moral thinking. James was all too aware of the fact that art as he understood it would be seen as likely to corrupt judgment. Mrs. Ambient, in James's "The Author of 'Beltraffio,'" finds the writings of her husband immoral and fears them as *contagiously* so. The object of this fear is his representation of life, the "distillation of the actual" (56), *not* brought under morality.

We have so far seen only part of the range of response that I am looking for. When Hume or others who reject what they call moralism (or what they think of in similar terms) are considered by those whom they would think of as moralistic, what does *their* mode of thinking look like? Dorothea Krook describes Hume's approach to morality as shallow, trivial, low, frivolous, unserious, unsolid, unreal, lacking any sense of the higher, lacking any genuine sense of evil. Hume's cheerfulness is the complacent comfortableness of the eighteenth-century clubman; reading Hume is like "being asphyxiated in an ocean of cotton wool." There is nothing in Hume for "the poor, the wretched, the deprived, and dispossessed," no place to be found for "those who are weary and heavy-laden" (*Three Traditions,* chapter 6, esp. 173–77). What Krook sees in Hume is a profound *irresponsibility.*

The passage to which Krook especially draws attention (as justifying the epithets she uses) is exactly the passage quoted by Baier in her contrast between Hume's nonmoralism and Kant's moralism—a passage (see note 4) in which Hume himself attacks moralistic writers as enemies of joy and pleasure. Krook's sense of being asphyxiated is tied to what she feels as the difficulty of objecting to Hume: "There is nothing solid [in that passage] to resist, nothing real to protest against" (174–75).[9] Her sense of Hume's thought about morality as *unsolid* is in part a response—very far from Baier's—to features of Hume's voice, "features of tone, emphasis, personal accent" (9). Krook and Kant differ in their responses to Hume, but both can be read as seeing in the Humean approach a denial of the *reality* of morality, and this is a source of Krook's perception of Hume as unserious, frivolous.

I want to pursue the idea that a feature of at least some of the approaches to morality that reject what they take to be moralism, when viewed by those who are seen as moralistic, is *frivolousness,* failure of (due) seriousness. One form that this idea takes is opposition to aestheticism. "Aestheticism," as a term of criticism, is no easier to pin down than is "moralism." An aestheticized version of morality does not allow morality to be itself; the seriousness of morality is gone.

In Henry James's fiction, Europe, Paris, and Europeanized Americans or Englishmen frequently represent aestheticized conceptions of life and of morality. Gabriel Nash in *The Tragic Muse* is one example; Paris in *The Ambassadors* is another, as in this passage:

> "You've all of you here so much visual sense that you've somehow all 'run' to it. There are moments when it strikes one that you haven't any other."
>
> "Any moral," little Bilham explained, watching serenely, across the garden, the several *femmes du monde.* . . .
>
> "I daresay, moreover," [Miss Barrace] pursued . . . "that I do, that we all do here, run too much to mere eye." (127–28)

James treats moralism and aestheticism, New England and Paris, as—both of them—distorted modes of thought and response to life.[10] For him, *frivolousness* and *lack of seriousness* are important notions not just in articulating the response of the *moralistic* to something they see or think they see in others but also in articulating a possible nonmoralistic understanding of what is the matter with aestheticism. New England may hate Paris, may not see what is splendid about Paris, but it is responding to unseriousness, failure of responsibility: various forms of failure of responsibility run through "aestheticized" thought. James, though, does not equate responsibility with what moralism makes of it. Genuine responsibility takes forms that moralism will not recognize, and moralism involves its own kinds of evasions. A great question for James is, then, the possibility of responsibility without moralism, the possibility of the quickened life of reflection and observation, in which neither the "visual" sense nor the sense of responsibility is scanted.[11] *The Tragic Muse* and *The Ambassadors* are especially interesting in this connection. Thus, for example, in the latter we see Strether's development, and the kind of moral thinking he reaches, in a complex contrasting relation not just to the moralism of New England but also to the aestheticism associated with Paris. To understand his moral journey, we must see it with the genuine attractiveness and the genuine limitations of *both* Paris and Woollett; we need also an account of the relation between the inadequacies of Paris and those of Woollett.[12]

Our *particular* moral views emerge from a more general background of thought and response. We differ in how we let (or do not let) moral concepts order our life and our relations to others, in how such concepts structure the stories we tell of what we have done or gone through. I have been focusing on the ways we respond to modes of moral thought that we do not share and that may appear to us as distortions of thought.[13] If it is indeed our forms of responsiveness that give rise to explicit moral thought and particular decisions, if it is indeed clashes in mode of responsiveness that underlie much moral disagreement, then it seems that moral philosophers and (more generally) people reflecting on ethics should attend to texture of life, to modes of responsiveness, and to the relation between texture of life and particular acts, thoughts, responses. That is indeed explicitly argued for by Iris Murdoch ("Vision and Choice"), and similar arguments are developed by Nussbaum. But the conclusion may be resisted; the kind of approach to morality that gets called *moralistic* can lead to a rejection of the argument that we should attend to modes of responsiveness to life. Here, I want to turn to *What Maisie Knew* and the moralistic criticism it inspired.

In *What Maisie Knew,* James portrays the freshness of Maisie's view and how she remarkably maintains that freshness within the morally corrupt world of her parents and their shifting sexual partners. From the point of view of good moral people (whom James refers to elsewhere as *bonnes gens*), this was an inappropriate subject for a novel. The world of the adults was morally disgusting, and the "mixing-up" of the child with that world aggravated the inappropriateness of subject: "nothing could well be more disgusting than to attribute to Maisie so intimate an 'acquaintance' with the gross immoralities surrounding her" (12). One part of James's response to this criticism (and to similar criticism of other writers, like Zola and Ibsen) is that the value of any subject cannot be seen in advance of its treatment, of what that treatment may have in it of responsiveness to life. Let us say that there is in the treatment a sense of the infinitude of character, a care for *that*; let us say that there is in the account we are given perhaps unexpected intensity of life: there is not then anything else that needs to be demanded of it. We cannot write off in advance, on the grounds that a *sympathetic* picture will be corrupting, the sympathetic treatment of, say, a wicked, diseased, disagreeable woman: of a Hedda Gabler.[14]

We might describe the clash between James and moralistic critics of his own work and that of others as a clash between views of life, or alternatively as a clash between James—taken as believing in the possible appropriateness and importance of representing any subject, the representation itself reflecting a responsiveness to life—and people who have a sort of metaview about views of life, who hold that *whether* it is appropriate or decent or useful to attend to a mode of responsiveness to life or to put a treatment of a particular subject before the public are questions to be judged on external moral grounds. In James's view the ground for such a judgment does not exist in advance of the treatment and what it has in it of the "quality of mind of the producer." On the fineness of that intelligence depends the achieving of "rightness" of discrimination (including moral discrimination) (*Critical Muse* 204–6). The view of life of James's critics was that views of life are to be judged by morality; James rejects the "grotesque finality" (*What Maisie Knew* 12) of the characterizations appealed to by those critics and their underlying, blinkered conception of morality. He takes moralism itself to be a human phenomenon and (like any other) to be judgeable only when we take it up in our thought, represent it, and understand it to whatever degree, at whatever depth. Our thought about moralism, or any judgment of it, grows out of a mode of responsiveness to life. *That* responsiveness has its moral character: it is morally alive, or dead, or obtuse, or shallow, or whatever it may be.

Henry James believed that the moralistic critics of such novels as *What Maisie Knew* failed to understand it. But then they did not want what he would regard as understanding; the effort to achieve such understanding they would take to be misplaced. Compare the idea, characteristic of moralism, that it is out of place to try to see the sinner or criminal in the light of a sympathetic understanding. The invitation to take up such an understanding is conceived as an invitation to feel sorry for such a person and to avoid making the judgment on her that she deserves. The route leading toward understanding seems (to the moralistically inclined) a route leading away from appropriate judgment, judgment depending on moral firmness that sympathetic understanding might soften. For James, in contrast, a consciousness that takes (as Lambert Strether's does), in all its difficulty and windingness, the route toward understanding is exercising a vital kind of responsibility. The disagreements I have been describing are disagreements in understanding, but also in the desire for understanding, the conception of its use, its place, its limits. These disagreements are then also reflected within moral philosophy. Thus, some contemporary followers of Kant take Kantian moral philosophy to be distinctively "agent-centered," but an essential element in their conception of "agency" is that a Jamesian appreciation of the actions and changing character, the passions and endurings of others, would be *contrasted* with the exercise of moral agency and not a fine and central case of it. To emphasize such appreciation would be to direct attention away from the "problems we have to face," but this is to hold that the real problems we have as moral beings, responsible agents, do not include those of achieving the kind of understanding that James sought. Moral agency is there tied by moral philosophy to principled choice; within such philosophy, the achieving of a Jamesian kind of understanding of things is described in a vocabulary that cuts it off from genuine exercise of moral responsibility in the face of real problems.[15] The Lambert Strethers, the Henry Jameses, go in for what is in these terms mere "moral connoisseurship," that is, a kind of spectatorship unconnected with the hardships of choice and dependent on the kind of leisure that would free one for mere appreciation. Here, we are back *within* the issues explored in *The Ambassadors* and elsewhere in James's fiction and criticism; we have not reached some neutral philosophical standpoint where inclinations toward or away from moralism no longer count.[16]

James's characters respond to moral things in life in an immense variety of ways; they find themselves at odds about everything from relatively simple, straightforward propositions (whether, for example, Morris Townsend, in *Washington Square,* is a decent young man) to life in general (Olive Chancellor and Basil Ransom, in *The Bostonians*). Philosophers, in their thought about moral disagreement, have focused almost exclusively on cases like the first. Because the judgments about which we disagree in such cases resemble ordinary factual judgments, philosophers have endlessly debated *how far* the resemblance to factual judgment goes. In this essay, I have looked at clashes in people's response to life, in their way of using moral concepts in understanding their own life and their relations to others. We may react very strongly to other people's mode of moral thought. What is being responded to is not this or that particular judgment. If we differ from others in *this* way, the disagreement does not resemble disagreements over admittedly factual matters. So the kind of philosophical question that arises about particular moral judgments—whether they are as much like factual judgments as they appear—does not arise in connection with *these* disagreements.

The idea that, phenomenologically, ethical thought resembles thought in which we judge how the facts stand is a starting point for much philosophical work. But the belief that that *is* the phenomenology of ethical thought is the result of ignoring much ethical thought—much ordinary unreflective, as well as reflective, thought. Ethical thought includes a variety of complex responses to what seem to us distorted or bad modes of moral thinking, modes of thinking that we may take (with greater or lesser awareness) to challenge or threaten our own sense of what is important. Although we may regard those from whom we feel thus distant as making false judgments about moral facts, the difference about those particular matters is not the heart of the disagreement, nor is it usually taken to be. The *character* of a mode of thought has great interest for us, not just as a matter of a disposition to reach or to miss accurate judgments. To call someone's mode of moral thought moralistic, or, on the other hand, to call it unsolid, evasive, frivolous, irresponsible, immoral, is in neither case to be claiming that the other person has some moral facts wrong. The phenomenology here is different; we need to be much more suspicious of philosophical remarks about *the* phenomenology of moral thought.

If James describes for us the varieties of forms that can be taken by our disagreements with each other on moral matters, philosophers should learn more from this than just that they had had an inadequate idea of the phenomenology of moral disagreement. Where did the apparent self-evidence of that initial philosophical reading of the phenomenology of moral life come from? It is hardly innocent of all connections with a moralistic inheritance. So what we need from James is also his portrayal of what these differences between us mean in our lives, what their significance is. His own complex response to the inheritance of moralism is in that complex portrayal of importances. It's all in the shades!—as some of his unmoralistic characters might say. But a dislike for shades is what marks us as philosophers.

I quoted William James at the beginning of this essay about our tendency as theorizers to oversimplify our material. He was thinking in particular of theories of religion and warning of the danger of taking there to be some essence of religion tied to the nature of religious experience *as such*. The will thus to oversimplify leads, he says, to "all that absolutism and one-sided dogmatism by which both philosophy and religion have been infested" (46). So, too, there is a need for philosophy not to oversimplify the phenomena of moral life and thought, not to look for some single basic characterization of moral experience. But in ethics the theorizing mind is not the only source of the tendency to oversimplify. A moralistic conception of morality—not just a theorizing mind—can lead us to say: this (whatever it may be) is what moral thinking in essence is; all else is not really moral thinking. The require-ments of morality, not just the requirements of theory, may seem to lead us away from any recognition of genuine variety within moral experience.[17]

Notes

1. Gaita's phrase is actually "philosophical and moralistic devaluing."

2. I am not concerned with the question whether Baier's account of Kant is fair but rather with the question what is involved in the characterization of a view, whether Kant's or not, as moralistic. It should, however, be noted that some defenses of Kant as not moralistic or even anti-moralistic appeal to a very narrow conception of what it is to be moralistic. Being moralistic may be identified with making or encouraging the mak-ing of moral judgments about other people and with failing to respect their choices; it may then seem easy to show that Kant is not moralistic. See, for example, Baron (98, 102).

3. The New Englander's intolerance of shades and ambiguities, of moral mixture, marks an important connection with Kant. Kant insists on the enormous importance of avoiding as far as possible in ethics the admission of anything "morally intermediate," any real (as opposed to merely apparent) mix of good and bad, in actions or human character: ambiguity undermines the precision and stability of moral maxims (*Religion* 18). For more about Henry James on shades and ambiguities, see Nussbaum (*Love's Knowledge*, esp. "Flawed Crystals"; see also Nussbaum's discussions of a related topic, the incom-mensurability of valuable things, in, for example, "The Discernment of Perception").

4. See especially chapter 3 of *The Ambassadors*. The complexity of James's use of "Europe" allows Chester to belong to Europe in one work, and Europe to be contrasted with England in others, thus demonstrating that Europe is a place in the American (or English) consciousness, not identical with any place on a map. The relation between Europe and England in *The Tragic Muse* allows James to make contrasts between philis-tinism and aestheticism that overlap but do not duplicate the contrasts between New England moralism and aestheticism. (Philistinism can, though, be tied quite directly to moralism, as in the character of Lady Agnes in *The Tragic Muse,* and even more clearly in the character of Mrs. Ambient in "The Author of 'Beltraffio.'") The hatred of art in the political/English characters is tied to a dislike of "discrimination of tones," just as is the hatred of Europe in James's moralistic/New England characters. The English liberal and the New Englander are equally appalled by iniquity, equally committed to active reform and improvement, equally suspicious of the aesthete's lack of commitment to reform, willingness instead simply to "feel," and utter lack of responsibility. For a sim-

ilar use of "place" in relation to the criticism of moralism, see Ibsen's *Ghosts* and the use of Norway/Paris in it; see also Ibsen's *Pillars of Society,* and the use of Norway/America.

5. See Krook on the role of lying in *The Europeans* (*Ordeal* 293n).

6. In "The Author of 'Beltraffio,'" James tells us nothing about what it is that the moralistic Mrs. Ambient objects to in "Beltraffio" and the other writings of her husband, but we are expected to recognize that what she objects to is the treatment of sex.

7. I am grateful to Julie Diamond for discussion of the issues in this paragraph.

8. We should note here the connection of Kant's idea that an otherwise admirable trait becomes abominable in the absence of a good will with his view (see note 6 above) that we must in ethics avoid as far as possible the very idea of a *mix* of good and bad in human character: if the absence of a good will makes an otherwise admirable trait *not* good, the presence of such traits in the absence of a good will cannot create a "morally mixed" character. Here, we can see further the contrast with Henry James: what interests him not just as author but also as critic, as for example in considering Hedda, is precisely the possibility of complex moral "mixtures" (*Critical Muse* 301).

9. The passage to which Krook objects so strongly is also one that Kant would condemn, although in different terms. In *Religion within the Limits of Reason Alone,* Kant tells us that our relation to morality is properly awe and not familiarity; he rejects the idea of morality as having "charm" for us. Hume's words for our relation to morality: "engaging charm . . . ease, familiarity, affection" (see note 4 above) would be seen by Kant as suggesting in two ways a kind of moral corruption: in their implicit rejection of the centrality of duty (duty tied to the moral law as having majesty) and in their consequent denial of the sublimity of our own destiny as moral beings. There is, though, a limited agreement between Kant and Hume in rejecting "monkish" self-immolation.

10. See, for example, the entirety of chapter 10, from which the quoted passage comes. I should note that, within the context of James's fiction, it is overly simple to identify moralism with "New England," as I have been doing. In two of his most interesting treatments of art in relation to a hatred of art tied to a sense of its immorality (*The Tragic Muse,* "The Author of 'Beltraffio'"), it is not New England but England that is the place associated with moralism and philistinism.

11. My phrasing draws on the first two chapters of *The Tragic Muse.* James's remarks, quoted above, about the novels of Scott and Fielding reflect related ideas: Scott is "irresponsible," Fielding a didactic, though amusing, moralizer. The possibility of responsibility without moralism is then important in James's understanding of his own aims as a novelist.

12. Nussbaum's discussion of *The Ambassadors* differs sharply from mine (see esp. 182, 185); it is framed in terms of *two* rival norms, two opposing conceptions of practical reason, Strether's and Woollett's. See also Hardy's description of the slow, complex, "eddying" process of moral transformation in which Strether rejects two moral cultures (27–31), and see Levenson's illuminating account of the three "moral attitudes" in *The Ambassadors* (1–77). Levenson makes clear the possibility of a critical perspective on "Paris" distinct from that of Woollett and essential to the novel's conception; he gives a detailed account of the "matching" failings of the two attitudes contrasted with Strether's. I am grateful to Conant for discussion of these issues.

13. It is important to note that the disagreements of which I have been speaking can be found within the mind of a single person. Two examples: fru Alving, in *Ghosts,*

has still within herself the woman, or the ghost of the woman, who refused, years ago, to see how her moralism was destroying her husband's life and her own. Her struggle during the period leading up to that of the play, and during the play, is to free herself from that woman's mode of thought. In Tolstoy the relation goes in the opposite direction: it is the inner moralizer who, in Tolstoy's later life, wants to put himself at a distance from the author of *Anna Karenina,* now seen as irresponsible, immoral, elitist.

14. We should note that, in James's defense of Hedda as subject, he defends Ibsen's choice of subject in exactly the terms that the moralistic would take to constitute a condemnation: Hedda, well acted, will no longer appear the wicked, disagreeable woman we may at first take her to be. We will become unsure of her wickedness and will indeed find her complicated, various, graceful; she suffers, she struggles, she is human; she is exposed to a dozen interpretations (*Critical Muse* 301). This description, from the point of view of Kant, would constitute all the justification needed for treating Ibsen's art as corrupt and corrupting. (The complicated, various, graceful bad woman who suffers, struggles, is human: this would also describe Kate Croy in *The Wings of the Dove.*)

15. Various passages in O'Neill would provide examples (see esp. 176); see also Korsgaard (186n).

16. Much of Nussbaum bears on the issues of this paragraph (see, for example, 26 and the whole of "Perceptive Equilibrium: Literary Theory and Ethical Theory"). Conant's account of the misunderstandings to which Nietzsche's perfectionism has been subject, as seen from a point of view that Nietzsche would have taken to be that of the moralism of moral philosophy, is relevant to all the questions I have examined. It is particularly relevant, too, to an important distinction made by O'Neill between the exercise of moral agency on the one hand and moral development and moral education on the other (176). Her understanding of that distinction is precisely what is called into question by perfectionism as described in Conant's essay. The relevance of this issue to James's understanding of moral life cannot be underestimated. See Hardy's description of *The Ambassadors* as a kind of Bildungsroman (28). Any attempt to separate Strether's real doings as a moral agent from his moral education and development (taking his enhanced capacity to appreciate and understand to belong to the latter) would again impose the point of view associated with moralism; compare also Murdoch's description of M's inner progress (*Sovereignty* 21–23).

17. I am very glad to have had the chance to present an earlier version of some parts of this essay at the Inter-Nordic Symposium on Ethics and Understanding in Turku, Finland, in 1993. An expanded version of the conference paper, overlapping this present essay, has been published under the title "Moral Differences and Distances: Some Questions." I was much helped by the discussion at the conference and by comments and suggestions afterward from Lars Hertzberg, Harald Johannessen, Kurt Baier, and Annette Baier. I am also grateful to A. D. Woozley and to James Conant for their helpful comments on various versions of the essay.

Works Cited

Alanen, Lilli, Sara Heinämaa, and Thomas Wallgren, eds. *Commonality and Particularity in Ethics.* London: Macmillan, 1991.

Baier, Annette. "Moralism and Cruelty: Reflections on Hume and Kant." *Ethics* 103 (1993): 436–57.

Baron, Marcia. "Was Effi Briest a Victim of Kantian Morality?" *Philosophy and Literature* 12 (1988): 95–113.

Conant, James. "Nietzsche's Perfectionism: A Reading of Schopenhauer as Educator." *Nietzsche's Postmoralism.* Ed. Richard Schacht. Cambridge: Cambridge UP, 2000.

Diamond, Cora. "Moral Differences and Distances: Some Questions." Alanen, Heinämaa, and Wallgren 197–234.

Edel, Leon. *Henry James: The Untried Years, 1843–1870.* New York: Avon, 1978.

Gaita, Rai. "The Moralization of Good and Evil." Alanen, Heinämaa, and Wallgren 235–59.

Goldberg, S. L. *Agents and Lives: Moral Thinking in Literature.* Cambridge: Cambridge UP, 1993.

Hardy, Barbara. *The Moral Art of Dickens.* New York: Oxford UP, 1970.

Hume, David. *Enquiry Concerning the Principles of Morals.* Oxford: Clarendon, 1902.

Ibsen, Henrik. *Ghosts. Ghosts and Other Plays.* Trans. Peter Watts. London: Penguin, 1964. 19–102.

———. *Pillars of Society. Hedda Gabler and Three Other Plays.* Trans. Michael Meyer. Garden City, NY: Anchor, 1961. 15–124.

James, Henry. *The Ambassadors.* New York: New American Library, 1960.

———. "The Author of 'Beltraffio.'" *Eight Tales from the Major Phase: "In the Cage" and Others.* Ed. Morton Danwen Zabel. New York: Norton, 1969. 29–78.

———. *The Bostonians.* New York: New American Library, 1980.

———. *The Critical Muse.* Ed. Roger Gard. London: Penguin, 1987.

———. *The Europeans.* London: Penguin, 1964.

———. *The Tragic Muse.* London: Penguin, 1978.

———. *What Maisie Knew.* London: Penguin, 1966.

———. *The Wings of the Dove.* London: Penguin, 1986.

James, Henry, Sr. *Moralism and Christianity; or, Man's Experience and Destiny.* New York: Redfield, 1850.

James, William. *Varieties of Religious Experience.* London: Collins, 1960.

Kant, Immanuel. *Groundwork of the Metaphysics of Morals.* Trans. H. J. Paton. London: Hutchison, 1956.

———. *Religion within the Limits of Reason Alone.* New York: Harper, 1960.

Korsgaard, Christine M. *Creating the Kingdom of Ends.* Cambridge: Cambridge UP, 1996.

Krook, Dorothea. *The Ordeal of Consciousness in Henry James.* Cambridge: Cambridge UP, 1967.

———. *Three Traditions of Moral Thought.* Cambridge: Cambridge UP, 1959.

Levenson, Michael. *Modernism and the Fate of Individuality: Character and Novelistic Form from Conrad to Woolf.* Cambridge: Cambridge UP, 1991.

Murdoch, Iris. *The Sovereignty of Good.* London: Routledge, 1970.

———. "Vision and Choice in Morality." *Proceedings of the Aristotelian Society* 30 (1956): 32–58.

Nussbaum, Martha C. *Love's Knowledge: Essays on Philosophy and Literature.* New York: Oxford UP, 1990.

O'Neill, Onora O. *Constructions of Reason: Explorations of Kant's Practical Philosophy.*
Cambridge: Cambridge UP, 1989.

Orwell, George. "The Art of Donald McGill." *A Collection of Essays.* Garden City, NY:
Doubleday, 1954. 111–23.

Richards, D. A. J. *A Theory of Reasons for Action.* Oxford: Clarendon, 1971.

Williams, Bernard. *Moral Luck: Philosophical Papers, 1973–1980.* Cambridge: Cambridge
UP, 1981.

HOW TO BE "IN TUNE WITH THE RIGHT" IN *THE GOLDEN BOWL*

J. Hillis Miller

ETHICS, EVEN ethics in its literary dimension, is a dangerous and slippery field, since it so tempts those who enter it to generalized speculation or prescription. Ethical prescription may claim to have a universal basis
but is likely to be no more than the reassertion of unconscious ideological
assumptions peculiar to a given society or person at a given time. All situations demanding ethical decision, it may be, are singular, not assimilable to
general rules or evaluations. One way to try, at least, to avoid the temptation
of generalization is to turn to a literary example with the presumption that
it may be *sui generis,* an example of itself, peculiar, particular. It might then
be exemplary of ethical situations in real life, not in the sense that it provides
universal rules but in the sense that we may learn from it how much on our
own we are when we are in a shrewd situation and must make an ethical
decision. I choose Henry James's *The Golden Bowl* as possibly providing
such an example.

The turning point or, to give it its austere Greek name, *peripeteia,* of *The
Golden Bowl* is a moment of double perjury. The word "perjury" is James's
own, or rather that of his deputy and delegate, the narrative voice. In a
carefully planned private encounter, Charlotte has found Maggie alone and
asks her if she has anything to complain of in her (Charlotte's) behavior.
Though Maggie knows—or thinks she knows, knows "more and more"—
that Charlotte, her stepmother, has betrayed her by renewing an old affair
with Maggie's husband, Prince Amerigo, Maggie swears that she has nothing to complain of to Charlotte: "I've *not* felt at any time that you've
wronged me." Charlotte, on her side, swears that she has not knowingly
wronged Maggie: "I'm aware of no point whatever at which I may have
failed you" (2:248). In both cases these assertions are outright lies. Maggie
believes she knows Charlotte has been sleeping with her husband, under
her nose, so to speak, and Charlotte, the reader is led to think, knows she has
wronged Maggie in the worst way possible: by sleeping with her husband.

At least the reader has been made to believe that is the case. We are never told this in so many words or shown a direct representation of the event. We have only indirect signs and insinuations. The reader no more has certain knowledge than does Maggie.

Though "lie" is a key word in *The Golden Bowl*, appearing far more often than "perjury," the narrator calls these particular lies "conscious perjuries": "With which she saw soon enough what more was to come. She saw it in Charlotte's face and felt it make between them, in the air, a chill that completed the coldness of their conscious perjury. 'Will you kiss me on it then?'" (2:251). Strictly speaking, neither a lie nor a perjury are, seen from one aspect at least, performative utterances. They are contrary-to-fact constative statements or statements that the speaker believes to be false. A performative utterance is neither true nor false. A lie or a perjury can, however, as J. L. Austin recognizes in *How to Do Things with Words*, have a performative function if it is believed or if those who hear it act as if they believe it. The lie or the perjury is then a way to do things with words.

What justifies the word "perjury" in the narrator's formulation? Or the adjective "conscious"? A lie may be a private matter, perhaps between two people only. It is even possible to "lie to oneself," or at any rate ordinary language permits saying that. Lying to oneself presupposes a doubling of the self into liar and the one lied to. Perjury, on the other hand, is necessarily public. It involves, at least implicitly, the minimum presence of one other person, the third as witness, testifier, *terstis*, potentially able to give testimony that the lie occurred. Unless a third is present, however vicariously or symbolically, an event in a sense does not occur for the community—for example, for the legal authorities—since no one can be forced to testify against himself or herself, at least not within United States law. If whatever Charlotte and the Prince have done together remains secret, it has for the community not happened. It has not happened as a social event, that is, as something for which they are answerable to the community. O. J. Simpson may possibly (who knows?) have killed his wife, Othello-like, in a fit of jealous rage, but for the community this did not happen (if it did happen), since a jury decided there was not enough evidence to convict him.

Perjury, moreover, involves, at least implicitly, an act of public and formal swearing or oath taking: "I swear I am telling the truth, the whole truth, and nothing but the truth, so help me God." This formula is carefully phrased. It forbids virtual lying by telling only part of the truth or by telling the truth mixed with some lies, fixing things up a bit, for example, to make a good story out of it, as when Huckleberry Finn, in the first paragraph of

Huckleberry Finn, says Mark Twain in *The Adventures of Tom Sawyer* has told the truth about him, "mainly." That "mainly" is disquieting and ominous. We want the whole truth and nothing but the truth. Perjury is lying under an oath, in defiance of a promise to tell the whole truth.

Perjury differs from lying, as the word "perjury" suggests, in being the violation of a prior oath. *Per* functions here as a prefix meaning "away," and *jure* means "swear." To perjure oneself is to swear away a prior oath or to swear away the truth, whereas I may lie on my own hook without having promised that I would tell the truth. Paradigmatic acts of perjury take place in a courtroom when someone has been served a subpoena and forced to testify under pain (that's what *sub poena* means in Latin) of imprisonment or fine. The whole machinery of law, justice, and the bonds of society are threatened by an act of perjury. That explains why it is taken so seriously and punished so severely.

Though both lies and perjuries are performative utterances, perjury is a speech-act crime that is punishable by law, whereas a private lie is not a crime, even though it may function as an efficacious speech act, as do many of the lies in *The Golden Bowl.* A lie works as well as a truth as a way of doing things with words if the lie is believed or if others can be brought to act as if they believed the lie. A lie may nevertheless radically endanger the community, as Kant presumed when he asserted that lying is never justified, not even to save someone's life.[1] One might argue, therefore, that all lies are perjuries in the sense that they violate a tacit social commitment never to tell a lie. Even so, a citizen is not jailed for lying as such, only for "lying under oath."

What Charlotte and Maggie say are perjuries as well as lies for two reasons. First, they are presented as secured by an explicit oath. Charlotte says, "I only wanted your denial," to which Maggie answers, "Well then you have it." This is followed by one of those repetitive stichomythias that are so important an ingredient in the grammar of dialogue in *The Golden Bowl.* Charlotte speaks first and Maggie echoes her, as though they were in a courtroom:

> "Upon your honor?"
> "Upon my honor." (2:251)

The second feature making this a scene of perjury is that the seal and signature of these lying oaths is publicly attested. "The prodigious kiss," a Judas kiss, "prodigious" in the root sense of being an omen, that Maggie receives from Charlotte is witnessed by Maggie's husband (also Charlotte's stepson and, presumably, her lover) and her father (also Charlotte's husband and, presumably, cuckold, in this quasi-incestuous tangle), as well as by their friends the Assinghams: "Her husband and her father were in front, and Charlotte's embrace of her—which wasn't to be distinguished for them either, she felt, from her embrace of Charlotte—took on with their arrival a high publicity" (2:252).

The word "conscious" in James's formulation "conscious perjury" is odd because it is apparently tautological. All perjuries, it would seem, must be conscious in the sense that they deliberately violate a prior oath that is remembered at the time of the perjury. Perjuries may not necessarily say what the perjurer knows to be false, but they swear what the perjurer believes to be false. The witness can always be making an honest mistake. Testimony is always an assertion of belief, not of knowledge, even if the witness has "seen with his or her own eyes." This makes the whole region of lies, testimony, and perjury partly a matter of belief, not simply of cognition, and therefore a domain of speech acts, not simply of constative statements. That is why the jury in a criminal trial is instructed to decide not on the basis of certain knowledge but "beyond reasonable doubt," that is, with strong inner conviction on the basis of the evidence as presented. The jury's decision is a collective act of conscience. Legal proof is always indirect. It is carefully staged by the lawyers within definite rules for what counts as legitimate testimony or evidence. Potential jurors are excluded, somewhat paradoxically, if they happen to have prior knowledge of the scene of the crime, since they are supposed to decide only on the basis of what is presented in the courtroom.

An "unconscious perjury," it seems, would therefore be a contradiction in terms, an oxymoron, like "heavy feathers" or "light lead." You always know you are doing it. The perjurer might, however, and often does, claim that he or she had forgotten in a prior testimony. One way perjury may be identified is by contradictions in a witness's testimony. The witness must in one assertion or the other be lying, therefore committing perjury, since it is a case of lying under oath. The witness, however, can always claim that he or she had not remembered right the first time and has now remembered correctly: "Now it all comes back to me. I remembered wrong when I first testified." This way out is not an option in *The Golden Bowl.* All the characters are presented as having total and accurate memories, even excessive, haunted, or hyperbolic memories, just as James himself did. Or thought he did, since how can we be certain that James's memories, in his autobiographical books, for example, are accurate? James's characters are haunted by ghosts of past moments. They are haunted by a "sense of the past" (to borrow the title of James's last, unfinished novel). This goes along with a sense of present possibilities that is immediate and almost material, as a ghost in broad daylight seems almost material, an immaterial materiality.

The image of memory or imagination as raising specters, revenants, ghosts returned from the dead, is James's own. It is used at crucial moments in *The Golden Bowl* and in its preface. In the preface, discussing the problematic custom of providing illustrations for novels, that is, representations in a different and competing medium, James speaks of the novelist's power as the ability to raise ghosts, to give the reader hallucinatory visions of the characters and actions he calls forth by force of the word: "That one should, as an author, reduce one's reader, 'artistically' inclined, to such a state of hallucination by the images one has evoked as doesn't permit him to rest till he has noted or recorded them, set up some semblance of them in his own other medium, by his own other art—nothing could better consort than *that*, I naturally allow, with the desire or the pretension to cast a literary spell." A moment later he says the novelist can so effectively cast this spell that his "figures and scenes" "become more or less visible appearances" (1:x).

In the novel itself a figurative strand defining the characters' imaginations as haunted or as raising ghosts, a line of images as evanescent and unnoticeable almost as a wisp of smoke, threads its way through the narration, appearing here and there like faint knots in an intricate embroidery. Maggie's perjuring lie to Charlotte seems to Charlotte to have been as performatively effective as a successful act of exorcism or the laying of ghosts would be: "her stepdaughter's word, wiping out, as she might have said, everything, had restored them to the serenity of a relation without a cloud. It had been in short by this light ideally conclusive, so that no ghost of anything it referred to could ever walk again" (2:279). A little later Maggie, so strong is her imagination of what Charlotte is suffering, thinks of herself as a specter following Charlotte about, though unseen: "Marvelous the manner in which, under such imaginations, Maggie thus circled and lingered—quite as if she were, materially, following her unseen, counting every step she helplessly wasted, noting every hindrance that brought her to a pause" (2:282–83). Though Maggie has learned only indirectly of the intimate relation between her husband and Charlotte, her projection of figures into the void of her ignorance is spoken of as a raising of spectral presences such as haunt the woods at night: "There had been through life, as we know, few quarters in which the Princess's fancy could let itself loose; but it shook off restraint when it plunged into the figured void of the detail of that relation. This was a realm it could people with images—again and again with fresh ones; they swarmed there like the strange combinations that lurked in the woods at twilight; they loomed into the definite and faded into the vague, their main present sign for her being however that they were always, that they were duskily, agitated" (2:280). A few pages further on Maggie is said to imagine all the main actors in her family drama to be living in a haunted house. They are haunted by what they are thinking about the others but cannot say: "They learned fairly to live in the perfunctory; they remained in it as many hours of the day as might be; it took on finally the likeness of some spacious central chamber in a haunted house, a great overarched and overglazed rotunda where gaiety might reign, but the doors of which opened into sinister circular passages" (2:288). About ghosts in James there would be much more to say, but I reserve that for another essay, observing now only that using words to raise ghosts is a speech act par excellence, an act of invocation or conjuration, just as laying ghosts to rest is in an act of abjuration, exorcism, or swearing away.

Maggie's "conscious perjury" is such an abjuration. By calling the perjury "conscious" James apparently means that by looking in one another's eyes and swearing falsely, then sealing those falsehoods with a public kiss, both Maggie and Charlotte are "coldly" and lucidly aware that they are perjuring themselves and aware also, coldly, that the other is also at that moment committing a respondent blatant act of perjury. Maggie's perjury is at the same time, it might be added, another kind of speech act. It is implicitly an act of renunciation. It is as though she were saying, "I hereby renounce my right as an injured wife to denounce you and my husband and to sue for divorce."

Why does Maggie perjure herself? Why does she renounce her right as the victim of her husband's presumed adultery? Is what she says a felicitous speech act, an efficacious way to do things with words? Does it make anything happen? If so, just what does it make happen? How could it do anything if each perjurer is aware of the other's perjury? Can it, finally, be justified? On what grounds? Does Maggie, as she claims, do the right thing when she perjures herself in this way? What would you have done in her place? Maggie thinks to herself, as reported in indirect discourse by the narrative voice, that she has successfully done something with her words: "The heart of the Princess swelled accordingly even in her abasement; she had kept in tune with the right, and something, certainly, something that might resemble a rare flower snatched from an impossible ledge, would, and possibly soon, come of it for her. The right, the right—yes, it took this extraordinary form of humbugging, as she had called it, to the end. It was only a question of not by a hair's breadth deflecting into the truth" (2:250–51). Is Maggie really "in tune with the right"? Is the right line for her not deflecting a hair's breadth into the truth? Can it ever be just, justified, or right to lie and perjure oneself in this humbugging way? How can this perjury be a felicitous speech act if Charlotte knows, or believes she knows, Maggie is lying, just as Maggie knows, or believes she knows, that Charlotte is lying? These are the central questions for the thoughtful reader of *The Golden Bowl*, the reader who sees reading literature as James in the preface sees writing it—as a particularly exigent and responsible part of "the conduct of life" (1:xxiv).

These questions can only begin to be answered on the basis of a prior understanding of the context within which the double perjury takes place. This context can be thought of as a field that lays down certain laws and rules determining the functioning of any speech act within its dynamic array of forces. The field includes the assumptions about society that are more or less mimetic of those in James's day (such as the impossibility of marrying without money, sharp class and gender distinctions, distinct national characteristics that make it hard, perhaps impossible, for Amerigo to understand Anglo-Saxons and hard, perhaps impossible, for them to understand him,[2] and a certain stage of high imperialism and late capitalism in England and the United States), assumptions about consciousness and language, about the way minds are related to one another, that are specific to this work, complex formal assumptions about the novel as a genre, and, within all that, tacit, and to some degree anomalous, assumptions about what makes a speech act felicitous or infelicitous. These laws, rules, and conventions are not laid down in so many words. They are tacit and exemplified concretely, so the readers are left to figure out for themselves the rules the examples obey. These laws are similar to those in other James novels, *The Wings of the Dove*, for example, but not identical. Each new work by James to some degree sets up conventions of its own, laws that operate only within that novel or short story. By the time careful readers reach Maggie's "I've *not* felt at any time that you've wronged me," they will have internalized the entire set of assumptions making up what I have called the dynamic field within which any enunciation takes place in the novel. This field may be compared to the vast expanse of untrodden snow that in the preface James proposes as a figure for "the clear matter" of the tale (1:xiii). It is at once bland and unspecified and at the same time absolutely compelling, just as James finds that there is only one right way to make the tracks in the snow that constitute the actual telling of the story, even though the field of snow is featureless, apparently an open space where one is free to walk as one likes.

Sharon Cameron, in the best and most brilliant essay so far written on *The Golden Bowl*, asserts, erroneously in my view, that James, especially in this novel and in *The Wings of the Dove*, characteristically assumes that a given character can by the sheer power of thinking, by a kind of telepathic thought projection, coerce another into behaving in a desired way, even against the other's will.[3] *The Sacred Fount* would seem to support this view of James in its dramatization of the way a given couple, married or in sexual liaison, may magically affect one another, the younger becoming older, the older younger, the dumb one smart, the smart one dumb, as though there were a single "sacred fount" of such qualities, with only so much youth and intelligence to go around, so that what is given to one person must be taken from some other. This supposition that James had a magic view of human relations provides a beguiling way of reading *The Golden Bowl* or *The Wings of the Dove*. It recognizes, at least, that these novels are exceedingly peculiar, that something strange is going on in them. I greatly admire Cameron, moreover, for having had the courage to say that *The Golden Bowl* is "unintelligible." I agree that it is "unintelligible" when read with her phenomenological presuppositions, but I claim it becomes if not intelligible, since speech acts are foreign to cognition and never "intelligible," at least explicable or able to be accounted for if readers shift their focus from consciousness or the power of thinking to language or, more broadly, to the proffering and reading of signs—that is, if readers shift their attention to the speech acts in the novel.

Cameron is right to note that *The Golden Bowl* puts great stress on each character's independent and solitary, ever-so-isolated power of thinking. The most salient and overt evidence of this is a passage in which Fanny Assingham asserts her recognition that Maggie is "deep," that a lot of hidden thinking is going on under her quiet surface, and later tells her that she thinks too much. Fanny tells Maggie, "I'm bound to confess I've never been so awfully sure of what I may call knowing you. Here you are indeed, as you say—such a deep little person! . . . What I've always been conscious of is of your having concealed about you somewhere no small amount of character; quite as much in fact . . . as one could suppose a person of your size able to carry" (2:110–12).

Much later, in a more extended interchange between Fanny and Maggie about the latter's thinking, Fanny tells Maggie that "It's your nature to think too much," to which Maggie replies that she needed to think because Amerigo and Charlotte "on their side thought of everything *but* that. They thought of everything but that I might think" (2:332). A little later in the interchange Fanny says of Maggie and her father, using another from the group of key words in the novel that includes "saved" or "safe," words that recur in connection with "knowledge" and "belief": "You think, both of you, so abysmally and yet so quietly. But it's what will have saved you," to which Maggie answers that it is rather what will have made her and her father lost, since their actions on the basis of their thinking will cause them to lose one another for good when her father returns alone to American City with Charlotte (2:333). A given character thinks of himself or herself as "safe" if he or she can get the others to believe or to act as if they believe in the way the first character wants.

Nevertheless, in spite of all the emphasis on the power of thinking in this novel, as in James's other works, solitary, private thinking in itself is powerless. This is as true in *The Golden Bowl* as in *The Wings of the Dove*. Thinking does not, pace Cameron, have some spooky telepathic effect, not even in *The Sacred Fount*. Thinking for James exerts influence over other people only when it has been "outered" in one way or another in words or other signs—for example, in Maggie's dressing in her best new dress and waiting for her husband in her drawing room or in her saying to Charlotte, "I've *not* felt at any time that you've wronged me" (2:249).

Just how does this work? The "felicity" of a normal or standard speech act, in Austin's view, depends on being grounded in a previously established set of conventions and rules. It also depends on being proffered at the right place and time by someone who has the right to perform that particular performative. I cannot, according to Austin, just casually walk up and christen a new British warship the *Joseph Stalin,* nor can I marry someone to a monkey, nor can I be writing poetry, or uttering a soliloquy, or acting on the stage, not if I want my speech acts to work, that is. A felicitous performative also depends (though Austin waffles on this point and is self-contradictory) on my good faith and sincere intentions. I must mean what I say, not be lying or perjuring myself. Maggie's speech acts or "sign acts," culminating in her resounding conscious perjury to Charlotte, disobey all of these conditions for a felicitous performative. Nevertheless, they work, they do something, they do what Maggie wants, they are felicitous, though the word has an ironic ring in this case, since their felicity inflicts "torment" on Charlotte and takes effective revenge on Amerigo by depriving him of his mistress.

How can Maggie's speech acts work if they have no precedent that grounds them, they obey no pre-established rules, they are based on her own private unsponsored, unauthorized decision to act, and they are accomplished through lies and perjuries? Moreover, these lies are not really believed, and they happen to occur in a work of literature, where, if Austin is right, nothing serious is ever supposed to be brought about by words. Literature, according to Austin, is frivolous, nonserious. It lacks purchase on the "real world." Nevertheless, Maggie's "sign acts" work. What Maggie does by saying or "signing" works to bring about the denouement of the novel and also to change the life of the reader, if he or she is a responsible reader, responsible to the demand made by the work. How can this be?

A parallel with the American Declaration of Independence may be useful here. As Jacques Derrida, in a brilliant short article, and more recently David Arndt, in a superb dissertation chapter, have shown, the Declaration of Independence is a peculiar document.[4] Its peculiarity is characteristic of such political acts of foundation. In spite of its appeals to precedent and to divine sanction as well as to "self-evident" truth, it is groundless and at the same time creates its own grounds, in a metaleptic speech act gesture that brings into existence as an immediate future, just after or in the same moment as the speech act, in speaking or by speaking, what it needed to have already in place in order to be efficacious. The "good people of these colonies" are brought into existence as a national community by the Declaration, just as is the right of Jefferson and the other signers to represent the states that are brought into existence as the United States by the document they sign. To say "We hold these truths to be self-evident," as Arndt argues, is to say two different incompatible things at once. The statement appeals constatively to the self-evidence of the "truths" that justify or are claimed or believed to justify the act of revolution, and at the same time it works, performatively, to "declare" or say "we hold" that these truths are self-evident. To say "we hold" is a speech act. The words bring about the thing they name.

Maggie's speech acts or sign acts are of the same nature. In their small way in their small arena they are truly revolutionary, inaugural. They bring about a radical change in the configuration of relations among the main characters. As Fanny Assingham says, "She'll take it [the responsibility] all herself" (1:380). For this reason it is proper to speak of what Maggie's speech acts do as a "declaration of independence." It is a declaration whose independence is signaled in James's trope of her getting off the coach that is bearing the four main characters irresistibly, it might seem, along.

Maggie's declaration of independence is felicitous only because she chooses not to exert her privilege as an injured wife and make public her grievance. If she had "gone public," she would have been "lost." She saves herself, however, only to be lost in another way, by losing her beloved father. Her choice is to pretend not to know, to be willing, like Fanny, to perjure herself by swearing that she knows nothing, and then to manipulate carefully the way she behaves and what she says to her husband, to Charlotte, and to her father in such a way that they are coerced into acting the way she wants by their not knowing for sure how much she knows or believes she knows, by their not knowing what she may do next, and by her creation of a precarious and delicate pretense among them all that nothing has happened. This keeps alive and functional the fiction that all is well. This fiction becomes the basis on which all the others must act. In one of her late face-to-face dialogues with Fanny, Maggie states that "Everything that has come up for them has come up, in an extraordinary way, without my having by a sound or a sign given myself away. . . . And that's how I make them do what I like!" Fanny replies, "My dear child, you're amazing. . . . You're terrible" (2:115). This gives another and proleptic meaning to Maggie's claim that it is always terrible for women. Maggie inflicts terror as well as passively suffering it. She makes the others do what she likes not by the solitary power of thinking but by what she says and does, by signs that she puts forth for them to see and try to read, in this case the lying signs that she knows nothing.

Later, in the scene in which Maggie brings Charlotte the right volume of her novel (she has taken the wrong volume outdoors to read), Charlotte tells Maggie she is "tired" and is going back to American City with her husband, Adam. "I place my husband first," says Charlotte (2:314). She tells Maggie that in order to keep her husband (Maggie's beloved father) for herself she must separate him from his daughter. Maggie asks, "You want to take my father *from* me?" (2:316), and ends by saying, "I've failed," meaning "I've failed to keep my father to myself." She says this but secretly thinks to herself that she has succeeded magnificently in getting Charlotte to do just what she wants: "Yes, she had done all" (2:318). This is an example of what I mean by saying that Maggie's thinking is always "outered," in however negative or mendacious a way, in speech or other signs. That is how she gets the others to act as she wishes.

Maggie has "done it all" in order to get Amerigo to herself. She has been willing to lose her father in order to secure her husband. The novel ends with a long suspense as Adam and Charlotte say goodbye to Maggie and the Prince just before leaving for America. This suspense is figured as Maggie's waiting to be "paid" for what she has done and wondering just what the figure of the recompense will be. Her reward is to get the Prince for herself. The last two pages make this clear in the talk about "the measure of her course and the full face of her act," her "terror that, when there has been suspense, always precedes, on the part of the creature to be paid, the certification of the amount. Amerigo knew it, the amount; he still held it. . . . She had thrown the dice, but his hand was over her cast. . . . then with her sight of him renewed to intensity she seemed to have a view of the number. His presence alone, as he paused to look at her, somehow made it the highest, and even before he had spoken she had begun to be paid in full" (2:367–68). Note that word "terror" again. It is echoed once more by a synonym in the Aristotelian formulation in the last sentence of the novel when Maggie, "for pity and dread" of what she sees in Amerigo's eyes, hides her own eyes in his breast. Maggie is being paid for not having made a fuss and for not having divorced him, for not having put him back in penury, for not ever having forced him to make a "confession" (2:368). In this bridge game (a figure dramatized in one scene in the novel) Maggie has made a grand slam, precisely by getting off the coach, by not playing in the game, to mix two of the salient figures the narrative voice provides. Her "act," which has been a speech act through and through, is recompensed at the very end by his act: "close to her, her face kept before him, his hands holding her shoulders, his whole act enclosing her, he presently echoed: 'See? I see nothing but *you*'" (2:369).

One final question remains, a question that circles back to the beginning of this essay. Has Maggie acted in justice, in tune with the right? Can what she has done be justified? No unequivocal answer to that can be made, any more than an unequivocal answer can be given to the question of whether the colonists were justified in declaring independence from England. In one sense the colonists were totally unjustified, since they had defied and disobeyed the laws and the sovereignty under which they lived. If the revolution had not come off, if the Continental Army had been defeated, all those who signed the Declaration of Independence would probably have been hanged. This would have been a just imposition of judgment according to the laws of England. Those who instigate a revolution are risking their necks. On the other hand, since the revolution worked, since it was secured by a military victory, the Declaration of Independence was justified in the event, as they say. It was a felicitous performative of that anomalous sort that is truly inaugural. It was a decisive break in history. Groundless in itself, it created its own ground and validation in a speech act that at the same time created a ground and did something on the basis of that ground. Maggie's act is like that. It is without precedent or justification, but it creates by the act itself the grounds that justify it. Maggie takes the situation on herself. She does indeed have a heavy burden on her conscience, something to confess to her priest that she has not confessed, as the novel in one place puts it.

Maggie finds herself in a location within her immediate social or intersubjective field in which only she can act to resolve the situation. The resolution inflicts torment on Charlotte, but it gets Maggie undivided possession of Amerigo, the purchase she told him early in the novel she would pay to keep. It also preserves intact the apparent successful acquisition of Amerigo and Charlotte that is so important to her father. It makes efficacious the public lie that these false works of art (as Amerigo and Charlotte are figuratively called) are genuine. In the last chilling exchange between Adam and Maggie, Adam says, "*Le compte y est* [The amount is there]. You've got some good things," and she answers, as they both look at Charlotte and Amerigo taking tea in Maggie's drawing room, sitting like "things," like wax figures "on one of the platforms of Madame Tussaud," "Ah don't they look well?" (2:360). In their last exchange Maggie says, "It's success, father," to which he answers, "It's success" (2:366).

This "success" could be defined as the triumph of the American ethical sense, its implicit assumption that each ethical act is autonomous, inaugural, an act of unjustified power, like the American Revolution, over the morality or immorality of old Europe. In acting as she does Maggie is acting in the spirit of the Declaration of Independence. She also acts as her father's daughter—that is, in the spirit of his ruthless business dealings and his unscrupulous acquisition of European artworks. Such an act is both justified and not justified. It is both in tune with the right and an unjustifiable act, a lawless taking of power, just as the Declaration of Independence was both justified and not justified by its precedent, the English "Glorious Revolution" of 1688 that brought a new dynasty to the English throne and gave new power to Parliament and the people, and just as Maggie is justified and not justified by the example of her father.

In a similar way, I claim, my reading of *The Golden Bowl* is justified by the text, while at the same time, if it is a responsible reading, if it is responsive to the demand the text makes, it is also to some degree interventionist, initiatory, inaugural, and in that sense unjustified. Nothing justifies, in the sense of prescribing it, the analogy I have drawn between Maggie's perjury and the Declaration of Independence. I draw the analogy on my own hook. I hold nevertheless that the analogy is a self-evident truth. The reader, in the end, is in a situation like Maggie's. The reader must act on his or her own, on the basis of a reading that has no fully prescribed basis, though that reading must try to follow as closely as possible the tracks James has made in the snow. The reader-critic must then take responsibility for what results from that act of retracing, in this case, the essay you have just been reading. I hereby take that responsibility.

Notes

1. See Immanuel Kant, "Über ein vermeintes Recht aus Menschenliebe zu lügen" ["On a Presumed Right to Lie out of Love for Humanity"]. This little essay is a jealous attack on Benjamin Constant, German against French, true philosopher against "philosophe." An oral seminar by Jacques Derrida of 26 May 1993, made available to me in a transcription from a tape, discusses Kant's opuscule. So far as I know, this seminar has not been published.

2. Amerigo tells Maggie, before they are married: "It's you yourselves meanwhile . . . who really know nothing. There are two parts of me. . . . One is made up of the history, the doings, the marriages, the crimes, the follies, the boundless *bêtises* of other people—especially of their infamous waste of money that might have come to me. Those things are written—literally in rows of volumes, in libraries; are as public as they're abominable. Everybody can get at them, and you've both of you [Maggie and her father] wonderfully looked them in the face. But there's another part, very much smaller doubtless, which, such as it is, represents my single self, the unknown, unimportant—unimportant save to you—personal quantity. About this you've found out nothing" (1:9). This personal quantity is one opacity. Another is racial, as the Prince is shown meditating about when he asks himself whether he is arrogant and greedy: "Personally, he considered, he hadn't the vices in question—and that was so much to the good. His race, on the other hand, had had them handsomely enough, and he was somehow full of his race. Its presence in him was like the consciousness of some inexpugnable scent in which his clothes, his whole person, his hands and the hair of his head, might have been steeped as in some chemical bath: the effect was nowhere in particular, yet he constantly felt himself at the mercy of the cause" (1:16).

3. See Sharon Cameron's chapter "Thinking Speaking: *The Golden Bowl* and the Production of Meaning" in *Thinking in Henry James*.

4. "Declarations of Independence," the preamble to a seminar on Nietzsche given at the University of Virginia in 1976 to help celebrate the two hundredth anniversary of the United States Declaration of Independence, was originally published, in French, under the title *Otobiographies: L'enseignement de Nietzsche et la politique du nom propre* (Paris: Galilée, 1984). For an English translation, see Jacques Derrida, "Declarations of Independence." See also David de Kanter Arndt's chapter "The Declaration of Independence" in *Ground and Abyss* (127–83).

Works Cited

Arndt, David de Kanter. *Ground and Abyss: The Question of Poiesis in Heidegger, Arendt, Foucault, and Stevens.* Ann Arbor: UMI, 1998.

Austin, J. L. *How to Do Things with Words*. 2nd ed. Ed. J. O. Urmson and Marina Sbisà. Cambridge: Harvard UP, 1997.

Cameron, Sharon. *Thinking in Henry James*. Chicago: U of Chicago P, 1989.

Derrida, Jacques. "Declarations of Independence." Trans. Tom Keenen and Tom Pepper. *New Political Science* 15 (1986): 7–15.

James, Henry. *The Golden Bowl*. 2 vols. New York: Augustus M. Kelley, 1971.

CONTRIBUTORS

CHARLES ALTIERI is Professor of English at the University of California at Berkeley. He is the author of a variety of important works concerning modern literature and literary theory, including *Canons and Consequences: Reflections on the Ethical Force of Imaginative Ideals* (1990), *Subjective Agency: A Theory of First-Person Expressivity and Its Social Implications* (1994), and *Postmodernisms Now: Essays on Contemporaneity in the Arts* (1998).

WAYNE C. BOOTH is Distinguished Service Professor of English Emeritus at the University of Chicago. He is the author of the celebrated *Rhetoric of Fiction* (2nd ed., 1983), which has now been translated into eight languages. Booth's other works include such significant volumes as *A Rhetoric of Irony* (1975), *Critical Understanding: The Powers and Limits of Pluralism* (1979), and *The Company We Keep: An Ethics of Fiction* (1988). His substantial contributions to literary study were underscored by the publication of *Rhetoric and Pluralism: Legacies of Wayne Booth* (1995), edited by Frederick J. Antczak.

G. THOMAS COUSER is Professor of English at Hofstra University. He is the author of such works as *American Autobiography: The Prophetic Mode* (1979), *Altered Egos: Authority in American Autobiography* (1989), and *Recovering Bodies: Illness, Disability, and Life Writing* (1997). His current project is "Auto/Bio/Ethics: Ethical Issues in Contemporary Life Writing."

TODD F. DAVIS is Associate Professor of English at Goshen College. The author of numerous articles and reviews in such journals as *Critique, Studies in Short Fiction, Mississippi Quarterly,* and *Yeats/Eliot Review,* Davis is currently composing a history of reader-response theory and formalist criticism (with Kenneth Womack).

CORA DIAMOND is William R. Kenan Professor of Philosophy and University Professor at the University of Virginia. She is the author of *The Realistic Spirit: Wittgenstein, Philosophy, and the Mind* (1991), as well as the editor of *Intention and Intentionality: Essays for G. E. M. Anscombe* (with Jenny Teichman, 1979) and *Wittgenstein's Lectures on the Philosophy of Mathematics* (1989).

SUSAN GUBAR is Distinguished Professor of English at Indiana University. She is the author and editor (with Sandra M. Gilbert) of some of contemporary literary theory and feminist criticism's most significant volumes, including *The Madwoman in the Attic: The Woman Writer and the Nineteenth-Century Literary Imagination* (1979), which was a runner-up for the Pulitzer Prize and National Book Critics Circle Award, as well as the three-volume *No Man's Land: The Place of the Woman Writer in the Twentieth Century* (1988–1994). Her latest volume is *Critical Condition: Feminism at the Turn of the Century* (2000).

KATHLEEN LUNDEEN is Associate Professor of English at Western Washington University. She is the author of *Knight of the Living Dead: William Blake and the Problem of Ontology* (2000). Additionally, she has published essays in such journals as *Word & Image, Keats-Shelley Journal, Review of English Studies, Film Criticism, Colby Library Quarterly, Connecticut Review,* and *Studies in Contemporary Satire.*

IAN MARSHALL is Professor of English at Penn State Altoona. He is the author of *Story Line: Exploring the Literature of the Appalachian Trail* (1998). Additionally, Marshall has published numerous essays on such authors as Henry Thoreau, Harriet Prescott Spofford, Robinson Jeffers, Robert Service, Colin Fletcher, and (yes, really) Dr. Seuss.

JAMES MEFFAN is Assistant Lecturer in the School of English, Film, and Theatre at Victoria University of Wellington, New Zealand, where he recently completed his dissertation, "Value, Identity, and the Ethics of Postcolonial Literature." His chapter on Coetzee and Gordimer, "Terror, Writing and Responsibility," is forthcoming in *Terror in the Arts: Changing Views of the Political.*

J. HILLIS MILLER is Distinguished Professor of English and Comparative Literature at the University of California at Irvine. A Fellow of the American Academy of Arts and Sciences, Miller has published a number of important works of contemporary literary theory and criticism, including *Fiction and Repetition: Seven English Novels* (1985), *The Ethics of Reading: Kant, De Man, Eliot, Trollope, James, and Benjamin* (1987), *Versions of Pygmalion* (1990), *Theory Now and Then* (1991), *Ariadne's Thread: Story Lines* (1992), *Topographies* (1995), *Reading Narrative* (1998), and *Black Holes: Cultural Memory in the Present* (1999).

ADAM ZACHARY NEWTON is Associate Professor of English at the University of Texas at Austin, where he also teaches in the Committee on Comparative Literature and the Center for Middle Eastern Studies. He is the author of *Narrative Ethics* (1995), *Facing Black and Jew: Literature as Public Space in Twentieth-Century America* (1999), and *The Fence and the Neighbor: Emmanuel Levinas, Yeshayahu Leibowitz, and Israel among the Nations* (2001). His articles have been published in *American Literary History, Narrative, Prospects, Social Identities, South Atlantic Quarterly,* and *Style.* His forthcoming project is entitled *The Elsewhere: On Belonging at a Near Distance.*

MARTHA C. NUSSBAUM is Ernst Freund Professor of Law and Ethics in the Law School of the University of Chicago. A member of the Council of the American Academy of Arts and Sciences, Nussbaum received the Brandeis Creative Arts Award for Nonfiction in 1990. Her numerous book publications include such celebrated volumes as *The Fragility of Goodness: Luck and Ethics in Greek Tragedy and Philosophy* (1986), *Love's Knowledge: Essays on Philosophy and Literature* (1990), *The Therapy of Desire: Theory and Practice in Hellenistic Ethics* (1994), *Poetic Justice: The Literary Imagination and Public Life* (1995), *Cultivating Humanity: A Classical Defense of Reform in Liberal Education* (1997), *Sex and Social Justice* (1999), and *Women and Human Development: The Capabilities Approach* (2000).

JAMES PHELAN is Professor and Chair of the Department of English at Ohio State University. He is the author of numerous books, including *Reading People, Reading Plots: Character, Progression, and the Interpretation of Narrative* (1989), *Beyond the Tenure Track: Fifteen Months in the Life of an English Professor* (1991), and *Narrative as Rhetoric: Technique, Audiences, Ethics, Ideology* (1996). Phelan is also editor of the journal *Narrative.*

DANIEL R. SCHWARZ is Professor of English and Stephen H. Weiss Presidential Fellow at Cornell University. He is the author of a number of books on modernism and literary theory, including a two-volume study of Joseph Conrad (1980, 1982), *The Humanistic Heritage: Critical Theories of the English Novel from James to Hillis Miller* (1986), *Reading Joyce's Ulysses* (1987), *The Transformation of the English Novel, 1890–1930* (1989), *The Case for a Humanistic Poetics* (1991), *Narrative and Representation in Wallace Stevens* (1993), *Reconfiguring Modernism: Explorations in the Relationship between Modern Art and Modern Literature* (1997), *Imagining the Holocaust* (1999), and *Rereading Conrad* (2001).

MARGARET URBAN WALKER is Professor of Philosophy at Fordham University. She is the author of *Moral Understandings: A Feminist Study in Ethics* (1998) and editor of *Mother Time: Women, Aging, and Ethics* (1999). Her current project is a book on responses to wrongdoing and moral repair.

KENNETH WOMACK is Assistant Professor of English at Penn State Altoona. In addition to coauthoring *Recent Work in Critical Theory, 1989–1995: An Annotated Bibliography* (1996) and coediting three volumes on British Book-Collectors and Bibliographers in the *Dictionary of Literary Biography* series (1997–1999), Womack has published numerous articles in such journals as *Mosaic, Biography, Studies in the Humanities, Literature/Film Quarterly, TEXT,* and the *Yearbook of Comparative and General Literature.* He is editor of *Interdisciplinary Literary Studies: A Journal of Criticism and Theory* and coeditor of the *Year's Work in English Studies.*

KIM L. WORTHINGTON is Senior Lecturer in the School of English, Film, and Theatre at Victoria University of Wellington, New Zealand. She is the author of *Self as Narrative: Subjectivity and Community in Contemporary Fiction* (1996). Her chapter "The Representation of Torture and the Torture of Representation: J. M. Coetzee" is forthcoming in *Terror in the Arts: Changing Views of the Political.*

INDEX